A HISTORY OF RUSSIAN MUSIC

IGOR STRAVINSKY

A HISTORY OF
RUSSIAN MUSIC

RICHARD ANTHONY LEONARD

With 17 Illustrations

GREENWOOD PRESS, PUBLISHERS
WESTPORT, CONNECTICUT

Library of Congress Cataloging in Publication Data

Leonard, Richard Anthony.
  A history of Russian music.

  Reprint of the 1957 ed. published by Macmillan,
New York.
  Bibliography: p.
  Includes index.
  1. Music--Russia--History and criticism.
I. Title.
[ML300.L45 1977]   781.7'47   77-6760
ISBN 0-8371-9658-2

Originally published in 1957 by the Macmillan Company,
New York

Reprinted with the permission of Macmillan Publishing Co., Inc.

Reprinted in 1977 by Greenwood Press, Inc.

Library of Congress catalog card number 77-6760

ISBN 0-8371-9658-2

Printed in the United States of America

ACKNOWLEDGMENTS

I should like to express my thanks to the various publishers and authors who gave their kind permission to quote copyrighted material from their books or periodicals: Constable & Co., Ltd., *The First Romanovs*, by R. Nisbet Bain (1905); Crown Publishers, Inc., *The Mighty Five*, by Victor I. Seroff, copyright, 1948, by Victor I. Seroff; Dodd, Mead & Co., *The International Cyclopedia of Music and Musicians*, Ed. Oscar Thompson, copyright, 1939, by Dodd, Mead & Co., Inc.; Harcourt, Brace & Co., Inc., *Discoveries of a Music Critic*, by Paul Rosenfeld, copyright, 1936, by Harcourt, Brace & Co., Inc.; Alfred A. Knopf, Inc.: *Moussorgsky*, by Oskar von Riesemann, translated by Paul England, copyright, 1929, by Alfred A. Knopf, Inc.; *My Musical Life*, by N. A. Rimsky-Korsakov, translated by Judah A. Joffe, copyright, 1923, 1942, by Alfred A. Knopf, Inc; *Sergei Prokofiev*, by Israel V. Nestyev, translated by Rose Prokofieva, copyright, 1946, by Alfred A. Knopf, Inc.; *Dmitri Shostakovich*, by Victor Ilyich Seroff, copyright, 1943, by Victor Seroff; the *Musical Quarterly:* "The Earliest Russian Opera," by N. Findeisen; "Victor Hartmann and Modest Musorgsky," by Alfred Frankenstein; "The Znamenny Chant of the Russian Church," by Alfred J. Swan; copyright, 1933, 1939, 1940, by G. Schirmer, Inc.; the *New York Times*, an interview with Serge Prokofiev by Olin Downes, copyright, 1930, by The New York Times Company; Ernst Krenek, author of *Music Here and Now*, copyright, 1939, by W. W. Norton & Co.; Oxford University Press, *Eight Soviet Composers*, by Gerald Abraham (1943); G. Schirmer, Inc., *A Century of Russian Song*, ed. Kurt Schindler, copyright, 191!, 1939, by G. Schirmer, Inc.; The Viking Press, *Monsieur Croche the Dillettante Hater*, by Claude Debussy, translated by B. N. Langdon Davies, copyright, 1929, 1956, by The Viking Press, Inc.

The extract from the poem *Seven, They AreSeven!* by Constantin Balmont is reprinted by kind permission of the Boston Symphony Orchestra and Mr. John N. Burk, editor of its historical and descriptive notes, copyright, 1927, by the Boston Symphony Orchestra, Inc.

It is also a pleasure to express grateful thanks to my friend Gerstle Mack for his invaluable editorial advice. For bearing literary burdens far too numerous and varied to mention, my thanks must go to my wife.

R.A.L.

Larchmont, New York
January, 1957

CONTENTS

LIST OF ILLUSTRATIONS

9

CHAPTER I

EARLY RUSSIAN CHURCH MUSIC

I

IN the West it is the custom to regard Russian music as a fairly recent phenomenon, which began with Michael Glinka and went through its luxuriant flowering all in the space of the past hundred years. Like so many generalizations about Russia this is only a half-truth. There have been not one but two great ages in Russian music. The first began with the introduction of Christianity to Russia late in the tenth century, and the bringing of the Byzantine chant of the Eastern Church into the pagan land. With centuries of use the Byzantine chant became slowly Russianized, developing and flourishing all through the Middle Ages into a richly ornamented liturgical art. It became known as the *znamenny* chant, and it was the first genuinely Russian art music.

The second age did not begin until centuries later, after the secular music of Western Europe at last seeped into Russia through the medium of the theatre—the drama of the West and Italian opera. The moment of great impetus for this movement occurred in the nineteenth century when Glinka visited the opera houses of Italy, and there was born in his mind a scheme for creating a Russian nationalist music based on, but not subservient to, the Western art.

There is a significant point to be made at the outset about both these epochs in Russian music. Both had a common origin— the impact upon the Russians of a foreign culture. It is a pattern which repeats itself again and again in the history of this country, whenever the barriers which have separated her from the rest of the world have been let down.

From any close study of Russian music, whether ancient or modern, two facts invariably spring forth. The most obvious is that the Russian is so strong a nationalist that when he seizes upon a foreign art which appeals to him he usually changes it into something which then seems to belong to him. The second is that, in spite of his strong nationalism, he is also by nature an eclectic, a

11

synthesizer, whose keen perceptions, if they are given free rein, will range over a very wide field. Modern Russian music shows these traits clearly. The most common generalization about this art is that it has a special character and a profuse variety, due to the way it uses ideas based on Russian folk music, church music, and to some extent the music of the Near East and the Orient. This is certainly true, but it is only half the story. Modern Russian music owes its variety and vitality equally to the way its composers have ranged without restriction over the whole field of Western music of the past two centuries. They have sampled avidly almost everything that Western composers have offered, and turned it to their own uses.

In the following pages a record will be set forth which shows these two forces of nationalism and eclecticism at work in the creation of Russian music. It would seem at first that the two are irreconcilable, that they must pull in opposite directions. But the greatest Russian composers, with special genius, have been able to make them work together and to the infinite benefit of their art.

II

The Russians have always been an isolated people. The Iron Curtain was not of course an invention of the Soviets, but has existed for almost a thousand years. Russia's long separation from the rest of Europe, moreover, was not the result of simple causes like distance, climate or her impingement upon Asiatic and Near Eastern peoples. The chief reason why Russia is geographically European and culturally only part-European derives from an event now remote and ossified in the pages of history—the breaking up of the Roman Empire. From that division Russia inherited not the Latin civilization of the West, but the Greek or Byzantine civilization of the East ; and her Christianity for nearly a thousand years thereafter was never that of Roman Catholicism, but of the Orthodox Eastern Church.

It was geographical position which determined Russia's early intercourse with the Eastern Roman Empire. In the ninth century the beginnings of a Russian state are visible in a dynasty, headed by Vikings from the North, which centred at the ancient city of Kiev. These early Slavs were a primitive people who lived by agriculture and herding. They were heathens, worshippers of wooden idols.

For centuries they had been in contact with the Eastern Roman Empire, moving down their natural waterways to· trade at Constantinople. They came bearing furs, honey, amber, wax, and— the inevitable prize of barbaric warfare—slaves. For these they purchased the fine Byzantine cloths and wine.

In the year 988 when the ruler of Kiev, Vladimir I, forcibly converted his subjects to Christianity, he called in priests of the Eastern Church to teach the new faith. As the religion quickly spread through the country it brought with it the seeds of Byzantine culture. Laws were established based on the Byzantine codes; churches arose modelled after the architectural plan sanctioned by Byzantium. With the Greek priests came the alphabet, and soon an infiltration of Byzantine literature. In the early monasteries appear the first Russian chronicles, and the beginnings of a literature of sacred writings. With the first priests there also came singers and choristers to teach the performance of the Byzantine chant.

Byzantine church music was an art of imposing splendour, comparable with the Gregorian music of the Roman Church. Music as an established part of the ceremonial had in fact entered the Christian Church through the Eastern branch, one of whose great figures, St. John Chrysostom, had helped to develop a liturgy of hymns and chants. During the centuries when the Ambrosian and Gregorian chants were flourishing in the Roman Church, there grew up in the Eastern Church an immense literature of religious poetry, of such wealth and beauty that it has been called "the chief artistic contribution of the Byzantine Empire to the world's literature". This poetry was created to be set to music, and thus ornament the liturgy of the church.

Among the greatest of the hymn-writers of the Eastern Church were: St. Romanus, who in the sixth century composed thousands of odes, and has been called the greatest master of the Byzantine chant; Sergius, Patriarch of Constantinople in the seventh century, another master of the ode; St. Andrew of Crete (seventh century) who invented the canon, a species of hymn which he expanded to the enormous length of two hundred and fifty strophes; and St. John of Damascus (eighth century) who was one of the most resplendent of early church scholars, a philosopher and poet, and one of the supreme masters of the canon.

The Byzantine chant was entirely vocal, with no accompaniment by instruments. The chant was monodic, the only hint of harmony being the occasional use of a drone. An important feature of dramatic effectiveness was the use of antiphony, the division of the choir into two groups which sang alternately.

III

The metamorphosis of the Byzantine chant after it had entered Russia is a subject only recently explored by music archaeologists. The difficulties encountered by these scholars have been enormous, since they involve researches extending back almost a thousand years into pre-Mongol days and the study of manuscripts the exact meaning of whose notations has been lost for centuries. The most important work was done by the Russian scholar, S. V. Smoliensky (1848–1909), whose studies of the old Russian church chant were exceptionally penetrating and thorough.

The principal chant of the Russian church in mediaeval times was known as the *znamenny* chant. Smoliensky began with this chant as it existed in the sixteenth century and was able to work backward, exploring its history to the thirteenth century, where he was balked by inability to decipher with certainty the old manuscript notations. In the opinion of most authorities the direct descent of the *znamenny* chant from the Byzantine chant is certain. There is some doubt, however, about the precise amount of change and amplification which the mediaeval Russian singers imposed on the product they had imported from the old Eastern Roman Empire. Again, most authorities agree that the change was considerable, and that with the slow passage of centuries the Russian choristers gradually transformed the chant to suit their own temperament and tongue, even colouring it with ideas and idioms borrowed from their native folk music, until the *znamenny* chant became a completely Russian art form.

Meanwhile, there had also been a change in language. The chant came from Byzantium with Greek words, but by the twelfth century the Russians were singing it partly in Greek and partly in their own tongue. In another two centuries the Greek words had disappeared, and the *znamenny* chant had become wholly Russian. For a period of about four hundred years—from the thirteenth to the seventeenth centuries—the *znamenny* chant melodies remained basically intact except for minor alterations.

The function of the *znamenny* chant was precisely that of the Gregorian and Byzantine chants—the illumination and adornment of the liturgy. In the complex and extended service of the Orthodox Eastern Church—the masses, vespers, matins, the various ceremonies for Sundays, holy days, saints' days, and Lenten days throughout the year—in all these music had an established place. In size and scope the *znamenny* chant grew to be enormous, with a variety of forms of differing lengths and elaboration—odes, *stichera* (or canticles), *heirmoi*, *troparia* and canons.

As for the exact musical nature of the earliest Russian chant, present-day knowledge is still limited by the problem of notation. Like its earlier prototypes, the *znamenny* chant was written in a neume notation, the forerunner of the modern staff notation which permits notes to be written indicating exact pitch. The neume notation was a kind of music shorthand, which gave rough indications of the direction the melody would take but could not indicate the exact pitch of every note. For that reason all early church music had to be memorized by the singers and passed on to other singers orally. Manuscripts could only be reminders of the melodies, and not exact representations as they are today. In spite of these difficulties modern scholars have been able to reconstruct even some of the earliest Russian chants in detail.

Like the Gregorian and Byzantine chants the *znamenny* was entirely vocal. Following the ancient restrictions of Eastern orthodoxy the Russian usage never permitted musical instruments, not even the organ, in the church service. The *znamenny* chant was likewise entirely monodic, with no supporting harmony except the holding of a single drone by a separate section of the choir, again a practice inherited from Byzantium. The *znamenny* was also diatonic. Each melody was cast in one of eight different *echoi* or *glassy*. According to Alfred J. Swan (one of the few modern authorities on the *znamenny*), these *glassy* were not modes like those of the Byzantine and Gregorian chants which were each based on a fixed succession of steps of the diatonic scale. The Russian *glassy* were rather melodic patterns, with as many as ninety different patterns in each *glas*. A *glas* was recognizable by certain melodic contours which gave it a prevailing mood—joyful, tender, mournful, plaintive, triumphant, etc.

The melody of the *znamenny* chant was made up chiefly of half and quarter notes, with occasional whole notes, and a very few eighth notes. This resulted, says Swan, "in a motion of great stateliness and nobility. . . . In the *znamenny* chant the text is treated with the utmost reverence. We never lose the feeling of being in the presence of a very exalted reading of the words." That indeed was the primary purpose of all this ancient church music—the glorification of the word; for the word itself, especially when it came from the Bible, was no mere text but a divinely inspired message—the very word of God.

The golden age of the *znamenny* chant appears to have been the sixteenth century, during the reign of Ivan the Terrible. In his youth, Ivan had studied music composition, and there exist manuscripts of two canticles which he is supposed to have composed at the age of seventeen. Later, the Czar became a patron of church music, importing a number of the finest singers of Novgorod to improve the singing in the churches of Moscow.

In form, the *znamenny* chant had been extended to a broad yet unified and finely-balanced structure. In spite of the rigidly careful treatment of the texts, the melodies (says Swan) were of "the supplest and most vivid kind". For some time, however, the fundamental principles of the chant had been threatened by innovations, among them the interpolation of elaborate coloratura passages. Fearful that the chant might be corrupted, Ivan ordered (in 1551) the creation of singing schools under the direction of the clergy, to provide instruction in the proper composition and performance of church music. In these schools and among the choirs which they sponsored, the *znamenny* chant is believed to have reached its zenith as an art form. The movement stimulated many new words in the old *znamenny* form, and the setting to music of portions of the liturgy heretofore unchanted.

IV

Even as late as the seventeenth century the *znamenny* was still the principal chant of the Russian church, but there were others in widespread use. The *znamenny* itself reigned supreme in the Moscow area. The Kiev chant, used in the south-west, resembled the *znamenny* in richness and elaboration. A Greek chant and a Bulgarian chant were simpler than the *znamenny* and more rhythmical, with prominent melodic qualities. There was also a lesser *znamenny*, a simplified version for daily church services that did not require elaborate ritual.

The fact that the *znamenny* chant, a species of ancient, monodic song, should still have been thriving as late as the seventeenth century calls attention to the extraordinary state of Russia herself at that time. The West had long since passed beyond the old Gregorian chant of the Roman Catholic Church. Gregorian chant had been on the decline since the thirteenth century when the development of harmony and counterpoint wrought its great change in all Western music. Four hundred years later that invention had not yet reached the music artists of Russia, because the nation itself had been virtually sealed off from Western Europe.

Russia's isolation had begun when she embraced the culture and religion of the Byzantine East, and not the Roman Catholicism of the West. Thereafter the gulf widened with the centuries, and to her great detriment. She shared in none of the rebirth of enlightened learning which carried Europe out of the Dark Ages and into the Renaissance ; she was plunged instead into the immeasurable disaster of the Tartar invasion.

The Tartars who conquered and imprisoned mediaeval Russia were part of the Mongol horde of Genghis Khan. Early in the thirteenth century they subdued all northern China and a vast territory of Central Asia. Then in a tremendous sweep which has been called the last and greatest of all raids of nomadism upon the civilizations of the East and West, they overwhelmed Russia and beat upon the doors of Eastern Europe. The tide finally spent itself in Hungary.

Europe was saved, but Russia remained under the Tartar yoke for three centuries. Before the invaders struck, she had been growing in vigour and prosperity. At least one of her cities, Novgorod, had developed a remarkably modern form of republican government ; another, Kiev, was the seat of an early Slavic culture. Kiev attracted the scholars of the church and other men of learning ; architects from Byzantium had built her first splendid churches ; her own artists were among the finest of the icon painters. After the Tartar invasion Kiev like scores of other Russian cities was a fire-blackened hulk, her wealth destroyed and the physical evidences of her culture in ashes.

The Tartar invasion impoverished Russia and set her back hundreds of years ; it cut her off completely from the rest of Europe. When the princes of Muscovy finally expelled the invaders in the fifteenth century and seized power over the entire nation they set up a czardom which was part Oriental and part Byzantine in concept. It was a despotism more fiercely repressive than anything ever seen in the West. And when serfdom, the curse of Russia, was finally clamped down upon the peasantry, the picture was complete of a great nation in a state of semi-barbarous isolation.

One other factor aggravated the cultural backwardness of Russia in the Middle Ages—the extreme dogmatism of the Orthodox Eastern Church. That side of Christendom had always been precisely what its name declaims—orthodox. For centuries it had maintained its stern, proud doctrine of a liturgy and a dogma utterly unchanged. Its control of the morals and the manners of the people was as severe as those of the czar; it put restrictions upon the arts which were all but stultifying.

Any Russian church of the seventeenth century was a monument of this orthodoxy which bound the people to a remote past. The building itself had Russian characteristics (e.g. its bulbous dome), but in the main it followed strict ecclesiastical regulations of form which had come down from Byzantium. Inside, no piece of sculpture, not even the crucifix, could adorn its walls, an ancient prohibition inherited from the iconoclasts of the ninth century. Separating the main body of the church from the *bema* (or sanctuary) was the *iconostasis*, a screen with images of Christ, the Virgin, or the saints. Here again the dead hand of the past froze the artist's inspiration. An icon might be a painting, bas-relief, or mosaic; but the postures and groupings of the figures, the vestures, and even the colours were all rigidly prescribed. God the Father could never be pictured at all. Finally, there was the sound of ancient music, the *znamenny* chant, which in its stark, monodic simplicity was like an echo of the age of St. Romanus, Sergius, or St. John Chrysostom.

v

It was not until the seventeenth century that the harmonized music of the West began to penetrate Russia. Meanwhile, a primitive form of polyphony had appeared in the Russian folk music when the peasants began a simple harmonization of their native tunes. What finally caused the downfall of the old *znamenny* chant, however, was a violent event inside the Orthodox Church itself. A great schism occurred midway in the seventeenth century when Nikon, the Patriarch of Moscow, tried to reform the rituals and purge them of errors and differences, from ancient Byzantine originals, which had crept in through the ages. A faction known as the Old Believers arose in fanatical revolt, and the holy war that swept through

Russia almost tore the nation apart. Rather than accept Nikon's tampering with orthodox beliefs thousands of the Old Believers died at the stake; others immolated themselves by the score in houses and wayside barns, sure that the advent of the Antichrist was at hand. Many went into hiding while their leaders were executed, banished, anathematized, or unfrocked. For a generation the struggle went on until the Old Believers were finally put down. The service books and rituals were corrected, and even the icon figures whose faces were not painted in accord with old Byzantine patterns were destroyed, or had the offending eyes of their saints gouged out.

One of the casualties of Nikon's church reforms was the ancient *znamenny* chant. It survived for a time as the Old Believers went into hiding and struggled to preserve the tenets of their faith; then it disappeared forever from the Russian church liturgy.

The next step in the evolution of Russian church music was a confused and hurried attempt at modernization, chiefly by the introduction of harmony. At the same time the old neume notations were abandoned and all Russian music was thenceforth written in the new staff notation. Russian scholars today are sceptical of the ultimate value of this wholesale grafting of Western ideas of harmony on to the native Russian church music. The change was hardly a natural one, but rather a headlong rush to adopt ideas which were alien to the old art, and for which the Russian musicians themselves were not prepared. For almost two hundred years, until the middle decades of the nineteenth century, Russian liturgical music lost most of its originality. It became instead weakly imitative of the music of Western Europe.

The *znamenny* chant itself, having practically disappeared with the Old Believers, did not undergo the harmonizing process. It was the later and simpler chants which, lending themselves more easily to harmonic structure, became the new music of the Russian church. All unison singing vanished. In their haste to reconstruct the chants according to Western theories of harmony and counterpoint, the adapters made no attempt to preserve either the essential contours or the spirit of the melodies. Much of the time they were influenced in their procedure by Italian opera, which entered Russia early in the eighteenth century to make another of its many conquests.

The Italian era in Russian church music is exemplified by the music of Dmitri Stepanovich Bortnyansky (1751–1825), the most noted of Russian ecclesiastical composers of the early nineteenth century. This man was a Ukrainian who began his career as a choir-boy in the Imperial Chapel. He became a pupil of Baldassare Galuppi when the Italian master was brought to Petersburg to direct the opera company of the Empress Catherine. When Galuppi returned to Italy in 1768 the Empress sent young Bortnyansky along for continued study. The Russian spent eleven years in Italy where he produced quantities of church music, instrumental works, and several operas. All this music was in the prevailing Italian style : Bortnyansky had mastered the foreign idiom, but it had also mastered him.

Bortnyansky returned to Russia in 1779 and was made director of the choir of the Imperial Chapel, where he remained for nearly half a century. He was a choirmaster of great ability. He trained his singers rigorously according to Italian methods until their ensemble singing became a marvel of unity, polished smoothness, and perfect intonation. Much of the pattern of Russian church singing as it is practised to this day stems from Bortnyansky. An appreciation of his work was left by no less an authority than Hector Berlioz, who heard the choir during his visit to Russia in 1847. This was more than two decades after Bortnyansky's death, but the singing was still so remarkable that Berlioz wrote about it with marked en-thusiasm after his return to France.

Bortnyansky's reputation as a composer was for many years a great one in his native land, where he was called "the Russian Palestrina". More than half a century after his death Tchaikovsky edited a ten-volume edition of his works. Even though some of his pieces are still sung in Russian church choirs the bulk of Bort-nyansky's work is commonplace and colourless, and far more Italian than Russian. It shows the extent of the domination of foreign music in Russia in the early nineteenth century. "Russian church singing," says Swan, "came to resemble very closely the state of affairs prevalent in Italian churches during the reign of the so-called Neapolitan Mass."

The Italian phase in Russian church singing lasted for the better part of a century, and for a considerable time after Bort-nyansky's death in 1825. A strong counter-movement, however, was inevitable and it came chiefly from the Orthodox Church monasteries where resentment against the corruption of the ancient chants had long smouldered. The church scholars finally gave their *imprimatur* to a simpler and more restrained type of singing. The chants were first of all shortened ; then all of them were harmonized in a simple style considered to be nearer to the spirit of the old Russian melodies. In the middle years of the nineteenth century this type of chant was taken over by the Imperial Court Chapel at Petersburg, where Bortnyansky had held forth for so long. There it was codified, and elaborated somewhat. Gradually it spread in use throughout the Russian churches, until it became the music most commonly heard wherever the Russian Orthodox faith was practised.

CHAPTER II

THE AGE OF ITALIAN OPERA

I

IT is one of the strange aspects of Russian life in the Middle
Ages that an art form as majestic as the *znamenny* chant could
have existed for centuries with no counterpart whatever in the field
of secular music. The fact is even more remarkable in view of the
variety and vigour of the Russian folk music, the other of the two
sources from which a secular art music of a superior nature should
have sprung. Until the eighteenth century a vacuum existed in
Russian music. That space between church and folk music should
have been filled as it was in Western Europe—by some form like the
madrigal which had engaged the artistry of many of the greatest
composers of the Renaissance period. No such art music appeared
during those centuries in Russia. The cause was, again, the authority
of the Orthodox Church and its stern control of every part of the
social structure.

For hundreds of years the Church in Russia fought fiercely against
all forms of art, entertainment, and recreation. In his study of the
nation under the early Romanovs, R. N. Bain recalls that

"the Church banned all music, profane songs, dances, and games
as sheer idolatry, akin to fornication. Draughts and chess were
anathematized because they were supposed to have been derived
from the Chaldeans, cards because they were known to be of
Latin origin. Dancing bears, hunting dogs and hunting birds,
together with jesters, mountebanks and minstrels who 'used
shameless words' (to wit, all popular, poetical expressions)
were also pronounced accursed."

The Church, it seemed, aimed at "making every house a monastery".

The Church's opposition to folk songs was especially severe,
because many of them were of ancient pagan origin and recalled
heathen rites and customs. But the native urge of the people toward
music was so strong that folk music and folk musicians thrived in
spite of all the Church could do. During the Middle Ages there
existed in Russia a whole population of roving minstrels. These

22

peasant performers were driven from the larger towns and cities by the clergy, so they moved in small bands among the towns and villages that clung to the banks of Russia's river systems; they reached the hamlets that dotted the waste spaces of the steppe and even the remote corners of the vast forests. The roving minstrels were usually received joyously by a populace so repressed that even laughter seemed a profane indulgence. They were secretly welcomed in many of the private estates of the aristocracy, where almost any diversion was a necessity to break the monotony of the long winter isolation.

The early Russian minstrels were made up of the classes usually found among primitive entertainers. First were the musicians, who played the native instruments like the gusli, the dumbra, the gudok, or the arfa. With them went the singers, to render popular folk songs, ancient mythical and historical ballads, and sometimes ribald jingles. In some of the larger troupes there were also dancers (the ancestors of the Russian ballet) and even jugglers and buffoons, boxers, and performing bears and apes.[1]

Minstrelsy in Russia never reached the stage of a fine art as it did in the West with the rise of the troubadours and trouvères in France, and the minnesingers in Germany. The Russian minstrels enjoyed neither privilege nor dignity. Hounded from place to place by church and state authorities they came at last to an unfortunate end. During the religious wars of the seventeenth century many of the halls of the aristocracy were closed to them, and they became no more than roving bands of thieves who terrified the peasantry. Their performances often degenerated into a low order of vulgarity. Nevertheless, the Russian minstrels performed a service to the culture of the nation. Theirs was a primitive rather than a fine art, but they kept alive many of the most ancient songs of the people, and they helped weave the immense web of Russian folk-lore.

II

Secular music of the kind known to Western Europe finally gained a foothold in Russia about the middle of the seventeenth

---

[1] Some of these popular Russian performances of the Middle Ages are believed to have descended from the Byzantine circus, which came into Russia with the spread of the Byzantine culture. The cathedral of St. Sophia at Kiev contains a fresco painted in the eleventh century and depicting circus acrobats, musicians, and dancers.

century, with the accession of the remarkable and liberal-minded Czar Alexis Mikhailovich (reigned 1645–1676). This man has been overshadowed in history by his son, Peter the Great, but it was Alexis who broke ground for much that Peter was later to do. From the middle of the fifteenth century there had existed in the suburbs of Moscow a small colony of foreigners, chiefly Germans, Englishmen, and Scots, whose homes became a small island of Western culture in a Russia still in the Dark Ages. These foreigners began to attract members of the Russian aristocracy who heard their Protestant church music, read their books, and even began to imitate their ideas of dress and decorum. Young Czar Alexis summoned to Moscow a group of foreign musicians to instruct the Russians in the playing of Western instruments.

The wrath of the Church was sudden and sharp. In 1648 a church ukase commanded, says Bain,

> "that all musical instruments were to be broken up and burnt, and all mountebanks and jugglers were to be whipped for plying their godless trade, with rods for the first, with a knout for the second offence".

Among the ensuing casualties were five wagonloads of musical instruments which were seized in Moscow alone, and were burned at a place behind the city marshes usually reserved for public executions.

It was only five years later that the Church itself, split by the great schism over Nikon's reforms, suffered a serious loss in ecclesiastical power and authority. The old order had changed, and one of the first manifestations of the new was the attitude of Czar Alexis. He aligned himself with those aristocrats, especially the influential boyar, Matviev, who wanted to pull Russia out of her mediaeval backwardness and orient her toward the West. Matviev had married a woman of Scotch descent, and in their home Czar Alexis saw for the first time European furniture, carpets, clocks, and paintings; he read books on mundane subjects considered scandalous by the Church. Alexis married Natalia, an adopted daughter of the Matvievs, and their child later became Peter the Great.

Czarina Natalia was interested in the theatre, an institution then unknown in Russia. In the Moscow foreign quarter she had seen performances by strolling players from Germany, and in 1672 she persuaded the Czar to establish a court theatre. He sent an emissary to the Baltic province of Kurland to recruit musicians and persons who knew how to organize theatricals. Meanwhile, to celebrate the birth of his son, Peter, he commissioned a group of Germans in Moscow to write and produce a play. They responded with what must have been one of the oddest hybrids in the history of the drama—a kind of mystery play on the Biblical subject of Esther, titled *The Acts of Artaxerxes*, written in a mixture of Russian and German dialogue, with incidental music performed by "organs, viols and other instruments", and a choir from the Court Chapel.

The play was performed privately for the Czar and his family in a room rigged up as a temporary theatre in a Moscow suburb. Later a permanent company was formed and the theatre was moved to a building in the Kremlin. In the next few years the Germans produced a series of similar plays, one of which, *How Judith Cut Off the Head of Holofernes*, has been called the ancestor of modern Russian opera. It set a pattern followed for the next hundred years, i.e. drama interspersed with musical numbers, and was a copy of the *singspiel* type of opera then on view in the German theatres. It permitted the interpolation of short comical interludes as a relief from the heavy drama; it further included, quite tactfully, strong references to the moral precepts of the Church.

Czar Alexis also influenced the future course of Russian church music. When the movement for the modernization of the old chants began he summoned to Moscow a group of Kiev musicians, who introduced to the Imperial Chapel the modern type of music notation to replace the ancient neumes. The Kievans also brought with them a new style of part-singing which they had learned from the Poles. Polish music was Western in style and construction. It was an entering wedge in the long isolation of the native Russian musicians and it helped pave the way for the forthcoming invasion of Italian opera.

III

It was Peter the Great (1672–1725) who permitted the first wave of Western culture to pour over the wall of Russia's isolation. Peter tried to modernize his country in one gigantic thrust, and to shake his people out of their mediaeval torpor; he tried to speed into a generation the slow progress of centuries by importing directly the science, industry, art, and manners of the West. Along with the thousands of skilled European craftsmen there now came into Russia, for the first time since the Byzantine influx, a stream of foreign artists—French, Italian, and German architects, Italian painters and composers, German actors and musicians—who were to teach the Russians the elements of their skills, and whose impact upon the ancient arts of the country was sometimes vitalizing and sometimes devastating.

Peter's service to the new art of music in Russia had more to do with the theatre than with music directly. During his journeys to Western Europe he had seen theatrical entertainments, including Italian opera ; on his return he took steps to revive the theatre which had been closed since his father's death. He sent out emissaries to attract foreign actors and musicians to Russia, and the call was first accepted by a German actor from Danzig, Johann Christian Kunst. This man appeared in Moscow in 1702 with his wife and a troupe of seven other actors. In return for 4,200 roubles a year and the title "Director of the Comedians of His Majesty the Czar", Kunst contracted to "entertain and cheer" his Majesty by theatrical divertissements, and to remain sober while so doing.

Only a year later Kunst died,[1] but his work was carried on by Otto Fürst, whose Russian name was Artemiem. Meanwhile, the Czar had a special wooden building erected near the Kremlin— the first public theatre in Russia—and he tried to encourage Russians of all social ranks to attend. The plays were pompous dramas or flimsy comedies based on antique themes, with songs and dances interpolated, and accompanied by an orchestra of seven musicians imported from Hamburg. The dialogue was delivered in German, and later in Russian. Rudimentary as they were, these early plays helped the drama and the music of the West to sink roots into Russian soil.

The real beginnings of opera in Russia must be accredited to the three women who ruled the nation during the greater part of the eighteenth century—the Empresses Anne, Elizabeth, and Catherine. In 1703 Peter the Great had laid the foundations of his new capital, Petersburg, at the mouth of the River Neva, "a window through which his people might look into Europe", and a means of making them forget the mediaeval Russia symbolized by the ancient capital city of Moscow. In the course of the next century Petersburg

---

[1] According to another account Kunst had to flee the country after a performance which displeased the Czar.

developed a court life of incredible luxury, housed in a series of vast palaces which were replicas of Versailles done in a Russian baroque.

An orgy of extravagance began in 1730 with the accession of Empress Anne, whose particular pleasure was to indulge herself in all manner of entertainments—balls, parties, masquerades, and theatricals. For the festivities of her coronation Augustus II of Saxony sent to Petersburg a company of Italian players. Their sparkling comedy delighted the Russians, who had tired of the German mystery plays. Empress Anne thereupon formed a permanent Italian theatrical company at her court. To direct the operatic performances she secured the services of an Italian composer, Francesco Araja (1700–1770), who arrived in Petersburg in 1732 with a company of singers and orchestral players, a scenic artist, a stage "machinist", a ballet master, and a group of dancers. Araja's company introduced the ballet as well as Italian opera to Russia. A ballet school was later established at the Court, headed by an Italian ballet master.

During the next twenty years Araja composed and produced a series of operas in the Italian style. These included *Abiazare* (1736), *Il Finto Nino* (1737), *Artaserse* (1738), *Seleuco* (1744), *Scipione* (1745), *Mitridate* (1747), *Bellerofonte* (1750), *Eudossa incoronata* or *Téodoro II* (1751), *Alessandro nelle Indie* (1755), and *Tzéfale i Procris* (1755).

At first Araja composed to Italian librettos which were then translated into Russian; later he was able to work directly from Russian texts. *Tzéfale i Procris* was the most revolutionary of all his operas, for in addition to a Russian libretto by the poet Soumarokov, it was produced with a cast composed entirely of Russian singers. "The music of this opera," writes the Russian musicologist Nicholas Findeisen, "was very much above the average, and the success of the Russian singers was great."

Araja's later operas were composed for Empress Elizabeth, who had succeeded Anne in 1740. This daughter of Peter the Great was a woman of regal beauty, with an exquisite face and a crown of auburn hair. She was pathologically extravagant. She loved Italian opera and French plays, but above all she loved the masked ball. At these entertainments (called "Metamorphoses") the women dressed in men's clothes while the men masqueraded as women. Elizabeth's favourite costume was that of a Dutch sailor, recalling her father's adventures as a shipwright in Holland.

Since wealth freely flowing has always been a tonic for art, the institution of Italian opera flourished amid the gaudy splendours of the Russian court. Araja was able to return to Italy with a handsome fortune. In 1762 he was recalled to Russia, but the affairs of the royal opera and of the nation were suddenly disturbed by a shocking event. Elizabeth's successor, Czar Peter III, was murdered and his throne usurped by his wife, Catherine II. Araja hastily reversed his plans and retired permanently to Bologna.

IV

The thirty-four-year reign of Catherine the Great (1762–1796) marked by far the most significant period in the growth of Italian opera in Russia. The remarkable Empress so greatly admired French culture that she made the manners of Versailles, its language, and some of its morals those of aristocratic Petersburg. In Catherine's palaces and in the town houses and the great country estates, life began closely to resemble the order of things in the mansions and châteaux of the West. Music was fashionable. Every wealthy aristocrat had to have a small orchestra or choir. At first most of the orchestral performers had been Germans, who played chiefly the lighter German and Italian instrumental works of the day. Under Catherine the craze for music became so intense that the performers were recruited from among the Russians themselves, many of them serfs who had been trained to sing and play.

The centre of this world of music for aristocratic pleasure was the Italian opera which Catherine maintained in her Court at Petersburg, and which she tried to make one of the most distinguished lyric theatres in Europe. Since Italian opera was then an institution controlled largely at its source, she sent again and again to Italy for the most celebrated composers and singers of the time.

The first of the group was Baldassare Galuppi (1706–1785), the harpsichord virtuoso whose music for that instrument was important in laying the foundations for the modern piano sonata. Galuppi also wrote many successful comic operas to librettos by Carlo Goldoni, the great master of modern Italian comedy. When Galuppi accepted Empress Catherine's call to Petersburg in 1766 he was already well known there and in Moscow. An Italian impresario named Locatelli had established public theatres in those cities for the performance of Italian operas, with the popular Galuppi-Goldoni pieces as drawing cards.[1]

On his own appearance in Petersburg as director of Catherine's court theatre Galuppi triumphed with his operas *Didone abbandonata* (1766), *Il Re pastore* (1766), and *Ifigenia in Tauride* (1768). The last was composed especially for the Petersburg company and had its première there. The comic opera, *La Cameriera spiritosa*, with libretto by Goldoni, was also performed at the court theatre in Moscow in 1767. During his stay in Russia Galuppi doubled in the post of Director of the Imperial Court Chapel. There he had the distinction of introducing the motet to the Orthodox Church service, and of composing other music to Russian ecclesiastical texts.

Following Galuppi there came Tommaso Traetta (1727–79), who composed with success in both the serious and comic forms, but is remembered chiefly for his important work in the field of opera seria. Traetta spent the years 1768–74 in Catherine's employ in Petersburg. He staged several of his own works, including *L'Olimpiade* (1769), *L'Isola disabitata* (1769), *Antigona* (1772), *Amore e Psiche* (1773), and *Lucio Vero* (1774).

A composer of great eminence followed in the person of Giovanni Paisiello (1740–1816), who shared with Piccini a leadership in the field of opera buffa. Paisiello went to Russia in 1776, remaining for eight years at a handsome salary as Empress Catherine's court conductor and "inspector of the Italian operas both serious and buffa". He revived several of his more notable successes, including *I Filosofi immaginari* (1779), *La Serva padrona* (1781), and *Dal finto il vero* (1782). He also composed a number of operas especially for the Empress, all to Italian texts. These included *Nitteti* and *Lucinda ed Armidoro* (1777), *Achille in Sciro* (1778), *Alcide al bivio*, *La Finta ciarlatana*, and *La Finta amante* (1780), and *Il Barbiere di Siviglia* (1782). The last work, *The Barber of Seville*, remained one of the most popular operatic works in European theatres until Rossini set the same Beaumarchais story to music a third of a century later.

Giuseppe Sarti (1729–1802), who followed Paisiello, was an operatic composer and conductor, church composer, choirmaster, and teacher. Cherubini was his pupil in Milan. Sarti also practised the art of court intrigue, which got him into serious trouble in

---

[1] These operas were *Il Mondo della luna* (Petersburg, 1758), *Il Filosofo di campagna* (Petersburg, 1758), *Il Mondo alla roversa* (Moscow, 1759), *Arcadia in Brenta* (Petersburg, 1759), and *Bagni d'Abano* (Petersburg, 1761).

Copenhagen and later in Petersburg. Summoned by Catherine in 1784 he remained for eighteen years in Petersburg, greatly improving the standards of performance at the opera. There was one short period when he was retired in political disgrace to the Ukraine, but he won his way back into favour with Catherine by organizing a conservatory of music at Katerinoslav, modelled on those in Italy.

Sarti produced a number of his own operas in Petersburg, including *Armida e Rinaldo* (1786), *Castore e Polluce* (1786), *Les Indiens et l'Anglaise* in French (1799), *The Glory of the North* (1794), and *The Early Reign of Oleg* (1790). The last two are of special interest. *The Glory of the North* was composed to a Russian libretto, while *The Early Reign of Oleg*, also in Russian, had a libretto written by Empress Catherine herself. Oleg was a legendary Varangian, and Catherine described her story on the title page of the score as "an imitation of Shakespeare, without the preservation of ordinary theatrical rules". In writing the music Sarti collaborated with a native composer, Vassily Pạskevich. The Russian is believed to have provided the choruses, which were based on familiar Russian folk songs.

During Sarti's long term in Russia[1] several other celebrated musicians were summoned to direct Catherine's Italian opera company, among them Vincente Martín, known also as Martín y Solar (1754–1810). This man was a Spaniard, born in Valencia, but he achieved a reputation as a composer of Italian opera. Martín went to Vienna in 1785, where his opera *Una Cosa rara* was an immense success, rivalling in popularity Mozart's *The Marriage of Figaro*, which was produced the following year.[2] Martín assumed the direction of Catherine's company in 1788. His work in Petersburg takes on a certain importance because a number of his operas were sung in Russian. These included *Una Cosa rara*, in a Russian translation by Dmitrevsky (1788), *L'Arbore di Diana*, in a Dmitrevsky translation of the original Italian libretto by Lorenzo Da

[1] A curious sample of Sarti's work in Russia was a Te Deum which celebrated a victory in the Turkish wars by a Russian army under Catherine's favourite, Potemkin. The piece was composed to a Russian text from the orthodox liturgy, for double chorus reinforced by bells, cannon, and fireworks. It was performed in the open air at Jassy in 1789, and the next year at Petersburg. Earlier in 1789 Sarti had also produced at Jassy his cantata, *Giove, la Gloria e Marte*, scored for two orchestras, chorus, soloists, drums and cannon. In these rare music forms the Italian maestro anticipated Tchaikovsky and his *1812 Overture*.

[2] Martín's reputation in Vienna is revealed in the fact that Mozart later paid the Spaniard the compliment of using a theme from *Una Cosa rara* in the finale of the second act of *Don Giovanni*. Mozart also wrote two arias, *Chi sa, chi sa, qual sia* (K. 582), and *Vado, ma dove?* (K. 583), for interpolation in Martín's *Il Burbero di buon cuore*.

Ponte, Mozart's famous collaborator (1789), *Le Preux chagrin Kossométovich*, which had one of Empress Catherine's librettos (1789), *Fedoul and her Children*, composed to another story by Catherine and with the music collaboration of the Russian composer Paskevich (1791), *La Mélomanie*, a comic opera with text by A. Khrapovitsky (1790), *A Village Festival*, Russian translation by V. Maikov (1798), and the one-act comic opera *Good Luke, or Here's My Day*, libretto by Kobyakov. *Il Burbero di buon cuore*, with libretto by Ponte, was produced in Italian in 1796.

The record of Martín's career in Petersburg gives evidence of the rising importance of the ballet during the closing decades of the eighteenth century. The Spaniard produced a number of elaborate ballets and ballet-pantomimes at Empress Catherine's Hermitage Theatre, including *L'Oracle* (1792), *Amour et Psyché*, a five-act ballet celebrating the marriage of Alexander I (1793), *Le Retour de Poliorcète* (1799), and *Tancrède*, an "heroic ballet-pantomime" in five acts (1799).

In 1788 Catherine succeeded in attracting to Petersburg one of Italy's great masters of opera buffa, Domenico Cimarosa (1749–1801), who spent three brilliantly successful years in Russia but then begged to be released because he could not stand the climate. For Empress Catherine he produced a so-called "dramatic cantata", *Atene edificata* (1788), a "pastoral cantata with ballet", *La Felicità inaspettata* (1788), a two-act "intermezzo", *Le Donne rivali* (1789), and two operas, *La Vergine del Sole* (1788) and *Cleopatra* (1789). Cimarosa is also supposed to have composed no less than five hundred short pieces for performance at Catherine's Court. His operatic works enjoyed great popularity in Russia and many of them, including *The Secret Marriage*, were performed after his departure.

Productions at the Petersburg court opera during the eighteenth century were by no means limited to works by the noted Italian masters who were its directors. There was a steady stream of performances not alone of operas but of ballets, cantatas, and oratorios by such composers as Piccini, Salieri, Pergolesi, Grétry, and Gluck. Moscow and a few smaller cities also had their opera theatres, and there were performances, sometimes on a lavish scale, in the private theatres of wealthy aristocrats.

Aside from the Italians already noted, Gluck was one of the most favoured composers in Russia during the eighteenth century. His *Ipermestra* was heard in 1760, followed by *Le Cinesi* (1761),

Alessandro (ballet-pantomime) (1767), *Orfeo ed Euridice* (1782), *Echo et Narcisse* (1785), *Alceste* (1785), *Iphigenia in Tauris* (circa 1786) and *Armide* (1787). Performances of Pergolesi's music included two of his most famous works—the comic opera *La Serva padrona* (1773), and the Stabat Mater (1774). *Livietta e Tracollo* had been performed in 1750. Mozart's *The Magic Flute* was heard in 1794, and *La Clemenza di Tito* in 1797. Grétry was represented by a number of works, including *Richard Cœur de Lion* and *L'Amant ʲaloux* (1795). Handel's oratorio *Samson* was performed in 1783 ; and Haydn's *The Seven Words of the Saviour on the Cross*, in 1789.

v

During the closing decades of the eighteenth century the meagre and often confused records of music affairs in Russia began to indicate an interesting phenomenon. In the company of the illustrious Italian composers appear the names of three Russians—Fomin, Matinsky, and Paskevich. These men were the first successful Russian imitators of the Italian opera style, and thus the ancestors of all modern Russian opera composers.

Very little is known of their private lives. Evstignei Ipatovich Fomin was born in 1741 in Petersburg and died there in 1800. He was by birth a serf, but was liberated and was sent to the Imperial Academy of Arts. Later he was sent to Italy where he studied with the celebrated Padre Martini at the Academy of Music in Bologna. When he returned to Russia, Fomin worked first at Moscow, but settled in Petersburg during the reign of Catherine II.

Fomin wrote a dozen or more operas and incidental music to many plays. He was possibly the composer of *Anyuta*, produced in Petersburg in 1772, to a libretto by M. V. Popov. This may have been the first truly Russian opera, with its composer and librettist both Russians. In 1786 Fomin was given the honour of composing music to one of Empress Catherine's librettos, *Buslaevich, the Novgorodian Hero*. This piece was produced at Catherine's Hermitage Theatre inside the great Winter Palace at Petersburg. By far the most successful of Fomin's operas was *The Wizard Miller*, a three-act comedy. After its première in 1779 it played twenty-seven performances to capacity audiences. For several years afterward, all over Russia, it was revived, acclaimed, and imitated.

The score of *The Wizard Miller* was an imitation of Italian opera buffa. Some of its numbers are charming. A feature of the score was the interpolation of several Russian folk songs. According to Findeisen, Fomin used folk tunes, "or good imitations of them", in his other operas.[1] "His recitatives (which are often nearer to actual melodic recitative than to *recitativo secco*), his arias, and even the instrumental music (overtures, interludes, and melodramas) in his operas are often superior to what his rivals . . . were turning out."

Michael Matinsky (1750 circa 1820) was also born a serf, and was liberated by his master, Count Yaguzhinski, who sent him to Italy to study music. In 1777 he collaborated with Fomin on an opera, *The Renaissance*, which was produced in Moscow. Matinsky later went to Petersburg where his opera *The Petersburg Bazaar* (or, *As You Live, So Will Be Your Reputation*) was produced in 1779. It was later revised by Paskevich. Findeisen praises this piece : "Matinsky shows us a racy, realistic picture of town life, of the life of the tradespeople and minor government clerks and officials." "His opera is alive and teems with interesting scenes."

Notwithstanding the success of his music Matinsky retired from the operatic field and became a teacher of mathematics. A man of wide interests and capabilities, he wrote books and articles on geometry, geography, weights and measures, and art.

In the early years of Empress Catherine's reign Vassily Paskevich (17??–1811) became a violinist in the court orchestra, rose to conductor, and finally became a successful opera composer particularly favoured by the Empress. In 1772 his first opera, *Love Brings Trouble*, was produced at the Hermitage Theatre. *The Misfortunes of Having a Carriage* (1779) had public performances both in Petersburg and Moscow. In 1786 Paskevich composed music to a libretto by the Empress, *Czarevich Fevei*, one of the many stories based on early Russian history and legend which Catherine wrote to please her two little grandsons, particularly the future Alexander I who was her favourite.

Paskevich is next found collaborating with two of Catherine's maestros, Vincente Martín and Giuseppe Sarti, on other librettos written by the Empress—*Fedoul and her Children*, and *The Early Reign of Oleg*. Other operas by Paskevich include *The Two Antons* (1804), and *The Miser* (1811). This composer also wrote a number

---

[1] In Fomin's opera *The Post Drivers*, there is a song and chorus based on the same folk tune which Tchaikovsky used almost a century later in the finale of his Fourth Symphony.

of songs, a few of which are still sung in Russia. Some of the
numbers from his operas are still fresh and charming, and show a
real creative imagination at work.

One of the tragedies of early Russian music is recorded in
the brief career of Maxim Sozontovich Beresovsky (1745–77).
He was born in the Ukraine and became a choir-boy in the Imperial
Chapel where his musical talent was observed by Empress Catherine.
She sent him to Italy in 1765 to study with Padre Martini. Beresovsky's progress was remarkable. He composed an opera, *Demofonti*
(to an Italian libretto), which was performed at Bologna and Livorno
in 1773—the first opera by a Russian ever to be produced abroad.
When Beresovsky returned to Russia he composed a considerable
amount of church music, but at the age of thirty-two in a fit of
despondency he shot himself.

VI

The arrival of the nineteenth century brought a sudden eclipse
in the vogue of Italian opera at Petersburg. Alexander I ascended
the throne in 1801, and the young czar's early admiration for the
French and his first flirtings with Bonaparte caused repercussions
in the affairs of the Imperial Opera. The popular French composer
Boieldieu arrived in Petersburg in 1803, and during an eight-year
stay in Russia he composed and produced ten operas in the gay and
frivolous French comic opera style of the period.

Boieldieu was succeeded by a German, Daniel Steibelt, who
was famous in his day as a pianist and composer, and infamous for
a private life of singular disrepute. In Vienna, in 1800, he achieved
a moment of immortality when he engaged in two pianistic duels
with a young rival virtuoso—Ludwig van Beethoven. In 1808
Steibelt turned up in Petersburg, thus putting a safe distance
between himself and an army of creditors. He became conductor of
Alexander's opera company, for which he composed several operas
and ballets in the French style.

During the tenure of French opera in Petersburg one of the
leading figures at the Imperial Opera was an Italian composer-
conductor, Catterino Cavos (1776–1840). This man was born in
Venice, and came to Russia in 1797 with a travelling opera company.
While still in his early twenties he was made court conductor, and
for the next forty years was prominent in the music life of Petersburg.

Cavos began to interest himself in Russian history and folk-lore as possible materials for opera stories. In 1804 he produced his *Rusalka of the Dnieper*, based on a Russian folk tale and sung in Russian. The piece was a success, and it decided Cavos' future. During the next quarter of a century he composed a succession of operas based on Russian stories, including *Ilya the Hero* (1806), *Ivan Susanin* (1815), and *The Bird of Fire* (1815). Musically these pieces were far more Italian than Russian, but their stories were the first extensive explorations of the rich vein of legend and history which the future composers of Russia were to work so avidly.

Cavos appears to have been a good music craftsman but never an inspired one. His pieces enjoyed great popularity in Russia, but in a few decades they had practically disappeared from the stage.

The most successful of all Russian composers before Glinka was Alexis Nicholayevich Verstovsky (1799–1862). He was the son of a country gentleman who sent him to Petersburg to study engineering. The young man turned instead to music, studying with Steibelt, several other German theory instructors, and John Field, the Irish composer-pianist, who was then living in Russia.

In 1824 Verstovsky was appointed director of the Imperial Opera at Moscow, the theatre around which his career was to centre for many years. At first he composed operettas and vaudevilles. His first serious opera was *Pan Tvarvodsky*, composed in 1828, but it was *Askold's Tomb* (1835) which made him famous. This piece enjoyed an enormous success, played hundreds of performances all over Russia, and was revived long after the composer's death.[1] A few of its songs are still in the repertoires of Russian opera singers and are available on phonograph records.

Askold's Tomb was a kind of *singspiel* vaudeville. Its music is now dry and faded with little left to recall the vitality that had charmed Russian audiences of a century ago. We see only a feeble blend of Italian and Russian melodies, set in harmonic clichés, and imitating Rossini, Bellini, and Donizetti. One point of novelty however deserves mention—the graveyard scene in Act III which gives the opera its name. This melange of thunder, lightning, departed spirits, and assorted nightmare horrors in the manner of E. T. A. Hoffmann, was clearly copied from the German stage—specifically from those romantic "magic" operas which reached their greatest success with Weber's *Der Freischütz*.

[1] *Askold's Tomb* was heard in New York City in 1869, played by a Russian opera company which failed after a few performances.

VII

So far as works of permanent value are concerned there is little to be treasured in the entire century of Russian music before Glinka. And yet, even in the groping attempts of pioneers like Fomin, Matinsky, and Paskevich a pattern of the future was already forming itself. Before they had really learned to master the foreign art, these composers were already trying to transmute it into something essentially Russian. This is clear both in their crude uses of Russian folk song and in their opera librettos in which they turn away from the antique and mythological subjects of Italian convention to work on purely Russian stories, even those with the local colour, comedy, and characterization of everyday life. Verstovsky takes a step further—by mixing Italian opera not only with Russianisms but with French operetta and with ideas borrowed from the early German romantic operas.

Thus these early Russian stage pieces are like embryos, misshapen and not a little monstrous, but with startling resemblances to the mature beings which were to come. What they presaged was the brilliant Russian art music of the later nineteenth century, which was to be remarkable both for its purely Russian characteristics and an eclecticism by which it fed upon a great variety of Western music sources.

Composers of the calibre of Fomin, Matinsky, Paskevich, and Verstovsky could give only the barest hints of the coming art because they were men of limited talent who could achieve only fair imitations of Western art. The far greater task—the development of a Russianized art music which would use the folk music with creative ingenuity and subtlety, with symphonic elaboration and richness—that was wholly beyond them. It required genius. Fortunately a man so gifted was awaiting on the horizon of the future. He was Michael Ivanovich Glinka.

CHAPTER III

GLINKA

I

IT has been so long the custom to begin any discourse on Russian music with the name of Michael Glinka that this composer now holds a priority almost like that of Genesis itself. He was the first identifiable Russian composer of genius; his work became the foundation for the entire modern edifice of Russian nationalist music; and he is still a symbol for the nineteenth-century concept of nationalism in the music art.

These facts are so strongly entrenched in music histories that it comes as a shock to realize that they have also given rise to popular misconceptions about Glinka's work. The creation of music with a special Russian flavour was not the sum and substance of his achievement. There was another side to his art, one which had just as powerful an effect on the composers of his country even when they themselves did not realize it. Glinka was also an eclectic, one of the first real eclectics in modern music. His achievement was actually twofold. He showed that a new art music could be created with an unmistakable Russian face; at the same time he established a tradition by which the mercurial mind of a Russian composer might run over a wide field of foreign music styles and idioms and put to use anything that appealed to him. Thus Glinka the nationalist was equally Glinka the cosmopolitan eclectic.

It is no disparagement of his genius to say that he was not wholly original, that he did not spring out of the air. He had the spur of historical events in Russia which surrounded him and carried him on. He had also a very powerful precedent. That precedent existed not so much in any previous music as in a literary source. It was Russia's supreme poet, Alexander Pushkin, who really wrote the prelude to Glinka's music. The two men were contemporaries and for a time friends. There are fundamental phases in Pushkin's art which also appear to be the basis of Glinka's.

The composer and the poet were born into a turbulent age in Russian history, the early reign of Alexander I. When the Russian armies, at first beaten and humiliated by Napoleon, finally repelled

37

the invader from Moscow in utter defeat and ruination, a wild patriotic fervour awoke the entire nation. It was the country's first great outburst of nationalist feeling, a counterthrust not merely to the French armies but to the Western cultural conquest which had begun in the days of Peter the Great. To the Russians the West has always been a giant magnet which alternately attracts and repels them. Now the polarity had suddenly reversed, and the time had come for a new era in Russian life and history.

No one contributed more to nineteenth-century Russian nationalism than Alexander Pushkin. Among intellectuals he gave the movement meaning and importance; by his literary mastery he seemed to prove at one stroke the strength of the native Russian genius when compared with the imported artistry of the West. His influence like his reputation was enormous, and it was by no means limited to literary men. For a hundred years Russian composers would use Pushkin's stories, poems, and plays with the same avidity that the romantic composers of the West went to Byron, Goethe, and Shakespeare.[1]

It was Pushkin's first excursion into nationalism which made him famous. His *Ruslan and Ludmila* (begun in 1817) is by modern standards only a mild sampling of Russian folk-lore; but thereafter in his stories, plays, and poems he ranged widely over the field of native life, history, and legend. At the same time there was no greater eclectic than Pushkin. His early passion for Byron is well known. Later he transferred his allegiance to Shakespeare (who, he said, overwhelmed him), and he studied the English poet to the end of his life. Pushkin admired the works of Voltaire, Molière, and André Chénier; he read widely the literatures of Germany and Italy. He used many subjects from Western art; he borrowed and transmuted ideas and methods at will, until in his own work "the finest traditions of the West are perfectly blended with the true spirit of Russia".

In his tribute to the poet, Dostoevsky pointed out this significant core to the genius of Pushkin, calling it "the miraculous reincarnation of his spirit in the spirit of other nations". We shall find that exactly

---

[1] Among the larger Russian music works based on Pushkin are *Ruslan and Ludmila,* by Glinka; *Rusalka,* and *The Stone Guest,* by Dargomyjsky; *Boris Godunov,* by Musorgsky; *Eugene Onegin, Mazeppa,* and *The Queen of Spades,* by Tchaikovsky; *Mozart and Salieri, The Tale of the Czar Saltan,* and *The Golden Cockerel,* by Rimsky-Korsakov; *The Captive in the Caucasus, A Feast in the Time of Plague,* and *The Captain's Daughter,* by Cui; *Egyptian Nights* (ballet), by Arensky; *Aleko,* and *The Miser Knight,* by Rachmaninov; and *Mavra,* by Stravinsky.

the same two hemispheres of interest, the national and the cosmopolitan, are present in the art of Michael Glinka.

II

Glinka was five years younger than Pushkin, having been born
on June 1 (May 20 O.S.), 1804. His birthplace was Novospasskoe,
a village in the Smolensk district. His father was a wealthy young
landowner who retired from the army to lead the life of a country
gentleman. In that branch of Russian society the landed gentry
lived in the luxury of large, rambling country houses on huge estates
worked by hordes of serfs. Since the gentry themselves were by
social dicta, if not by natural disinclination, forbidden to work, they
fought a constant struggle against boredom and inaction, and the
loneliness which isolation on the sparsely settled land forced upon
them.

The future composer was the product of an artificial, hothouse
existence which in curious ways warped his later life. Glinka was not
an eccentric, but he was an odd and colourful man. He was indolent
and self-indulgent, a hypochondriac and a libertine, who wasted
years of his life in dissipation, the pursuit of women, or simple idle-
ness. Much of his career could be written down as a comedy, were
it not for the tragedy of his misspent genius.

In early childhood Glinka was given over to his grandmother,
with whom he lived until he was six. The old lady was an invalid who
pampered the child as she did herself, seldom permitting him in the
open air. These years spent in overheated sick-rooms may have
prolonged the grandmother's life, but they possibly shortened the
grandson's. In manhood he suffered from an endless series of
illnesses, both physical and mental, real and hypochondriacal.

When he returned to his parents' home the boy's education
was in the charge of a German governess from Petersburg, who
also gave him his first piano lessons. Years later Glinka recorded in
his memoirs the awakening of his passion for music. An uncle who
lived on a neighbouring estate maintained a private orchestra. This
band occasionally visited the home of Glinka's father, and during
dinner they would play Russian songs, arranged for two flutes, two
clarinets, two horns and two bassoons. The composer wrote: ". . . it
may be that these songs, heard in childhood, were the first cause
of my later love of Russian folk music."

When he was thirteen years old Glinka was sent to Petersburg to attend a school for aristocratic young men. At that time no music conservatory existed in the country, but the boy's parents provided him with some of the best private teaching in music that Petersburg could afford. He had three lessons on the piano from John Field before the Irishman left Petersburg; then he went to several German teachers.

In Petersburg Glinka heard his first operatic performances, including works by Cherubini, Méhul, and Rossini. He also made the acquaintance of a beautiful young lady, the first of a large company who were to grace the composer's life. This girl played the harp. Young Glinka was moved to try his hand for the first time at composing, but his pieces (a set of variations for harp and piano on a theme by Mozart) only convinced him that he knew little of the harp and less of the science of music composition. Accordingly, he studied for a time with another German theorist, J. L. Fuchs.

When he was eighteen Glinka left school, and the next few years became a psychological struggle between the young man and his father. Glinka was powerfully drawn toward music but got no sympathy from his parent, the reason being that for a Russian aristocrat music could offer no career whatever. Young Glinka responded to this impasse by falling ill. His father sent him to take a cure at Patigorsk, a fashionable place in the Caucasus, where the young man found the scenery inspiring but the mineral waters revolting. He returned home and sprang back to health when he was permitted to pass his time conducting rehearsals of his uncle's orchestra in overtures by Cherubini, Méhul, and Mozart, and three symphonies—one by Haydn, the G minor by Mozart, and the D major by Beethoven.

Glinka's father next forced him to take a job in the Ministry of Communications in Petersburg, which for a time resolved the difficulty. These posts in the swollen governmental bureaucracy were often sinecures for the aristocracy, and Glinka's work left him free to indulge himself in music, poetry, birds (he had a small private aviary), and the society of various ladies. He continued his music studies and took voice lessons from an Italian teacher. He began to compose songs. He also wrote an immature string quartet in D, and the first movement of a sonata for viola and piano.

It was at this time that Glinka formed a friendship with the poet, Pushkin, among a group of young intellectuals in Petersburg. He also got himself involved, indirectly, in the ominous Decembrist uprising, a revolt of a small group of army officers which broke out in 1825 with the accession of Nicholas I to the throne. The revolt was put down, and Nicholas proceeded to make himself one of the worst despots in modern history. Thereafter to the end of his long reign this "Iron Czar" stifled every whisper of liberalism or reform. He established a secret police (the terrible Third Section) which combed through the government services, the press, and the universities for the slightest hint of political heresy. Following the Decembrist uprising one of Glinka's intellectual friends was arrested for complicity and the composer himself was closely questioned, and thoroughly frightened. He was able to extricate himself from suspicion, and then discreetly composed a short cantata to celebrate the coronation of the new czar.

During the next few years Glinka was constantly in the company of the poets Khukovsky, Alexander Rimsky-Korsakov, and Pushkin, and other fashionable young men who moved in the aristocratic drawing-rooms of Petersburg. At times they gave vent to their romantic ardour by serenading from small boats along the River Neva, or by giving private operatic performances. Glinka toyed continually with composition. He wrote a number of songs, most of them weak and uninteresting, and a few "dramatic scenes" for voices and orchestra, some of which he later worked into his operas.

In spite of his pleasant life and its rather aimless drifting, all was not well with the young composer. He appeared to be chronically ill and was morbidly afraid of death. A modern psychiatrist might suspect as a source of his various pains his passionate desire to travel abroad and his father's adamant refusal. Finally, a noted doctor examined the young man and found "a whole quadrille of ailments" which could only be dispelled by three years in a warm climate. The father capitulated. Young Glinka left Russia in 1830 for a long visit to Italy, a sojourn which had little effect on his health but which did bring him to a turning point of immense significance in his music career.

III

Glinka was by no means the first northern musician whose entire life seemed suddenly to ripen under the golden warmth of the Italian skies, but for this young Russian, emerging for the first time from his country's harsh isolation, the experience must have been especially glorious and exhilarating. For three years the beauty of the Italian scene—the art and culture, the illustrious music and musicians, the lovely women—all unfolded before him as a series of fascinating pictures.

In September, 1830, Glinka went for instruction to the head of the Milan Conservatory, Francesco Basili, whose dry lessons in counterpoint soon repelled him. But when the opera season opened, a new and ravishing experience suddenly unrolled at his feet. He heard Italian opera performed by the most renowned singers of the day, and he heard Donizetti and Bellini conducting performances of their own works. Two historic premières took place that winter—Donizetti's *Anna Bolena*, and Bellini's *La Sonnambula*. At the latter performance Glinka shed "torrents of tears—tears of emotion and enthusiasm". Later in the year he went on to Naples with a young Russian friend who studied with the great singer, Nozzari. Glinka was permitted to attend the lessons and to absorb the master's elucidation of the art of bel canto. In Naples the Russians also met Bellini and Donizetti, and Glinka was moved to try his hand at various pieces in the Italian style. In the year 1832 he was back in Milan, attracted by two beautiful and musically-gifted young ladies. Inevitably more composition resulted, serenades on operatic themes, and a sextet for piano and strings.

After three years in Italy Glinka became restless and acutely homesick. He suffered such agonies from "pains in the head and stomach, aggravated by insomnia and even mental aberrations", that he finally left Italy in July, 1833. A new crisis had also developed in the composer's mind. The impact of the Italian operatic art, especially the mastery of Bellini and Donizetti, had at once inspired and discouraged him. He suddenly knew himself for what he was— a tyro and a dilettante ; and yet he had the courage to examine his failure and to discern why as an imitator of the Italians he was fore-doomed. "It cost me some pains," he wrote afterwards, "to counterfeit the Italian *sentimento brillante*." He did not feel life with the easy-going, light-heartedness of the southerner ; he was a northerner, and "with us, things either make no impression at all, or they sink deep into the soul ; it is either a frenzy of joy or bitter tears . . . with us, love is inseparable from sorrow". For Glinka the realization of these facts was the beginning of wisdom.

After a disheartening experience taking the waters at Baden he went on to Berlin. There he went to Siegfried Dehn, a theorist of wide repute, who gave him in five months a concentrated dose of harmony, counterpoint, fugue, and instrumentation. Glinka afterwards said that Dehn "not only put my musical knowledge into order but also my ideas on art in general, and after his lessons I no longer groped my way along, but worked with the full consciousness of what I was doing".

The immediate fruits of these studies were a group of pieces based on Russian themes—a *Capriccio on Russian Themes*, for piano duet; two movements of a Symphony in D minor; and one of his finest songs, *The Rustling Oak*, to words by the poet Zhukovsky. Glinka was also stirred by the first vague notions for a bold project. He wanted to write an opera. In a letter to a friend in Petersburg he said: "I fancy I have the ability to enrich our stage with a big work. . . . In every way it will be absolutely national. And not only the subject but the music."

In the spring of 1834 Glinka's studies with Dehn, his operatic project, and a love affair with an eighteen-year-old girl with "a Madonna-like face", were all interrupted by the death of his father at Novospasskoe, requiring the composer's immediate return to Russia.

IV

The next two and a half years of Glinka's life were largely dedicated to the planning, composition, and production of the great scheme which became his first opera, *A Life for the Czar*. He had intended to return to Berlin, but in the autumn of 1834 he met in Petersburg the lovely young Maria Petrovna Ivanova to whom he became engaged the following year. He remained in the capital, renewing his friendships with Pushkin, Zhukovsky, and other intellectuals, and meeting Nikolay Gogol, whose *Evenings on a Farm Near Dikanka* was the new sensation of Russian literature.

Glinka discussed his project for a Russian opera with Zhukovsky, who suggested the story of the peasant-hero Ivan Susanin, a subject already well known in Russian music circles from its successful treatment by Catterino Cavos, twenty years previously. The idea struck Glinka with explosive force and he set to work composing various numbers for the piece even though he had no libretto. Zhukovsky had been his choice for librettist, but after providing a few verses the poet retired in favour of one Baron von Rosen, a German secretary to the Czarevich.

In the spring of 1835, amid his work on *A Life for the Czar*, Glinka married Maria Petrovna Ivanova. The union has been compared with the marriage of Pushkin, for it ended in a disaster almost as costly to the artist involved. At first Glinka was deliriously happy with his seventeen-year-old bride who seemed to him "an angel and a miracle of beauty". Accompanied by his angel and her less-than-angelic mother the composer journeyed to Novospasskoe, and while travelling in the coach he began composing *Spring Waters Flow o'er the Fields*, the bridal chorus in 5/4 time in Act III of his opera. At his old family home composition proceeded apace. "Every morning," he related in his memoirs, "I sat at a table in the big sitting-room. . . . My mother, my sister and my wife—in fact the whole family—were busy there, and the more they laughed and talked and bustled about the quicker my work went. The weather was lovely, and I often worked with the door open into the garden, drinking the pure fragrant air."

Glinka completed *A Life for the Czar* during the following winter in Petersburg. He brought it to Cavos who was still active at the Imperial Opera, and the Italian praised the opera so generously that it was accepted for performance. Rehearsals under his direction continued through the summer and autumn of 1836. Glinka had originally titled the piece *Ivan Susanin*, but after Czar Nicholas attended one of the final rehearsals and indicated his pleasure both in the work and its dedication to him, the name of the opera was changed to *A Life for the Czar*.

The first performance of *A Life for the Czar* took place at the Grand Theatre in Petersburg, December 9 (November 27 O.S.), 1836. After the Polish scenes the audience sat in utter silence because the Czar's presence made it unwise to applaud his historic enemies even when portrayed by actors; but thereafter the enthusiasm was boundless. At the end Glinka was summoned to the Czar's box for congratulations, and later he was rewarded with a ring worth four thousand roubles and the post of Kappellmeister to the Imperial Opera.

The story of *A Life for the Czar* (which is based on an old tale that may or may not be historically true) begins in the year 1613 when Russia was torn by civil wars and threatened by Polish armies. Michael Romanov, the first of the Romanov line, had been chosen czar but was hiding in a monastery. The commanders of a Polish army corps try to force a Russian peasant, Ivan Susanin, to lead them to the monastery but Susanin secretly sends his foster son to warn Michael, and then leads the Polish soldiers astray into the depths of a snowy forest, knowing that death awaits him when his deception is discovered. In the final scene of the opera Czar Michael is hailed by the people before the Kremlin in Moscow, and all do honour to the dead body of Susanin.

Musically, Glinka's first opera is a crude work, but it exhibits quite clearly those features which were later to become the essentials of his art. On the one hand the piece is a true pioneer example of Russian nationalist music. On the other it shows that Glinka was also by nature an eclectic and that he knew by instinctive artistry how to reconcile the diverse phases of his talent. He had begun by aiming to write "a Russian opera", music "in which my beloved countrymen would feel at home". But this really meant a Russian version of an Italian form. When he finally hit upon the story he wanted, he said that "the plan of the whole opera and the idea of the antithesis of Russian and Polish music . . . flashed into my head at one stroke". Thus the piece was from the beginning a purposeful mingling of Russian, Italian, and Polish music styles.

In spite of its Russian flavour and its story, *A Life for the Czar* is predominantly Italian. Glinka was not yet strong enough either as technician or aesthete to escape the weight of two centuries of Italian procedure. The general form of the piece follows the old formulas. Each act is made up of set numbers—solos, choruses, duets, trios, dances, etc.—bound together by recitatives. The various numbers are built up conventionally with long repeats, so that a minimum of material may be spread over a large area. Much of the melody is imitation Italian, especially the parts of Antonida and Sobinin, the soprano and tenor, which attempt weakly to be vocal showpieces.

The Polish materials are most striking in the opening of the second act, which represents a festival at the Polish capital and is made up of a group of dances—polonaises, mazourkas, and waltzes. These now sound commonplace when compared inevitably with Chopin's treatment of the same forms. Some original touches in the orchestration remain their best feature.

It was quite naturally the Russian elements of *A Life for the Czar* which first gave the opera its great distinction and its success. Russian audiences quickly recognized that this was no formless vaudeville with interpolated folk songs, but a professionally conceived art work with a semblance of musical unity and a strong dramatic force. Glinka used Russian folk songs both as complete entities and as thematic seeds. An example of the latter procedure is found in Susanin's opening recitative in Act I, whose phrases are taken from a cab-driver's song. A less obvious example occurs in Act IV in which a robber's song, *Down by Mother Volga*, is moulded into an accompaniment figure in the orchestral part. Most of the Russian themes appear to be Glinka's own invention, and they are often admirable imitations of the folk style—for example, the *Bridal Chorus* in 5/4 time, a charming melody cast in one of the typical Russian rhythms ; and the *Slavsya Chorus* in the final act, a glorification of the czar, which has real power and majesty.

Glinka used other devices to give his score a native flavour. In Act I there is a unison chorus famous for its pizzicato accompaniment which strongly suggests balalaikas, an effect which Tchaikovsky may have remembered in writing the Scherzo of his Fourth Symphony ; and there are other uses of unaccompanied choral singing in the folk manner. Act III contains a marked reference to the antiphonal singing of Orthodox Church choirs.

At least passing mention should be made of Glinka's use of a scheme of leading motives in his first opera, an anticipation of the idea which Wagner was later to exploit so prodigiously. The Russian composer's treatment of recurring themes is hardly more than rudimentary, but it reveals a facet of his mind—his receptiveness to new ideas, and his eagerness to give his music a distinction and a character of its own.

After its successful first performance the popularity and prestige of *A Life for the Czar* continued unabated for many years. At one stroke it made a reputation for Glinka as the "first composer of Russia". The early critical opinions were for the most part enthusiastic, although there were notable dissensions. The attempt to create a work of art from folk materials inevitably invited ridicule. The Russian sophisticates of the day, still bemused with the refinements of Western culture, could find only vulgarity in things Russian. With disdain they referred to *A Life for the Czar* as "coachman's music".

Outside Russia *A Life for the Czar* is today hardly more than a museum piece, but within the country it retains a vitality that is likely to endure. In 1939, when a successful revival of the work in Leningrad was broadcast to Europe and America, it appeared that the opera had been refurbished by the Soviet authorities. It was announced that "the original title was misleading", and that "the libretto written by Baron von Rosen had catered to the wishes and

whimsy of the czar, perverting the true event of Susanin's heroism".
Accordingly, with the change of the title back to *Ivan Susanin*,
came a rewritten libretto, the work of the young Soviet poet, Sergei
Gorodetsky. In this new version Susanin's devotion to his country
and his fellow-Russians rather than to his ruler becomes the basic
theme; and words like "Glory, glory to the Czar" (in the Fifth Act
hymn) become "Glory, glory to the fatherland".

V

Two months after the first performance of *A Life for the Czar*
there occurred a black day in the history of the Russian arts. On
February 8 (January 27 O.S.), 1837, Alexander Pushkin, then
only thirty-eight years old, was killed in a duel. The tragedy which
robbed Russian literature of one of its supreme talents had also a
depressing effect upon the fortunes of Michael Glinka. The composer
had in mind a second opera, to be based on *Ruslan and Ludmila*,
Pushkin's charming and satirical fairy tale. Whether the two men
actually discussed the project is not known for certain, but in later
years Glinka recalled that Pushkin's death lost for him the chance of
having the poet's guidance in drawing up a scenario.

Glinka required six years for the completion of *Ruslan and
Ludmila*. He afterwards said that he worked in "snatches and
fragments", with periods of intense and hurried composition
followed by long spells of inactivity. For a long time he had no
libretto at all, but only a vague general plot; nevertheless, he
would dash off numbers for various parts of the story as the spirit
moved him, without waiting for verses to be written.

The most serious distraction came from the collapse of Glinka's
marriage. It would be hard to place the blame on either party, for
while the composer would have been a trial for any woman, being
undependable, indolent, and a libertine, his wife Maria was extravagant and frivolous. The girl's German-born and dictatorial
mother who lived with the couple only completed the picture of
marital calamity. The quarrelling became frequent and nerve-
shattering, after which the composer would take himself off for days
at a time to the homes of various friends.

Glinka was especially attached to Nestor Kukolnik, a minor
poet, at whose house there were meetings of intellectuals, some of
dubious authenticity—Kukolnik and his brother, several singers, a

caricaturist, and a colonel of artillery who tried to compose. At these gatherings Glinka heard performances of Beethoven's last string quartets, and he was moved to write a number of songs to Kukolnik's words. Not infrequently the meetings ended in "orgies" which shocked the composer's more respectable friends.

The doom of the Glinka marriage was sealed in the spring of 1839 when the composer fell in love with a pale, neurotic girl named Ekaterina Kern. For several years they carried on a fleeting affair, both ill from various nervous disorders and balked in their desires to marry by the presence of Maria. Glinka finally secured proof of his wife's infidelity and sued for a divorce in 1841. It was not until 1846 that the marriage was legally ended, but by that time the romance with Ekaterina was also dead.

Meanwhile, the composition of *Ruslan and Ludmila* continued on its perilous course. Glinka was still lacking a scenario when one night he happened to play some excerpts from the opera. Present was a man named Constantine Bakhturin. "He undertook," wrote Glinka, "to draw up a plan of the opera, and although drunk, did it in a quarter of an hour." This plan seems to have served as a scenario for a considerable part of the piece. Following Bakhturin, Glinka secured the services of a Captain Shirkov, who wrote a number of verses.

In the autumn of 1840 there occurred a considerable interruption when Glinka obliged his friend Kukolnik by writing an overture and some incidental music to a tragedy called *Prince Kholmsky*. The play died after three performances and before Glinka had completed his task. The next year Kukolnik helped the composer with verses for *Ruslan and Ludmila*, the libretto of which was now in a deplorable state of confusion. Glinka finally wrote some of the words himself, and the score was completed in April, 1842.

The misfortunes that had attended the creation of *Ruslan and Ludmila* continued through its première on December 9 (November 27 O.S.), 1842, the sixth anniversary of the first performance of *A Life for the Czar*. During the final rehearsals mutilating cuts were made in the score, the scenery was poor, the conductor was incompetent, and at the last moment one of the leading singers became ill and had to be replaced by an inadequate understudy. The audience, remembering the patriotic splendours of *A Life for the Czar*, sat bewildered and disappointed by Glinka's fairy-tale opera, whose story they could not understand and whose music left them cold. At the end there was hissing. Later the reviews were nearly all bad, the work being described simply as a bore. Glinka remarked with bitterness that *Ruslan and Ludmila* "would probably be recognized in a hundred years". Certainly it found no appreciative audience during his own lifetime and for years thereafter.

Pushkin's original story was the poet's first important work, and was a scintillating piece of wit and fantasy. Unfortunately for Glinka, his librettists captured little of the story's original flavour and succeeded only in making the plot hopelessly diffuse.

The opera begins with an introductory scene in which a bard of legendary days in pagan Russia is telling the story. Ludmila, the beautiful daughter of Prince Svietozar of Kiev, has three suitors— the knights Ruslan and Farlaf, and Ratmir, a young Tartar prince. Ludmila's love is given to Ruslan, but during the ceremonies preceding their marriage, Chernomor, a wicked sorcerer, appears in a clap of thunder and carries the bride away. Prince Svietozar offers his daughter in marriage to the man who will rescue her. At this point, which closes Act I, the three suitors (and the opera plot itself) proceed to wander off in all directions.

In Act II Ruslan seeks help at the cave of the kindly old wizard, Finn, who first relates his own pathetic story. Years before he had wooed the sorceress, Naina, changing himself into a shepherd, a fisherman, a warrior, and finally into a wizard. This last transformation won Naina's heart, but alas, they realized that now they were both too old for love. Finn advises Ruslan to arm himself with a magic sword, and to attack a fearsome Giant's Head, as one of the steps by which he may rescue Ludmila. The third scene is an ancient, moonlit battlefield, covered with whitened bones and shrouded in mist. Here Ruslan encounters the terrible apparition of the Giant's Head, which he slays with the magic sword.

Act III depicts the ensnaring of Ratmir by Naina's enchantments. The act begins with a Persian Chorus of women's voices, and later Ratmir meets the seductive Gorislava whom he had jilted for Ludmila. There are dances by the women of the harem, but later the entire lovely scene, which was the work of Naina's sorcery, fades away and leaves Ratmir alone on the empty steppe.

Act IV takes place in the evil sorcerer Chernomor's enchanted garden. There are Oriental dances and ballets, after which Ruslan defeats Chernomor in an aerial combat. The hero then awakens Ludmila from a magic spell.

In Act V the lovers are again separated when Farlaf carries off Ludmila by treachery. At her father's palace he claims the hand of the princess, who is again in a magic-induced sleep. Meanwhile, Finn enlists the help of Ratmir, urging him to carry a magic ring to Ruslan, by means of which Ludmila may again be aroused from her sleep. At the moment when Farlaf is about to marry the princess, Ruslan arrives, to awaken his beloved—and conclude the opera.

Even though the libretto of *Ruslan and Ludmila* was a dramatic botch, it was not in the long run fatal to the opera itself. The piece failed at first chiefly because of its remarkably modern music for which the Russian audience of the time was unprepared. Glinka had made astonishing strides as a composer. He had gained facility and sureness of craftsmanship, and an abundant flow of creative ideas; his music now had a style, character, and individuality that were new to this art.

A Life for the Czar had been primarily an Italian opera, with a thin layer of Russian ornamentation. *Ruslan and Ludmila* was a far more Russian work and much of it could never have been written by anyone but a Russian. But again, Glinka's achievement was twofold : *Ruslan and Ludmila* was the composer's masterpiece as a pioneer work of nationalism and it created almost at one stroke the essential style of modern Russian music; it was also Glinka's most powerful effort as an eclectic—a synthesist who drew upon ideas from a dozen different sources, blending them effectively with his Russian material.

Ruslan and Ludmila contains countless details of melody, harmony, rhythm, form, instrumentation and style which all became a kind of Russian musical language and which would be spoken by composers for the next century. At the bottom of it all was a central problem which Glinka had to solve first. Russia's folk music and her ancient church music were based on old modal scales which Western music had centuries ago abandoned for the major-minor scales and their principles of tonality. The problem was to reconcile and join the two systems, and this extended beyond melody and harmony into basic principles of tonal relationship and form. In *Ruslan and Ludmila* we see Glinka's solutions of the tentative experiments he had begun in *A Life for the Czar*. He had no precedent; he had to feel his way. What guided him, fortunately, was a creative instinct of a high order.

Ruslan and Ludmila has been known so long as the fountainhead of pure Russianism that its other great characteristic—its eclecticism—usually goes unnoted. Poured into the score are gleanings from Glinka's adventures in a dozen different music sources, both of the East and the West. This eclecticism begins with the very first page and continues on and off to the last. The Overture, now a standard concert piece, has distinctive Russian melodies and rhythmic verve, set in a German framework. The neat contrapuntal effects and the rushing scale passages are remindful of Weber and Mozart. Act I begins with the wholly Russian song of the Bard in the archaic *bilini* style, with harp and piano imitating the gusli. Ludmila's Cavatina, a farewell to her father, is an Italian coloratura piece with conventional florid decorations.

The choral Invocation to Lel, the pagan God of Love, is Russian to the core, and most original. Cast in 5/4 rhythm, it achieves an effect of primitive harshness and garish brilliance, with the melody often set forth boldly in simple octaves or in consecutive sixths, both in the chorus and the orchestra. After the thunderclaps which lead to the abduction of Ludmila by the black wizard Chernomor we come to an exercise in German counterpoint. For more than a hundred measures the horn holds a pedal point on E flat, around which is constructed a four-part canon, sung by the three suitors and Svietozar.

Finn's Ballad in Act II has a pure folk quality, being based on a Finnish postillion's song which Glinka had noted down years before on a trip to the Imatra Falls. Farlaf's Rondo is right out of Italian opera buffa—a *Largo al factotum* with Russian words. Ruslan's Aria is made up of wholly Russian melodies but is built on the classic sonata form, the second subject being the broad second theme of the Overture. The fantastic and highly imaginative scene with the Giant's Head is clearly related to the magic operas of German romanticism, but with ideas that were Glinka's own. He created his Giant's voice by placing inside the head a small chorus of men's voices, singing in unison.

Act III opens with a Persian Chorus of women's voices, one of the most admired numbers in the opera. The charming and delicate melody was a genuine Persian air which Glinka heard in 1828 from a Persian secretary of the Foreign Ministry. The tune is sung in unison and is repeated again and again against orchestral variations that grow constantly in richness and elaboration. Ratmir's Nocturne, with its answering phrases in the English horn, is based on a Tartar melody. It was one of three such melodies given to Glinka by Ayvazovsky, the noted marine painter. The ballet scene which follows is a curious mixture, with rococo dances in the French opera style making their odd appearance in an Oriental garden.

Soon after the beginning of Act IV there is a Chorus of Flowers whose sweet melodies and luscious harmonies Tchaikovsky must have remembered decades later. This alternates with an air for Ludmila that is decidedly gypsy-like. After a Russian lullaby in the simple folk style, Chernomor and his magicians take over and the German magic style returns, but again metamorphosed by Glinka's own imaginative genius. Chernomor's March was so startling in its originality that it delighted Franz Liszt, who transcribed it for piano in 1843. Of the Oriental Dances that follow, the first is based on a Turkish song while the second is imitation Arabian. By far the most remarkable dance movement in the entire opera is the third Oriental dance, the Lezginka. (The Lezghians were a tribe of Caucasian mountaineers.) Here Glinka used two more Tartar themes given him by Ayvazovsky, and he worked up a movement of immense vigour and speed. His bold use of dissonance was so disturbing, moreover, that the piece was often cut in early performances.

"We are all sprung from Gogol's 'The Cloak'," said Dostoevsky in a famous remark about Russian writers. The same could be said of modern Russian composers and *Ruslan and Ludmila*. It became their source-book of nationalist procedure. It was just as much their guide to eclecticism. In all music it would be hard to find another score made up of such a miscellany, one which still congeals into unity. And it would be hard to exaggerate the way in which Glinka's procedures—both nationalist and eclectic—lodged themselves in the thought of his descendants. Much of the variety and distinction of Russian music in the next hundred years, as well as some of its weaknesses, spring from Glinka's cosmopolitan tastes and his adventurous mind.

In his handling of the orchestra Glinka earned the respect of its greatest modern masters. By intuition, it seemed, more than by serious study he evolved a style that set the standard in Russia for many years. In the main it was characterized by crystal clarity, by brightness, with telling contrasts between thin and piercing high registers and a bass of massive dignity and power. Rimsky-Korsakov, himself a prince of orchestrators, had nothing but adulation for Glinka after his meticulous work as editor of his predecessor's scores:

"How subtle everything is with him and yet how simple and natural at the same time! With avidity I imbibed all his methods. I studied his handling of the natural-scale brass instruments, which lend his orchestration such ineffable transparency and grace; I studied his graceful and natural part-writing."

VI

The failure of *Ruslan and Ludmila* had a disastrous effect upon the career of its composer. Although Glinka was then only thirty-nine with fifteen years yet to live he never again completed a large-scale work. He became restless and unsettled. Russia no longer pleased him and to escape the boredom of his life he made several journeys to Western Europe, living for long periods in Paris, Madrid, Warsaw, and Berlin.

On his travels abroad Glinka found that he was a new phenomenon in the world of music, a Russian composer. Liszt had paid him handsome tributes and played the transcription of Chernomor's March all over Europe. In Paris, Berlioz played excerpts from his operas and later praised the Russian fulsomely in a press article. Meyerbeer sought his friendship and played his music at the court of the King of Prussia. Nothing, however, could rouse Glinka's ambitions for more than the meagrest effort at composition.

The breakdown of his marriage contributed to the dissolution of the composer's personal life, which became a succession of transient affairs with women he chanced to meet on his travels—various young Spanish girls in Madrid, an Andalusian singer in Granada, a dancer, and, later, the daughter of a restaurant-keeper in Warsaw, an actress, a grisette, and a milliner in Paris, to say nothing of a large company of servant girls. Unfortunately the composer contracted syphilis, the disease which finally killed him.

In the summer of 1844 Glinka went again to Paris, and during the next year the interest shown his works at Berlioz' concerts convinced him that he should try his hand at a new type of orchestral piece, which he termed *Fantaisies pittoresques*. He decided shrewdly that the established repertoire of concert pieces—quartets, symphonies, concertos, variations, etc.—were usually too abstruse or complex to engage a wide public interest. He wanted instead to write pieces "equally accessible to the connoisseurs and to the general public". These would be short, picturesque or fanciful, and not too heavily freighted with intellectual difficulties. With his eye for the exotic and the colourful, Glinka decided that Spanish melodies and folk tunes might yield just the material for his *Fantaisies*. It might be that even a Spanish opera would result.

He set out for Spain in the summer of 1845, and was immediately captivated by what he saw and heard. The entire apparatus of Spanish music and dancing—the complex and insinuating rhythms, the guitars and the castanets, and above all the melodies that were either soft, throaty, and languorous, or burning coals of love and hate—these impressed themselves vividly upon the receptive mind of the Russian. He spent almost two years in Spain, with visits to Madrid, Granada, Aranjuez, and Toledo ; he listened to the popular music in the theatres, the songs of the guitarists, the folk tunes of muleteers ; he watched the dancing of the gypsies. His researches were enlivened by the native company (invariably feminine) whom he met on the way. The gypsy dancing even fired him with a sudden ambition to learn the flashing steps himself, but he failed. "My feet were all right," he said, "but I couldn't manage the castanets."

The results of Glinka's studies of the popular music of Spain were not immediately spectacular. He wrote but one work in Madrid, the Spanish Overture No. 1, in which he used the Aragonese *jota*, an ancient folk tune. The rest of the experience lay dormant in his music consciousness until 1848, when in Warsaw he wrote *A Night in Madrid*, Spanish Overture No. 2, based on four Spanish melodies. At the same time he failed in an attempt to construct a work on Andalusian tunes, because he could not manipulate the Oriental scales on which they were based. No Spanish opera, moreover, was ever forthcoming from Glinka's pen.

At first glance it would seem that the Spanish works hardly justified the effort of the two-year sojourn. The first Overture, on the *jota* Aragonese, is a melodious and spirited piece, richly coloured with the hues of its origin ; but the second, *A Night in Madrid*, is somewhat disappointing. Nevertheless, the works have real historic significance. They reveal once more Glinka's eclectic bent and his pioneering genius, and they are à definite part of his important spadework in the vast field of nationalism in music.

Glinka was not wholly without models for his experiments, for nationalist airs had been coming into prominence in Western art music. Mozart and Beethoven had both imitated the so-called "Turkish style", to give an exotic colour to short movements, and the latter had also made use of Hungarian and even Russian themes. Weber touched lightly on Hungarian and Chinese airs. Chopin's mazurkas and polonaises in the Polish style clearly anticipate Glinka. Moreover, in 1845, the year of the Russian's Spanish journey, Franz Liszt was also in the Iberian peninsula on a concert tour, one result of which was his Spanish Rhapsody for piano.

What gave Glinka's Spanish pieces distinction was the composer's success in retaining much of the native flavour of his material. His work with Russian music had taught him how to extract the essential melodic contours of folk music, to use its characteristic harmonies and its rhythms, and even to imitate the charm of native instruments. The result with the Spanish pieces was wholly picturesque—evoking with vividness the image and the atmosphere of the native locality.

Glinka left Spain in May 1847, returning finally to the family estate at Novospasskoe. There restlessness and nerves again beset him. He started for Petersburg but suffered a relapse and had to spend a winter at Smolensk, attended by his devoted sister, Ludmila Ivanovna Shestakova. The next spring (1848) found him in Warsaw. Here he had the companionship of his birds which flew around his flat, two hares which also had the run of the place, and a young girl named Angelique. It was in these congenial surroundings that the composer was moved to write his second Spanish overture, *A Night in Madrid*, and the best known of his orchestral works, the *Kamarinskaya*. The latter piece employs two tunes, a song and a dance, derived from Russian folk weddings. The first is lyric and flowing, the second briskly spirited. With these two simple airs Glinka pieced together a short work which is still fresh and engaging in its characteristic Russianness. Tchaikovsky paid tribute to the little piece when he said that from it "all Russian composers who followed Glinka (including myself) continue to this day to borrow contrapuntal and harmonic combinations directly they have to develop a Russian dance tune". Another feature of *Kamarinskaya* which the composer's descendants widely copied has been described by the English musicologist, Gerald Abraham, as a method of building up a folk tune "without destroying either its form or its spirit". The tune is repeated, "with little or no modification, against ever new but always sympathetic backgrounds of harmony and instrumental colour".

Kamarinskaya marked the virtual close of Glinka's life as a composer. In the following eight years he moved aimlessly in and out of Russia, his health broken, his ambitions at their lowest ebb. When he became seriously ill his sister Ludmila usually sped to his side to nurse and comfort him; once he recovered, her place was taken by some young lady friend of charm if not virtue.

On a few occasions Glinka tried to fan the dying embers of his creative life. In the summer of 1852 he set out once more for Spain, but remained instead in Paris. There he began work on what he called a "Ukrainian" Symphony, a programme piece based on Gogol's story, *Taras Bulba*. The idea progressed no farther than part of an allegro in C minor when the composer lost heart and gave it up, "being unable to get out of the German rut of development". In Petersburg, in 1855, he considered writing an opera to be based on his friend Kukolnik's drama, *The Bigamist*. After a few preliminary sketches this idea was also abandoned, the reason being Glinka's dislike of his librettist and his inability to escape the music style of *A Life for the Czar*. If he could not invent something new, he preferred not to write at all.

The last struggle took place in Berlin. The composer had left Petersburg in May 1856, spitting contemptuously at the city he had grown to detest. In the Prussian capital he went once more to his teacher, Dehn. He had been studying the old ecclesiastical modes, his interest in church music having been aroused by a performance of the Crucifixus from Bach's B minor Mass. Like so many romantics he turned at last to the font of classicism. With Dehn he studied the *Well-tempered Clavier*, and wrote two fugues himself. What music metamorphosis might have resulted from the impact of classicism upon this eclectic-romantic-nationalist we shall never know, for on February 15, 1857, Glinka suddenly died. At least one event must have brightened the melancholy of his last days. A few weeks before his death he had been honoured at a Court Concert of the King of Prussia, at which Meyerbeer produced the trio from *A Life for the Czar*.

VII

There was an epilogue to the life of Michael Glinka, a remarkable drama in which the protagonist was the composer's sister, Ludmila Ivanovna Shestakova. This woman was fourteen years younger than her brother, and she outlived him almost fifty years. To the moment of her death in 1906, at the age of eighty-eight, a single passion ruled her life—the belief that her brother's work constituted one of the major glories of Russian art.

For some years before his death Ludmila had been one of the main props of Glinka's existence. She urged him constantly to compose; she collected and preserved his carelessly treated manuscripts; she even badgered him into writing his memoirs, which relate with such disarming candour the achievements and the wasted opportunities of his strange career. It was after the composer's death that the strength of the sister's character and her zealot's faith in his greatness began to impress themselves upon the music chronicle of the times. She had his body removed from Berlin to a place of honour in the cemetery of the Alexander Nevsky Monastery in Petersburg; and then, for half a century, she fought an unrelenting battle to keep his name and his work alive.

For Glinka's masterpiece, *Ruslan and Ludmila*, the sister performed an incalculable service. A single copy of the full score remained in existence at the composer's death. Ludmila commissioned young Mili Balakirev, a disciple of her brother's, to supervise the making of two new copies. The work had hardly been completed when the composer's original copy was destroyed in a fire at the Marinsky Theatre. To remove the stain of failure from the opera itself, Ludmila waged a campaign that lasted more than a decade. When she could not force a revival of the work in Petersburg she sent Balakirev to Prague, in 1866, hoping to get it performed there with a success that would awaken interest in Russia. When Balakirev failed she went herself to Prague and in a short time made the arrangements for the performance. In 1872 she finally won her point in Petersburg, when a significant revival of *Ruslan and Ludmila* took place at the Marinsky Theatre.

Ludmila's next project was the publication of a definitive edition of the scores of her brother's operas. She hired Balakirev, Liadov, and Rimsky-Korsakov as editors. They worked for two years at the task, correcting errors and, in *Ruslan and Ludmila*, restoring cuts that had been made at the first performance. Ludmila sent copies of the new editions to libraries, opera houses, and other music organizations all over Russia and even abroad. She paid the costs herself, from money received from the sale of her land.

Hardly less significant than her work as active propagandist for Glinka's music was Ludmila's position as matriarch of the brilliant and ambitious group of young musicians who were later known as "the Five". Her home became a salon where they foregathered; she was their friend, correspondent, and confidante; over Balakirev and Musorgsky especially, she exerted a powerful influence. She became a vital communicating link between her brother—the charming, profligate, genius-wasting Glinka, the prophet of modern Russian music—and the men who were destined to become its gods.

CHAPTER IV

DARGOMYJSKY

I

ALEXANDER DARGOMYJSKY has been called "the mystery man of Russian music", a fitting title for a composer whose theories were among the most novel and influential of his time, but whose major works are long since entombed in the silences of library shelves. Dargomyjsky was like an inventor who had constructed a balloon according to radical principles, but his balloon refused to go up. Other men, coming later and using his principles, succeeded in building balloons which made perfect ascents.

Dargomyjsky's early life ran parallel in many respects to Glinka's. He was born in 1813 on a country estate in the Government of Tula. As a child he received private instruction in piano and violin playing, but none in composition. In early manhood he took a government job in the Department of Justice, where, like Glinka, he tried to be a musician on the side. He was a talented performer on the piano and violin, but a tyro as a composer. In 1834 came a turning point in Dargomyjsky's life—his meeting with Glinka in Petersburg. From the famous composer he borrowed the five note-books on harmony, counterpoint, and instrumentation which recorded Glinka's instruction from Professor Dehn in Berlin. Thus fortified, and with Glinka's encouragement, Dargomyjsky set out to be a composer.

The story of his career is one of the most disheartening in music, a long succession of disappointments and frustrations which the composer bore with fortitude. He finished his first opera, *Esmeralda*, after a story by Victor Hugo, in 1839, and for eight years it lay in the files of the Imperial Opera, under consideration but never performed. "Eight long years of waiting in vain," wrote Dargomyjsky, "during the very keenest and most fervid period of life! This experience weighted heavily upon the whole of my artistic career." When *Esmeralda* was finally performed in 1847 it failed after three performances.

In 1840 Dargomyjsky had begun a one-act opera ballet, *The Triumph of Bacchus*. This was not produced until 1867 when it failed, never to be revived or even published. His next opera, *Rusalka*, finished in 1855, seemed to break the chain of misfortune. It was well received on its première in Petersburg in 1856, ran briefly, and after a revival in 1866 remained among the most popular works in the Russian repertoire.

Meanwhile, Dargomyjsky had staked everything on his *magnum opus*, *The Stone Guest*, based on Pushkin's version of the Don Juan story. This piece, which was to be a testing-ground for the composer's radical theories about opera, was begun in 1866. But Dargomyjsky's health had meanwhile broken down. He worked with feverish haste, "ailing and all twisted by rheumatism", struggling to finish one of the most difficult tasks ever attempted by an operatic composer. In 1869 he died, leaving *The Stone Guest* unfinished. At his request the work was completed by César Cui and orchestrated by Rimsky-Korsakov. One final defeat at least the composer was spared. When *The Stone Guest* received its première performance in Petersburg in 1872 it failed in spite of a superior cast and production.

Both as man and artist Dargomyjsky seemed marked for misfortune. He was hardly more than five feet tall, with an abnormally large head; his nose was short, his eyes small and continually blinking; his face was pasty and unhealthy looking. He never married but he loved the society of women, whose flattery and adulation he craved. He would accept only women as pupils. The composer lived in Petersburg with his wealthy father, and several afternoons each week he entertained lavishly. The guests were usually women. Dargomyjsky prepared elaborate music programmes made up chiefly of his own works, which he sang in a high-pitched squeaky voice. Disappointment in his career made him abnormally sensitive and overbearing; he continually overrated his own music, comparing it with Glinka's to the latter's detriment.

Dargomyjsky was a man of keen intelligence. It was his great misfortune, in fact, that his mental capacities and especially his gift for inquiry, speculation, and enterprise in the technical side of music far outran his creative talent. The "singing soul", the sheer natural outpouring of music ideas, was denied him.

II

Dargomyjsky's revolutionary theories about opera developed slowly. His first opera, *Esmeralda*, showed no originality and the composer himself later said of it, "The music is slight and often trivial—in the style of Halévy and Meyerbeer." In 1844 Dargomyjsky travelled abroad, visiting Brussels, Paris, and Vienna, where he met various important persons in the music world and gave private performances of his own works. He returned to Petersburg ardently pro-Russian and determined like Glinka to write a purely Russian opera. He would emulate his predecessor—but with one important reservation. Glinka, he felt, had touched only one side of Russian folk music, the lyrical and the melancholy; Dargomyjsky planned to tap the dramatic, realistic, and comical side.

He chose as his subject Pushkin's *Rusalka* (The Water Nymph). "Russian folklore," remarked Rosa Newmarch, "teems with references to the *rusalki*, or water nymphs, who haunt the streams and the still, dark forest pools, lying in wait for the belated traveller. . . ." Pushkin's story involves a miller's daughter who is betrayed by her lover, a Prince, and drowns herself in the mill-stream. Years later, as a water nymph, she haunts the Prince, drawing him back to the ruined mill. Her father, old and insane, finally throws his daughter's betrayer into the stream and drowns him.

Dargomyjsky's piece has a certain importance because it was the only operatic work of any consequence to be composed in Russia between Glinka's *Ruslan and Ludmila* and Musorgsky's *Boris Godunov*. It held a place in the repertoire for years and was the only opera by Dargomyjsky to be produced abroad. In *Rusalka*, Dargomyjsky's workmanship is competent, but never inspired. For all his attempt to create a Russian opera his piece remains simply an odd specimen of the Italian genre. It follows the familiar pattern—arias, choruses, set numbers, interspersed with recitatives. The composer's attempts to create Russian music are pallid. Most of the tunes are reminiscent; few stay in the mind.

Dargomyjsky was too intelligent not to realize that for all his theorizing he was still in the grip of Italian opera. Meanwhile, he had been speculating about the new concept of realism in art, then exemplified in Russia chiefly in the stories of Gogol. The idea of "realistic truth" in literature bridged a gap in the composer's mind to "realistic truth in music". Dargomyjsky finally convinced himself that "truth" in vocal music could be achieved if the music could be made to mirror the precise meaning and mood of the words. He composed a number of songs embodying this idea. He had also made a start on the procedure in the recitatives in *Rusalka*, which were a move toward a kind of melodic declamation, with the music following closely the natural contours of the spoken words.

Gradually this scheme rooted itself in Dargomyjsky's mind with the tenacity of religious dogma. He explained the public coldness toward his music by his refusal to "seek for melody which is merely flattering to the ear. This is not *my* first thought. I have no intention of indulging them with music as a plaything. *I want the note to be the direct equivalent of the word. I want truth and realism.*"

The first lukewarm reception of *Rusalka* turned Dargomyjsky away for a time from the field of opera. He had begun a "magical-comic opera", *Rogdana*, but abandoned it, composing instead three short orchestral works—*Kazachok, Baba Yaga*, and *Fantasia on Finnish Themes*—all of which show the composer's sharp sense of humour and his urge to try novel effects of harmony, rhythm and instrumentation. It was not until 1866 after a second trip abroad[1] that Dargomyjsky began work on *The Stone Guest*, the opera which was to bring to fruition all the composer's years of theorizing about realistic truth in music.

There is hardly another operatic score at once as remarkable and as paradoxical as *The Stone Guest*.[2] It is in all probability the most influential failure in the history of the lyric stage. As music it is a dull and frigid work, undramatic, dogmatized to the point of sterility, lacking essential music beauty ; but as a piece of pioneering it is engrossing, and invaluable to the story of modern Russian music.

Dargomyjsky's scheme for this opera was based on two main theories : first, he aimed to depart utterly from the conventions of Italian opera by abandoning all semblance of its outward structure— its arias, recitatives, choruses, set pieces, etc. ; second, he would create an entirely new structure simply by setting Pushkin's pla, to

[1] While in Brussels Dargomyjsky composed his curious "*Tarantella Slav*, for persons who are unable to play the piano". The secondo part of this piano duet consists of a single bass note repeated throughout. The piece was intended as a compliment to a young lady dancer who had attracted the composer's fancy, but could not play the piano.

[2] In 1826 Pushkin planned to write ten short plays, or "little tragedies". He finished only three—*The Miser Knight, The Stone Guest*, and *Mozart and Salieri*, which treat successively the themes of avarice, lust, and envy. *The Stone Guest*, with Don Juan as its chief character, has been called the most perfect of the group. Its source was a famous seventeenth-century Spanish play, *El Burlador de Sevilla y convidado de piedra*, by the immensely prolific dramatist Tirso de Molina. Many later writers copied the Spaniard's piece, including Molière, Goldoni, and Lorenzo Da Ponte, whose libretto for Mozart's *Don Giovanni* is the best-known adaptation. Pushkin's Don Juan has been called "an epicurean", who is "in love with love rather than with women", and is said to portray not a little of the poet himself.

music word for word and without the slightest change. The general form of his opera would thus be a continuous recitative, or rather, dramatic declamation. The vocal line would have rhythms and contours characteristic of melody; at the same time it would be born of and controlled by the precise inflections and meanings of the words. Many years later Debussy built his opera *Pelléas et Mélisande* according to these principles.

Considering the time when he wrote and his own limitations as a composer, Dargomyjsky had undertaken a task of terrifying difficulty. He came gradually to realize this, saying that "for every single phrase he had to devise a new musical idea, whereas the usual method consisted in the working out of a few themes". Besides its general form *The Stone Guest* contains other remarkable innovations. The entire score is written without key signatures, a practice which was to be handed down, through Musorgsky, to a whole generation of modern composers striving to escape the tyranny of clearly-defined tonalities. There are also uses of the whole tone scale and whole tone chords, and innumerable attempts at unorthodox modulations and radical harmonies.

The similarity between Dargomyjsky's theories in *The Stone Guest* and those by which Wagner revolutionized modern opera must be instantly apparent. Both composers were seeking release from the prison of Italian opera form; both hit upon the same general escape device. Dargomyjsky's "melodic declamation" and Wagner's "endless melody" are also related to an evolutionary process that had been going on for a long time in the realm of the German art song. The primary type, known as the *Volksthümliches Lied*, grew from the simple folk song which used the same music for each stanza of the poem. Late in the eighteenth century there began to appear a second and more complex type, the *Durchcomponiertes Lied* (meaning, literally, "composed through"), in which the melody was not bound at all by the stanza form of the poem, but varied itself with complete freedom to reflect in minute detail the thoughts expressed by the words. The genesis of the *durchcomponiertes* type is usually traced to Mozart's famous song, *Das Veilchen* (The Violet), but it received its greatest impetus from Franz Schubert.

Schubert's songs in the *durchcomponiertes* style are often miniature music dramas which unfold with romantic freedom and completely ignore the old stanza-like matrices. For an opera composer seeking a way out of the old closed forms of Italian opera the example of the *Durchcomponiertes Lied* offered a solution, albeit a formidable one. It is possible to see in the mature music dramas of Wagner the *Durchcomponiertes Lied* enormously magnified. The same is true of Dargomyjsky's *The Stone Guest*.

It was actually through Dargomyjsky and not Wagner that this new type of opera composition made its way in Russia. Wagner's later music dramas were slow in reaching that country, and meanwhile the man who was to create the greatest of Russian operas had already imbibed the theories and acted upon them. During the late eighteen-sixties when Dargomyjsky was at work on *The Stone Guest* he was on terms of intimate friendship with a young musician, Mili Balakirev, and a group of amateur composers who formed Balakirev's Circle. One of their number, Modest Musorgsky, was fascinated by Dargomyjsky's opera and his radical theories; at private performances in the composer's home he sang the role of Leporello. Into the mind of Musorgsky, a mind of far greater creative power than Dargomyjsky's, were implanted both the vague doctrine of "realistic truth in music" and the more tangible scheme of dramatic declamation which mirrored the full meaning of the words. After Dargomyjsky was dead and his dull and dogma-ridden scores were speeding on their way to oblivion, it was Musorgsky who would transmute and vitalize their substance, and thus create a living monument.

III

In spite of his misfortunes as an operatic composer Dargomyjsky's life work was by no means a total loss. He composed about ninety songs for voice and piano. Some of these have beauty and distinction, and are still alive in the Russian repertoire. As a songwriter Dargomyjsky has, again, historical significance, for he shares with Glinka the honour of opening the rich field of the modern Russian art song. Before them the ground was barren; after them came a harvest of song composers of talent and even genius—Balakirev, Borodin, Musorgsky, Rimsky-Korsakov, Tchaikovsky, Rachmaninov, Gretchaninov.

A number of Dargomyjsky's songs are realistic and satirical types in which he anticipated Musorgsky's great essays; but the majority are early romantic examples like Glinka's. They established in fact a particular genre, the so-called "romance", which blended the simplicity of Russian folk-song melody with ideas borrowed from the Italian opera and the canzonet, from Schubert, and even Beethoven. No one has expressed the beauty and significance of these romances more aptly than Kurt Schindler, who wrote:

"Glinka's and Dargomyjsky's ballads represent the period of romanticism in Russian music; they are elegiac, despairing, sentimental; they were written to move hearers to tears, and they did so unfailingly. Wonderful is the atmosphere of the Russian salons of 1840–50, that these ballads exhale: young men with romantic lofty ideas, hypersensitive, *schwärmerische* ladies; desperate passions and infinite longings. All the *milieu* of Eugene Onegin, of which Pushkin and Tchaikovsky sang. It is strange to see how the styles of Beethoven and Schubert become amalgamated with Russian melodic strains, and with what appealing results, as in Dargomyjsky's *Elegy* (on a Moonlight Sonata accompaniment), or in his *Prisoner in Siberia*, which apostrophizes the 'heavenly clouds' that are banished and homeless like himself."

CHAPTER V

BALAKIREV AND HIS CIRCLE

I

THE death of Czar Nicholas I in 1855 removed from Russia's throne a despot who for three decades had had a throttling effect upon the progress of the country. In the coming half-century —roughly between the reigns of Nicholas I and Nicholas II— Russia was to make a great leap out of her semi-feudal stagnation. She would double her population, expand her agriculture and industry enormously, begin a wider dissemination of public education, and for the first time begin to break the shackles of serfdom. The intellectual life of the country would thrive as never before.

It was in the eighteen-sixties that a spirit of liberalism, long fiercely suppressed by Nicholas I, joined with a new outburst of nationalist feeling. In various fields of art—literature, painting, architecture, music—the movement became one of renaissance, of rebirth, and the artists went for their materials to two main sources: first, the common life of the simple Russian man, the colour and the drabness of his surroundings, the drama and pathos and comedy of his daily existence, the decorative richness and naïveté of his handicraft, his folk songs, and his folk tales; and second, the vast pageant that lay behind in the history of mediaeval and ancient Russia, a story of sombre beauty through which was interlaced the history of Byzantium, Islam, and the Tartar Orient, and all the ecclesiastical solemnity of the great Church of Eastern Christendom.

The illustrious group of nationalist composers known as the Five were a part of that spiritual awakening of the eighteen-sixties. The original member of the band was Mili Balakirev, a disciple of Glinka. He was the founder, mentor, and for a time virtual dictator, and one of the names commonly given to the group, "The Balakirev Circle", indicated his pre-eminence. Balakirev and his four associates—Cui, Musorgsky, Rimsky-Korsakov, and Borodin— were as queerly contrasted a group of personalities as only that romantic age could have brought together. The music talents of the Five (or the "Mighty Handful", as they were also called) ranged from the powerful but misunderstood genius of Musorgsky whose art forecast much of twentieth-century music, to the puny, ineffectual gifts of Cui whose works are now a catalogue of forgotten failures.

Besides the Five one other remarkable man stood within the Circle. Vladimir Stasov was not a composer, but he was one of those rare spirits who move with ease and understanding through the entire realm of art. He was an historian, critic, and connoisseur; he was also the ablest propagandist for the new nationalist movement through all the Russian arts.

It is a pity that Balakirev's music can no longer compare in interest to the man's life, or to his personality that burst like a fiery spark over Russian art circles in the eighteen-sixties. This composer was one of the oddest characters in the gallery of nineteenth-century romantics. He was dominating and forceful, a leader of his group and a moulder of his times; he was also a recluse who withdrew from his friends and from his art for years at a time. He was born with music talents of a prodigious order, but he was never able to gear them to a consistently strong creative machine. Over his life-effort must be placed that most unsatisfying of epitaphs: His influence was greater than his work.

Mili Balakirev was born on January 2, 1837 (December 21, 1836 O.S.), in the ancient city of Nijni-Novgorod. His father was an impoverished nobleman. The son showed such talent for music that at the age of ten he was taken to Moscow for lessons with one of John Field's pupils. Two years later the boy had the good fortune to acquire a patron in the person of Alexander Dmitrievich Ulibishev (1794–1858), a wealthy landowner whose passion for music is indicated by his biography of Mozart, the writing of which occupied him for more than ten years. Ulibishev's home in Nijni-Novgorod was a small island of culture in the dull commercial life of the town. He had a large library, an important collection of orchestral scores and other music, and a private orchestra. Ulibishev took young Balakirev into his home and for years treated him as his own son. At the age of fourteen the boy became conductor of Ulibishev's private orchestra.

In Balakirev's early music career there is proof that a significant change had taken place in Russian music circles. The Italian influence had greatly waned; German music and musicians had moved into prominence. Balakirev himself recalled in later years that in his youth most of the music teachers in Russia were German.

His own piano teacher was one Karl Eiserich who had been conductor of Ulibishev's orchestra. The latter's interest in Mozart
(and later Beethoven) indicated the new order. It was also significant that the works which young Balakirev conducted or performed in the Ulibishev home included sonatas, chamber music, and
orchestral works by Mozart, Beethoven, Mendelssohn, and Hummel.

After studying mathematics and physics for two years at the
University of Kazan young Balakirev decided to make music his
profession. He had been giving music lessons at the University to
earn a slender living, and he had tried his hand at composition.
Late in 1855 his friend Ulibishev took him along on a trip to Petersburg, and there the brilliant young man found the place where his
genius was to take root.

It seemed that from the beginning Balakirev was destined to
meet great men. The first of these was Glinka. When Ulibishev
brought his young protégé to the famous composer of *A Life for
the Czar* and *Ruslan and Ludmila* the meeting was like that of
Schumann and young Brahms. Glinka was astounded by Balakirev's
prowess as a pianist and pleased by his recently composed Fantasy
on themes from *A Life for the Czar*. During the next few months
the embittered Glinka felt a new glow of hope, which the failure of
Ruslan and Ludmila and his own indulgence had destroyed. From
his notebook he gave Balakirev two Spanish themes as material
for another fantasy; he remarked to his sister, "He is the first man
in whom I have found views on music corresponding to my own . . .
believe me, in time he will become a second Glinka." What might
have been a fruitful friendship was cut short the following spring
when Glinka bade his contemptuous farewell to Russia and went on
to Berlin, and to his death.

II

It was through Glinka that Balakirev met a second man of
destiny in the intellectual life of the time—Vladimir Stasov. The
future historian and art critic was then thirty-two years old, and
was doing research for the Director of the Petersburg Library.
Stasov had been educated in the School of Jurisprudence in Petersburg but his travels in Western Europe and especially in Italy had
turned his interests to art. He had a mind of immense vigour and
scope; he was a linguist, a writer of skill and conviction, a born

debater and propagandist. When Balakirev first met Stasov the latter's home (in which lived a sprawling family of brothers, sisters, wives, daughters, and aunts) was a meeting place for the intelligentsia of Petersburg. Stasov's knowledge of music was formidable. He and young Balakirev played four-hand piano arrangements of the classic repertoire and they discussed Balakirev's ideas for a new nationalist music in Russia. It was Stasov who awakened the younger man's interest in the history and literature of the West; together they read Homer and Shakespeare.

The real moment of birth of the Balakirev Circle came in 1857 at a concert in a private home in Petersburg where Balakirev chanced to meet César Cui, a young officer in the Engineering Corps of the Russian Army. Cui had had some slight instruction in music theory but his general knowledge of the art was small. Balakirev set about expounding to his new friend his ideas for a new Russian music; he also instructed Cui through many hours spent at the piano reading music or playing duets.

Balakirev's next recruit was Modest Musorgsky, a young officer in a fashionable regiment, who had struck up a friendship with Cui at the home of Dargomyjsky. Musorgsky was a talented pianist but he had never had regular instruction in music theory. In 1857 he too began taking lessons from Balakirev. Three years later a shy young midshipman at the Naval Academy, Nicholas Rimsky-Korsakov, joined the group. He was ignorant of composition, barely able to play the piano, but was drugged by his love of music and hypnotized by the genius of Balakirev. The last to join was Alexander Borodin, a young scientist from the Academy of Medicine, who came into the group in 1862.

Rimsky-Korsakov, many years later, left in his *Chronicle of My Musical Life* a record of those first historic meetings of the band, the Saturday evenings at Balakirev's home during which the young men began their rearrangement of music's cosmos. One is struck by their vast seriousness. There were occasions when Stasov read aloud passages from the *Odyssey*, Musorgsky read Kukolnik's *Prince Kholmsky*, and the painter Myasoyedov read Gogol's *Viy*. "Balakirev, alone or four-hands with Musorgsky, would play Schumann's symphonies and Beethoven's quartets. Musorgsky would sing something from *Ruslan and Ludmila*. . . ." Balakirev also played excerpts from his piano concerto (then in the course of construction), or he would expound instrumentation or form, or discourse on composers from Bach to Chopin.

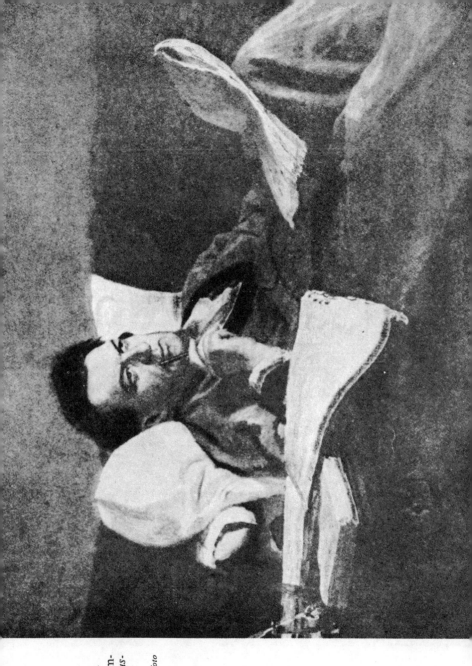

M. I. GLINKA
at the time he com-
posed the opera *Rus-
lan and Ludmila*

Sovfoto

ALEXANDER DARGOMYJSKY

In this coterie of serious young thinkers Balakirev was the central sun who held the others in their orbits by sheer intellectual domination. Even his personal appearance was remarkable. He was heavily built, with a squarish head and Mongolian-like features that suggested (wrongly) descent from the Tartars. His cheekbones were high, his mouth large with thick lips. In that heavily-bearded epoch Balakirev assumed a beard when hardly out of adolescence. Even then he had been mature and in deadly earnest, born, it would seem, an old man. A passion for dominating and leading could hardly be mistaken in a boy of fourteen who had enough self-assurance to conduct an orchestra.

Balakirev had one talent which held the members of the Five enthralled—his prodigious and intuitive knowledge of music. Rimsky-Korsakov's description of his colleague is a famous one :

> "Balakirev, who had never had any systematic course in harmony and counterpoint and had not even superficially applied himself to them, evidently thought such studies quite unnecessary. . . . An excellent pianist, a superior sight reader of music, a splendid improvisor, endowed by nature with a sense of correct harmony and part-writing, he possessed a technique partly native and partly acquired through a vast musical erudition, with the help of an extraordinary memory, keen and retentive. . . . Then, too, he was a marvellous critic, especially a *technical* critic. He felt instantly every technical imperfection or error, he grasped a defect in form at once . . . forthwith seating himself at the piano, he would improvise and show how the composition in question should be changed exactly as he had indicated, and frequently entire passages in other people's compositions became his and not their putative authors' at all."

In those early days the others obeyed him unquestioningly : "He held us absolutely spellbound by his talents, his authority, his magnetism."

Balakirev's teaching methods, his disdain of textbook instruction in harmony and counterpoint, his insistence that learning should come instead from the study of great works, and above all his despotic handling of his pupils' efforts have all been the subject of endless debate. He was often blamed in later years for what seemed to be technical crudities in Musorgsky's music ; Rimsky-Korsakov later decided that Balakirev was "absolutely wrong" and that he himself made little progress until he threw over Balakirev's methods and schooled himself rigorously in every branch of technique.

III

Very soon after Balakirev and his four friends had formed themselves into the circle, things began to happen in Petersburg which threw them into sudden prominence. They made several important enemies. One was the composer-critic, Alexander Serov; another was Anton Rubinstein, the internationally famous pianist and composer. A battle began to shape up between the comparatively unknown young nationalists and the highly-influential conservatives.

Serov was born in Petersburg in 1820, studied jurisprudence, and tried to be a composer with only an amateur's equipment for the task. In the law school his closest friend was young Vladimir Stasov. Together they planned a number of bold music projects for Serov, but he was hopelessly handicapped by his technical ignorance. Later he took a short course in counterpoint by mail, corresponding from the Crimea (where he held a sinecure in the legal bureaucracy) with a teacher in Petersburg. In 1850 he completed an opera based on Gogol's story, *May Night*, but when Stasov expressed dislike of the work he is said to have burned the five-hundred-page manuscript of the score.

In 1851 Serov returned to Petersburg, where he began writing controversial articles about music for the press. He had no enthusiasm for the pan-Slavic ideas of the nationalists, and this cleavage brought about a notorious rift in his friendship with Stasov. From inseparable friends they became deadly enemies, carrying on for years a bruising warfare in the press. Serov was not otherwise a conservative for he liked the new music of Berlioz and Liszt, while Wagner's music almost dissolved his reason. He became the first Wagnerite in Russia, his adoration reaching such a pitch that on several trips to the West he was warmly welcomed into Wagner's personal circle of disciples.

When he was past forty Serov was finally goaded by his enemies into composing an opera. By sheer force of intellectual effort he overcame his technical deficiencies and produced a lyric drama, *Judith*, based on the Biblical story. It was mounted in Petersburg in 1862, with surprising success. Serov followed with *Rogneda*, based on a story of ancient Russia at the time of the conversion to Christianity. Produced in 1865, it became immensely popular and remained in the repertoire for many years. Serov was engaged in the writing of a third opera, *The Power of Evil*, when he died suddenly in 1871.

The popularity of Serov's operas can be explained only by the way the composer had his eye firmly fixed on the "grand" operas of Meyerbeer. His procedure is reminiscent of Wagner's in *Rienzi*, the imitation of Meyerbeer which had once captivated Germany like an operatic circus.

"Serov knew how to catch the crowd," commented Tchaikovsky, "and if his opera suffers from poverty of melodic inspiration, want of organic sequence, weak recitative and declamation, and from harmony and instrumentation which are crude and merely decorative in effect—yet what sensational effects the composer succeeds in piling up!"

Russian audiences, like those of the Paris Opera, relished Serov's operatic spectacles, which contained almost nothing of enduring music substance.

Something of Anton Rubinstein's prodigious reputation still clings to his name. The present age remembers him, however, almost solely as a sovereign pianist. Of his vast catalogue of compositions—including fifteen operas, four "sacred" operas, six symphonies, eight concertos, and a flood of smaller pieces—very little remains in the modern repertoire. The great pianist was born in Podolia in 1829. He was a child prodigy, making his first public appearance at the age of ten. He studied composition with Dehn in Berlin, but much of his early manhood was spent in Moscow. For almost half a century until his death in 1894 he was a leonine figure in the concert halls of Europe.

A study of Rubinstein's voluminous compositions is now only depressing. He had immense facility but little else. His style was essentially German rather than Russian and he seldom departed beyond the horizon of Mendelssohn, without ever commanding Mendelssohn's lyric gift. In the latter part of his life Rubinstein attempted what he hoped would be a new art form, called *"geistliche Oper"*, or sacred opera—a hybrid of opera and oratorio based on Biblical subjects. These grandiose by-products of Wagner's *Ring of the Nibelung*, were among the more conspicuous failures of the nineteenth-century lyric stage. They found a few performances in Western Europe but none in Russia.

IV

Anton Rubinstein's leadership in Russian music circles began when he founded the Russian Musical Society in 1859 and its subsidiary, the Petersburg Conservatory, in 1862. In the latter venture his purpose was especially laudable—to create an academy devoted to higher music education (which did not then exist anywhere in Russia), to maintain standards of pedagogy on a par with those of music schools in Germany, to make Russian musicians true professionals instead of amateurs, and by raising their cultural level to improve their social standing.

In Russia under Nicholas I noblemen were still forbidden to engage in most professional work. The penalty was loss of social rank. A stigma of this kind on the art of music galled brilliant men like Rubinstein. Years before, Catherine II had raised painters and architects to the rank of Free Artist, which gave them important social privileges. Rubinstein's aim was a similar status for musicians, but he knew that a cultural and intellectual background was the first step.

In spite of some of his aims Rubinstein's founding of the Petersburg Conservatory had a violent effect upon the group of young nationalist musicians. Rubinstein's sympathies were wholly cosmopolitan; he had no use whatever for the new nationalist ideas. He had even declared that the failure of Glinka's *Ruslan and Ludmila* proved the inevitable doom of such "barbaric" theories. His school, which had government endowment and patronage, was modelled on the conservatories of Western Europe. When the youthful members of Balakirev's circle noted the membership of the faculty of the new school they were revolted by its Germanic character— "not a Russian in the whole lot". For them the place was no more than "a den of professors", and a monument to conservatism of the most stultifying type. Balakirev countered with a bold move. He organized what he called a Free Music School. It was free, moreover, in two senses. Tuition was offered to anyone of talent without charge, with evening classes to accommodate persons occupied in other jobs and professions. The teaching was not to be the strict, old-fashioned German type, but Balakirev's own freer style of instruction, with wide latitude given to individual inclination.

Balakirev had no money to finance his venture, but he hoped to raise funds from a regular series of public concerts. At first the plan flourished and pupils from every walk of life crowded into the New School—men and women from government bureaux, university students, and even tradespeople and workmen. An orchestra and a chorus slowly grew and in the first five years of the school a dozen concerts were given, several conducted by Balakirev himself. The programmes published Balakirev's creed, for they presented both the standard classics and what was the new music of the day—works by Berlioz, Liszt, and Schumann. Most significant of all were performances of Russian works by Glinka and Dargomyjsky, and the early efforts of Rimsky-Korsakov, Musorgsky, Cui, and Balakirev himself.

It was not long before the battle of the music schools spread beyond the city itself. In 1866 Nicholas Rubinstein, a gifted younger brother of Anton's, founded the Moscow Conservatory. The first member of the new faculty was a young graduate of the Petersburg Conservatory, Peter Ilych Tchaikovsky. Naturally the conservative standards of the Rubinsteins were transplanted to the new school. Its curriculum was described as "cosmopolitan" rather than national. In a curious way the rivalry of the two music factions now became the rivalry of cities.

All this was another phase of the familiar issue which has so often split Russian intellectuals—Slavophiles versus admirers of Western culture. But here there was an important difference. Slavophiles were usually looked upon as the conservatives, standing on the old ground of autocracy in the state, orthodoxy in the church, and nationalism in culture; while the Westerners were considered cosmopolitan liberals. But in the music life of the eighteen-sixties the opposite was true. The nationalists were the progressives, and the cosmopolitan Westerners were the conservatives. Even the cities became switched around, adding to the complication. Petersburg, itself a newly-manufactured imitation of the West, became the centre of nationalism in music; while the old conservative ultra-Russian Moscow became the seat of a cosmopolitan eclecticism.

In the early years of the quarrel between the Five and the Rubinstein party, Russian music circles quivered and the press rang with the excitement of the noisy battle. At first things went rather badly for the Balakirev group, and not only because their neo-Russian theories antagonized many admirers of Western culture. It is clear in retrospect that the young radicals had far more to offer in the way of promise than actual performance. Their own music in its early stages simply could not live up to their ambitious preachments.

As for the exact nature of Balakirev's creed, it is important to note that it is now too often reduced to the simple, singlephased proposition of Russian nationalism in music. It was actually much more than that. Various other issues claimed almost equal significance, and each represented a stand squarely against convention and reaction.

First of all, the Five stood for Russian nationalism—the proposition that the native music of the people, both folk and religious, was a worthy basis for an intellectual art music. Second, they assumed the right to ignore if they wished the strict rules of Western technical procedure, the "severe German counterpoint" et al, and to operate instead with more latitude and freedom. Third, they allied themselves with the spirit of the new music of the West, that of Berlioz, Schumann, Chopin, and Liszt, which had marched away from the old territory of eighteenth-century classicism and into the new domain of nineteenth-century romanticism. Fourth, they embraced the newest doctrine of all in music, that of realism. This idea, which they derived from Dargomyjsky and which only Musorgsky was to exploit to the full, was a wholly new approach to the problems of opera and its method of joining music and drama. Fifth, they took the familiar stand against Italian opera as a mere glorification of vocal display. Instead they proposed (as Wagner was proposing) a more serious treatment of the drama and a richer exploitation of all music's resources. In Cui's words, "everything seductive in the music art should be utilized—the charm of harmony, the science of counterpoint, the richness of polyphony, the colour of the orchestra". At the same time they rejected as overbalanced Wagner's symphonic treatment of the orchestra. Finally, they attacked the frozen conventions of abstract forms like the symphony, its inevitable four parts, its submission to the eighteenth-century sonata matrix. "The time has come," said Stasov, "for this to pass into oblivion."

When these various theories of the Five are separated it becomes plain that nationalism was only a part of what they stood for. Their quarrel with the Rubinstein party really resulted from the fact that they were progressives, forward-lookers; while their opponents were in the main old-fashioned conservatives. The nationalist issue only beclouded this more fundamental difference. The Five were far from rejecting Western culture. To them Russian nationalism was a vital new force and they wanted to join it with other new things in Western music, not water it down with the old. Unfortunately, they did not always make themselves clear. For many years a great deal of confused arguing went on in Russian music circles because the nationalism of the Five, being linked with half a dozen liberal theories, could mean different things to different people.

It requires no great perspicacity to see that what was needed during those vigorous early years was a measure of tolerance on both sides. Instead the world of Russian music became little more than a battle-royal, with three sets of antagonists having at each other. There was Serov, for whom there could be no god but Wagner; Rubinstein the conservative, detesting both Wagner and the national-ists; and the nationalists, unwilling to see the slightest virtue in any cause but their own.

V

All during the eighteen-sixties Balakirev's manifold activities went on at a furious pace. He made a collection of Russian folk songs which appeared in 1866. He went to Prague at the instigation of Ludmila Shestakova and in the spring of 1867, in spite of immense difficulties (including much wrangling with Bedrich Smetana), he conducted historic performances of Glinka's *Ruslan and Ludmila*. Back in Petersburg he took over the direction of concerts by the Russian Musical Society founded a decade before by Rubinstein, but in 1869 he had to resign. Balakirev's rude tactlessness alienated the members of the orchestra, the press, and the Grand Duchess who was the Society's patroness. Meanwhile, the Free School was travelling along a familiar route—through artistic success toward financial disaster—with Balakirev trying to stave off the inevitable out of his own meagre income.

In 1870 he began to crack under the strain. The first outward sign came when he made a sudden and incomprehensible move: he took a job in the freight office of the Warsaw railway. Except for a few music lessons which he was forced to give to augment his miserable income, he abandoned his great career in music entirely. Balakirev's friends had not realized what frustration and overwork had done to the razor edge of his mind. The crisis came after a cruelly hurtful episode at Nijni-Novgorod, where the composer had gone with the hope of restoring his finances by giving a concert. His native city ignored him and the concert hall was almost empty. "My Sedan," was Balakirev's laconic remark.

After that began the composer's withdrawal from the world—a strange interregnum that lasted for the better part of five years. He retired into the isolation of a bleached and spiritless existence in which his disordered mind searched for the landmarks of truth and comfort but found neither. He became a mystic and an ascetic, refusing to smoke, eat meat, or wear fur clothes; the welfare of animals and even insects agitated him morbidly. A religious fanaticism seized him and he prayed constantly before icons. Strangest of all, he began consulting a professional soothsayer—a handsome, black-eyed young woman who was described by his friends as "a witch". This woman held ghostly seances; apparitions appeared in a mirror, bringing the composer messages from the dead. The sorceress further complicated the queer and occult proceedings by falling in love with Balakirev. Meanwhile, the composer's old friends were shocked by the change that had come over him. On the infrequent occasions when they saw him he remained unresponsive and even silent, as if his whole electric personality had been extinguished. Said Stasov, "I felt I was confronting a coffin...."

It was a long time before light shone through the darkness that had descended upon Balakirev's mind. In 1876 he began to compose again, taking up his tone poem *Tamara*; he also began the work of editing Glinka's scores for publication. In 1882 he resumed the directorship of his Free Music School. But "the Balakirev of the eighties", said Rimsky-Korsakov, "was not the Balakirev of the sixties". The music mind had regained its old vigour and acuteness, but the powers of leadership had dwindled. Balakirev could no longer rule the Five; they had begun to go their separate ways without him. He began to gather a new group around him, among them the young composer Liapunov. In 1883 he assumed a venerable post, the directorship of the Court Chapel, where he did valuable work in making modern arrangements and transcriptions of the ancient liturgical chants. It was after he had retired from this post that Balakirev found the leisure to return to composition. There began a twilight period in the composer's life during which various large works appeared, some of them new, some projects he had abandoned a quarter of a century before.

In this closing decade of his career Balakirev moved into the

MILI BALAKIREV
from the drawing by Léon Bakst

CÉSAR CUI

Sovfoto

shadow of the public neglect which was soon to overtake his music. He continued to press the cause of other men's music rather than his own; Glinka, Chopin, and Berlioz remained his gods to the end. The cause of Russian nationalism was by that time a triumphant reality, and Balakirev was himself no more than an embodied memory of its great days. Of the circle itself only he and Cui remained alive.

Death came for Mili Balakirev on May 29, 1910. A month later, in Paris, there occurred an event which would be a signal flash for the arrival of a new epoch in Russian music—the first performance of Igor Stravinsky's ballet *The Firebird*. Thus had Balakirev's life stretched out like a bridge between two great salients—between the first tentative nationalist efforts of Glinka and the internationalist art of Stravinsky, the most influential music in the modern world.

VI

The music of Balakirev is often as unsatisfying and contradictory as the man's personality itself. It is uneven in quality and small in quantity; it gives only indirect evidence of the great goals toward which we know the composer strove; and yet the few pieces that survive in modern concert halls outside Russia do hold a certain interest. They are like pieces in a museum—reminders of an age in music history notable for its originality and brilliance.

There were only two short periods of creative activity in Balakirev's life, separated by a gap of about twenty-five years. The first began in the late eighteen-fifties and extended through the sixties. The works of this early period include his best-known pieces: the tone poems, *Tamara* and *Russia*, and the piano piece, *Islamey*; the three Overtures on native themes (Russian, Czech, and Spanish); the incidental music to *King Lear*, and many of the composer's best songs. Among the works begun at this time and worked over many years later were the First Symphony and a Piano Concerto. A giant choral symphony in honour of the twenty-fifth anniversary of *A Life for the Czar* got no farther than the planning stage, and the same fate befell Balakirev's only projected opera. The subject of the latter was the Firebird, the same legend which Igor Stravinsky was to use for his ballet. Balakirev progressed no further than the improvising of a few episodes.

The works of Balakirev's second creative period, which began late in the eighteen-nineties, were nearly all in the classic forms.

He completed his First Symphony, in C major, in 1898; and his Second Symphony, in D minor, in 1908. To this period also belong the Piano Sonata in B flat minor, published in 1905, and a Cantata written for the Glinka centennial, celebrated in Petersburg two years late, in 1906. Balakirev also finished two movements of his Piano Concerto which he had begun in the sixties; the final movement was written from his sketches by Liapunov, after his death.

As for the general nature of Balakirev's music, it advances a logical step beyond the music of Glinka. Balakirev resembles his predecessor in being both a nationalist and an eclectic. He was especially fond of the orientalisms which had attracted Glinka; otherwise his music reflects his deep affections for native Russian music and for a few Western composers and their methods—the powerful dramatism of Liszt, Chopin's chromatic lyricism, Berlioz' orchestration. In the closing period of his career when he turned to the classic forms the Russian composer showed his reverence for the thematic development procedures of Beethoven and the polyphony of Bach.

The works of Balakirev's first period are almost all romantic in feeling and form. The tone poem for orchestra, *Russia*, was composed in 1862 (revised in 1882) for the celebrations commemorating the thousand year anniversary of the Russian nation. It was based on three folk tunes from Balakirev's collection, which were meant to illustrate "the three principal elements in our history: paganism, the Muscovite state, and the quasi-democracy of ancient Russia". The tone poem is one of Balakirev's best works and one of the most successful of the early nationalist genre.

The orchestral rhapsody *Tamara* owed its inception to an Oriental tune which Balakirev and Rimsky-Korsakov heard while visiting the barracks of the czar's regimental bodyguard. Rimsky-Korsakov wrote in his memoirs, "I vividly recall the men, Orientals, making music on a balalaika-shaped or guitar-like instrument." Balakirev used the theme for the first allegro of *Tamara*, going on to develop a work which long remained the prototype for Russian composers beguiled by the exotic music of the Orient—sensuous in mood, garishly coloured, and full of the embroideries and arabesques of Eastern decoration.

Islamey was based on a group of themes taken from Armenia and the Caucasus. This time the simple materials were magnified into one of those monstrous machines of piano technique for whose original pattern Franz Liszt must bear the responsibility. For many years virtuoso pianists used *Islamey* as a club to stun audiences into open-mouthed awe. It is still possible to admire the composer's sheer cleverness in devising this technical display, which rings from the piano a whole carillon of brilliant sonorities.

None of Balakirev's late works ever achieved the popularity of these early colourful essays. Despite a few interesting innovations they remain only mildly interesting. The first movement of the First Symphony displays an astonishing skill at the development of a single unpromising theme into a long, complex, and cleverly contrived structure; but the piece as a whole droops for lack of melodic vitality. The most striking feature of the Piano Sonata is the first movement which attempts boldly to fit fugal subject matter into the general structure of the sonata-allegro form. In the four other movements (all beautifully written for the instrument) the ghosts of Balakirev's past—Chopin and Liszt—mingle in strange affinity with Russian folk themes.

In one form at least the composer was consistently inspired throughout his long career. Balakirev's songs often contain the true glimpses of the man's creative spirit; Calvocoressi has dared to say that "he was the first Russian to compose songs that rise to as high a level as Schubert's and Schumann's. . . ." Nearly all the Balakirev songs are romantic in feeling and subject matter and show that the man, however difficult and refractory an outward personality, had the ardent nature of a poet and a painter. Many of these pieces are exquisite and deserve frequent performance. Among the best are *O, Come to Me!*, *Song of Georgia*, *The Song of the Golden Fish*, *Hebrew Melody*, *A Vision*, *Spring Night*, *Invocation*, and *The Call to Freedom*. Balakirev's natural mastery of the piano is evident in his beautifully constructed accompaniments.

Any final measurement of Balakirev's stature must take into account more than the great debt which the other members of the Five owed him as the prime mover in their nationalist cause. He was the first Russian composer of consequence to centre his art not in vocal music but in instrumental music, and this in spite of the superior nature of his songs. He was totally disinterested in opera, which made him a curiosity among the Russian composers of his age. Instead he tried to explore a territory which lay away from all the ancient Russian traditions of music as essentially a vocal art. Balakirev's first interest was the orchestra, and after that the piano. If he had not quite the creative strength to produce works of lasting vitality in the instrumental field he was still a pioneer who left his countrymen an example of boldness, discernment, and adventure.

Lastly, Balakirev established what may well be the most fruitful of all traditions in modern Russian music—that composers should also be teachers. In no other country is there such a record of music pedagogy. In an unbroken chain, from Balakirev to Miaskovsky, the composers have passed on at first hand their wisdom and their skill to the succeeding generation. With Balakirev teaching was far more than a means of livelihood or even a duty. It was a form of self-expression, at times almost a passion. To this day we have not seen the end, fortunately, of the power of this remarkable man's example.

VII

It would be difficult today to undervalue the music of César Cui. As a composer he was the weakest member of the Five, and by so wide a margin that we wonder at the respect and even deference which he commanded from the group. He was a power in Russian nationalist music for more than half a century, although he had been born in Poland with no drop of Russian blood in his veins. A mere handful of Cui's songs might today illustrate in miniature the great cause which he espoused so long; the rest of his output has joined the music of his old enemies, Rubinstein and Serov.

Cui's case is interesting because it so neatly illustrates the confusions which often becloud a new art movement. The clear-cut issues, like the precise evaluations, usually come only in retrospect. It is often hard for contemporaries to distinguish between the greater artists in the new movement and the lesser. In this case, moreover, the Five were by no means a homogeneous group, aiming together at one target. They all reacted differently to Balakirev's original nationalist idea; after the first decade they went their separate ways, developing their varied talents and often becoming severely critical of each other's works.

For the students of those times who were trying soberly to evaluate the cause which the Five espoused, Cui must have been a singularly disturbing element. He was at once the poorest composer and the loudest talker. For many years he was a music critic on a large newspaper in Petersburg, and while he was composing music which hardly ever rose above mediocrity and impressed itself only faintly upon the nationalist art, he was assuming a pontifical position in the press with pieces that now appear narrow, opinionated, and often wrong-headed.

Cui was born in Poland, in the town of Vilna, on January 18, 1835. His father was a Frenchman who had been a member of Napoleon's Grand Army in the march on Moscow in 1812. Wounded and almost frozen to death at Smolensk, the elder Cui could not join in the terrible retreat. He remained in Poland, married a Lithuanian girl, and became a teacher. His three sons, all named after military geniuses, were Alexander, Napoleon, and César. At the age of sixteen César showed great talent for music, but his parents sent him to the school for military engineers in Petersburg. He was commissioned in 1855, had a long and distinguished career in the Russian Army, and ultimately became a general and an authority on the subject of fortifications. His meeting with Balakirev, however, aroused his passion for music composition, a career which he was to follow along with military science to the end of his long life.

Cui's army income was at first so small that he was forced to operate a preparatory school for candidates to the engineering school. Later he held professorships in the army academies of engineering and artillery; he wrote technical books on military science, and he contributed music critiques to the Petersburg newspaper. In spite of these manifold activities Cui still found the time and energy for composition. For many years he studied and composed steadily, until his output exceeded in bulk that of any other member of the Five. His works include ten operas, a number of short orchestral pieces, some thirty choruses of various types, three string quartets, many short pieces for the violin and for the piano, and more than two hundred songs.

Cui's operas engaged most of his efforts as a composer, and in the early days of the Five the lyric stage was regarded as his province. In 1859, two years after he began studying with Balakirev, he completed a two-act opera based on Pushkin's poem *The Captive in the Caucasus* (revised and performed in 1881). The previous year he had finished a short comic opera, *The Mandarin's Son*. This was performed privately[1] on the occasion of his wedding to

[1] The role of the Mandarin was sung by Musorgsky, "with such life, gaiety", wrote Stasov, "with such adroitness and comic quality of singing, diction, pause and gesture, that he made the whole company of friends and comrades roar". A study of the score itself makes Musorgsky's accomplishment appear even more remarkable.

Malvina Bamberg, a German girl who was a singer and a pupil of Dargomyjsky.

In 1861 Cui began work on an opera based on Heine's tragedy, *William Ratcliffe*, but the difficult task was not completed until 1868. During those years the small band of nationalists, fighting their early battle for recognition, put strong faith in Cui's efforts. Musorgsky wrote to him, "*Ratcliffe* is not only yours, but ours." It was indeed the first large-scale work by the Five to receive a public performance. But its première, at the Marinsky Theatre in Petersburg, in February 1869, was a crushing disappointment. Cui's attacks in the press against Italian opera and the Rubinstein party had aroused strong resentment and *William Ratcliffe* gave his opponents their perfect moment for revenge. At the close of the performance when the composer arose in his box to bow he was struck by a wave of booing, hissing, and whistling. After eight performances the opera was withdrawn at his request. Thirty-one years later, in 1900, it came to life for a brief revival at Moscow; since then it has reposed undisturbed in the vast mortuary of operatic failures.

Cui appeared undaunted by the fall of *William Ratcliffe* for he completed his *Angelo*, based on a drama by Victor Hugo, in 1876.[1] It was produced with only fair success at Petersburg and later at Moscow. Almost two decades passed before Cui tried again, with *Le Filibustier*, based on a comedy by Richepin and composed especially for performance in France. It was produced in January, 1894, at the Opéra-Comique, but ran only four nights. Cui carried on with *The Saracen* (1899), after a play by Dumas; *A Feast in the Time of Plague* (1901), a one-act opera based on a poem by Pushkin; *Mam'zelle Fifi* (1903), from the story by Maupassant; *Matteo Falcone* (1908), after Daudet's story; and *The Captain's Daughter* (1911), after Pushkin. All were failures.

Cui's last major effort as a composer was his arrangement of *The Fair at Sorochintzi*, the comic opera which Musorgsky had left unfinished at his death a third of a century before. It was produced in Petersburg in October 1917, when Cui was in his eighty-second year. The composer died the following spring, March 14, 1918. Russia at that moment could give little heed to the last survivor of the small band of men who had revolutionized her music. Over the whole

---

[1] That same year at La Scala in Milan, the Italian composer Ponchielli had much better luck with his opera *La Giaconda*, which was based on the same play by Hugo.

nation there had descended the fiery curtain of political and social revolution.

The mere listing of Cui's operas and the origins of their librettos indicates the split in this composer's music personality. Only three of his lyric dramas were based on Russian stories; of the rest the majority were from French sources. When Tchaikovsky heard *William Ratcliffe* in 1869, he wrote:

> "It contains charming things, but unfortunately it suffers from a certain insipidity. . . . By nature Cui is more drawn towards light and piquantly rhythmic French music; but the demands of 'the invincible band', which he has joined, compel him to do violence to his natural gifts and to follow those paths of would-be original harmony which do not suit him."

That very nearly sums up Cui's entire effort as a composer.

Even Cui's work as propagandist for the Five no longer withstands scrutiny. It is true that his articles were widely read and that he also spread the news of the nationalist movement abroad with his pieces in French and Belgian journals; nevertheless, he was often so bigoted that he made more enemies for his cause than friends. For all his espousal of a progressive idea, Cui's mind was narrow and conservative. He never even penetrated to the core of Russian nationalism: Musorgsky's finer works confused and repelled him. He contributed to an early misappraisal of Wagner's music in Russia by diatribes that now seem only foolish, and he lived long enough to ridicule Debussy's *Prelude to the Afternoon of a Faun*.

Modern critics have noted that it was not Cui but Vladimir Stasov who deserved from history the honour of being the first propagandist and literary interpreter of the Five. Stasov was opinionated too, but he had the advantage of a far greater intellectual capacity, more cultured tastes, and sounder judgments. No artist himself, he yet enjoyed a subtle perception of the refinements of art. The clue to the stature of Stasov is his understanding of Musorgsky —his long and loyal friendship with the unhappy man, the valuable contributions he made to the composer's stage works, and his early appreciation of the enduring greatness of Musorgsky's music.

CHAPTER VI

MUSORGSKY

I

MUSORGSKY was that most appealing and yet most tragic of artists—a misunderstood genius. His case was not simply the familiar one of a man ahead of his time. He was the victim of a whole series of events and misfortunes which for years caused not merely his purposes as an artist to be obscured and deprecated but his music itself to suffer actual disfigurement. Today it is no longer necessary to argue his rank among the leading creative spirits of his age. But even today the public know comparatively few of his works as the composer himself created them. Most of his music is still heard either as bowdlerized by an editor or transcribed to other mediums by arrangers.

To understand why Musorgsky and his music should have undergone so long an ordeal of disparagement and neglect it is necessary to observe closely the unusual circumstances that surrounded him. There was first of all his place in the moving stream of liberal nationalism which agitated intellectual Russia in the eighteen-sixties. In the highly controversial field of music the Five were of course the leaders of the nationalist movement, and they were widely looked upon as radicals. Within the Five itself the most uncompromising nationalist, surpassing even Balakirev himself, was Musorgsky. It was Musorgsky who made by far the most extensive and penetrating use of the Russian folk idiom; it was he who broke most violently with the technical conventions of the older Western music; finally he was the only one of the Five who espoused the new doctrine of realism in art as opposed to the prevailing romanticism.

The significance of Musorgsky's interest in realism needs close study. It is a peculiar fact that the enormous force of realism, which succeeded romanticism in nineteenth-century literature and the drama, made but small impression upon the music of that age. By comparison, romantic music could hardly have come into existence without its literary prototype; with the exception of Chopin there was no romantic composer of consequence whose music did not depend in large measure upon the fertilizing germ of romantic literature. But realism brought with it no such immediate cross-fertilization. No nineteenth-century French composer is remembered today for an opera based on "Madame Bovary", or "Nana"; there were no enduring transformations into music of Ibsen's realistic plays, either by Scandinavians or Germans; strangest of all, in nineteenth-century Russia where literary realism reached its greatest heights, the stories of Tolstoy, Dostoevsky, and Turgenev found no composer willing to attempt a setting in opera. Realism did not become a force in modern music until the advent of the twentieth century. The point to be made here is that Musorgsky's pioneer interest in the concept of realism actually set him apart not only from his own group but from every other important composer in and out of Russia.

The very nature of his art, then, served to make Musorgsky seem a radical among radicals, even an eccentric. The man's own personality had the same effect. In spite of a manner of great outward charm, he was difficult to fathom. Many of his closest friends thought him talented but shallow; to others he was merely a poseur who had not the capacity to master the intricacies of music technique. Few suspected the profundity of his thought or the enormous creative force which spurred him on. And when with the passage of years his whole life disintegrated from acute alcoholism many took it for granted that what was strange in his music must have been the result of either bungling ineptitude or mental disorder. The cruelty of that judgment is not wholly wiped out to this day, when musicians are still content to perform "corrected" versions of his music rather than Musorgsky's own.

II

Modest Petrovitch Musorgsky was born on March 21 (9th O.S.), 1839, at Karevo, a village in the Toropets district of the Pskof Government. He was descended from an ancient family of wealthy landowners. His father was the illegitimate son of a serf woman by an army officer, the birth being later legitimized by a decree of the Senate after the marriage of the parents.

The composer himself once wrote a short autobiographical sketch in which he described his early music life as follows:

"Under the direct influence of his nurse he became familiar with Russian fairy tales. It was this acquaintance with the spirit of the folk-life which chiefly impelled him to improvise music before he had learned even the elementary rules of piano playing. His mother gave him his first piano lessons and he made such progress that at the age of seven he played small pieces by Liszt, and at nine played a grand concerto by Field before a large audience at his parents' house."

When Modest was ten years old the family moved to Petersburg. There he studied the piano privately with the German pedagogue, Anton Herke, who drilled him for several years in piano technique but taught him nothing of composition. Improvisation became a favourite diversion of the boy. He spent hours at the piano creating a spontaneous music of his own, but "never suspecting the existence of any sort of musical theory or science". In spite of his ignorance young Musorgsky actually tried to compose an opera based on Victor Hugo's *Han d'Islande*, but he soon abandoned the project. He was then seventeen years old.

In that year, 1856, Musorgsky entered the Preobrajensky Guards, a famous and ancient regiment in which many of his ancestors had served. It transpired that no greater catastrophe could have overtaken the young man. At the most formative stage of his life he found himself in a group of men whose chief interest was not military science but dissipation. In his efforts to keep up with this fast-living, hard-drinking set, Musorgsky acquired the beginnings of alcoholism, the scourge which would later ruin his life and damage his art.

It was during his early months in the Preobrajensky Guards that Musorgsky met Alexander Borodin, then twenty-three years old and a doctor on the staff of a military hospital in Petersburg. Years later Borodin recalled the appearance and personality of his new friend:

"M.P. was at that time quite boyish, very elegant, the very picture of an officer; brand-new close-fitting uniform, shapely feet, sleek, pomaded hair, immaculate nails and aristocratic hands. Refined, aristocratic manners, conversation the same, sprinkled with French phrases, rather affected. Some traces of foppishness, but very moderate. Extraordinarily polite and well-bred. The ladies made a fuss over him. He sat at the piano and, coquettishly throwing up his hands, played excerpts from *Trovatore*, *Traviata*, etc., very sweetly and gracefully, while the circle around him murmured in chorus, 'charmant, delicieux!' and so on."

At this time Musorgsky's interest in music led him to make other new friends—Alexander Dargomyjsky, César Cui, Mili Balakirev, and Vladimir Stasov. In 1857 he urged Balakirev to give him music lessons. It appears that in these early instructions Balakirev concentrated upon form and general construction. The two men played through four-hand arrangements of Beethoven's symphonies, and works by Schumann, Schubert, Glinka and others, Balakirev pointing out details of structure and Musorgsky absorbing and analysing. There was no instruction in harmony, and apparently none in counterpoint; these the pupil was left to absorb by himself.

Very soon Musorgsky began to compose. The novice works of the man whose later music was to be drenched in Russian nationalism were at first merely exercises in the standard classic and romantic styles. He tried to write two piano sonatas which have disappeared, and then two Scherzos for the piano (B flat major, and C sharp minor) which have survived. These were followed by an Allegro from a projected Piano Sonata in C, composed in 1860, and piano arrangements of several movements from Beethoven's last string quartets. Sketches for a Symphony in D, abandoned by the composer and now lost, practically sum up the classic phase of Musorgsky's efforts.

Far more significant are his early songs. The first half-dozen of the group of works by which Musorgsky was to change the course of the modern art song had an unfortunate early history, one which foretold the fate of much of this composer's music. They had been composed between 1857 and 1860, but after the composer's death in 1881 they disappeared and were believed to be lost. Twenty-eight years later, in 1909, a manuscript of these and eleven other Musorgsky songs was unearthed in Paris. In general these first songs are romantic in style, and several are strongly flavoured by Russian folk melody. None of them is distinguished, but in all the workmanship is good. Very little of Musorgsky's gift for lyric writing is evident here; instead the melodic ideas seem to be subordinated to the young composer's special interest in harmony. Already he was trying for bold key contrasts, modulations, and chord constructions. Many of these effects are immature and clumsy; a few, however, clearly presage the imagination of the artist who was to come.

In 1860 Musorgsky made an attempt to write incidental music to a drama, *Œdipus*. This was long believed to be the Sophocles tragedy, but recent researches by Gerald Abraham reveal that it was more probably a version by the Russian dramatist, V. A. Ozerov (1769–1816), which was produced in 1804. Musorgsky composed an overture and several choruses of which only a single chorus in F minor survives. But Abraham demonstrates that two other choruses had a later and curious history. Musorgsky appears to have incorporated them first in an unfinished opera based on Flaubert's *Salammbô*, and after that, and along with other *Salammbô* music, in his great music drama, *Boris Godunov*.

III

So far Musorgsky's career as a composer had been hardly promising; nevertheless, he had resigned his commission in the army in 1858, resolved to follow music. At this time he had suffered a serious illness, a siege of nervous depression and melancholia which was to return in more violent form in the later years of his life. Musorgsky's character as it emerged during his callow years was one of unusual complexity. It would be nearer the truth to say that as he grew older his true character never emerged; rather the man himself became submerged under a thickening veil. The elegant and affable young officer who had charmed Borodin was also sensitive and introspective, filled with the morbid passions that moved many romantic intellectuals of his age. Byron's *Manfred* excited him wildly; he wrote to Balakirev that he had been "so electrified by the sufferings of that lofty spirit" that he had cried out, "How I wish that I were Manfred!" . . . "I became literally 'Manfredized' and my spirit slew my flesh."

As he matured Musorgsky lost some of these affectations, only to take on others more enigmatic. His letters reveal his habit of "putting on masks" (as one biographer has termed it), of appearing in various comical roles, and inventing nicknames to caricature himself and others. His correspondence is often difficult to understand because he obscured his real thoughts by elaborate double meanings. The reader is reminded at times of Robert Schumann who also loved to be slyly whimsical, both in his prose writings and his music. Musorgsky's humour was usually more extravagant and bizarre.

The involutions of Musorgsky's personality did not always permit the young man to appear in his best light. Within the Balakirev circle there was at first respect for his ability as a pianist and singer but for little else. In 1863 Stasov wrote in exasperation to Balakirev: "What is there for me in Musorgsky? . . . I didn't hear from him a single idea or a single word expressed with real profundity of understanding, with the profundity of a raptured, moved soul. Everything about him is flabby and colourless. To me he seems a perfect *idiot*." Balakirev agreed that "Musorgsky is practically an idiot". Cui found several of his early songs "rather ridiculous". . . . "In his work, of course, I don't believe."

In 1863, when he was twenty-four years old, Musorgsky faced a serious crisis in his personal life. Two years before, Czar Alexander II had issued the famous ukase which was intended to emancipate the Russian serfs. It was also a serious blow to the nobility and the land-owning class who had to divest themselves of much of their wealth. The Musorgsky family found themselves impoverished, so the young composer joined hundreds of other sons of land-poor nobles by taking a job in the government service. This became his life for the next eighteen years—a bureaucratic clerk, working at a salary that barely kept him alive. A grindingly-dull routine occupied him every weekday from eleven to four; only in the evenings and on Sunday was he free to compose.

A few months before he entered his government job in the Ministry of Transport, Musorgsky had begun work on his second opera project. He was living at the time in a Commune—a large apartment shared by six young men who were intellectuals with liberal political and artistic ideas. The talk of the moment was Flaubert's newly published novel, *Salammbô*. The brilliant re-creation of life in ancient Carthage deeply impressed Musorgsky, and he made considerable progress on what was the largest music task he had yet attempted. He made elaborate scenic and costume sketches and he devised a libretto made up of strangely-compounded elements. It contained, in addition to lines from the novel, verses by the composer himself and also verses by Heine and three Russian poets. Musorgsky's procedure was unorthodox, but with him it became common practice whenever he set words to music. He did not consider a poet's lines to be inviolate; he reserved the right to change a text in any way, with the sole purpose of creating a more powerful union of words and music and thus a more vivid final result.

Musorgsky's version of *Salammbô* progressed haphazardly, the composer working on three different acts without finishing any of them. Even the few completed scenes exist only as piano arrangements. After three years he lost interest in the work and abandoned it. The fragments that remain show that the young composer's real interest lay in the large ensemble scenes and the massed choral effects. He was clearly groping toward a new conception of the opera chorus—as an independent and powerful dramatic protagonist. The chief weakness of his *Salammbô* music lay in the characters, whom he could not bring to life. Like so much of Musorgsky's music, *Salammbô* had an extraordinary history. In later years the composer incorporated parts of it into other works, most of it going into his opera, *Boris Godunov*.

During the years when he was struggling with *Salammbô* the young composer's personal life had been badly disrupted by a series of misfortunes—the loss of the Musorgsky income which had sent him out drudging for a living, the death of his mother to whom he was devoted, and finally, in 1865, a complete collapse from acute alcoholism. He suffered his first attack of delirium tremens. Thereafter Musorgsky gave up the corrupting life in the Commune and made his home for several years with his brother. Being young and resilient and secretly burning with ambition, Musorgsky rebounded from all these misfortunes. Though he may not have been aware of it, his art had begun to find its natural outlets—in the field of song.

IV

Musorgsky produced some eighty songs in his short career in music. That he was the greatest Russian master of this art form is now beyond dispute, but for a long time the variety, originality, and strangeness of the Musorgsky songs stood in the way of their wide acceptance.

The first harvest of great songs came roughly between the years 1863 to 1870, a time when the composer was growing toward the mastery which would yield his first version of his opera, *Boris Godunov*. Even though it is not possible to group them in any significant chronological order, these pieces as a whole show clearly the new direction in which the composer was moving. While the other members of the Five talked much and practised some of Russian nationalism, of realism in music, of progressive freedom from outworn Western formulas, it was Musorgsky who put their preachments into actual practice.

Musorgsky did not make a sudden break with the romantic and eclectic past, that is, with the type of song then favoured by his Russian colleagues. Several of his songs of the eighteen-sixties show him making exotic experiments with Oriental and Hebrew themes; a few others are typically romantic interpretations of Goethe and Byron. Thus, *King Saul* (composed 1863) was based on a poem from Byron's *Hebrew Melodies*. It is a powerful dramatic piece depicting Saul's farewell before the battle, and is noteworthy for its Oriental-Hebraic colour. The later *Hebrew Song* (or *The Song of Solomon*), composed in 1867, is based on an original Jewish theme from which Musorgsky created an exquisite melodic poem, passionate and languorous, suffused with melancholy and longing. *The Harper's Song*, from Goethe's *Wilhelm Meister* (1863), is another of this eclectic group; while *By the Don a Garden Blooms* (1867) is one of Musorgsky's few "love" songs, a dreamy picture of a garden by the river, and the path along which the fair Masha passes with her water-jar on the way to the well.

In spite of the romantic beauty of these pieces, they are in the minority and not at all representative of the series as a whole. Another and entirely different concept of the song as an art form had seized Musorgsky's imagination, and it yielded two main types—the realistic song, and the song of satire. Both were, in effect, protests against the prevailing romanticism of the time.

Realism was a new and disturbing art phenomenon in young Musorgsky's world of the eighteen-sixties. It had taken powerful hold of Russian writers, and would produce in the next few decades the greatest realistic literature of modern times. Among composers, only Musorgsky was at all eager to desert the old romantic pastures and follow Dargomyjsky into this strange new territory. What urged him on was his overwhelming interest in life, in people around him, and especially the life of the Russian serf.

"The whole vast world of Russian serfdom" (writes the composer's biographer, Riesemann), "with its various personalities, its manifold activities, its want and misery, the intolerable burdens of daily life embittered by every conceivable form of degradation, torture, oppression—all these had hitherto had no existence so far as the world of music was concerned."

Musorgsky made Russian national life his great theme, and his realistic songs are a series of portraits and human episodes, created in tone, but often as vivid and as authentic as anything found in the Russian novel or the drama. The composer once wrote to Ilya Repin, exponent of realism in Russian painting:

"It is *the people* I want to depict; sleeping or waking, eating and drinking, I have them constantly in my mind's eye; again and again they rise before me in all their reality—huge, unvarnished, with no tinsel."

The song *Kallistrat*, composed in 1864 to words by Nekrassov, was the first of Musorgsky's essays inspired by his sympathy for the Russian serfs. A young peasant recalls the cradle song which his mother sang to him: "Kallistrat, you were born to be happy; blithe and carefree shall your life be." But his life has dealt with him cruelly. He lives in poverty; his wife and children are hungry and in rags. The melodic lines of this song are folk-like in character, and are poignantly harmonized. Rhythms have a primitive irregularity, with measures of 4/4, 7/4, and 3/2 alternating freely. In similar vein are *Cradle Song* (1865), and *Eremushka's Cradle Song* (1868). *The Orphan Girl* (1868) depicted a common sight in Russia's cities at that time—a beggar child roaming the streets and imploring passers-by for pennies lest she die of cold and hunger. The words are by Musorgsky, and the theme is based on a melody he had heard sung by groups of wandering beggars.

The most startlingly original song in this group inspired by sympathy for the Russian peasantry is *Savishna: The Love Song of the Idiot* (1865). The composer had actually witnessed from the window of a farmhouse the scene which he depicted in music. An imbecilic cripple who was the butt of village jokes had secretly loved one of the prettiest girls, and in a moment of anguish blurted out to her his adoration. Musorgsky was struck with pity at the strange and moving scene, and he remembered and set down the droning, imploring contours of the boy's voice. A single, short motive is repeated again and again in 5/4 rhythm, breathlessly and without rests, to the end of the song; the tune rises and falls over a pattern of discordant harmonies, chiefly empty fourths and fifths. Even Musorgsky's contemporaries, who constantly misjudged and underestimated his work, were moved by this astonishing song.

The Banquet (or *The Country Feast*) (1867) re-creates a peasant celebration:

> "The mighty doors of oak open wide to receive the guests. The host and hostess lead them to the great hall where they sit down for the feast. Among them passes the young wife with soft black eyes, offering the bowl of hospitality; the sweet daughter passes mead to them. The guests eat and drink and laugh until the midnight hour."

There is a bardic quality to the poet Koltzov's words, which Musorgsky transformed into a melody of archaic dignity and charm. The rhythm is a distinctive one of eleven beats (5/4 alternating with 3/2).

Hopak (1866) is the song of a young peasant woman who dances with wild abandon to forget her life with an old Cossack husband whom she hates. "Out of your house your wife will stray, and a handsome lad will come her way." This was the first of a series of songs of comedy by which this composer revealed himself as a satirist of the first order. The next year, 1867, he wrote five more in the same vein—*The Magpie*, *The Seminarian*, *The Ragamuffin*, *The Goat*, and *Gathering Mushrooms*.

The Magpie was put together from two poems by Pushkin. The chattering bird, hopping through the garden gate, reminds the poet of a gypsy-dancer at the fair, who beats her tambourine, waves her kerchief and offers to tell fortunes with her cards. Another scherzo-like essay is *The Ragamuffin*, a humorous counterpart of *The Orphan Girl*. This time the young beggar is an impudent boy who jeers at an elderly lady, calling her "Grandma" and "old scarecrow", until the outraged dame takes him by the ear.

The mood of satire cuts deeper in *Gathering Mushrooms*. A young peasant woman picking mushrooms in the forest entertains the idea of throwing in a few toadstools for her worthless husband, thus making way for a fair-haired lad whom she loves. *The Goat*, with Musorgsky's own words, is titled "a fable of high society". A sweet young girl is chased in the fields by a goat, a mean shaggy old beast from whom she flees in panic into the bushes. But presently we find the same girl on her way to the altar—to be married to an older, shaggier, and more repellent husband. "It's a love match!" she declares demurely.

The most famous of all Musorgsky's satires is *The Seminarian*. The composer's own words describe a pale young divinity student struggling with his Latin declensions:

> *"Panis, piscis, crinis, finis ;*
> *Ignis, lapis, pulvis, cinis . . ."*

But all the while a more desperate wrestling match is taking place with Satan, who brings before the student's eyes the vision of Father Simeon's young daughter. Even at a special Mass while he was intoning a psalm in the sixth liturgical mode, the seminarian's eye strayed toward the lovely Stiosha as she stood praying. Father Simeon saw it all, and afterwards in the hall served "a three-fold benediction" on the young man's head. For punishment he must cram on Latin grammar:

> *"Orbis, amnis et cannalis,*
> *Sanguis, unguis et annalis."*

The Seminarian shocked the ecclesiastical censor when Musorgsky sought to publish the song in Russia. Publication or circulation were banned because of its "blasphemous spirit". A publisher in Leipzig brought the song out in 1870, but it was not admitted to Russia for many years after the composer's death.

Two other satires, *The Classic* and *The Peep-Show*, represent Musorgsky as a champion of Russian nationalism and opposed to the music tories of his day. *The Classic* (1867) was a blast aimed at the composer-critic Famintzin, a local Hanslick who had been alarmed by the modernism of young Rimsky-Korsakov's symphonic poem, *Sadko*. *The Peep-Show*, a much longer and more elaborate piece, was aimed at a group of reactionaries whom Musorgsky set up for lampooning in a musical waxworks—Serov, the composer; Zaremba, the director of the Petersburg Conservatory; the music critic, Tolstoi; and again the unfortunate Famintzin.

Between 1868 and 1872 Musorgsky composed seven songs about children, later published as a cycle called *The Nursery*. These were his only works to become known outside Russia during his lifetime. In 1873 Franz Liszt received copies of some of them from the Russian publisher, V. V. Bessel, and they completely charmed the old abbé. Stasov subsequently urged Musorgsky to make a trip to Western Europe to meet Liszt; the idea intrigued Musorgsky but he never went. Many years after his death when his music still lay unplayed and virtually unknown outside Russia another great composer of the West would take pains to point out his unappreciated genius. Wrote Claude Debussy of *The Nursery*, "It is a masterpiece"; and of Musorgsky: "No one has given utterance to the best within us in tone more gentle or profound; he is unique, and will remain so, because his art is spontaneous and free from arid formulas. Never has a more refined sensibility been conveyed by such simple means. . . ."

The songs of *The Nursery* are miniature dramas which depict life as seen through the eyes of a small child. They contain no hint of the precious, and no trace of sentimentality. Realistically they mirror the moods and fancies of the child mind, not with conventional melodies but with recitative-like voice parts which imitate childish inflections. The piano part is a nimble alter ego which takes every possible liberty with harmonic, rhythmic and structural rules to paint the scenes and deftly suggest the characters and their actions—the bogy man gnawing the bones of children, the king who limps, the queen sneezing, the naughty child unwinding the nurse's wool, the buzz of the terrifying beetle with the big moustaches, the hobby-horse, the cat, the bird. Debussy noted that in these songs Musorgsky could convey "shadowy sensations of trembling anxiety which move and wring the heart"; and again, "an amazing power of sympathetic interpretation and of visualizing the realms of that special fairyland peculiar to the mind of a child".

v

Contemporary accounts of Musorgsky the man refer constantly to his skill in the performance of his own songs. Besides a pleasing voice he had superb talents as an actor and mimic, and when he sang he held his listeners breathless. This extraordinary theatrical gift was but one phase of a far greater gift—his genius for creating drama in terms of music. Musorgsky was at heart a dramatist, whose overwhelming interest was humanity. Thus his creative instincts led him to those two music forms which are concerned in the highest degree with human life—the song and the opera. But even these, as he found them, were unsatisfactory because they interposed between him and his subject matter a stone wall of formula. In only one way could he achieve a fusion of words and music to express an idea white-hot with life-like truth, and that was to smash the old conventions of music technique which had become for him a senseless road-block.

Musorgsky's maturity as an artist came with the realization that for him content was more important than form. He began working with increasing boldness and ingenuity, not only exploring ideas of melody, harmony, and rhythm which were new to the syntax of music but also departing radically from the old song forms which gave a standardized symmetry to construction. For Musorgsky, every song should create its own form. Unity and structural beauty did not depend upon geometrical design; rather each song became a small drama in which the form was determined by the forces of dramatic tension, suspense, climax, and resolution.

Musorgsky's ideas of rhythmic freedom came from his study of Russian folk song which was full of unusual cadences, these being in turn the result of the strong influence on the primitive song-makers of the Slavic language and the ancient church chant. The composer began to use primitive folk rhythms like the 5/4 in *Savishna*, and the eleven beat rhythm in *The Country Feast*. Later he broke the convention that a single rhythmic pulse must prevail through a long series of measures. His music became at times multirhythmic, with the metre changing rapidly every few measures. Thus he forecast the rhythmic complexity which is a characteristic of much twentieth-century music.

Of all his purely technical procedures it was Musorgsky's harmony which made his music in its day seem so radical. Although he lived through the Wagner era he seems to have known little of the later Wagnerian music dramas and their expansion of the technique of chromatic harmony. Musorgsky's harmonic innovations were distinctly his own, and some of his boldest strokes seem to have been arrived at empirically. He used a great variety of scales—modal, irregular, and incomplete—developing an elaborate complex of unusual harmonies. He used chords of the ninth, eleventh, and thirteenth; he employed dissonance freely, as well as open fourths and fifths, consecutive fifths, and unconventional doubling. He used a variety of enharmonic modulations, but an even greater variety of completely abrupt modulations with no enharmonic foundation. Often he moved from chord to chord with complete disregard of formal preparation, for example, his continual use of plain major and minor triads in series. In these practices he anticipated Debussy by at least three decades.

Although his tonalities are always strongly defined Musorgsky used keys with the same freedom that he applied to chords, so that in his music there is often a continual shifting of tonality. Extremely sensitive to the "colour" of certain keys, he soon ceased to consider the key of a certain piece or song to be a rigid framework. "His music," writes Calvocoressi, "teems with examples of light and darkness, of tension and relaxation, produced by changes of key." In the course of a song he did not bind himself to any tonality, often ending in a different key from that in which he had begun. He experimented ceaselessly with endings. He tried to vary the old cadences and to round off his songs with endings arrived at by bold means, or by modulations from remote keys or chordal constructions. His final chords are often not tonic chords at all, and there is one early example (in *The Harper's Song*) that is actually polytonal —a startling anticipation by a third of a century of Strauss's ending for *Also sprach Zarathustra*.

So much of Musorgsky's procedure is now an established part of modern music that the present-day listener finds it hard to believe that it was once considered radical and ugly. Even his fellow nationalists, although avowed progressives, were puzzled and often repelled by what he was trying to do. Even when they agreed that his work had power and imagination they deplored its lack of "finish". Since they knew that Musorgsky had had little technical instruction they assumed that his music was full of mistakes due to ignorance. For many years afterward the notion was current that this composer was a kind of unkempt primitive—a bungling genius, who botched his work by his failure to master even the simpler rules of composition. Stasov was apparently one of the few of his contemporaries who realized that the composer was actually an artist of exquisite discernment and taste. Far from being crude, the sensibilities which governed his art were exceedingly fine. Above all, he was an individualist who hated the obvious and hackneyed. "Musorgsky was an enemy of every sort of routine and commonplace," said Rimsky-Korsakov's wife, "not only in music, but in every phase of life, even in trifles." That is the aesthetic key to almost every measure of his music.

VI

In the autumn of 1860 while he was engaged upon his *Œdipus*, Musorgsky had written his friend Balakirev of an idea for an "extremely interesting work". This was to be music for a scene from a drama called *The Witch* by Baron Mengden, and was to depict a witches' sabbath. No trace remains of any music which Musorgsky may have set down for this effort, but it seems likely that some of these early ideas found their way, by a strange and circuitous route, into the orchestral piece now known as *A Night on Bald Mountain*.

Almost seven years later Musorgsky confided to Rimsky-Korsakov that he had completed (appropriately on June 23, the eve of St. John's Day) a piece called *St. John's Night on Bald Mountain*. The composer acknowledged that a recently published book, *Witchcraft*, by M. S. Khotinsky, had given him inspiration. According to Rimsky-Korsakov's later testimony the work was written for piano and orchestra, but the existence of a piano part has since been questioned.

Musorgsky was proud of this piece, which he had composed in only twelve days and in a fever of inspiration. He called it "Russian and original", and his "first large work". He delighted in certain bold clashes of dissonant harmony, "thoroughly foul and barbarous". "The whole thing is fiery, brisk, close-knit without German transitions." To him it was "something new, and ought to produce a satisfactory impression on any thinking musician".

Unfortunately, *St. John's Night* produced none of the results hoped for by the composer. It brought him only anguish and disappointment. It became part of the chaotic stream of misfortune and disfigurement which was later to immerse almost the whole of his magnificent art.

Musorgsky's first disappointment came when his piece repelled Balakirev, who refused to perform it. Musorgsky in turn politely refused to make any of the changes suggested by his mentor, though he did soften the percussion parts. The score lay untouched until 1871 when Musorgsky, with Cui, Borodin, and Rimsky-Korsakov, embarked on the curious *Mlada* project. They were asked by S. A. Gedeonov, director of the Imperial Theatres, to compose collectively an opera-ballet, each man to write the vocal music for a single act. (The ballet music was entrusted to one Ludwig Minkus, the official ballet composer of the Theatres.) Part of Musorgsky's assignment called for a witches' sabbath scene, so he went to his *St. John's Night* score and revamped it, adding chorus parts. Then Gedeonov called off the entire *Mlada* project for lack of funds.

Balakirev later tried to persuade his friend to rewrite the *St. John's Night* score. "There are such powerful and beautiful things in it," he admitted to Stasov, "that it would be a pity to leave it in its present disorder." In 1880 Musorgsky only added to the confusion when he decided to incorporate the music in his comic opera, *The Fair at Sorochintzi*, as an orchestral interlude between Acts I and II, depicting the nightmare of the Peasant Lad. When the composer died some months later no note of the *St. John's Night* score had ever been heard as the composer originally wrote it. But the strange story of the piece had by no means come to its end.

Five years later Rimsky-Korsakov took the last version of the material in hand and arranged, edited, and orchestrated it to his own satisfaction, forming a tone poem or symphonic fantasy which he called *A Night on Bald Mountain*. This Rimsky-Korsakov version[1] remained for many years the only work ostensibly by Musorgsky to appear in the programme of symphony orchestras. Rimsky-Korsakov prefaced the score with the following argument:

"Subterranean sounds of unearthly voices. Appearance of the Spirits of Darkness, followed by that of the god Chernobog. Glorification of Chernobog, and the celebration of the Black Mass. Witches' Sabbath. At the height of the orgies, the bell in the little village church is heard from afar. The Spirits of Darkness are dispersed. Daybreak."

It would be a source of satisfaction to lovers of Musorgsky's music to be able to hear the original score of *St. John's Night on Bald Mountain*, as it poured from his pen in the early summer days of 1867. The piece has special interest because it was one of the few works in which he showed an interest in Russian folk-lore and fairy-tale, a subject soon to become the stock-in-trade of so many Russian composers. The score exists in the definitive edition of all Musorgsky's works in their original form, as prepared by the Russian scholars Paul Lamm and Igor Glebov, and published

---

[1] Another version of *A Night on Bald Mountain* was made by Leopold Stokowski and was used in Walt Disney's film, *Fantasia*. Its orchestration is wilder, more grotesquely fantastic than Rimsky-Korsakov's.

in recent years by the Soviet Government; but the closing of the Iron Curtain has made these volumes difficult if not impossible to obtain. *St. John's Night on Bald Mountain* meanwhile remains one of the empty spaces in the chronicle of Musorgsky's art.[1]

VII

In 1868 Musorgsky made his third attempt at writing an opera. He had been so impressed by Dargomyjsky's *The Stone Guest* that he proposed to make an opera of Gogol's comedy, *The Marriage*, and to imitate closely Dargomyjsky's procedure. The older composer was carrying his theories of truth and realism in music to an unheard-of extreme by not altering a single word of Pushkin's dialogue, and by writing dramatic declamations which followed the precise meaning of the text. Musorgsky proposed to go even farther. His text would not be poetry but colloquial prose, the simple everyday speech of Gogol's middle-class Russian characters.

Musorgsky loved Gogol's work and his appreciation of the

[1] Musorgsky's letters show that he was at least partly inspired by reading the book, *Witchcraft*, by Khotinsky. This popular history of demonology in Russia fascinated the composer, especially the account of a trial in the sixteenth century of a woman who was later burnt at the stake. Her testimony included, wrote the composer, "a very graphic description of a witches' sabbath", and her confession that she had indulged in "love pranks with Satan himself . . ." "From this description I stored up the construction of the sabbath."

The Bald Mountain depicted in Musorgsky's tone poem is an actual locality —Mount Triglav, a three-pronged, bald peak near Kiev in Southern Russia, named after a three-headed god. It was the legendary scene of the Slavic *Walpurgisnacht* which took place each year on the eve of the feast of John the Baptist. During those hours the peasants barred their doors and placed kettles in their windows to charm away evil spirits, while far away on the mountain-tops all the creatures of demonology—spirits, ghosts, witches, sorcerers, vampires, and other assorted fiends—assembled to pay homage to Satan. They were joined by members of his retinue who were transformed into wolves, toads, and reptiles; while the arch-fiend himself appeared as Chernobog, in the form of a monstrous black goat.

The revels were unspeakably vile, ending in the supreme blasphemy of the Black Mass. During the evening's entertainment the witches, "stark naked, barbarous and filthy", were especially honoured. In one of his letters Musorgsky described how they would assemble on the mountain—

"gossiping, playing lewd pranks, awaiting their superior—Satan. Upon his arrival they would form a circle around the throne, where he sat in the guise of a he-goat, and would carol glory to their superior. When Satan became frenzied enough at the witches' glorification, he would order the start of the sabbath, whereupon he would select the witches who caught his fancy to satisfy his needs."

After the title on his original score of *St. John's Night on Bald Mountain* Musorgsky included the following programme: "1. Assembly of the witches, their chatter and gossip; 2. Cortege of Satan; 3. Unholy glorification of Satan; and 4. Witches' Sabbath."

droll comedy was keen. He was also drawn to Dargomyjsky's method because it resembled his own procedure in writing songs, that is, to let content determine form. He followed *The Stone Guest* plan resolutely, setting Gogol's dialogue to music without the slightest alteration, and in the form of a continuous recitative-like melody. The accompaniment is a discreet yet cleverly illuminating commentary which subtly reflects the dialogue, the four characters, and the stage business.

Musorgsky abandoned *The Marriage* after completing a vocal score of the first act, but he seems to have learned much from the attempt. The modernity of the piece is astonishing, not alone in the main scheme which discards all formal operatic conventions for a continuous melodic dialogue, but also for the harmonic and rhythmic freedom and the deft strokes by which the subtleties of the play are mirrored in music. What was to be the orchestral part represents an extreme, even for Musorgsky. It is so completely subordinated to the text, so pithy and attenuated that it appears broken into fragments, often without clear musical unity. There is no doubt that the composer himself relished the task he had set for himself; nevertheless in his later works he compromised and in part abandoned the strict scheme of *The Marriage* for one in which the orchestral part expands into a more dominant voice and with much longer lines of unbroken music continuity.

Calvocoressi points out the extensive use of leading motifs in *The Marriage*, and the fact that Musorgsky was the first Russian composer to employ them freely and methodically: "All the themes except one are 'characterizing' themes associated with one person, their shape and rhythm being suggested by that person's demeanour, attitudes and gestures; in other words, they are descriptive and pantomimic."

The Marriage brought Musorgsky to a point of mastery toward which he had long been striving. In his own words this was "to make my characters speak on the stage as living people really speak . . . my music must be an artistic reproduction of human speech in all its finest shades". "All Russian critics agree," writes Calvocoressi, "that Musorgsky was the one and only composer whose musical thinking was governed throughout by the influence of everyday Russian speech, which affected the shape of his melodies, the pace, the punctuation and the cadences." In his music for the Gogol comedy he achieved some of his most remarkable translations of speech into music.

VIII

While Musorgsky was still intent upon *The Marriage* and apparently planning the second act, it happened that a friend whom he met one evening at the home of Ludmila Shestakova changed the entire course of his music destiny. The man was Professor V. V. Nikolsky, an authority on the work of Pushkin. He suggested to Musorgsky the poet's drama based on the career of Boris Godunov as a possible subject for an opera. Mme. Shestakova presented the composer with a copy of the play, but he needed little encouragement. The idea had suddenly set Musorgsky's ambitions and his imagination ablaze.

The ensuing history of this opera, the greatest Russian work for the lyric stage, could hardly be more strange if it were itself a work of fiction. Musorgsky began the task with immense energy and concentration. He wrote his own libretto, making extensive revisions in Pushkin's original drama. With the help of Stasov he made historical researches into the reign of Boris Godunov, seeking data on costumes, properties, and folk songs. The composer's music inspiration (in his own phrase) "went boiling and bubbling" at such a pitch that within a year he had completed the opera in piano score. The orchestral scoring required less than six months, so that early in 1870 what was to be known as the first version of *Boris Godunov* was finished.

The completion of the task was a tremendous accomplishment for Musorgsky. Only a few months before he had begun, the composer became assistant to the chief clerk of the Forestry Department of the Ministry of Agriculture. "In the archives of the department," notes Riesemann, "there was found a heap of about twenty bundles of documents drawn up by Musorgsky in his fine, regular handwriting" . . . "they serve to show that Musorgsky's official duties were by no means a sinecure and that his complaints of a senseless occupation that wasted so much of his time and strength were fully justified." Thus a dull and stultifying job was necessary to keep the composer alive; only what was left of his energies could be given to the creation of his operatic masterpiece.

In July, 1870, Musorgsky submitted his *Boris Godunov* for production at the Imperial Opera. After a long and anxious wait the opera committee rejected the work. The reasons given now seem only ludicrous, the typical reaction of small minds coming into collision with a great though unfamiliar art. The committee objected to the lack of a female part in the play and to the story as a whole, which seemed too unconventional and too sombre; the music repelled them by its "modernism".

Musorgsky accepted some of the committee's criticism and set about making revisions. He added an entire act (known as the "Polish Act") to give variety to the opera and to include the part of Marina, a Polish princess. He added several songs and episodes to provide a contrasting lightness of mood; he revised the order of certain scenes; he made various cuts and changes and he left one important scene out entirely. It was during this period in the composition of *Boris Godunov* that Musorgsky took lodgings with Rimsky-Korsakov, who was then hard at work on his early opera, *The Maid of Pskov*. The association was a congenial one and lasted for several years. Neither composer could have foreseen the part which Rimsky-Korsakov was to play years later in the strange fate that befell *Boris Godunov*.

Musorgsky finished his second version of the opera in 1872, and there ensued another long delay before the work was finally accepted for performance. The première took place at the Marinsky Theatre in Petersburg on January 27 (O.S.), 1874. The opera was variously received. Friends like Stasov felt that "it was a great triumph for Musorgsky"; Rimsky-Korsakov said, "We all triumphed." The victory, however, was by no means complete. Musorgsky was prepared for the ridicule that arose from reactionary quarters, but he was hurt and bewildered by a condescending review published by his friend Cui.

Boris Godunov remained a centre of controversy but it was produced fifteen times during the composer's lifetime. When he died in 1881 it was withdrawn and not heard again in Petersburg for fifteen years. It seemed that the opera was dead. It still lingered however in the memories of his friends who could recall the strange power of the music when the composer himself had played and sung it in private homes. For Rimsky-Korsakov it held a special fascination. "I hated *Boris*," he said, "and yet I worshipped it."

In 1895, amid his task of editing all Musorgsky's music for publication, Rimsky-Korsakov went to work on the score of *Boris Godunov*. What he did to his friend's masterpiece, at that time and in a later revision in 1908, was an astonishing performance, one which ultimately raised a small war in the world of musicology.

In his preface to the edition of 1896, Rimsky-Korsakov said that he had been guided by a twofold purpose: first, he aimed to simplify the work technically, to make it easier to sing, play, and conduct and thus facilitate its performance in opera houses; second, he sought to rescue it from what he and its original detractors considered to be "technical weaknesses and mistakes", and thus se it above the reproach of academic criticism. However sincere the editor's purpose, it unfortunately got him into very deep water.

Rimsky-Korsakov did not merely edit *Boris Godunov* in the accepted sense of the term; he made instead a sweeping revision of the entire opera "correcting" every detail that could not meet the test of academic practice. He simplified Musorgsky's bold rhythmic schemes; he altered melodic lines to remove "difficult" intervals; he reorchestrated the entire score. He shifted the keys of whole sections, thus changing the original colour schemes; wherever he could he erased harmonies, modulations, and especially dissonances which he considered "ugly" or "barbaric". For example, Musorgsky was a pioneer in the free use of intervals of the fourth and fifth in his chord constructions, and he used them freely in *Boris Godunov*; Rimsky-Korsakov, being a traditional harmonist, hated those intervals, and wherever he could he changed them to conventional thirds or sixths.

It should be said at once that Rimsky-Korsakov's labours on his dead friend's behalf actually brought the opera back into the repertoire in Russia and ultimately to public acclaim in opera houses all over the world. But that does not alter the fact that his method, in many instances, was to take Musorgsky's most potently original ideas and turn them back into the very clichés which Musorgsky must have striven to avoid. In removing what he considered mistakes and evidences of "the bumptiousness of the amateur", Rimsky-Korsakov now seems like a teacher of draughtsmanship correcting "distortions" in a canvas by Cézanne, or a Lord Tennyson coolly rewriting *Leaves of Grass* to purify its vocabulary of words not considered poetic by Victorian standards.

Above and beyond all controversy about *Boris Godunov* and its various versions there remains one fact—the unassailable greatness of the original music itself and its imperviousness to change. For all his tinkering and retouching Rimsky-Korsakov could not improve the work, nor in the long run did he really mar it. In any version *Boris Godunov* remains one of the monuments of the lyric stage, and one of the greatest works of art ever to come out of Russia.

IX

Pushkin's original drama on the subject of Boris Godunov was written in 1824 while the poet was a political exile. The work was partly the fruit of his study of Karamzin's *History of Russia* and of the historical plays of Shakespeare. The similarity between the characters of Boris and Macbeth has often been noted. Both men are driven by an overwhelming ambition to murder; both are hounded to ruin by remorse and retribution.

In the political chaos which followed the reign of Ivan the Terrible one man had remained a symbol of strength and authority. He was the boyar, Boris Godunov, a descendant of a Tartar family, who was chosen to act as regent for Feodor, the weak-minded son of Ivan. It seemed that Boris himself might one day rule, except that Feodor's six-year-old brother, Dimitri, stood in his way to the throne. In 1591 Dimitri was mysteriously murdered, and later Boris became czar. At first he ruled with wisdom, but his conscience was deeply troubled. Finally a pretender appeared, a monk Gregory, who claimed to be Dimitri grown to manhood; Polish armies taking advantage of the crisis marched toward Moscow. Boris meanwhile was driven almost insane by the terrible dilemma on which he was impaled. If the child Dimitri had not really died, then Boris and his own son had no claim to Russia's throne. Boris could lawfully rule only if the cruel murder occurred as he had ordered, and if the blood of the child was on his soul. After appointing his son to succeed him, the czar was finally released from his torments by death.

Musorgsky reduced considerably Pushkin's original drama, forming his libretto as follows:

The opening scene of the Prologue is in the courtyard of the Novodievichy Monastery. The police intimidate the people, ordering them to entreat Boris Godunov to accept the throne. In the second scene Boris appears at the Kremlin for his coronation, but even amid the celebrating chants and wildly ringing bells he is depressed. He promises to strive for the future greatness of Russia.

Act I opens some years later in a cell in the Chudov Monastery, where the aged monk Pimen is writing historical chronicles. A youthful novice, Gregory, wakens from a strange dream in which he saw himself raised to power and glory. From Pimen, Gregory hears the story of the murder of Dimitri and is startled to learn that had the boy lived he would now be exactly Gregory's age. The young monk resolves to impersonate the dead Czarevich. In the second scene, at an inn near the Lithuanian border, Gregory tries to cross the boundary in the company of two vagabond friars, Varlaam and Missail. The police enter the inn with a warrant for Gregory's arrest, but he escapes into Lithuania.

Act II is in the apartments of Czar Boris in the Kremlin. Musorgsky's second version of this act (a considerable expansion of the first version) depicts the children of Boris, Xenia and Feodor, in several songs and episodes with their nurse. In a corner of the room is a chiming clock with moving mechanical figures. Scenes with Boris follow, revealing the Czar's affection for his children; with Feodor he studies a map of Russia, describing his far-reaching domains. But later, in a long monologue ("I have attained the highest power"), the Czar broods over his guilt. Prince Shuisky brings news of the appearance of Gregory, the Pretender, and when Boris is left alone he gives way to terrible despair. The clock begins to strike, and as a ray of moonlight falls upon one of the moving figures Boris, in a moment of frenzied hallucination, imagines that he sees the ghost of the child Dimitri.

Act III is the "Polish Act", not included in Musorgsky's original version. Its two scenes depict the Polish princess Marina, and her love for Gregory, the Pretender. A proud, ambitious woman, she hopes to ascend with him the throne of Russia. In her scheming she is abetted by Rangoni, a Jesuit priest, who aims to spread through her the power of his church.

Act IV began, in Musorgsky's original version, with a powerful scene before the Church of St. Basil in Moscow. The people are starving. They gather before the church to hear news of the excommunication pronounced on the Pretender, and in the crowd is an imbecilic boy, tormented by street urchins. As Boris leaves the church people beg him for bread, and then the imbecile calls out to the Czar to cut the throats of his tormenters, "as thou did cut the throat of the little Dimitri". Boris spares the imbecile's life and asks his prayers. Musorgsky omitted this scene from his second version of the opera, and it was not included in either of Rimsky-Korsakov's versions.

Musorgsky closed his first version of the opera with a scene in the reception hall of the Kremlin. Boris, now a dying man, appears at a council of the boyars. The aged monk Pimen is brought before him to relate the story of a miracle which once took place at the tomb of Dimitri. Boris is convinced of the child's murder and of his own guilt. He calls for his children, bequeaths his throne to his son, and dies.

In composing his second version of the opera Musorgsky discarded the scene before the Church of St. Basil and instead opened the final act with the scene of Boris's death. Then he wrote a new closing scene, using some of the music from the St. Basil scene. This new close is set in a forest near Kromy. The starving peasants have been driven by their sufferings to open revolt; they capture a boyar and torture him, and they seize two Jesuit priests. When the Pretender appears they shout allegiance and follow him toward Moscow. Only the imbecile boy is left behind, weeping in the snow and wailing: "Woe, woe to Russia! Soon the foe will come and darkness will set in; black, impenetrable darkness."

In his versions of the opera Rimsky-Korsakov reversed the order of scenes in the final act, beginning with the Kromy revolt and ending with the death of Boris.

In Musorgsky's time *Boris Godunov* was recognized as a genuine although seemingly eccentric piece of Russian nationalism. Today we may observe that in a still larger sphere it was also the first piece of operatic realism, the first important step away from the prevailing romanticism of the nineteenth century. This was no romantic picture gallery or historical pageant, but an intense and sombre drama which approaches the outposts of reality. It was the beginning of the modern opera of naturalism, which would not again find expression in the lyric theatre until the twentieth century brought forth works like Strauss's *Elektra*, Berg's *Wozzeck*, Shostakovich's *Lady Macbeth of Mzensk*, Brittain's *Peter Grimes*, and Menotti's *The Consul*.

No small part of the realistic force of *Boris Godunov* is due to Musorgsky's gift for human portraiture, already strongly revealed in his songs. Except for the persons in the Polish act, who are weak and conventional by comparison, the composer paints character after character with extraordinary penetration and refinement— the children of the Czar and their nurse, the venerable Pimen and the ambitious unstable Gregory, the drunken friars, the scheming Shuisky, and above all the Czar himself, a man of majestic stature ruined and brought down by a psychological force within him.

As a work of nationalism *Boris Godunov* remains unsurpassed in the history of the lyric stage. It is so rich in native historical colour, so drenched in the idioms of Russian song that it stands as a master-piece of sheer evocation. Mediaeval Russia comes to life, a fierce, dark, and melancholy country, long vanished into the past and yet still existing in the turbulent present. It is noteworthy that, although there is some genuine folk song in the score and some direct quotation from the music of the Russian Church, by far the greater part of the thematic material is Musorgsky's own invention.

In addition to its intense nationalism and its realism *Boris Godunov* shows in many other details that Musorgsky was the only artist of the Five bold enough to carry out their pioneer ideas to the limit. In its general form, for example, the piece deserts Italian opera for a new type of music drama. Although it does not go to the extreme of *The Marriage*, it employs in a modified form a continuous melodic dialogue. The speeches and actions of the characters are lifelike and unhampered by what goes on in the orchestra. Where choruses, songs, duets, and even arias do exist they do not obtrude as set pieces, but are woven into the continuous unbroken texture of each scene. Except in the Polish act there is no grand opera vocalism.

Musorgsky's use of a leit-motif scheme in *Boris Godunov* is further proof of his willingness to experiment with what was then a radically new idea. It is also a refutation of the notion that he was technically ignorant. Recurring themes in *Boris Godunov* are not employed as persistently or as openly as in the Wagnerian method; some seem only vaguely touched upon, or they are deeply embedded in the texture of the music, as in Debussy's *Pelléas et Mélisande*; nevertheless, they germinate the entire score. Calvocoressi notes that in the first scene of the opera "all the music is derived from the melody with which the Prelude opens, all the patterns of this melody being used in turn for structural (not symbolic or allusive) purposes with extraordinary thoroughness and appositeness". The themes do not always appear at first in full panoply; sometimes the composer "prepares their appearance in such a way that we are able to feel them gradually taking shape—at times long before they are actually asserted".

It was in the field of harmony that Musorgsky's pioneering got him into most trouble with his contemporaries. Even his fellow nationalists, though dedicated to the new harmonic freedom as they found it in the music of Chopin, Liszt, Berlioz, and what little they knew of Wagner, found it hard to accept Musorgsky's dissonances, his chords employing fourths and fifths, his uninhibited modulations.

The original score of *Boris Godunov*, before Rimsky-Korsakov's editing, contains measure after measure of these innovations. No longer strange, they add immeasurably to the richness, colour, and dramatic power of the score. Like Wagner and Debussy, Musorgsky was acutely sensitive to harmony; of all the components of music he could use it, he found, most subtly and for the greatest expressness.

When he began work on *Boris Godunov* Musorgsky was thirty years old, a young man of unsteady character, little conventional training, and a limited knowledge of music precedent. Yet the force of his genius was enormous and his convictions about art hung before him like a fiery ball. He produced a score of such magnitude and originality but, at the moment, of such strangeness that the work could at first find no home. Russia was still too immature, musically, to appraise it. *Boris Godunov* had to wait the passage of time and the birth of a new age before its stature could be revealed.

X

In the summer of 1873 Musorgsky lost one of his dearest friends, Victor Alexandrovitch Hartmann. This man was an architect, designer, and water-colourist, and his place in Russian architecture corresponds roughly to that of the members of Balakirev's circle in music. He was an avowed nationalist, dedicated to the renaissance of Russian art in all its forms and of the folk arts in particular. When only thirty-nine and at the height of a thriving career he died suddenly of a heart attack.

In an often-quoted letter to Stasov, Musorgsky revealed his own grief and self-reproach: "My very dear friend, what a terrible blow! 'Why should a dog, a horse, a rat have life,' and men like Hartmann die!" The composer went on to relate a poignant incident. A short time before, he had been walking with Hartmann on the street when the architect suddenly leaned against a wall and turned pale, saying, "I can't breathe." Musorgsky remarked carelessly, "Rest a bit, little soul, and then we'll go on"—words that now filled him with bitter regret. His fear of frightening Hartmann and his own "cowardly fear of sickness" had made him appear unconcerned at a moment when he should have realized that his friend's death warrant had been signed.

In the spring of 1874 Stasov arranged in Petersburg a huge public Memorial Exhibition of some four hundred specimens of

Hartmann's work—water-colours, sketches, architectural drawings, and designs. Musorgsky visited the show, and was later moved to pay homage to his dead friend by composing a suite of short pieces for piano, which he called *Pictures at an Exhibition*. It was a labour of love, and the composition moved with such speed that on June 22, 1874, after a few weeks' work, the series was completed.

The fate of *Pictures at an Exhibition*, Musorgsky's only large work for the piano, was again typical of what happened to so much of this composer's music. It was not published until 1886, five years after his death, and was then neglected for almost half a century. In 1923 it was splendidly revived, but not in its original form. Ravel transcribed the work for orchestra, and the result was an instrumental *tour de force* of such brilliance that conductors everywhere set upon it avidly. *Pictures at an Exhibition* in the French composer's orchestral form soon became the best-known of Musorgsky's works and it contributed greatly to the steady revival of interest in all his music.

From the huge collection of pictures at the Memorial Exhibition Musorgsky had chosen ten examples. Only a few of these original ten pictures by Hartmann now survive, so that for years the only clues to their exact nature were a few short descriptive notes written by Stasov for the first edition of the piano work. Recently, however, Alfred Frankenstein's scholarly researches on the subject of Hartmann, his work, and the various pictures at the exhibition have unearthed much new data.

Musorgsky's suite begins with an introduction called *Promenade*, which was not based on a Hartmann picture but was the composer's portrayal of himself as he strolled through the gallery. In the opening measures the rhythm is 5/4 alternating with 6/4, "an awkward, waddly effect," remarks Frankenstein. "Musorgsky was no sylph". The Promenade recurs four times, variously metamorphosed, between the succeeding movements and is also heard in the finale, thus acting as a binder for the loose-leaved structure of the entire piece.

The ten pictures proceed as follows :

I. *Gnomus*. Stasov wrote that this was "a drawing representing a little gnome walking awkwardly on deformed legs". It was actually a design for a toy nutcracker for a Christmas tree, and was an example (says Frankenstein) "of Hartmann's fantastic craft work". Musorgsky's movement, in a sombre E flat minor, is by turns violent, eerie, threatening, and darkly spiteful—perfectly recalling the little monster and his sinister purpose.

II. *Il Vecchio Castello.* "A Mediaeval castle before which stands a singing troubadour," is Stasov's description. Hartmann had spent the years 1864–67 visiting France, Italy, Germany and Poland, and the present picture, says Frankenstein, "was obviously one of Hartmann's architectural water-colours done in Italy". Musorgsky's movement (the least interesting musically of the set) is built over a pedal point on a low G sharp which is maintained through the entire piece. The long-flowing melody is darkly coloured and melancholy, over a throbbing accompaniment that vaguely suggests a singer with his lute.

III. *Tuileries.* A memory of Hartmann's visit to Paris, and described by Stasov as "a walk in the garden of the Tuileries with a group of children and nurses". Musorgsky's movement is a scherzo which depicts the noisy children at their monotonous sing-song play.

IV. *Bydlo.* This title is the Polish word for "cattle", and Stasov's note reads, "A Polish wagon on enormous wheels drawn by oxen." The picture is believed to have been one of a large group which Hartmann painted in 1868 during a month's visit to the Polish town of Sandomir, an ancient, historic place and the scene of the Polish act in *Boris Godunov.* Musorgsky's tone picture is that of a huge, lumbering ox-cart as it slowly comes into view and then disappears down the road. The tune is a "folksong in the Aeolian mode, evidently sung by the driver". Heavy, laboured themes are heard over massively reiterated chords in the bass.

V. *Ballet of the Chickens in their Shells.* This is a remnant of Hartmann's work as stage and costume designer. In 1871 he made costume sketches for an elaborate ballet production of *Trilbi* (after Charles Nodier, not du Maurier), with choreography by Marius Petipa. The sketch which inspired Musorgsky survives, and shows ballet dancers encased in costumes made to resemble large egg-shells and with their heads covered by helmets that look like canary heads.[1] Musorgsky's music is a *Scherzino*, set chiefly in the upper registers of the piano and deftly imitating the peeping and cheeping of the chicks.

VI. *Samuel Goldenberg and Schmuyle.* Several small confusions, of the kind which darken the minds of programme annotators, cling to this section. The origin of the title is doubtful, though it is usually

[1] Remarks John N. Burk, the programme annotator of the Boston Symphony Orchestra: "Mixed ornithology in ballets and descriptive suites is apparently of no consequence."

ascribed to Stasov in the first piano edition, since in his original manuscript Musorgsky left this section untitled. There is also doubt about the precise nature of the Hartmann picture. It may have been a single drawing portraying two Polish Jews in the Sandomir ghetto; or it may have been two separate drawings which the Exhibition catalogue noted as belonging to Musorgsky himself, one being titled "A rich Jew wearing a fur hat: Sandomir", and the other "A poor Sandomir Jew". Whatever the origin, Musorgsky's representation of the two characters is masterly, the high point in inspiration of the entire work. The composer used themes based on the Oriental scales of ancient Jewish music. The man of wealth appears dignified, ponderous, disdainfully aloof, and is drawn by a melody of bold and decisive contour. The poor man is a pitifully insignificant creature; his theme cries and bleats as he seems to beg his more fortunate brother for alms.

VII. *Limoges, The Market Place.* "Frenchwomen furiously disputing in the market place," noted Stasov. Hartmann made many drawings during his visit to the French town, but nothing is known for certain of any market-place scene. Musorgsky's representation of the quarrelling, gossiping women is another scherzo, chattering like a breathless toccata.

VIII. *Catacombs.* The catalogue of the Memorial Exhibition contained the following description of this picture: "Interior of Paris catacombs with figures of Hartmann, the architect Kenel, and the guide holding a lamp." Musorgsky's catacombs are a series of heavy, sustained chords alternating between fortissimo and pianissimo, moving ponderously and slowed by suspensions, as if groping through the heavy, oppressive darkness.

Con mortui in lingua mortua (sic). This section is a restatement of the Promenade theme, but transformed to make it a lugubrious appendage to the *Catacombs.* On the margin of his manuscript Musorgsky left the following note: "A Latin text: with the dead in a dead language. Well may it be in Latin! The creative spirit of the departed Hartmann leads me toward the skulls and addresses them —a pale light radiates from the interior of the skulls."

IX. *The Hut on Fowl's Legs.* Baba Yaga, the proverbial witch of Russian folk-lore, lived in a hut perched on huge fowl's legs. Hartmann's picture on the subject was actually a design for a clock. It was done in the Russian style of the fourteenth century, and the drawing (which survives) shows the clock in the centre of a hut, which has a long gabled roof and stands on fowl's legs, with elaborate and fantastic ornamentation. Stasov noted that "Musorgsky has added the ride of Baba Yaga in her mortar". The composer recreates the scene in a fantastic movement full of weird colour and grotesque figurations, but with few of the more obvious devices of conventional "witch" music.

X. *The Great Gate at Kiev.* On April 4, 1866, Czar Alexander II escaped assassination at Kiev, and three years later Hartmann submitted designs in a competition for a massive gateway to commemorate the event. The project was never carried out, but Hartmann considered these designs to be his finest work. The drawing which inspired Musorgsky still exists. It shows a front view of a huge stone gate in the old Russian style, adjoined by a bell tower. The main archway is supported by unusually short columns, which "seem sunk into the earth as though weighted down by old age," wrote Stasov, "and as though God knows how many centuries ago they had been built". The arch is crowned by a huge design of an ancient Slavic war helmet, ornamented like chain mail and rising to a pointed peak. A Slavic headpiece also tops the bell tower. Musorgsky's tone picture is one of monumental splendour and grandiosity. The majesty of the czardom through a thousand years is proclaimed in massive chords; alternating with these are softer antiphonal passages, chorale-like and prayerful, as if the Church were the other foundation stone upon which rested the edifice of ancient Russia.

Some of Musorgsky's *Pictures* seem to have no ancestry in piano music; they are originals. The Russian composer thought independently even of Liszt and Chopin, whose styles dominated the piano music of his time. One thing Musorgsky shared with Chopin—a penetrating knowledge of the piano as an instrument capable of infinitely varied sonorities. The *Pictures* are full of inventions in pure piano sound, e.g. in *Gnomus, Bydlo, Samuel Goldenberg and Schmuyle, Catacombs, The Hut on Fowl's Legs,* and *The Great Gate at Kiev.* Here the chords are often deployed in a wholly original manner; there are startling combinations of melodic and accompaniment material, and unusual contrasts in dynamics.

The pure picture value of the various pieces is astonishing. The subjects leap from the music sharply defined, and seldom by obvious means. It is remarkable, for example, that two characters so alike and yet so contrasting as Samuel Goldenberg and Schmuyle could be drawn in music at all; it is almost inconceivable that Musorgsky was able to accomplish the feat in only twenty-five measures.

Pictures at an Exhibition is important historically, for it marks the beginning of a new era in the progress of Russian music. It shares a distinction with Tchaikovsky's Piano Concerto in B flat minor (composed the same year, 1874), the two pieces being the first large-scale piano works of enduring quality to come out of Russia. They were the forerunners of a new literature of Russian piano music which would flower in later decades in the works of Scriabin, Rachmaninov, Stravinsky, and Prokofiev. The long reign of vocal music in this country was coming slowly to an end. Thereafter the instruments, especially the piano and the orchestra, would begin to have their day.

XI

In the summer of 1872, after he had finished the revision of *Boris Godunov*, Musorgsky was eager to begin work on another opera. It was Stasov who suggested that he go for a subject to another grim and critical era in Russia's history—the end of the seventeenth century when young Peter I was awaiting accession to the throne. At that time the whole sky of Russia's political, social, and religious life was black with storm clouds, for the great schism of the Church and the revolt of the Old Believers which had convulsed the nation a generation before had still not resolved. The old Russia was dying and the new Russia, its face turned toward the West, was struggling to be born. Moscow and the Czardom were a snake-pit of political intrigue. One central episode was a revolt by the Streltzy, a savage, undisciplined regiment of musketeers whose leader was the powerful Prince Ivan Khovansky. This man and his son Andrew aimed to seize the throne, but the revolt failed and the Khovanskys died on the gallows. Musorgsky chose this episode as the subject of an opera to be called *Khovanshchina*, which was Czar Peter's contemptuous term for the machinations of the two princes.

The composer plunged at once into the project and for the better part of a year made researches into the complex history of the period. No play such as he had had in Pushkin's *Boris Godunov* existed for *Khovanshchina*; he had to devise a drama of his own from a mass of historical material and from Stasov's suggestions. Musorgsky never did plan to condense his story into a simple, unified plot of the kind upon which the drama of the West depends. Rather he chose the technique which many other Russian opera composers were to use and which is essentially that of the great Russian novels, i.e. a series of isolated scenes, mosaic-like episodes, not too closely connected but adding up to an epic panorama. Musorgsky had also a dramatic precedent for this method in Pushkin's *Boris Godunov*, which was loosely constructed after the chronicle plays of Shakespeare. In the old chronicles the purpose was to reveal and glorify some great historical epoch or person, to recreate out of the surrounding darkness of history a whole series of scenes with sudden brilliant flashes of drama or portraiture, each illuminating a small segment but forming together a glowing canvas that teemed with life and colour. Unfortunately for the opera librettist there is a trap which surrounds this method, and Musorgsky fell into it. He did not know where to stop.

He began the work of composition apparently in the summer of 1873. There came an interruption in January 1874, with the first production of *Boris Godunov*, and then for the next six years there were sporadic periods of work and long pauses. In 1875 the complex task began to weigh the composer down and he dropped it entirely for a new operatic project. This was *The Fair at Sorochintzi*, a comic opera based on Gogol's story. After composing a series of fragments for this piece the composer again lost interest and set the comedy aside. Like *Khovanshchina*, it was never finished. Musorgsky returned to *Khovanshchina* and worked through a haze of alcoholic dissipation until the summer of 1880 when he wrote to Stasov that the opera was finished "except for a little piece of the final scene of self-immolation".

After Musorgsky's death in 1881 Rimsky-Korsakov took over the task of completing and preparing *Khovanshchina* for performance. Musorgsky had composed almost twice the material for an average length opera; very little of it was orchestrated. Rimsky-Korsakov made many cuts in the work; he composed a final scene, and he orchestrated the entire opera. In the course of his ministrations he also made many revisions and "corrections" of Musorgsky's harmonies. In 1885 he offered his version of *Khovanshchina* to the Imperial Theatre but that body, remembering its difficulties with *Boris Godunov*, turned it down. It was first performed by an amateur company in Petersburg, in 1886. Thereafter it remained practically in oblivion until the Imperial Theatre revived it belatedly in 1911, with Chaliapin in the role of Dosifey. Since then the opera has held a place in the repertoire in Russia but is not often performed elsewhere.

Diffuse and uneven though it may be, *Khovanshchina* is still one of the monumental works of the Russian lyric theatre and a repository of much of Musorgsky's finest music. Its theme is lofty and full of symbolic meaning—the epic tragedy of a nation struggling to free itself from the dead past, the conflict which still tears at the heart of Russia. The chief protagonist is the young Czar Peter who never appears but who personifies the force which is to pull the reluctant nation out of its mediaeval torpor. Against him are ranged three princes: Ivan Khovansky, whom Stasov described as "the representative of the ancient, gloomy, fanatical, dense Russia"; Golitzin, the clever, unstable schemer, his veneer of Western culture thinly covering his half-barbaric heritage; and the venerable Dosifey who had abandoned his title and worldly goods to become the leader of the Old Believers, a holy man whose mystical faith in the sternest tenets of orthodoxy carries him and his followers to final self-immolation.

As these powerful men struggle among themselves and against the Czar, each thinking he holds Russia's salvation, the people of the nation are put through an ordeal of sorrow and suffering. Two are followers of Dosifey—a young widow, Marfa, who has strange gifts of prophecy, and whose guilty passion for the profligate Prince Andrew Khovansky makes her life a torment until she seeks the cleansing penance of death by fire ("a Potiphar's wife", Stasov called her); and Suzanna, "withered, yellowed, malicious, fanatical".

The music fabric of *Khovanshchina* differs noticeably from that of *Boris Godunov*. It is less complex; its general structure is simpler and even slightly nearer the old operatic conventions; its harmonic schemes lack the opulent richness of the former work. The recitative is so melodious that with certain characters it becomes almost pure song. This was Musorgsky's aim. "I am now deep in the study of human speech," he revealed to Stasov, "I have come to recognize the melodic elements in ordinary speech and have succeeded in turning recitative into melody. I might call it 'melody justified by the meaning'. . . ."

Though it does not match *Boris Godunov* for concentrated dramatic power or originality, *Khovanshchina* achieves its effect by an accumulation of riches, the piling up of scene upon scene, each with a special beauty, until the whole grows at last into grandeur, e.g. the serene orchestral prelude which paints the pale sunrise over Moscow; the brutal, thundering tramp of the soldiery and their shouting trumpets which echo through the entire drama; the stately leit-motif that limns the portrait of the old Prince Khovansky in all his towering arrogance; the sorrowful declamations of Dosifey, and the choruses of the Old Believers which Musorgsky based on ancient liturgical chants; Marfa's divination scene, her song of lamentation in Act II, her passionate confession of a "soul-consuming love"; the boyar Shaklovity's aria, a prayer that Russia may be delivered from her sufferings; Act IV entire, with its unforgettable scene on Khovansky's country estate when the great prince, brushing aside a message of danger, calls for dances by his Persian slave girls, an interlude that has been called "the most precious pearl of oriental music in the world"; and then the exquisite Song of Praise (actually a folk wedding song) sung by the peasant girls an instant before an assassin knifes the old prince to death; the scene before the Church of Vassily Blajeny when a coach carries Prince Golitzin to exile, and the theme of Marfa's divination which foretold his downfall is transformed into a dirge of tremendous power; and finally, Marfa's last radiant proclamation of the triumph of love in death.

It is true that *Khovanshchina* has never achieved anything like the worldwide appreciation now enjoyed by *Boris Godunov*, but in any serious evaluation of Russian music the two must be placed together, like major columns supporting the edifice of nationalism in art. The discerning Paul Rosenfeld wrote of *Khovanshchina*:

"Like *Boris*, this folk drama is a glowing portrait of the collective entity, the Russian people; one not only steeped in the deep colours of its subject, but executed with a feeling and a truthfulness and a power matched by no other of its musical portraitists and by only a few of the composers who have enriched the world. Like that of *Boris*, the music of *Khovanshchina* is vocal of the very essences of the people, its forces, its sense of the starkness of life, and of the inevitability of suffering, its Asiatic fatalism. . . ."

XII

The last half-dozen years of Musorgsky's life were a prolonged alcoholic debauch which finally sent him at the age of forty-two into delirium tremens, epilepsy, and death. What psychological crisis first drove the composer to alcohol and then left him its helpless prey no one can now say with certainty. His letters offer no positive clue. Involved, rambling, obscured by elaborate devices of irony and whimsy, they often becloud rather than reveal the man's inner existence. It seems fairly clear that Musorgsky's alcoholism was his unfortunate means of releasing himself from periods of mental torture, the depressions which seize the Russians with especial virulence. It may be that that torture stemmed in Musorgsky's case from disappointment and frustration, from a general lack of public appreciation of his art; or it may have had its roots in some loss even more personal. The composer never married and little or nothing is known for certain of a romance with any woman. He seemed to have an abhorrence of the very idea of marriage for he once wrote, "When you read in the papers that I have put a bullet through my head or hanged myself, you may be certain that I married the day before."

It appears likely that Musorgsky's music itself was part of his undoing. His was an art of the most demanding kind—a constant struggle to avoid the conventional, and instead to invent and explore. He brought to this task a powerful imagination, but he lacked the sheer strength of character necessary for such prolonged battling. It would seem that moments came when, balked or exhausted by his efforts, he had to thrust his music from him, defeated by obstacles he could not surmount. Musorgsky periodically escaped into the dual life of the alcoholic.

For days at a time he would disappear, even his closest friends having no knowledge of his whereabouts. Ilya Repin, the painter, described how the composer

"sank, sold his belongings, even his elegant clothes, and soon descended to some cheap saloons where he personified the familiar type of 'has-been', where this childishly-happy, chubby child, with a red potato-shaped nose, was already unrecognizable. . . . Was it really he? The once impeccably dressed, heel-clicking society man, scented, dainty, fastidious. Oh, how many times V.V. (Stasov) . . . was hardly able to dig him out of some basement establishment, nearly in rags, swollen with alcohol. . . ."

In the summer of 1873 Musorgsky began to share the lodgings of a young friend, Count Golenishchev-Kutuzov. The count was twenty-five years old and a poet of some distinction. His association with Musorgsky was a happy one, particularly because the composer used a group of poems by Kutuzov for a number of his finest songs —the two cycles, *Sunless*, and *Songs and Dances of Death*.

The six songs of the *Sunless* cycle for voice and piano were composed in the summer of 1874. Their titles (every translator seems to have his own version) comprise : *In My Attic*, *Thine Eyes in the Crowd*, *Retrospect*, *Resignation*, *Elegy*, and *On the River*. The despairing mood of all these pieces is established in the first—a grey hopelessness, a brooding introspection that finds solace in the very loneliness of a little attic room. *Thine Eyes in the Crowd* is a moment of pain caused by a glimpse of a loved one on the street, and the memory of a passion of long ago. *Retrospect* is another backward glance into the past, whose magic once enthralled but is now dead. *Elegy* contains one of the few moments of dramatic climax in the entire cycle, when the poet is haunted by echoes of the "great sad bell of Death". *On the River* completes the set in a mood of black despair.

The music of the *Sunless* cycle marks a break with Musorgsky's nationalist past. Little is left of the contours of Russian folk song which permeated so much of this composer's music. These are also romantic songs and their spirit that of the romantic tradition of the time, rather than the realism of Musorgsky's own past. The music workmanship of the cycle is fastidious, almost elegant throughout, and many of the effects are attained by means of extreme subtlety. In several of the songs the mood of desolation, of emptiness, is suggested by the texture of the music, which becomes so attenuated that little is left of formal structure. Musorgsky's harmonies are as usual imaginative and free, with many anticipations of modern procedure. In *Resignation* there is an effect which has been noted by students of Debussy's work, and which may indicate that the French composer during his sojourns in Russia as a young man had opportunity to study the music of Musorgsky. A descending chromatic figure in thirds and sixths in the accompaniment of *Resignation* is a startling anticipation of the opening measures of Debussy's *Nuages*.

Musorgsky's last cycle and his greatest achievement in the art of song is the series of four *Songs and Dances of Death*. The first three, *Death's Lullaby*, *Death's Serenade*, and *Trepak*, were composed in the spring of 1875 ; the last, *Field Marshal Death*, in June, 1877. Musorgsky was attracted to these essays because they afforded him variants on a supremely tragic theme—the paradox of

Death, with its irony and degradation, its lacerating cruelty for the living, its spiritual justification.

In *Death's Lullaby* a mother waits through a long night beside her dying child. As dawn breaks Death knocks at the door. The pleadings of the mother are in vain; Death lulls the child to sleep. In *Death's Serenade* the spectre of Death stands beneath the window of a young girl. Her eyes are bright with fever, her sleep fitful. In the guise of a romantic young knight, Death sings his serenade in praise of her beauty. Closer he draws to his loved one, then triumphantly claims her in a smothering embrace. In *Trepak*, an old peasant, drunken and weary, loses his way in the forest; as the storm descends he dances a wild trepak until he falls exhausted in the snow. Death claims him as he dreams one last dream—that summer has come again with fields warm in the sunlight, and "sweet voices in the hay, happily singing, echoing far away". *Field Marshal Death* begins with the clash and din of battle. Night falls on the ghastly field and then in the moonlight, "his bones all glittering white and stark", Field Marshal Death rides forth. His grim and mocking commands ring out exultant: "Mine is the battle! . . . Friend and foe shall pass in review . . . March by me solemnly, greet your commander!"

If nothing were left of Musorgsky's operatic writing these *Songs and Dances of Death* would prove the composer's genius as a music dramatist. They are in fact compact music dramas in which the singer must perform not merely as a narrator but as an actor playing several parts. Present are all the elements vital to musico-dramatics: the establishment of a scene with its prevailing mood and colour, the delineation of characters and the projection of their various emotions, and finally the development of a theme or story with rising interest, suspense, climax, and resolution.

In these four pieces Musorgsky expanded the small frame of the art song to give it a new and overwhelming expressiveness. "Here we find," wrote Kurt Schindler, "a descriptive power uncanny in its visual correctness; melodic lines of undreamt-of boldness; harmonies that none other heard or felt before him; and a masterful handling of technical resources and of declamation." In other hands these scenes might have become over-romanticized, had they been attempted at all; but Musorgsky was able to depict the gravest and most poignant experiences in man's existence without trace of sentimentality. Always there is tenderness, and yet an uncompromising directness and force. The composer evokes the pity and the tragedy of human life and death in terms of the highest art.

Musorgsky had planned several more songs to be included in this cycle, but they were never composed. One other song, *After the Battle* (or *Forgotten*), might be joined with them, because of its subject matter and its treatment. It was composed in 1874. The original poem was also by Kutuzov and was inspired by a famous picture by the Russian painter Vereshchagin, who was noted for his battle scenes. This canvas depicted the corpse of a soldier on a battlefield, and was so realistic and shocking that Czar Alexander II recoiled from it in horror. The picture was removed from the gallery, and it was falsely rumoured that the painter had destroyed it fearing the Czar's displeasure. Even Musorgsky's song could not be published during the composer's lifetime.

The words of the song describe a soldier lying dead on a battlefield in a distant land. His comrades have departed victorious; he lies alone and forgotten. In the skies above, the vulture wheels, ready for the feast. Far away at home a lonely mother rocks her child to sleep with a lullaby, promising that soon the father will return, safe and happy. But somewhere far away, under the open sky, he lies alone.

XIII

The disorganization of Musorgsky's life during its closing years is shown by his entanglement in no less than three operatic projects, none of which he was able to finish. *Khovanshchina* progressed slowly, seeming to grow more complex as the years went on; *The Fair at Sorochintzi* he had laid aside, giving the excuse that he, a Great Russian, could not really comprehend the nuances of speech of Little Russia (the Ukraine). Nevertheless, in 1876 the composer resumed work on *The Fair* and in the following year he finally wrote out a brief libretto. In 1877 he also began making notes for still another opera, *Pugachevshchina* or *Pugachev's Men*. This idea derived from Pushkin's story, *The Captain's Daughter*, which was based on Pugachev's rebellion during the reign of Catherine II. Musorgsky had many discussions with Stasov regarding the development of a libretto, but beyond that made no visible progress.

The year 1880 marked the composer's last work on *The Fair at Sorochintzi*. For many years after his death the fragments of the uncompleted comedy lay untouched. With the successful revival of

Boris Godunov in 1908 came an awakening of interest in all Musorgsky's music, and in the succeeding decades there began to appear various versions of *The Fair*, completed and orchestrated by other composers. One such version has been mentioned, that of Cui, which received a performance in Petersburg in 1917, just a week before the outbreak of the Bolshevist Revolution. Cui composed music of his own to the scenes Musorgsky had left blank. A more successful attempt was that of Nicolas Tcherepnin, a modern Russian composer and pupil of Rimsky-Korsakov. Tcherepnin filled out the score by developing Musorgsky's unfinished sketches and using material from his other works, so that only Musorgsky's music was used throughout. The Tcherepnin version was produced by the Metropolitan Opera Company in New York, in 1931. Another version, by the Russian conductor, Emil Cooper, was performed in New York in 1942 by the New Opera Company. Still another version was prepared by the Soviet composer, Vissarion Shebalin, in collaboration with Paul Lamm, the distinguished musicologist and editor.

All the various versions of *The Fair at Sorochintzi* serve to accentuate the fascination and the frustration which attend any unfinished work by a great artist. Fortunately, Musorgsky left enough material for his comedy to make fairly clear his ultimate intentions. The better versions all reveal a gay and lyrical work, with much of the native colour and charm of Gogol's original story. The piece is redolent of Russian folk song and it reveals again Musorgsky's unique mastery of that idiom. *The Fair* avoids the extreme stylization of *The Marriage* for a much more conventional treatment of the dialogue. No attempt is made to mirror speech in music or to preserve the absolute integrity of the text; instead, the general form is that of a series of songs, choruses, and set pieces.

In 1879 Musorgsky was in such straits that his friends began to despair of his life. Balakirev wrote to Stasov, "Musorgsky is such a physical wreck that he can hardly become more a corpse than he is at present." He was also beginning to disintegrate mentally. In the summer of that year a singer named Daria Leonova persuaded him to act as her accompanist on a tour of southern Russia. They travelled as far as the Crimea, and the composer seemed to enjoy the experience. At the concerts he played solo arrangements of scenes from his operas and a strange improvisation which he called "a grand musical picture: Storm on the Black Sea". This work was never written down, but Rimsky-Korsakov described it as "a rather long and confused fantasia".

Back in Petersburg, Musorgsky became more than ever dependent upon Mme. Leonova at whose singing school he earned small sums as accompanist and teacher. His government job had ended and most of the time he was desperate for money. At Stasov's suggestion a group of his friends agreed to subsidize him to the extent of one hundred roubles a month on condition that he finish *Khovanshchina*. Another group, unknown to the first, agreed to give him eighty roubles a month if he would finish *The Fair at Sorochintzi*. And so the composer struggled on with both scores, through a daze of alcoholic confusion.

On a day early in February, 1881, the unfortunate man came to Mme. Leonova in great agitation, saying that "he had no place to go, that nothing was left for him but to walk the streets". That night he acted as accompanist for one of Leonova's pupils at a party in a private home, where he was suddenly taken with an epileptic fit induced by acute alcoholism. Two days later he was removed to the Nikolaevsky Military Hospital in the suburbs of Petersburg. There a kindly young doctor who knew and grieved for the great artist behind the wreck of the man, saw that he received decent care. The composer had moments of lucidity and others of completely insane ravings. The doctors indicated that he might have lived that way for as long as a year but, mercifully, his sufferings were cut short. "Terribly weak, changed and grown grey," he had the strength to sit up while Repin painted his shocking portrait, and in the early morning of March 28 (16 O.S.), 1881, Musorgsky died.

XIV

Russians themselves agree that of all musicians Musorgsky comes closest to the heart and spirit of their country. He was at once the most powerful nationalist and the least eclectic of Russian composers. Among the Five he seems to have paid the least homage to the West; he had not Borodin's grasp of classic procedure, Balakirev's sympathy with the great romantics, or Rimsky-Korsakov's purely syntactical skill. None of these phases of Western music absorbed Musorgsky; hence there is little that is secondary or borrowed in his art. He is one of the least derivative of composers.

Even before he was a nationalist Musorgsky was a stylist. His instinct was not to use materials as he found them but to put them through a moulding, a transforming process. This is the sea change wrought by all artists with a high sense of personal style; it exaggerates, it intensifies, it adds a touch of strangeness which is the magic ingredient of all great art. This stylization, exemplified in what seemed like broken textbook rules, was what really troubled Rimsky-Korsakov, himself not great enough an artist to apprehend the beauty inherent in the strangeness of his friend's creation.

Musorgsky was thus one of the genuine originals of music history. He followed a course of his own, one which often seems to have little connection with the past but springs from creative processes of remarkable depth, subtlety, and ingenuity. For him the pursuit of art meant the understanding of man. This explains why he worked as he did and where he did—chiefly in the realms of song and opera.

As for Musorgsky's place as a pioneer of modern realism in music, it is important not to exaggerate. There is no doubt that the literary concept of realism affected him powerfully and that this, coupled with his instincts for drama in music, led him to create music of a wholly new kind, e.g. many of his finest songs, much of *Boris Godunov*, all of *The Marriage*. But Musorgsky never did wholly renounce romanticism. He wrote many specimens of high romantic beauty. The songs of the *Sunless* cycle, many of the *Pictures at an Exhibition*, parts of *Khovanshchina*, all composed at a time when his interest in realism was at its height, show his mastery of the opposite genre. Taken as a whole, therefore, Musorgsky's music flows back and forth between the realistic and romantic poles. He could follow either course because the soul of his music is always its lyric character. Musorgsky was a superb melodist, but one who seldom used his gift in the more obvious lyric designs.

The tragedy which destroyed Musorgsky's life and left his art so long under a cloud had its effect on the course of all modern Russian music. The composer who could have left to a succeeding generation the most powerful example of sheer natural genius was instead bereft of influence. It would appear, though we shall never be certain, that the composer who learned most from him was not a Russian but a Frenchman, and that in the mind of the youthful Debussy germinated the seeds of Musorgsky's thought.

CHAPTER VII

BORODIN

I

ALEXANDER BORODIN was a member of that select but regally accomplished circle which claims Leonardo da Vinci as its most distinguished fellow. He was an artist-scientist. Borodin's contemporaries used to speak of him as a professional scientist and an amateur musician, for science was his trade and music his avocation. The passage of time, however, has reversed the order of precedence. Even though Borodin's work in organic chemistry was a valuable contribution to nineteenth-century Russian science it is now almost forgotten; while his music, the product of his spare time and his hours of indisposition, is a living part of the art of his country.

Borodin was endowed with natural gifts of a high order. Among the members of the Five he had the finest mind, the widest intellectual capacity, and his music talents were surpassed only by those of Musorgsky. Admirers of his art view his scientific life only with regret for it reduced his music output to a mere token of the man's genius. Even so, the small number of works which he did produce made their way quickly, especially in the West, where he became the first Russian composer to gain an international reputation.

Borodin was born in Petersburg on November 12 (October 31, O.S.), 1833, of distinguished lineage but out of wedlock. His father was the sixty-one-year-old Prince Ghedeanov whose family descended from the ancient kings of Georgia in the Caucasus, monarchs who claimed descent from David and "bore on their coat-of-arms the quarterings of the harp and sling". Borodin's mother was Eudoxia Kleineke, a middle-class girl of twenty-four. As was customary with illegitimate children of noblemen, Alexander was registered as the son of one of his father's serfs, Porphyri Borodin.

The boy's childhood was dominated by his mother, a woman of culture and refinement, who saw that her son received all the advantages that affluence and social prestige could afford. He was reared carefully, not permitted to go to school but taught at home by private tutors. His music education, however, was haphazard. A

125

flutist from a military band gave him lessons on that instrument, and later he had some instruction on the piano and the 'cello. At the age of fourteen, and apparently without any instruction whatever in composition, he wrote a concerto for flute and piano, and a trio for two violins and 'cello on a theme from Meyerbeer's opera, *Robert le Diable*. It was at this time that science and art began their cohabitation in Borodin's life. He became passionately interested in chemistry, set up a laboratory in his room and experimented in making fireworks.

In 1850 young Borodin's scientific career began in earnest when he entered the Academy of Medicine and Surgery at Petersburg. He distinguished himself as a student and in 1856 was appointed assistant to the professor of pathology and therapeutics. Two years later he received the degree of Doctor of Medicine. In 1859 he was sent abroad to study, spending the winter at Heidelberg and making a summer journey to Italy and Switzerland. One of his friends among a group of young Russian scientists was Mendeliev, who later became one of the greatest of chemists. At Heidelberg Borodin met his future wife, Catherine Protopopova, a frail young girl from Moscow, whose ill-health had brought her to the German town for a cure. She was an excellent pianist and her playing of Chopin and Schumann aroused the intense interest of Borodin, both in herself and her music. Two years later, after their return to Russia, they were married.

In 1864, at the age of thirty-one, Borodin became a professor of organic chemistry at the Academy of Medicine, and his life at that moment moved into the channel it was never to leave until his death twenty-three years later. He and his wife had a spacious apartment in the Academy building itself, where they enjoyed a chaotic but happy domesticity, and where Borodin remained absorbed in his teaching and his chemical researches. It seems incredible that in those busy years during which he also wrote important scientific papers and made occasional trips to Western Europe on matters of scientific importance, Borodin yet found the time to become one of the most distinguished of Russian composers.

II

Borodin called himself "a Sunday composer", who worked at his art only in odd hours. "In winter," he said in a letter long prized by his biographers, "I can compose only when I am too unwell to give my lectures. So my friends, reversing the usual custom, never say to me, 'I hope you are well,' but 'I do hope you are ill'." Nevertheless, music and chemistry intermingled in Borodin's life with strange affinity. Rimsky-Korsakov's accounts of Borodin, both as man and artist, are among the gems of the former composer's autobiography. The following is but a sample :

"On visiting him I often found him working in the laboratory which adjoined his apartment. When he sat over his retorts filled with some colourless gas and distilled it by means of a tube from one vessel into another, I used to tell him that he was 'transfusing emptiness into vacancy'. Having finished his work, he would go with me to his apartment, where he began musical operations or conversations, in the midst of which he used to jump up, run back to the laboratory to see whether something had not burned out or boiled over; meanwhile he filled the corridor with incredible sequences of successions of ninths or sevenths."

Unlike Musorgsky whose work in the Government service was drudgery, Borodin's career in science brought him the keenest pleasure. He loved his life at the Academy, his researches, and his contacts with his pupils. He was especially active in a campaign to admit women to higher education, a cause which he espoused for many years. He was one of the founders of the School of Medicine for Women in Petersburg, where he gave courses in chemistry.

Even during his busiest student days Borodin had never relinquished his desire to play and to compose. He studied fugal writing ; he played the 'cello in an amateur quartet (carrying his instrument seven miles in all kinds of weather) ; and he tried his hand at songs and small instrumental works. All this was done on his own and without professional instruction. Borodin met Musorgsky briefly in 1856 and again in 1859 but his real introduction to the Balakirev Circle came in 1862, when he began teaching at the Academy. He became Balakirev's pupil, plunging almost immediately into writing his First Symphony.

Like all Borodin's major works the First Symphony, in E flat, progressed very slowly and was not completed until five years later. The young composer was not unlike an apprentice carpenter trying to learn his trade by building an entire house. He had to master not only the rudiments but the refinements of harmony, counterpoint, form, and orchestration, guided only by Balakirev's highly-opinionated advice and his own music instincts. The work proceeded at a most leisurely pace, for Borodin never hurried. Only at the end was he forced to rush the copying of the instrumental parts in time for the first performance of the symphony. This took place on January 16, 1869, under Balakirev's direction, at a concert of the Russian Musical Society. The work was well received, and the name of Alexander Borodin was formally introduced to the world of Russian music.

Borodin's First Symphony has found no place in the modern orchestral repertoire outside Russia, for it is an immature work. It owes its importance as a minor landmark in nineteenth-century music to certain details of its construction, first pointed out in recent years by Gerald Abraham. Outwardly the symphony follows orthodox lines, but the inward structure of the first movement is revolutionary. Instead of the usual sonata form with its two contrasting themes, Borodin drew all his melodic material from a single basic theme; and instead of the usual complete statement of the thematic ideas in the exposition Borodin's melody is exposed only partially, in fragments as it were. These fragments are spun about through the orchestra and juxtaposed in counterpoint in typical development fashion, but it is not until the coda, a quiet contemplative *lento*, that all the various parts of the theme fall together to form a satisfying melodic whole.

Twentieth-century composers seeking a release from the conventions of the symphonic first movement now make constant use of this procedure—the invention of the half-amateur Borodin in the eighteen-sixties. Sibelius has been one of its more successful employers, and several movements of his symphonies and some of his tone poems are built by a series of exposures of a theme in part, with the complete statement reserved for a climactic close.

Borodin was so encouraged by the public reception of his First Symphony that he began work on a second, roughly planned as early as 1867. But for all his scientific training the composer carried little of order or system into his music life: he composed not only in a leisurely manner but with an almost chaotic lack of long-range direction or plan. His ambitious Second Symphony had to wait while he veered over suddenly into the field of opera. In the years 1866–67 he had composed a short opera farce, *The Bogatyrs* (The Valiant Knights), which parodied Serov's opera *Judith*,

MODEST MUSORGSKY
A photograph taken in 1870

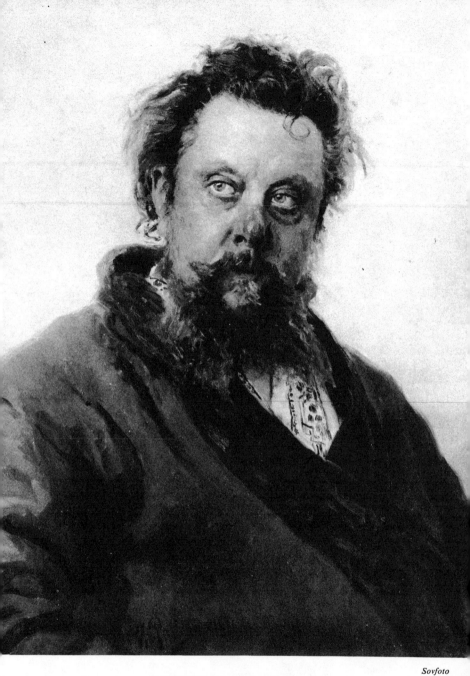

MODEST MUSORGSKY

From the portrait by Repin, painted about ten days before
the composer's death, in 1881

and was written in the styles of Rossini, Offenbach, Meyerbeer, and Serov himself. It was produced anonymously in Moscow, but was a failure.[1] In 1867 he attempted, and very soon abandoned, an opera based on Mey's tragedy, *The Czar's Bride*, which his friend Rimsky-Korsakov later utilized. Then in 1869 Stasov came forth with a grandiose idea. He sent Borodin a short sketch or scenario for an opera to be based on the ancient Russian epic of Prince Igor. The composer was entranced with the idea, and began studying the history and documents of the period and collecting folk melodies of Central Asian tribes. He made fair progress with a first act, but then ran into trouble with his libretto. He struggled and floundered, revised his story in mid-stream, but still could not form the details of the epic into a workable drama. Composition also proceeded haphazardly with Borodin working at various numbers which attracted him but without regard to their place in the story.

Borodin gradually realized his own shortcomings as an opera composer. He became disheartened and abandoned *Prince Igor*, turning instead to his Second Symphony. He completed the first movement in 1871, only to lay the whole thing aside for the collective opera-ballet *Mlada*, which he, Musorgsky, Cui, and Rimsky-Korsakov, undertook as a joint enterprise. Borodin's share was the fourth act. He reworked some of his *Prince Igor* music and was devising new material when the enterprise collapsed for lack of funds.

The composer returned again to his Second Symphony. In 1874 he made another try at *Prince Igor*, reworking his *Mlada* material and struggling with his libretto. And thus he proceeded, like a cook with many pots on his stove—symphony, operas, chemistry, medicine, teaching—but at last, in 1876, the Second Symphony was finished. Its first performance, in Petersburg on February 26, 1877, was a failure. Rimsky-Korsakov recalled that Borodin had originally scored the work too heavily for the brass; this error the composer later corrected and soon the symphony began to make its way in the world. It was one of the first major works in Russian music to find favour in Western Europe, scoring successes there even before it was accepted in Russia.

---

[1] The manuscript of *The Bogatyrs* remained lost until 1922. In 1936 the opera was produced in Moscow in a version orchestrated by Alexander Medtner, brother of the composer, Nicolas, and with a libretto by the Soviet poet Demyan Bedni. Because the piece satirized the mediaeval knights and heroes of Russian legend it outraged Commissar Molotov, who walked out on the première performance. The piece was banned and Bedni publicly disgraced.

The B minor Symphony begins with a bold leap into its famous motto theme—a magnificent gesture from the string choir in octaves —startling in its originality and full of native brawn. The movement which unfolds thereafter is rich in drama, colour, and romantic individuality. The form is fairly orthodox with a graceful lyric second theme for contrast; but it is the thunderous motto theme which dominates the movement and impresses its remarkable character on the entire piece. With this movement a new voice speaks out in the art of music. This is unmistakably a Russian symphony, dyed with the hues of a new nationalism.

In his second movement, *Molto vivo*, Borodin sends the orchestra flying like the wind, propelled by a series of reiterated Cs, and with the thematic material scudding about like leaves in the blast. Gusty rhythmic effects trip all but the most expert orchestral players. For contrast there is a central *Allegretto*, a delicately plaintive melody reminiscent of the Orient. The slow movement, a romantic *Andante*, is one of Borodin's finest lyric flights. The themes are exquisite, with unusual refinements of harmonic colour. The closing movement, *Allegro*, is one of dazzling brilliance.

Stasov wrote that "Borodin is an epic poet . . . whose unfettered imagination needs a text as a positive idea". He went on to describe the "national character" of the Second Symphony.

> "The old heroic Russian form predominates, as in *Prince Igor*. I may add that Borodin himself has often told me that in the *Adagio* he intended to recall the songs of the old Slavonic *bayans* (like the Troubadours, or Minnesingers); in the first movement, the assembling of the old Russian princes, and in the finale, the banquets of the heroes, to the tones of the *gusla* and bamboo flute, amid the enthusiasms of the people."

The B minor Symphony shows that of all the members of the Five Borodin stood closest to Balakirev. The Russian nationalist style of the piece is marked, but it has little of Musorgsky's sharp, personal stylization of that idiom; it is warm, rich, dramatic, tinged at times with Orientalisms. It has also what Balakirev's music lacked—a fund of beautiful melody, the fruit of Borodin's natural lyric gift. For his harmonies in this symphony Borodin for the most part followed Balakirev's suit: none of Musorgsky's radicalisms, but a mixture of the modal style of Russian folk and Church song with the chromaticisms of progressive Western music. The orchestral style is taken from Liszt and Berlioz, but with ideas that were Borodin's own.

The B minor Symphony has never enjoyed popularity, but that is no measure of its worth. It was one of the most original works of its time and it still deserves more performances than it gets. Its historical significance moreover is lasting: it was the first enduring Russian work for symphony orchestra.

III

In 1877, the year of the first performance of his B minor Symphony, Borodin journeyed to Germany on matters concerning the chemistry department at the Academy and his own researches in chemical subjects. He made a side trip to Weimar to visit Franz Liszt. At several felicitous meetings the Russian entered the great man's circle (which he described as "a Venusberg in which Liszt was Venus") and he received advice which had the ring of historic truth. On hearing that Borodin had been urged to "correct" his music because it had been criticized as amateurish, lacking in form and employing excessive modulation, Liszt exclaimed: "Heaven forbid! Do not touch it; alter nothing. Your modulations are neither extravagant nor faulty. Your artistic instinct is such that you need not fear to be original. Do not listen to those who would deter you from following your own way. You are on the right road. Similar advice was given to Mozart and to Beethoven, who wisely ignored it. Despite the adage that 'there is nothing new under the sun', your Second Symphony is entirely new. Nobody had done anything like it. And it is perfectly logical in structure." Liszt later proved the sincerity of his words when he helped to introduce the B minor Symphony and other works of Borodin to Western Europe.

A record of Borodin's meetings with Liszt is preserved in a series of letters which the Russian composer wrote to his wife and to César Cui in the summer of 1877, and during a later visit to Germany in 1881. The gem of this remarkable correspondence is the portrait of Liszt—the amazing old man, still the king of pianists, with his boundless vitality and his omnivorous appetite for music, holding court at Weimar amid the adulation of various Baronesses, Countesses, Grand Dukes, and a company of charming young ladies. "Evidently he has a weakness for the fair sex," remarked Borodin after describing the happy salutations and the kissing which concluded each two-hour music lesson.

The affinity between Liszt and Borodin was part of a much deeper bond of understanding which included the members of the Five as a group. Part of their creed was the very thing which Liszt stood for in the West—progressive freedom in art, individuality, forward movement. Their eyes were not closed to the facile emptiness of some of his music but they admired his originality, his creative vigour. Pieces like the *Mephisto Waltz*, and the Episodes from Lenau's *Faust*, especially the *Totentanz*, captivated them; they took ideas from his symphonic poems, his orchestration, his pianistic style, his harmonies. Liszt, indeed, is the key to the attitude of the Five toward all Western music, the fact that they were not blindly anti-Western Slavophiles as their conservative opponents of the Rubinstein party insisted.

It is not surprising that a few years after his first visit with Liszt at Weimar Borodin produced a work in that form which the renowned abbé had invented—the symphonic poem. Borodin called his piece *In the Steppes of Central Asia*, and he dedicated it to Liszt. It was originally intended as incidental music to one of a series of *tableaux vivants* presented in celebration of the silver jubilee of Czar Alexander II, in 1881. It is thus described in a note in the score :

> "Over the broad, sandy steppes of Central Asia come the sounds of a peaceful Russian song. From the distance is heard the tramping of horses and camels, and then the sound of an Oriental melody. A native caravan draws near. It pursues its way through the boundless desert, safely escorted on the long journey by a troop of Russian soldiers. The caravan moves farther and farther away. The song of the Russians and the melody of the Asiatics blend to form a common harmony, finally dying away in the silence of the steppe."

The piece begins with a long-sustained high E, played in octaves by two violins and evoking the emptiness, the silence, and the sadness of the vast plain. A folklike Russian theme is heard from the clarinet, and then from the English horn comes the mournful Oriental tune which revolves, characteristically, around a few notes. 'Cellos and basses play a pizzicato figure whose rhythm suggests plodding of horses or camels. These are the simple means which the composer develops into a picture of the meeting of East and West in the waste spaces of the Asian continent. Many composers, Russians and others, have since copied Borodin's ideas—his delicate uses of oboe, English horn, 'cellos, and violas for his Oriental theme, the monotony of the inverted pedal point on E, the effective contrast of the mournful Eastern theme and the simple Russian folk tune, the exotic colouring of the whole piece.

At the present time when romantic picture music has fallen into disrepute *In the Steppes of Central Asia* is infrequently heard. It played an important part, however, in the early spread of public interest in Borodin's work and that of his fellows. It was among the first of his orchestral works to receive wide popularity abroad, helping to arouse an international interest in the new phenomenon of Russian music.

IV

In spite of his natural gifts for polyphonic writing and his student activity in chamber music, Borodin as a mature artist did not attempt a large-scale chamber work until comparatively late in his career. He wrote his first string quartet between 1877–79 and his second between 1881–85. A third was left unfinished when the composer died.

The student pieces in chamber forms were by no means inconsequential. While at Heidelberg Borodin had composed a string sextet which was performed there in 1860, but was afterward lost. A piano quintet followed in 1862. This is preserved in manuscript and is described by Calvocoressi as showing "signs of originality". All during this student period Borodin was engrossed in German music, and in his own phrase "impregnated with Mendelssohnism". After his meeting with Balakirev his interest in the German classics gave way to the new nationalism; he forgot chamber music while he busied himself with his first two symphonies and his early attempts at opera. It was not until 1875 that he began planning a string quartet. Actual composition was begun in 1877 and two years later the work was completed.

Borodin's String Quartet No 1, in A Major, has been called the earliest example of first-rate chamber music to be written by a Russian composer. At the same time it proves that the labels which Russian composers of that day pinned on themselves and on each other were often meaningless. Here is a work composed in the very citadel of nationalism and by a supposedly leading Slavophile, yet it bears almost no sign of its Russian origin. Borodin, it would seem, had gone back to the days of his youth when German chamber music engrossed him. The composer himself indicated that his quartet was inspired by a theme from Beethoven's String Quartet in B flat, Op. 130, and the first subject of Borodin's opening movement is a paraphrase of the German master's theme. The entire work, although lyrical as all of Borodin's writing is basically lyrical, is remarkable chiefly for its contrapuntal ingenuity. Here was one Russian, reputedly a radical nationalist, who understood the abstract art of polyphony as if he were a German.

Borodin's early love for Mendelssohn comes to life again in this quartet, especially in the elfin Scherzo, a faery piece which the youthful composer of music to *A Midsummer Night's Dream* would have relished. There is much originality in Borodin's skilful creation of new tonal colours for the four instruments. The romantic slow movement (which Calvocoressi believes influenced Debussy and Ravel) is full of whispered, ghostly sonorities; while the harmonics in the trio of the Scherzo are glints of silver and starlight also in the manner of the coming French impressionists.

Borodin's String Quartet No. 2, in D major, remains one of the finest Russian works in chamber form, in which the composer again maintains an equipoise of lyric beauty and polyphonic skill. His part writing seems effortlessly smooth; the four instruments sing with a continual euphony and grace. There are some traces of nationalism in this Quartet's moods and themes, especially in the romantic slow movement, a Nocturne which has recalled "the heavy, languorous atmosphere of a summer night in Russia". On the other hand, part of the Scherzo is based on a waltz-like figure which would almost persuade us that the Russian composer on his travels abroad had enjoyed an unforgettable sojourn in Vienna. But these are not major considerations. What the Borodin String Quartets prove is that this composer had an intuitive understanding of this rarefied art. He did not have to rely upon nationalist idioms, or colour or romantic pictures, but was wholly equal to the demands of abstract musical design.

v

Borodin's songs were for many years among the least heard of his important works, and even at the present time they are not well known outside Russia. They are a slender company, comprising a mere dozen songs in all, yet even within this tiny compass the composer was able to display his refined and eclectic tastes, his natural lyric gift.

The first songs were written in the 1850s, when Borodin was a medical student at the Academy and still a tyro as a composer. These efforts, including a setting of Heine's *Fishermaiden*, remain unpublished. His first published song was *The Sleeping Beauty* (1867), a recounting of the familiar fairy-tale of the princess slumbering in the enchanted forest. Borodin's version is a dreamy, lyrical tone-picture (the words are his own) whose most unusual feature is the copious use of dissonant seconds, softly reiterated in syncopation. These, and the use of whole-tone scales in the bass line, startled and antagonized the anti-nationalist critics of Borodin's day and stamped him as an insurgent.[1]

The next year, 1868, Borodin published four more songs: *The Queen of the Sea*, *Dissonance*, *My Song is Fierce and Bitter*, and *The Song of the Dark Forest*. All four pieces are written with mature skill, and the last three are among the composer's masterpieces in the song form. *The Queen of the Sea* (words by Borodin) is another fairy-tale picture piece, close in style and mood to *The Sleeping Princess*. The same feeling of delicate fantasy prevails and there is again a use of dissonant seconds, a harmonic device which recurs so often in Borodin's piano accompaniments that it becomes almost a trade-mark.

Dissonance is also set to words by Borodin himself, although the terse, epigrammatic style (the entire song comprises only seventeen measures) and the romantic irony are remindful of Heine. To indicate the "false note in her voice and in her heart" Borodin maintains the note F above middle C through the entire piece. What saves the song from being a mere technical trick is the unusual harmonic scheme which revolves around the single note, and the expressive strength of the compressed and fragmentary melodic material. *My Song is Fierce and Bitter* is a companion piece. The words are Heine's, and again only a handful of measures is needed for a compressed lyric epigram. These songs reveal Borodin's study of the music of Chopin, for we hear more than a trace of Chopin's *appassionata* style—"sonorously tragic, troubled by fevered visions, capricious, irregular . . ."

---

[1] Harmonic innovations based on these intervals appeared a generation later in Debussy's music, and may have been part of the legacy which the French composer is believed to have received from his several visits to Russia and contacts with Russian music during his student days.

In *The Song of the Dark Forest* Borodin departed from fairy-tales and Byronesque romanticism for a Russian primitivism which might have come from the pen of Musorgsky. The words again are the composer's and they tell a "tale of long ago, of ages past and gone". Imitation of the Russian folk style is achieved with bold ruggedness and simplicity. The piano underlines in octaves much of the broad melodic line ; the rhythms, irregular measures of 7/4, 5/4, 3/4, and 6/4, maintain an illusion of bardic declamation. In this song Borodin was clearly influenced by Musorgsky's early excursions in the folk idiom. He ignored formal rules and instead let his music go straight to the heart of the text.

The Sea (1870) was for a long time the composer's most famous and widely-performed song, but the Lisztian pyrotechnics in its accompaniment material have weakened its appeal. This seascape is painted largely by means of pounding and rumbling figures in the bass register, prolonged until the effect is as much a piano etude as a lyric essay. The result is overdrawn and somewhat blatant, one of the few lapses in taste which may be charged against this composer.

Ten years passed before Borodin turned again to the song form. Between 1880 and his death in 1887 he produced six more songs, but in general they are inferior to the finer examples of his first period. In 1880 came a setting of Heine's *Aus meinen Tränen* (Of my Tears), a rather pallid song and hardly comparable with Schumann's setting of the same poem in the *Dichterliebe*. The following year the death of Musorgsky moved Borodin to write *For the Shores of Thy Far Native Land*, to words by Pushkin. This song is conventional in its imitation of Germanic sentimentality, an estimate apparently shared by the composer himself who refused to allow the work to be published during his lifetime. *Arabian Melody*, written sometime in the 1880s, is Borodin's only song employing the Eastern idioms which he used with such ravishing effect in *Prince Igor*. Borodin's own words were based on genuine Arabian songs. The union of these words with a languorous and exotic melody and an accompaniment which is like the strumming of some instrument of the East, gives the song a singular charm, a redolence of Oriental romance and passion.

Two "character" songs completely different in style from Borodin's others were composed in the 1880s. *Master Pride* (words by Alexey Tolstoy) is a satirical picture of a pompous, ostentatious little man, as proud of his new wealth as he is ashamed of his humble beginnings. The caricature is clever, but not as deeply cut as the prototypes by Musorgsky. *Rich and Poor* (1884) is a setting of a poem by Nekrassov, in which the poor Russian serf dreams for a fleeting moment of the luxuries he would enjoy if he were rich.

The Magic Garden (1886) closed Borodin's brief excursion into the art of song. It was written after the composer's two visits to Belgium where he was lionized and his music acclaimed. It paid tribute specifically to a patroness of Russian music in Belgium, the Comtesse de Mercy Argenteau, at whose castle near Liége Borodin had been an honoured guest. In *The Magic Garden* he returned to the style of his early fairy-tale pieces, recapturing the dreamy mood and elusiveness of outline which vaguely foreshadow the coming impressionism of Debussy.

VI

No account of the career of Alexander Borodin would be complete without some description of his home life, the incredible domestic symphony amid which the artist-scientist lived and worked for a quarter of a century. The apartment at the Academy was a large one and was supplied to the Borodins rent-free; but there its advantages ended. Rimsky-Korsakov said that it was like a corridor, for it never permitted Borodin to "lock himself in or pretend he was not at home to anyone". In consequence people swarmed through it at all hours of the day or night—students seeking advice, friends seeking company, relatives (both near and distant) seeking shelter. The relatives especially came often and in large numbers, sometimes choosing Borodin's home as a convenient hospice in which to "fall ill or even lose their minds". When all the beds were taken they slept on couches or on the floor or dozed in chairs; not infrequently they took Borodin's bed. The apartment itself was usually a litter of disorder and disarray. Five years after they moved in the Borodins still picked their way around piles of books and music, half-unpacked trunks and suitcases; on one occasion when carpenters and plumbers came to repair defective drain-pipes they left holes in the floor that remained uncovered for months.

Since Borodin seemed never to remember whether or not he had eaten, meals were fantastically irregular with dinner often begun as late as eleven o'clock at night. Along with transient guests, relatives, and partial strangers, the Borodins shared their meals with a colony of cats—bold animals of both sexes and varying sizes which walked on the table, examined the food, leaped onto the backs of the diners and in general treated the Borodin ménage as a feline liberty hall.

Even though he lived amid this carnival with outward tolerance and calm, never seeming to mind even the most outrageous invasions of his privacy, the composer was actually an extremely nervous man who was a prey to minor ailments. He came down with a succession of headaches and colds, stomach disorders, toothaches, and boils. His wife suffered cruelly from asthma and as many of her nights were sleepless she often slept through much of the day. When her malady became intolerable she would desert Petersburg for long visits with her mother in Moscow, leaving the composer to struggle along as best he might in the incredible apartment.

It was during one of Catherine's Moscow visits that Borodin became deeply involved with a young woman, Anna Kalinin, who had the misfortune to fall in love with him. Anna was an intelligent girl, interested in music, science, and social problems. For a time she attended Borodin's classes in physics and chemistry. When they met she was twenty years old and married to a boorish landowner. As Anna became more infatuated with the composer her husband became more repellent to her; soon she began suffering from nervous ailments including epilepsy, partial paralysis, and unaccountably large bumps on her skull.

For Borodin the girl created an insoluble problem, and at the same time a situation which might have come from the pages of Turgenev. The composer was powerfully drawn to the suffering Anna, but his love for her, he assured himself, was wholly unsensual. Most amazing of all, he wrote his wife a candid day-by-day account of his passion.

> "I put my face into the pillow and wept bitterly, talking aloud to myself. 'Why isn't she my sister, my daughter, or my cousin? How happy I would be then! I could love her without bringing unhappiness to anyone.'" . . . "When I am with her I am absolutely tranquil. Not a single sensual thought touches my soul." "I love to look at her. I love to listen to her thin childish voice, to look at her light darling eyes, which become alive every time she looks at me. I even like to see her wrinkle her nose."

To allay any possible qualm of doubt which might arise to disturb his wife, Borodin finally remarked, "Don't forget that from the moment of our first meeting (when we kissed each other) I never kissed her again, although I had plenty of opportunities to do so."

Borodin's wife reacted to the chaste affair in a way which left the unhappy man gasping with shock. Catherine was ready to rush back to Petersburg at once, and not to her home but to a hotel. "For God's sake, be calm," returned the distracted husband; and then: "My darling, please come quickly. Cry on my breast, and let me cry with you. Do you hear me? I am waiting. Come quickly." Catherine finally returned. Anna soon faded from the composer's life, leaving him momentarily saddened but wiser in the ways of feminine psychology.

The last half-dozen years of Borodin's life were crowded and eventful, even though they marked a slow slackening of his creative pace. His only important achievement in music was his D Major String Quartet, which he finished in 1885. In that year he began a Third Symphony, in A minor, and by 1886 had almost finished the first two movements. They were completed and orchestrated after his death by Glazunov. Work on *Prince Igor* had come almost to a standstill. One reason for the slackening of Borodin's creative efforts was an attack of cholera in 1884 which left him with a weakened heart. He was worried and depressed, too, about his wife who had become so ill that she had to remain permanently in Moscow. Meanwhile, however, he had reason to be elated by the steady progress of his music in the public esteem, both in Russia and abroad. In 1885 he journeyed to Belgium where his work had made a fine impression. The next year he went again, accompanied by César Cui whose opera *The Captive of the Caucasus* was performed at Liége. On both visits Borodin and his music were received with enthusiasm; he had too the satisfaction of knowing that in other European cities and in the United States his works were being played and admired.

On his return from the triumphant Belgian journeys Borodin plunged again into his scientific and musical work. In 1886 he published the last of his chemical monographs (recording his researches on the subject of nitrogen) and he worked on his Third Symphony. During the early days of 1887 he wrote a few numbers for *Prince Igor*. On the night of February 26, Borodin attended a dance given by one of the Academy professors. He came dressed in a Russian costume with red blouse and high black boots; he joined in the gaiety and the dancing and he gave jocular imitations of a friend. Later in the evening the composer stood aside talking, and when he suddenly fell backward to the floor his friends thought for a moment that he was joking. But his long-over-taxed heart had stopped, and he died instantly.

VII

With Borodin's death his greatest project in music, the opera *Prince Igor*, remained unfinished although it had lain upon his work-table for eighteen years. Certain numbers were finished and orchestrated; some existed as finished piano sketches, others as fragmentary rough drafts only; still others were missing entirely. There was no adequate libretto or scenario. The amorphous mass of manuscript was taken in hand by the composer's friends, Rimsky-Korsakov and Alexander Glazunov, who spent many months bringing the work to a finished state. It was first performed, at Petersburg, on November 4, 1890. *Prince Igor* is surely one of the most famous scores in Russian music; just as surely it contains much of Borodin's most prized music. Yet the opinion prevails (outside Russia, at any rate) that as an opera it is a beautiful failure.

The epic, *The Tale of Igor's Expedition*, is the work of an unknown bard of the twelfth century, and has been called "the greatest extant monument of Kievan literature". The original manuscript was found in 1795, the property of a monk. It was published in 1800, but in the burning of Moscow in 1812 the original was lost. Thereafter some scholars doubted its authenticity, suspecting it to be a late eighteenth-century imitation like the poems of Ossian; but today its validity seems assured. Writes Professor Ernest J. Simmons:

"This prose-poem . . . reveals in abundance the very essence of Old Russian literature, its symbolism and ecclesiastical elements. Not at all inferior in artistic quality to similar mediaeval works in the West, such as 'Beowulf', and the 'Chanson de Roland', 'The Tale of Igor's Expedition' provides convincing proof of the high degree of cultural development and national consciousness attained by the Russians in this early period of their existence."

The Prince Igor story is an echo after hundreds of years of a tremendous human drama which had taken place during the twelfth century on the Eurasian steppes, and which Arnold Toynbee has

expounded as the ancient recurring struggle of the nomadic peoples
who roamed the land and the peasants who cultivated it. Prince
Igor of Seversk led the forces of the Slavic husbandmen, and the
epic is an account of his expedition against the Polovtsy, a wandering
tribe of Tartars who had invaded the regions of the River Don.

The libretto which Borodin fashioned from the epic is simple
enough. In the Prologue, Prince Igor accompanied by his son
Vladimir sets out with his army against the Polovtsy, undeterred
by an ominous eclipse of the sun. In Act I his brother-in-law,
Prince Galitsky, tries treacherously to arouse the populace against
the absent ruler. He is denounced by Igor's wife, Princess Yaroslavna, just as news is brought of the terrible defeat of Igor's army
on the banks of the Kayala. The second and third acts take place
in the camp of the Polovtsy, where the Tartar captors treat Igor and
his son with chivalrous courtesy. The son Vladimir falls in love with
Konchakovna, daughter of the Tartar Khan. Prince Igor finally
escapes from the camp of the Polovtsy, but at the last moment
the son remains behind in the arms of the beguiling Konchakovna.
In the fourth act Prince Igor is reunited with Yaroslavna, amid the
ruins of their palace.

Both in its general outlines and in its details *Prince Igor* differs
radically from the realistic music dramas of Musorgsky, returning
instead to the earlier pattern of Glinka. Borodin himself described
his work as "nearer to *Ruslan* than to *The Stone Guest*". There is no
attempt at realistic drama for the reason that Borodin was little
interested in character study or development. "I am by nature a
lyricist and a symphonist," he said with perfect appreciation of his
gifts. In his *Prince Igor* he purposely subordinated the symphonic
side of his art.

"In opera" (he said), "as in decorative art, details and
minutiae are out of place. Bold outlines only are necessary ; all
should be clear and straightforward and fit for practical performance from the vocal and instrumental standpoint. The
voices should occupy the first place, the orchestra the second."

Having reduced the interest of the drama *per se* and purposely
subordinated the orchestra, Borodin concentrated on the lyric side
of his task with the result that his opera is largely a succession of
songs, many of them among the most splendid and colourful the
composer ever wrote.

The undramatic qualities of Borodin's libretto have undoubtedly weighed heavily against the acceptance of *Prince Igor* in opera houses of the West. Like Musorgsky in *Khovanshchina*, Borodin apparently did not attempt to concoct a strong central plot, relying instead on a series of dramatic mosaics. But if *Khovanshchina* was related to the diffuse and somewhat wandering style of the old chronicle plays, *Prince Igor* sprang from an even more rambling form, the ancient epic. Russian critics are agreed that Borodin's music is a magnificent spiritual re-creation of his archaic subject, and that his deep love of its poetic, lyric, and allegorical beauty bore rich fruit. But if *Prince Igor* is to succeed as opera it must apparently be on its own ground, among the people of whose heritage it is a part. As static as an oratorio, it needs even there the splendour of brilliant staging to bring it to life in the theatre. Meanwhile, its individual numbers keep it green : many stirring choruses, arias which are in the repertoires of all Russian singers, and the incomparable dances.

Borodin was obviously captivated by the Eastern scenes in his story and thus the second and third acts surpass in interest the other two. The Polovtsian Dances are opera ballet music at its zenith of sheer brilliance. With the vividness of a painting they evoke the wild scene on the Eurasian plain ; they vibrate with the life and colour of the half-barbaric Orient. Borodin was in his element here, blending lyric beauty with breathless rhythm, exotic harmony, and dazzling colour ; while Rimsky-Korsakov's instrumentation is a classic example of that art.

VIII

In his own day Borodin was flayed by conservative critics as a music anarchist, and his work was called "unhealthy, shapeless and extravagant", "infested with the poison of dissonance", and "the bitter fruit of inadequate musical education". Any tribute to the man's art and to his character must include recognition of the steadfastness with which he held to his course. That course, as we may see it today, was simply the one which Balakirev had inherited from Glinka. Borodin is thus a true descendant of Glinka, an artist who could be widely eclectic and still remain a strong Russian nationalist.

As an eclectic he followed Glinka and Balakirev in going both to East and West. His Oriental imitations are the best in Russian music, and it may be that a natural heritage from his father's ancestors was at work here. When he turned to the West his inquisitive mind took him over a wide field. For his symphonies and chamber works he went to the German classics, both for structural ideas and for polyphonic texture; he was the first Russian, indeed, to succeed as a polyphonist. We have seen his indebtedness to Liszt, and he also owed something of the harmonic richness of his music to Chopin's chromaticism. For operatic form he borrowed chiefly as Glinka did, from the Italians.

In his use of the Russian folk idioms Borodin was seldom a bold stylist like Musorgsky but he contrived to flood much of his music with a rich native colour. Calvocoressi notes that the influence of the old modal scales is quite evident not only in his melodic and harmonic style but also in his structural schemes:

> "The tonal plans of his symphonies, for instance, are founded on modal relations, not on the tonal relations of the major-minor system, the main features of which originate in the pull of the dominant and of the leading note. So he played an important part in the modern evolution of music outside Germany, an evolution characterized by the gradual extension of the limits of tonality and a growing awareness of the possibilities of the old modes, further and further away from which Western musical art had been proceeding for centuries."

Borodin had one of the finest lyric gifts which has yet appeared in Russian music. Melody seemed never to fail him whether he worked in opera, symphony, chamber music, or the song; and with it went a gift for harmonic colour, compounded of diatonic, chromatic, modal, and at times dissonant hues. These, and a remarkable sense of form and an instinct for polyphony, produced an art which in any country would be natural, spontaneous, and well rounded. Above all, Borodin had taste—the sound aesthetic judgments and the fastidious instincts which are part of the unconscious equipment of all superior artists.

CHAPTER VIII

RIMSKY-KORSAKOV

I

ANYONE who writes of the life, the times, and the music of Nicholas Andreievich Rimsky-Korsakov must admit at the outset a considerable handicap. The work has already been done, and incomparably, by the composer himself. Rimsky-Korsakov's autobiography, *My Musical Life*, is a work as priceless in its way as the autobiography of Berlioz. The Russian composer had not the great Frenchman's exuberant fancy, his wit, or his astonishing command of literary expression; nevertheless Rimsky-Korsakov bequeathed to history a detailed and vivid record of his age and his own place therein. His was the first and the finest account we have of the genesis of the group known as the Five, their personalities, their aspirations, and the creative force they generated in Russian music; and any writer who travels over that ground must acknowledge a debt to the composer.

Rimsky-Korsakov was the youngest member of the Five and his career as a practising musician lasted for almost half a century. It was an enormously abundant career, contrasting sharply with the brief years that Musorgsky and Borodin were able to give to music, and with the thin yield of Balakirev's life work. Rimsky-Korsakov in fact took over the direction of the movement that Balakirev started, not long after the latter's breakdown in the early eighteen-seventies. His influence over the Russian music of the later nineteenth century and the early twentieth century was very great, and it still colours the creative thought of present-day Soviet composers.

Rimsky-Korsakov was born on March 18 (March 6, O.S.), 1844, in the town of Tikhvin in the Novgorod Government. His family was an old and aristocratic one, but its distinctions were removed from the field of art. The composer wrote, "My parents . . . rarely coming in touch with prominent literary and artistic people, naturally were far from the thought of making me a musician." His father was a Governor-emeritus in retirement; an uncle and a great-grandfather had been admirals in the navy, and his older brother also became an admiral. Young Nicolas Andreievich was

144

ALEXANDER BORODIN

NICHOLAS
RIMSKY-KORSAKOV
from the painting by
V. A. Serov

Sovfoto

entered in the Corps of Naval Cadets in Petersburg when he was twelve years old.

During the first dozen years of his life he showed unusual interest in music, but his parents did not realize the significance of the fact that from an adjoining room he could recognize and name any note on the piano. He was given only mediocre instruction. It was after his residence as a cadet in Petersburg that he first heard great music adequately performed. He attended the opera and symphony concerts, and he took piano lessons. It was Glinka's music which set his mind ablaze: "I truly began to love the art of music when I came to know *Ruslan and Ludmila.*" The young man began studying scores and even trying to orchestrate and to compose, with only a second-rate piano teacher as a guide. He had practically no instruction in music theory.

When he was seventeen years old Rimsky-Korsakov was introduced to the Balakirev circle in the latter's home. There he met Cui, Musorgsky, and Stasov, and very soon he became a regular member of the group which was later to form itself into the famous Five.[1] The young naval cadet was entranced by the personality and abilities of Balakirev ("I was literally in love with him"), and the latter quickly assumed the role of teacher and mentor. At Balakirev's urging the cadet attempted nothing less than the composition of a symphony. Rimsky-Korsakov later wrote:

> "I who did not know the names of all the intervals and chords, to whom harmony meant but the far-famed prohibition of parallel octaves and fifths, who had no idea as to what double counterpoint was, or the meaning of cadence, thesis and antithesis, and period—I set out to compose a symphony."

Studying and imitating a few works of Schumann and Glinka, and with one eye on Berlioz' *Treatise on Instrumentation*, the seventeen-year-old cadet actually got down on paper a first movement, a scherzo, and a finale, but was defeated by the slow movement.

> "My attempts to write an Adagio met with no success, and it was useless to hope for any; in those days one was somehow

[1] There had been a previous member of the group, one Gusakovsky, a young graduate chemist whose music talents Balakirev greatly admired. He was described by Rimsky-Korsakov as a "queer, extravagant, and sickly character", who composed in a style imitative of Beethoven and Schumann, but seemed incapable of finishing any of his compositions. He left a place for Rimsky-Korsakov when he went abroad for a long stay, thus removing himself from possible immortality in the field of Russian music.

ashamed to write a cantabile melody; the fear of dropping into the commonplace precluded any kind of sincerity."

At this moment the plans of the Russian Navy took precedence over the young man's music career. In April, 1862, he was assigned to the clipper *Almaz* which left Russia the following autumn for a three-year cruise. For an account of those voyages the reader must go to the composer's autobiography where the story is told vividly, and all too briefly, of his visits to London, to the East coast of America during the Civil War, to Rio de Janeiro, the Cape Verde Islands, the Mediterranean, and his final return to Russia in 1865.

During this period the sea and its adventures almost obliterated the young man's serious interest in music. It was not long, however, before contact with Balakirev and his group rekindled the flame, and Rimsky-Korsakov set to work finishing his first symphony. It was performed late in 1865 under Balakirev's direction at a concert of the Free School of Music. Like so much of Rimsky-Korsakov's early music this Symphony in E flat minor was in later years completely revised by the composer who was unwilling to leave for posterity a record of his rash amateurishness.

During the next few years Rimsky-Korsakov's assignment to shore duties in Petersburg permitted him ample time for music. Balakirev at the time was at work arranging and harmonizing his collection of Russian folk songs. These, and a group of Oriental melodies and dances which Balakirev heard in the Caucasus, impressed and delighted young Rimsky-Korsakov. They marked, he said, the origin of his love for folk music. He composed a group of songs (among them the Oriental fantasy, *The Rose Enslaves the Nightingale*), an Overture on Three Russian Themes (1866), a Fantasy on Serbian Themes (1867), the symphonic poem, *Sadko*, (1867), and the programme symphony *Antar* (1868). In his later years Rimsky-Korsakov completely revised and re-orchestrated these works.

During the year 1868 the entire Balakirev circle began attending the musical soirées of Alexander Dargomyjsky, who was then furiously at work on his opera, *The Stone Guest*. Here Rimsky-Korsakov met the two talented Purgold sisters, one a singer and the other a pianist. The latter, Nadezhda Nikolayevna Purgold, later became Rimsky-Korsakov's wife. At Dargomyjsky's parties the composer and his friends would perform sections of *The Stone Guest* as he completed them. Rimsky-Korsakov was so fascinated that he decided to attempt an opera himself. At the suggestion of Balakirev and Musorgsky he chose as his subject Mey's drama, *The Maid of Pskov* (*Pskovityanka*), known outside of Russia as *Ivan the Terrible*. After many interruptions the piece was finished four years later, in 1872.

This first of Rimsky-Korsakov's long list of works for the lyric stage had a revealing history. The première performance, in Petersburg on the first day of the year 1873, met with gratifying success. Four years later the composer spent many months completely revising and re-orchestrating the work, but in 1878 the directors of the Imperial Theatres refused to produce the new version. A decade later the still-unsatisfied composer returned once more to *The Maid of Pskov* for further revisions. It was not until 1898 that a third version was produced brilliantly both at Moscow and Petersburg. In these cold statistics is contained a clue to the essential character of Rimsky-Korsakov—the man and the artist. Few composers have been more remorselessly self-critical, few more persevering in the pursuit of technical knowledge and skill. Rimsky-Korsakov's entire career, as we shall presently see, was a series of steps in which the artist gained, after exhaustive study, proficiency in some branch of music technique. With each step he sought not only to apply his finely-wrought skill to his work of the present but also to improving and purifying what he had done in the past.

II

In the summer of 1871 when he was in his twenty-seventh year, an event occurred which changed the entire course of Rimsky-Korsakov's life. He was offered the professorship of practical composition and instrumentation at the Petersburg Conservatory. During his deliberations the young composer came to the realization that for a long time he had been unhappy as a disciple of Balakirev. His methodical mind rebelled against the free and easy instruction ; he craved instead to learn the technique of music from the ground up and according to the methods of standard pedagogy—the very thing which Balakirev disdained. And so he took a daring step. Even though he was almost completely ignorant of textbook harmony, counterpoint, and form, he accepted the professorship. First he had to teach himself, and this he did in secret while he managed by evasion and bluffing to keep just ahead of his first pupils.

The studies which began with the professorship at the Conservatory never really ended during Rimsky-Korsakov's lifetime. He started with the most elementary harmony exercises and then went on to counterpoint, fugue and canon. "Counterpoint and fugue absorbed me altogether," he wrote. During the spring and summer of 1875 he filled a large blank book with counterpoint exercises, and he composed some sixty fugues. Obviously, he was a born student and a born technician. His mind was precise and well organized, capable of long and intense concentration; it seemed that no task was too heavy for him.

In 1873 Rimsky-Korsakov was appointed Inspector of Bands of the Navy Department, a post he held until 1884. The appointment, he said, "stirred in me a desire of long standing, to familiarize myself thoroughly with the construction and technique of orchestral instruments". Familiarize was hardly the word. He went into the subject exhaustively, buying a number of the instruments and learning to play them himself. In the next fifteen years he became one of the most assured and brilliant orchestrators of his age.

Of great importance to modern Russian music were the years which Rimsky-Korsakov gave to editing, finishing, and orchestrating works of other composers. His earliest task of this kind was done in 1868 when he orchestrated several numbers of the opera *William Ratcliffe* for César Cui. The next year he orchestrated *The Stone Guest* when Dargomyjsky died leaving his magnum opus unfinished. Then in the eighteen-seventies he and Balakirev spent several years preparing for publication the full orchestral scores of Glinka's operas, *A Life for the Czar* and *Ruslan and Ludmila*. After Musorgsky's death came his extensive ministrations on the scores of *Boris Godunov* and *Khovanshchina*, his best-known (and most severely criticized) operation in the editorial field. Finally, after Borodin's death he brought *Prince Igor* to completion, orchestrating a large portion of it.

It was typical of Rimsky-Korsakov that in his mature years he not only criticized severely his own early work as editor and orchestrator but actually went back and did much of it over again. He was so troubled by his youthful orchestration for *The Stone Guest* that in 1902 he rescored the entire opera. Unfortunately, he also "softened here and there the extreme harshness and harmonic follies (sic) of the original". In 1906 he made a second version of his edition of *Boris Godunov* restoring numerous cuts he had made in the version of 1895.

In addition to his posts at the Conservatory and as Inspector of Naval Bands, Rimsky-Korsakov also filled several other important positions. In 1874 he took over the direction of the Free School of Music after Balakirev had resigned. In 1883 he became assistant to Balakirev as superintendent of the music of the Imperial Chapel. In these posts he functioned for a number of years both as teacher and conductor, schooling himself rigorously in the latter art ("Conducting is a thing shrouded in mystery," he remarked). During the course of his busy life he conducted innumerable symphonic and choral concerts and many performances of his own operas. As a teacher Rimsky-Korsakov exerted an immense influence through the next generation of Russian composers. Among his pupils were Alexander Glazunov, Anatol Liadov, Anton Arensky, Michael Ippolitov-Ivanov, Nicolas Tcherepnin, Alexander Gretchaninov, Igor Stravinsky, Serge Prokofiev, and Nicholas Miaskovsky.

In a separate category of the composer's manifold projects may be included his works as textbook author, musicologist, and historian. In 1884 he wrote his Textbook of Harmony, a manual originally intended for his classes at the Imperial Chapel. The famous treatise, Principles of Orchestration, was conceived as early as 1873 when the composer's work with the naval bands so fired his interest in instrumentation that he became eager, he said, "to tell the world no less than *all* on this subject". He spent two years making notes and even studying the works of Tyndall and Helmholtz on the laws of acoustics, but then gave up the task. Twenty years later he started and abandoned another draft. Then, during the last four years of his life, he brought to near-completion a text illustrated by more than three hundred music examples from his own works. The book set a new standard in its scientific treatment of the subject. Rimsky-Korsakov's publications in the field of Russian folk music comprise two works produced between 1875 and 1877—his editing and harmonizing of forty folk songs collected by T. I. Filippov, and his compilation and harmonization of his own great Collection of a Hundred Russian Folk Songs (Opus 24). Finally, there remains his incomparable autobiography, *My Musical Life*, at which he worked during many of the "spare" hours of his career, and which is one of the treasures of music history.

Among the few unfinished projects of this man's gigantic life-work were two books which he conceived during a strange crisis in his career in 1892, when he suffered a shattering nervous break-down. He planned the writing of "a comprehensive article or even book on Russian music . . ." but in his then confused and tired mental state the work became lost in a maze of reading on philo-sophical and metaphysical subjects. During the same period the composer started another book whose subject remains a mystery. He wrote in a letter, "I've torn up a book I was writing, in a fit of stupid bitterness, and . . . I can't remember what I'd written." In a career notable for its long series of ambitious projects, all ably carried out, these two unfinished efforts remain curious exceptions.

III

In the early years of his career when he abandoned Balakirev and subjected himself to a strict course in music theory, Rimsky-Korsakov created a deep rift in the unity of the Five. Only Borodin defended him; the others felt that he had deserted their cause of artistic freedom and nationalist distinction to become a conservative pedant. His obvious joy in the study of technique and his discovery of the great classic past in music gave every indication that his own work would reflect a sharply classic bent. Instead, Rimsky-Kor-sakov's art soon began to illustrate one of the strangest of paradoxes. When he tried to compose in the purely abstract forms—the sym-phony, the string quartet, the concerto—he had no success whatever. It was only when he turned to the romantic overture, the tone poem, the picture suite, the folk opera, and the fantastic fairy-tale opera, that his talents flourished and his work took on distinction.

Rimsky-Korsakov was thus a psychological puzzle, for behind his pedantic façade lay a creative imagination which yearned for the dream world of fantasy. In this world the composer lived a second life, full of the enchantment of fairy-tale and fable which he tried to transmute into his operas and his symphonic works. Here, as in so much of Russian folk-lore, the real and the fanciful, the historical and the supernatural were all grotesquely intermingled —warrior princes and blood-thirsty czars, sea kings and mermaids, fabulous swan queens and snow maidens, peasants and village dancers, hunters, wood-cutters, minstrels, gusli players and bandoura players, wizards, and sorcerers who dealt in love potions, *rusalki* who haunted mill streams and waterfalls, devils and witches who flew off with the moon and the stars. Behind this stream of queer and wonderful inhabitants lay the great panorama of nature—the vast steppes and the wintry forests, lakes flashing in the sunlight, birds in spring flight, swarms of bees, nightingales, and golden fish; and through it swept the sounds of marvellous processions, real and visionary, the thunder of Tartar armies, the bedlam of the market-place and the Oriental bazaar, the toll of ancient Russian bells.

Rimsky-Korsakov's love of fantasy manifested itself in his music as early as 1867, two years after he completed his first symphony. He composed a symphonic poem, *Sadko*, based on the legend of the famous gusli player of Novgorod. Years later he expanded the same idea into one of his most successful operas. In the tone poem the vessel of Sadko is becalmed at sea, until the minstrel is thrown overboard with his gusli to placate the Sea King. At the bottom of the sea Sadko finds a great festival in progress celebrating the marriage of the Sea King's daughter to the Ocean. The minstrel plays upon his gusli until the monarch and all his court dance wildly, stirring up a tempest on the ocean. Only when Sadko breaks the strings of his instrument does the dancing stop and the sea resume its calm.

Rimsky-Korsakov made two revisions of his *Sadko* (in 1869 and 1891). In his autobiography the composer spoke rather slightingly of the piece. With his usual candour he related that the music describing Sadko's fall into the sea was reminiscent of a moment in Glinka's *Ruslan and Ludmila*; the feast in the Sea King's realm recalled Balakirev's beautiful song, *The Song of the Golden Fish*, and a recitative in Dargomyjsky's *Rusalka*; other passages came from Liszt's *Mephisto Waltz* and Balakirev's *Tamara*.

Following *Sadko*, Rimsky-Korsakov made an abortive attempt at another symphony. He confessed that the beginning of the first movement recalled the beginning of Beethoven's Ninth Symphony, and that the second subject had "an unwelcome resemblance" to a chorus by César Cui—a juxtaposition of ideas which would have brought any work to ruin. Meanwhile, another symphonic plan had crowded into his mind and it had, significantly, a programme background. This Symphony No. 2, titled *Antar*, was based on an Arabian story by Syenkovsky. It was composed in 1868, but it was twice revised and reorchestrated (in 1876 and 1897), and its title finally changed to "symphonic suite", because the scrupulous composer believed it to be no symphony in the meticulous sense.

In the story by Syenkovsky, Antar is a recluse in the Arabian desert who one day saves a beautiful gazelle from the attack of a monstrous bird. Antar is then transported to a great palace where the gazelle is revealed to be a Fairy Queen. By way of reward she promises her rescuer the three supreme pleasures of life—Vengeance, Power, and Love. It is during the enjoyment of the last of these pleasures that the Queen's passion burns away the heart of Antar, and he dies.

Rimsky-Korsakov's first movement paints the scene of Antar in the desert and his encounter with the gazelle and the bird. The three succeeding movements describe the rewarding pleasures of Vengeance, Power, and Love. The scenario is followed only in a vague and general way, so that the piece is simply a series of movements in a pseudo-Oriental style with interrelated thematic material. Melodies lean to the minor mode; some are languorously Oriental in mood and ornate with Eastern arabesques; keys, harmonies, and orchestration all seek for colour contrasts and brilliance.

Rimsky-Korsakov's next large orchestral work was his Third Symphony, in C minor, composed in the years 1873 and 1874. Progress was slow and beset with difficulties. "I strove to crowd in as much counterpoint as possible," he wrote, "but being unskilled in it and hard put to combine the themes and motives, I drained my immediate flow of imagination considerably." The work evoked little enthusiasm when performed in 1874. The composer's First String Quartet belongs to the same period of his furiously intense study of counterpoint and fugue. He was ashamed of the work when he finished it and did not attend the première performance. The next year, 1876, he undertook a String Sextet in A Major. One movement contained "a very complicated six-part fugue", while another had a fugue in tarantella time. The same year came a Quintet in B flat for piano, flute, clarinet, horn and bassoon. The last movement had an interesting innovation in the form of virtuoso cadenzas for three of the instruments, but still, said the composer, "this composition did not express my real individuality".

IV

Slowly Rimsky-Korsakov came to the realization that the abstractions of chamber music were for him no more than sterile exercises. It was not until the eighteen-eighties when he was past forty that he finally struck his stride. He had composed his second opera, *May Night*, and then *The Snow Maiden* (*Snegurochka*), his first and one of his finest operas in the fantastic fairy-tale genre. Then in 1887 and 1888 came three brilliantly successful orchestral works—*Spanish Caprice*, *Scheherazade*, and the *Russian Easter* Overture—all picture pieces in the romantic vein, coloured by the magic brush of his wonderful orchestration, and unclouded by the pedantries of German counterpoint.

The *Spanish Caprice* grew from the composer's original intention to write a virtuoso piece for violin which would be based on Spanish themes. The work is in five short movements: (I) Alborada, an aubade or morning serenade; (II) Variations on a theme; (III) Alborada, an orchestral variation of the first movement; (IV) Scene and Gypsy Song, the first part presenting a series of cadenzas for horns and trumpets, solo violin, flute, clarinet, and harp; (V) Fandango and Asturias, a vigorous elaboration of an old Asturian dance theme.

Rimsky-Korsakov's *Spanish Caprice* was written some decades before the school of music impressionism would wholly renovate the procedure for handling both nationalist idioms and picture pieces. His work therefore has none of the subtle understatement, the refinements, and the elisions of more modern Spanish studies by Debussy, Ravel, or Falla. By comparison the Russian composer's essay is all glare and glitter; but it is still a buoyant and exciting piece. The composer himself had a perfect appreciation of its values:

"The opinion formed by both critics and the public, that the Caprice is a *magnificently orchestrated piece*, is wrong. The Caprice is a brilliant *composition for the orchestra*. The change of timbres, the felicitous choice of melodic designs and figuration patterns, exactly suiting each kind of instrument, brief virtuoso cadenzas for instruments solo, the rhythm of the percussion instruments, and so on, constitute here the very *essence* of the composition and not its garb or orchestration. The Spanish themes, of dance character, furnished me with rich material for putting in use multiform orchestral effects. All in all, the Caprice is undoubtedly a purely external piece, but vividly brilliant for all that."

In the winter of 1887–88 when Rimsky-Korsakov was occupied with his work on Borodin's *Prince Igor* his thoughts travelled beyond the realm of the wandering Tartar tribesmen to the borders of Araby, and "A Thousand and One Nights". He was inspired to write an orchestral work based on several episodes from the Eastern romance. When completed the following summer the piece had become a symphonic suite in four movements, the immensely popular and successful *Scheherazade*.

The composer prefaced his score with a note which reminds the listener of the plot of the Arabian Nights Entertainments : The Sultan of the Indies, wrathful at the infidelity of wives, made a vow to take a new wife each night and put her to death the following morning. The Sultana Scheherazade, however, saved herself by telling her husband a long series of fabulous stories. After a thousand and one nights the Sultan recalled his vow.

When his *Scheherazade* was first performed Rimsky-Korsakov gave its four sections descriptive titles : (I) The Sea and Sinbad's Ship ; (II) The Tale of the Prince Kalender ; (III) The Young Prince and the Young Princess ; (IV) Festival at Bagdad—The Sea—The Ship is Wrecked on a Rock Surmounted by a Warrior of Bronze— Conclusion. As a unifying device there are brief cadenza-like introductions to the first, second, and fourth movements and an intermezzo in the third movement which are all played by a solo violin with harp accompaniment, and are intended to delineate Scheherazade herself, "telling her wondrous tales to the stern Sultan".

When we consider that *Scheherazade* has had countless performances during the past half-century by symphony orchestras all over the world, that it has been and still is an assured success in the recording industry, that is has been imitated by countless composers, pilfered by motion-picture arrangers, and perverted by ballet masters—we realize that Rimsky-Korsakov's piece is not only indestructible, but is a work of beauty and distinction. We need not look far into this guileless and charming music to discover why the public has found it so attractive. First of all, Rimsky-Korsakov had succeeded in a form for which there was practically no pre-cedent. The repertoire of romantic music was full of short pieces in the picturesque fairy-tale genre, but no one had produced a long work of this type which was symphonic in plan and elaboration.

Besides its exotic Eastern colouring which originally gave a new titilation to Western ears, *Scheherazade* has two advantages as picture music—its delightful melodic material and an orchestration of surpassing brilliance. No one would claim rare excellence for the melodies of *Scheherazade*, but they do have charm, especially those which are decorative in a quasi-Oriental way. With his orchestration the composer reached the first of two climaxes which marked the growth of his mastery of the instruments. *Scheherazade* is the finest example of his skill during the first half of his career when he was working (as he described it) essentially in the instrumental framework he had inherited from Glinka, and before he came under the influence of Wagner's scoring. Everything is transparent as crystal or glowing with the brightness of primary colours. The handling of the instruments is so masterful that the work almost takes on the attributes of a concerto. The violin, flute, oboe, clarinet, bassoon, horn and trumpet are given passages which exhibit both their most luscious tone qualities and their dexterity and fleetness.

Scheherazade also abounds in expert usage of the instruments in combinations to form new and exotic tonal effects, in contrasts between various instruments and groups of instruments, and finally in contrasts between the tonal colour of the same instruments in different registers.

More than passing mention should be made of the rhythmic schemes of *Scheherazade*. The last movement, with its noisy hubbub and confusion of the Bagdad Festival (all planned with masterly precision), is clearly an anticipation of much modern rhythmic procedure. There are sections with rapid changes of rhythm every few measures, and at times even mild poly-rhythmic effects. Rimsky-Korsakov had a phenomenal memory, and it is possible that all this sprang from an experience of a dozen years before. On a visit to the Crimea he had been captivated by the sights and sounds of the ancient town of Bakhchisaray near Sevastopol:

"its shops, its coffee-houses, the shouts of the vendors, the chanting of the muezzins on the minarets, the services in the mosques and the Oriental music . . . all made the oddest impression on us". . . . "It was while hearing the gypsy musicians of Bakhchisaray that I first became acquainted with Oriental music in its natural state, so to speak, and I believe I caught the main features of its character. By the way, I was particularly struck by the quasi-incidental beats of the big drum, in false time, which produced a marvellous effect."

The complexities of Rimsky-Korsakov's character which produced such ambiguities in his art extended, it would seem, even to the depths of the man's spiritual nature. Through much of his adult life the religion of the Orthodox Church left him unsatisfied; he was fascinated instead by the ancient Slavic paganism, while his love for nature also led him at times to the borders of a more mystical pantheism. All these are happily reconciled from the artistic viewpoint in the composer's *Russian Easter* Overture which he produced in the summer of 1888.

The experience which inspired Rimsky-Korsakov to write this Overture (and which he prescribes for any listener who would appreciate it) was attendance at the Easter morning service in a great cathedral of the Russian Orthodox faith. But the composer hoped to capture something deeper than simply the outward spectacle of a vast church thronged with worshippers intent upon the gorgeousness of ancient ritual and mystical celebration. He wanted, he said, to combine in his music reminiscences of Isaiah's ancient prophecy of the resurrection, the Gospel story of the risen Christ, and finally a picture of the Easter service with its "pagan merrymaking".

In his autobiography Rimsky-Korsakov made particular reference to these pagan implications of his Overture.

> "The capering and leaping of the Biblical King David before the ark, do they not give expression to a mood of the same order as the mood of the idol-worshippers' dance? Surely the Russian Orthodox chime is instrumental dance-music of the church, is it not? And do not the waving beards of the priests and sextons clad in white vestments and surplices, and intoning 'Beautiful Easter' in the tempo of *Allegro vivo*, etc., transport the imagination to pagan times? And all these Easter loaves and twists and the glowing tapers—how far a cry from the philosophic and socialistic teachings of Christ! This legendary and heathen side of the holiday, this transition from the gloom and mysterious evening of Passion Saturday to the unbridled pagan-religious merry-making of the morn of Easter Sunday, is what I was eager to reproduce in my Overture."

The music materials for the *Russian Easter* Overture are largely based on themes from the *obikhod*, which is a collection of the most important canticles of the Orthodox Church service. The first two of these themes, "Let God Arise!" and "An angel wailed", appear in the solemn introduction which is intended to evoke thoughts of Isaiah's prophecy. Later the gloom of the holy sepulchre is dispelled by an "ineffable light at the moment of resurrection", as harp glissandos and shimmering strings depict the radiant scene. The music bursts into a spirited Allegro, based on the theme, "Let them also that hate Him flee before Him." There follows a long fantasia in which various scenes and moods are revealed— "the solemn trumpet voice of the Archangel" (horns and trumpets) ... "the joyous, almost dance-like bell tolling, alternating now with the sexton's rapid reading and now with the conventional chant of the priest's reading the glad tidings of the Evangel" (trombone solo). In the stunning coda, and amid the brazen trumpet voices and the wildly ringing bells, is intoned the *obikhod* theme, "Christ is risen."

The orchestration of this Overture makes plain once more the fact that with Rimsky-Korsakov this science had become an art. The very choice of an orchestral setting for his evocation of a Russian church service was in a sense precarious. For a thousand years the unrelenting edicts of orthodoxy had banned musical instruments from the church; nevertheless the composer proved that these small profane machines could be made the implements of faith, and that with them no less than with the human voice the glory of God might be celebrated. It may be that he remembered the words of the Psalmist:

> Praise the Lord with the sound of trumpet
> Praise Him with psaltery and with harp!
> Praise Him with timbrel and with dance;
> Praise Him with stringed instruments and organs!
> Praise Him with sounding cymbals;
> Praise Him with loud clashing cymbals!

V

The fourteen operas which Rimsky-Korsakov composed over a period of forty years comprise by far the most important part of his life's work, and are the largest single contribution which any Russian has yet made to the lyric stage. The present generation has almost forgotten that this composer's operatic work was so extensive and in its day so influential. This is because only a few of these pieces (notably *The Snow Maiden*, *Sadko*, and *The Golden Cockerel*) have achieved international acceptance; some of the rest found favour only in Russia, while a few are patent failures.

In spite of two revisions in his mature years Rimsky-Korsakov's first opera, *The Maid of Pskov* (or *Ivan the Terrible*), remains a testament to his youth and his allegiance to the early nationalist-realist standards of the Five. The work pays homage to Dargomyjsky in its conscious use of melodic declamation ; subconsciously, however, the composer was imitating his friend Musorgsky. *The Maid of Pskov* appears today as a pale replica of *Boris Godunov*. Held taut on the leash of official censorship, Rimsky-Korsakov had to romanticize his figure of Ivan, and the half-insane czar never achieves stature. The assembling crowds of the people of Pskov, with the deep-tolling tocsins and the choruses in the Russian folk style are all reminiscent of *Boris Godunov*, but all are on a lower scale of beauty and imagination.

The second of Rimsky-Korsakov's operas, *May Night*, was composed in 1878, after he had passed through his first period of intense technical study, including his dry contrapuntal phase and its abortive chamber works. His study of Russian folk song and his editorial work on Glinka's scores suddenly led the composer back to nationalism. At his wife's insistence he took up the subject of *May Night*, from Gogol's cycle of stories of Little Russia, *Evenings on a Farm near Dikanka*. Personal sentiment was strongly at work here, for the composer and his wife remembered reading *May Night* together on the day of their betrothal in 1871. Composition of the opera progressed with ease and fluency ; the composer had shaken off, he said, "the shackles of counterpoint". The whole work is simply conceived, very lyrical in the folk-song manner, and scored in the light, transparent style of Glinka. The composer had deliberately, almost defiantly, turned his back on Dargomyjskian realism ; he created instead the Glinka type of Russian opera based on the old Italian formula—simple melodies, recitatives, ensembles and choruses, with every number "rounded off".

The subject matter had a dual attraction for the composer. He loved Gogol's tale of life among the Ukrainian villagers, with its boisterous humour and its pastoral scene-painting. He also added a note of his own, "that ceremonial side of folk-life which gives expression to the survivals from ancient paganism". *May Night* was the first of the Rimsky-Korsakov operas which evoke the worship of the sun and the sun gods and other vestiges of an ancient pantheism surviving in the songs, games, and ceremonies of Russian peasant life. All the choral songs in *May Night* have, according to the composer, "a ceremonial colouring or a game colouring"

The Snow Maiden (Snegurochka), Rimsky-Korsakov's third opera, is one of his most ingratiating works for the lyric stage. He had read the dramatist Ostrovsky's poetic fairy-tale based on the old epic of the Snow Maiden, delighting in its fantasy and its pagan pantheism. Then in 1880 the composer and his wife and children spent a memorable summer on an estate in a village near Looga, where the whole pastoral scene enchanted him—the groves and forests, the fields of rye, buckwheat and flax, the rivers and lakes, the tiny villages with charming antique Russian names. Near the comfortable old house, he recalled, was a garden "with a multitude of cherry trees and apple trees, currants, wild and garden strawberries, gooseberries, lilacs in bloom, an infinity of field flowers and the incessant singing of birds—everything was somehow in peculiar harmony with my pantheistic frame of mind at the time and my passion for the subject of *Snegurochka*". Here, during a sultry summer "dense with thunderstorms", the beautiful opera came to fruition.

The Snow Maiden is the daughter of King Winter and the Fairy Spring. She lives hidden in the snowy forests of the mythical land of the Berendeys, for the summer sun has foretold that when the first rays of sunlight touch her cold beauty she must die. Beguiled by songs of the shepherd Lel, the Snow Maiden begs her parents to grant her the life of a mortal; but in that life she meets only sadness and disillusion. Lel is indifferent to her, but she is passionately wooed by Mizguir, a young Tartar merchant. The Fairy Spring finally grants her unhappy daughter's wish—the power to love like a mortal. Just as Mizguir claims the Snow Maiden as his bride and the warmth of love grows within her, a ray of sunlight pierces the clouds and the vision of beauty is melted into the spring torrent.

With *The Snow Maiden* Rimsky-Korsakov created something essentially new in the field of lyric drama. It is not strictly the magic opera of German romanticism which Glinka had followed in *Ruslan and Ludmila*. In spite of its mortal characters *The Snow Maiden* is pure fairy-tale. The Maiden herself is the embodiment of a fanciful pantheistic goddess, and so are the Fairy Spring, King Winter, and the Faun; while the birds, trees, bushes, clouds, snowflakes, the wind and the sky are all a living part of the enchanting tale. Even the Czar Berendey, as he sits on his golden throne surrounded by blind gusli players and their ancient instruments, is far nearer the realms of legend than reality.

In his autobiography Rimsky-Korsakov gave an absorbing review of this opera from its technical aspects. He revealed that the piece abounds with Russian folk tunes, most of them taken from his Collection. These are used both in their entirety and as a profusion of "minor motives and tunelets". There are also genuine bird-calls —the cuckoo, the merlin, the cock and the bullfinch. The greater part of the melodic material, however, is the composer's imitation of the folk idiom. In his harmony he made copious use of the ancient modes (Dorian, Phrygian and Mixolydian), and he succeeded in inventing "some new things" in harmony, e.g. unusual chords based on whole tones.

VI

After the composition of *The Snow Maiden* there came a lapse of almost a decade during which Rimsky-Korsakov created nothing for the theatre. At first he was absorbed in the task of editing works of Musorgsky and Borodin after their deaths, and later in his own series of notable orchestral works. Then in the winter of 1888–89 occurred in Petersburg the performances of Wagner's *The Ring of the Nibelung* by Neumann's company under Karl Muck's direction. The impact of Wagner's mature music upon Rimsky-Korsakov was nothing less than profound. It turned the Russian composer back to the lyric stage and for the next two decades he produced opera after opera, to the exclusion of almost every other form except the song.

Rimsky-Korsakov's orchestration was first to be affected by the Wagnerian apparatus and soon other changes followed—a more extensive use of the leit-motif system, a bolder use of chromatic harmony and other colourful harmonic effects, a general enrichment of the orchestral part, and the employment of extensive scenic effects. Thus after long delay the most powerful force in nineteenth-century music had at last reached Russia, and Russian music like that of the West would henceforth react to its enormous weight and impact.

Rimsky-Korsakov resumed operatic composition with the opera-ballet *Mlada*, composed in 1889–90. He decided to make his own version of the piece which he, Borodin, Musorgsky, and Cui had started and abandoned as a joint enterprise back in 1872. The story is an odd miscellany involving a Slavic kingdom on the Baltic Sea during the ninth century, and is replete with pagan rites, dances, and ceremonies, and a dash of demonology. For contrasting Oriental colour there also appears the shade of Cleopatra. The piece was originally intended to be not so much an opera as a series of brilliant scenic effects and ballets, interspersed with grand opera vocalism. Rimsky-Korsakov took advantage of the opportunity and with the aid of a gigantic Wagnerian orchestra (the largest he had ever used) he produced a gallery of elaborate tone pictures. The most famous number, the Procession of the Princes, survives today for an occasional performance; but in general *Mlada* has long since faded. Its première was an ordeal by misfortune, the Marinsky Theatre in Petersburg being strained by the glut of stage effects. In his autobiography Rimsky-Korsakov left a classic account of the sufferings of a composer who must sit by helpless as his child is brought into the world by the bungling accoucheurs of the opera house.

After he finished *Mlada* and before its production in 1892 Rimsky-Korsakov suffered a serious nervous and mental breakdown which for a time threatened his whole career. Neither the exact cause nor the true nature of his illness are known, but the composer went through long spells of deep melancholia. His mind was weary and unsteady and all work became impossible; his own music revolted him, and there are dark hints in his autobiography about the fact that he dared not be alone. The lowest point in the unhappy man's life came in the autumn of 1893 with the loss of one of his children, his little daughter Masha, who died at Yalta after a long illness.

The next spring found the composer in a more rational mental state. He began work on the opera *Christmas Eve*. Gogol's story[1] of the capricious village beauty Oxana who refuses to marry the smith, Vakula, until he brings her a pair of the Empress's shoes, gave the composer ample chance for boisterous peasant humour; and he tried to take advantage of such fantastical tone pictures as the snow-covered Little Russian village on the radiant eve of Christmas, the revels of the stars and comets, the flight of the Devil and the witch with the moon and stars, and the festivities in the palace of the Empress. But his heart was not in the work, and the melodic ideas simply would not flow. A few moments of genuine lyric beauty,

---

[1] Tchaikovsky had previously composed an opera, *Vakula the Smith*, based on this Gogol story. It was a failure, but Rimsky-Korsakov did not feel free to attempt a version of his own until after Tchaikovsky's death in 1893.

like Oxana's lament in the final act, only serve to expose the long stretches of dull and arid writing.[1]

One reason for the weakness of *Christmas Eve* was the fact that the composer lost interest in the work lòng before he finished it. The musicologist N. F. Findeisen had suggested to him the subject of Sadko, the legendary gusli player of Novgorod, which he had used in his early tone poem. This idea so delighted him that soon all manner of musical ideas began to shape in his mind. The work was composed between 1894 and 1896.

Sadko is part fairy-tale and part historical evocation, in which the composer attempted to recreate the old legendary *bylina* or bardic style with its blend of ancient history and fantasy. The story is taken from the Novgorod Cycle of the eleventh century, and recalls the glories of the City of Novgorod, the thriving port whose fleets of red ships brought the riches of the earth to her wealthy merchants. The poor but adventurous minstrel Sadko, 'the night-ingale of Novgorod", lays a wager with the merchants that he can catch golden fish in the beautiful Lake Ilmen. By his singing he has already charmed a Princess of the Sea, and she has promised him that when he casts his net in the lake he will catch little fish with golden scales. By this means Sadko wins a vast treasure from the Novgorod merchants, then sails away for years of adventurous wandering. At last he descends to the depths of the sea, beguiles the Sea King with his songs, and marries the Sea Princess at a great celebration attended by all the fabulous creatures of the ocean deep.

Sadko is one of the most brilliant pieces of operatic picture painting Rimsky-Korsakov ever achieved, and it is one of his works which blends most happily a fine lyric invention and the composer's mastery of technique. Here he is at once lyric poet, tonal painter, technician, and scholar. The City of Novgorod with its throngs of merchants, "wandering pilgrims, merry andrews, soothsayers, gay women, etc.", is re-created with many splendid choral numbers in the Russian folk style; the submarine kingdom with its "dancing of little rivers and little fishes, processions of water monsters, and its wedding around the cytisus bush", is achieved by veritable sym-

---

[1] *Christmas Eve* also suffered a harrowing première (1895). At the dress rehearsal two Grand Dukes became incensed because they believed their great-grandmother, Empress Catherine, was represented on the stage, and because a cathedral which contained tombs of their ancestors was painted on a back-drop. The part of the Empress was hastily changed to a "Most Serene Highness" to be sung by a baritone instead of a mezzo-soprano, and the picture of the cathedral was daubed out. Rimsky-Korsakov could only show his contempt for these disfigurations by remaining away from the première.

phonic poems woven in complex harmonies from a system of leading motifs and set off by a scintillating orchestration. Moreover, "running through the opera like a scarlet thread," says the composer, is a peculiar type of recitative which is given chiefly to Sadko and which is modelled after the declamatory style of the old *bylina*—"a sort of conventionally regulated narration of parlando singing. . . ."

In spite of lyric beauties which are notably high for Rimsky-Korsakov, *Sadko* depends for success more upon its spectacle and its sumptuous orchestral and choral fabric than upon the vocal interest of individual singers. Thus it remains a lavish period piece, seldom revived in these lean operatic times. It is a reminder of a golden age when opera impresarios had fortunes to spend on a single production, and stage managers were undaunted by seven massive scenes in the Wagnerian manner, each with stage effects that would strain the capabilities of a circus.

VII

After the completion of *Sadko* in 1896 operas continued to flow in a steady stream from Rimsky-Korsakov's pen, and in the next eleven years he produced no less than nine works for the lyric stage. Unfortunately, this immense facility was not always joined with inspiration and several of these pieces fall among the poorest in his catalogue.

Mozart and Salieri (1897) seems to have been an experiment. It is a short opera based on one of Pushkin's dramatic miniatures which recounts the erroneous (though once widely believed) story that Mozart was poisoned to death by Antonio Salieri, a rival Italian composer in Vienna. As if surfeited with the grandiloquence of *Mlada* and the nationalist panoramas of *Sadko*, Rimsky-Korsakov reversed himself completely and turned to dramatic realism and a spare, attenuated scheme of melodic declamation in the style of Dargomyjsky's *The Stone Guest*. He set Pushkin's dialogue to music without altering a word. The results were unfortunately no better than *The Stone Guest*; *Mozart and Salieri* remains unexpressive and doctrinaire, and little more than a curiosity.[1]

[1] Wrote the composer of his *Mozart and Salieri*: "The composition was purely vocal: indeed, the melodic web, following the sinuosities of the text, was composed ahead of all else; the accompaniment, fairly complicated, shaped itself later, and its first outline differed greatly from the final form of its orchestral accompaniment." Feodor Chaliapin, the eminent singer, scored his first great success in this opera, in 1899, in Petersburg.

The next year, 1898, came a work of reconstruction. When Rimsky-Korsakov made his final revision in 1893 of his earliest opera, *The Maid of Pskov*, he had omitted the Prologue contained in his original version. He now reworked this material into a one-act opera, *Boyarina Vera Sheloga*, intended to precede the performance of *The Maid of Pskov*. The style reverts to that of the composer's maiden effort—melodic recitative of a more lyric and less realistic type than Dargomyjsky's.

Rimsky-Korsakov tired quickly of the restrictions of operatic realism but in his next work he went to another extreme—an old-fashioned, Glinka-like imitation of Italian opera. He said that the style of *The Czar's Bride* (1899) "was to be cantilena par excellence" ; with "vocal ensembles, genuine, finished", and with no nod whatever in the direction of the modern type of "quasi-dramatic truth". The composer's urge to write in this simpler style came partly from his realization (while writing a group of songs) that in much of his previous operatic music his melodies had been born of instrumental and even harmonic ideas. In *The Czar's Bride* he hoped for a flow of purely vocal melody. He did compose far simpler music for this opera (which was based on a sluggish play by the dramatist Mey) but the result was only manufactured dullness broken by a single number of beauty—the famous aria sung by Marfa in the second act.

In *The Czar Saltan* (1899–1900) the composer returned to his favourite field of fantasy, and instantly his inspiration rose buoyantly. The story came from Pushkin and its rambling and picturesque nature is indicated by its full title, "The Tale of the Czar Saltan, of his Son the famous and mighty Warrior, Prince Guidon, and of the beautiful Swan Princess". Here in the realm of folk-lore and fantasy, bizarre episodes and naïve, childlike comedy, Rimsky-Korsakov was again in his element. He avoided the massive proportions of *Sadko*, seeking instead refinement of workmanship and a child's picture-book quality of intimacy and beguilement. The composer realized that in *The Czar Saltan* he had again accomplished something worthy of his art for he arranged from this work an orchestral suite called *Little Pictures from the Fairy-tale of the Czar Saltan*, which unaccountably omitted what was to become the most famous portion of the score—*The Flight of the Bumble Bee*.

The Czar Saltan was quickly followed by three failures—*Servilia* (1900–01), *Kashchey the Immortal* (1901–02), and *Pan Voyevoda* (1902–03)—in which Rimsky-Korsakov's work for the lyric stage sank to its nadir. The first of these was based on a drama (again by the redoubtable Mey) which had to do with ancient Rome and the singularly unadventurous theme of conflict between a Roman maiden's love for a Tribune and her conversion to Christianity. Rimsky-Korsakov seems to have chosen the subject because he was deathly sick of Russian nationalism.

In *Kashchey the Immortal* the composer returned, uncrestfallen, to the familiar ground of Russian folk-lore; but the ogre Kashchey (who was to appear a decade later in the ballet *The Firebird* by Rimsky-Korsakov's pupil, Igor Stravinsky) led him into a morass of good-and-evil symbolism and an even worse swamp of imitation Wagnerian chromaticism.

In *Pan Voyevoda* Rimsky-Korsakov went off on a Polish tangent. In an attempt to pay homage to Chopin, whose music he had always loved, he succeeded only in adding another failure to the catalogue of Russian composers' attempts to imitate Polish idioms.

VIII

The strange unevenness which marked the progress of Rimsky-Korsakov's art is nowhere more strikingly displayed than in the sudden great leap which he took after *Pan Voyevoda*. With his two final operas, *The Legend of the Invisible City of Kitezh* (1903–04), and *The Golden Cockerel* (1906–07), he stood once again upon the heights where, as superb technician and serious scholar, he found also a resurgence of creative power.

The story of *Kitezh* combines two ancient legends, those of the Invisible City of Kitezh and of the Maiden Fevronia of Murom, the two being woven into a kind of miracle play. Fevronia is an embodiment of goodness and truth, a child of nature, who, like St. Francis, finds God in the forests and among the creatures of the earth and sky.

The orchestral prelude and the opening act create a tone painting of the forest near little Kitezh where Fevronia sits among the tall grasses singing hymns in praise of the beauty and wonder around her. The creatures of the forest join her and are her friends—a bear, a crane, an elk, the birds. Fevronia is found in the forest by a Prince who brings her to little Kitezh to be his bride. Here the girl becomes a symbol of love as it impinges upon a harsh and unpitying world. A band of Tartars overruns and destroys little Kitezh, seeking the way to the sacred city of Kitezh the Great. Fevronia is made a prisoner. She prays for the salvation of Kitezh the Great and through her supplications the city is transported to the skies. The fear-stricken invaders see only its reflection in a lake. In the battle with the Tartars the Prince is slain, but his spirit appears to Fevronia and she joins him in death. In a final scene the Prince and his bride enter the cathedral in the sacred city while the people intone anthems of praise.

That the story of *Kitezh* moved Rimsky-Korsakov deeply is evident in almost every measure of the long score, which burns with a heat of inspiration rare with this composer. The finest portions are those dominated by the character of Fevronia. Weakness in drawing human character convincingly had dulled much of this composer's operatic work, but here he created in his saintly heroine one of the most exquisite portraits in the whole field of Russian opera. Here his music takes on a deep expressiveness, perfectly evoking the girl and her mystical innocence.

Kitezh has many moments which sustain the composer's inspired vision of Fevronia—her ordeal at the hands of the Tartars, her prayers for the deliverance of Kitezh, her transfigured ecstasy as the little lamps appear in the trees, and gold and silver flowers spring up in the grass as she receives the message of death—"sweet Death, my long desired one"—and finally, the miracle of apotheosis.

It was inevitable, considering the time of its composition and its subject matter, that *Kitezh* should be called "the Russian *Parsifal*"; but that comparison need not be explored. More significant is the fact that in this opera Rimsky-Korsakov made his most successful general use of the Wagnerian theories and apparatus of music drama. There is little doubt that for the Russian composer the impact of Wagner's greater works had been a mixed blessing. The revelation of *The Ring of the Nibelung* back in 1889 had taken Rimsky-Korsakov at a psychological moment. He was a master in his own right and of his own distinctive style; then suddenly this new and overwhelming art rose up before him. For the next decade he was trying alternately to imitate Wagner's music or to escape from it. With *Kitezh* he found again his own equilibrium.

Early in 1905 the entire Russian nation was shaken by a political and social upheaval which had been rising with the shocking defeats of the Russo-Japanese War. Strikes, riots and assassinations were on the way, and a deadly conflict between terrorists and the secret police. "Political ferment seized all Petersburg," wrote Rimsky-Korsakov. "The Conservatory too was affected; its students were in turmoil." Soon afterward cordons of police surrounded the Conservatory building, a hundred students were expelled, and Rimsky-Korsakov who had sympathized openly with them was dismissed from the faculty. Performance of his compositions was later forbidden in Petersburg. Instantly an outcry arose all over Russia from liberals and intellectuals who deluged the composer with letters of sympathy. For the better part of a year the conflict went on and Rimsky-Korsakov, wearied and shaken, began to believe that his career as composer was at an end, that he was in fact written out.

The composer went abroad with his wife and three of his children and spent the summer of 1906 in Italy. At Riva on Lake Garda he wrote the final passages that brought the great Chronicle of his music life to a close. Then two months later, back at Petersburg, he recorded in his notebook the first sketch of a now-famous theme, that of the Golden Cockerel: "Kiri-koo-koo! Reign lying on your side!"

Rimsky-Korsakov's last opera, *The Golden Cockerel* (*Le Coq d'Or*), is based on a poem by Pushkin.[1] The poet had adopted a classic ruse for getting even with an autocracy which had repressed and tormented him—that of ridiculing it under the guise of fairy-tale. Rimsky-Korsakov was obviously attracted to the story because of his own recent experience. His opera was composed during the years 1906–07, but when it was ready for performance the censors refused to sanction the work unless certain lines were cut. Not many weeks later the composer suffered a serious heart attack. His condition (a combination of angina pectoris and asthma) was aggravated by his anger at the officials who would mutilate not only his music but words by Pushkin. He put his hopes in Serge Diaghilev who was staging historic productions of Russian opera in Paris. But Rimsky-Korsakov did not live to see a performance

---

[1] Between 1831 and 1834 Pushkin wrote a group of *Fairy Tales* in verse, in which, says Janko Lavrin, "he made an attempt at adapting the themes taken from non-Russian folklore in such a way as to make them an organic part of both Russian literature and the Russian people". An earlier attempt (1828) had been his Russian version of the Scottish ballad, *The Two Corbies*. Some of Pushkin's *Fairy Tales* are wholly Russian, including the finest, *The Tale of the Czar Saltan*. Two are taken from the Grimm brothers—*The Tale of the Fisherman*, and *The Tale of the Dead Princess*, the latter being based on *Snow White*. The source of *The Golden Cockerel* was the legend of the Arab astrologer in Washington Irving's *The Alhambra*. A French translation of this book, together with one of Grimm's stories, was found in Pushkin's library.

of the work which many were to consider his masterpiece, for he died suddenly on the night of June 21, 1908.

The story of *The Golden Cockerel* takes place in a mythical Oriental land whose inhabitants have beguiling Italian names. King Dodon is the "hero"—an empty-headed, gluttonous old monarch, who rules his kingdom "with his hands folded, lying on his side". Dodon fears nothing more than the necessity for action or the making of decisions; he therefore welcomes the gift offered by an Astrologer—a marvellous Golden Cockerel which will sit upon a spire and sound a warning in the event of danger from invading armies. For a time Dodon is able to sleep blissfully, "forgetting that in this world there are calamities". Suddenly the Cockerel sounds his cry of alarm and King Dodon, after first sending his sons off to battle, unwillingly prances off himself. The King encounters not an enemy but the bewitching Queen Shemakha, who delivers such a breathtakingly frank recital of her personal charms that the monarch is undermined. He escorts her back to his palace preceded by a cavalcade of fantastic splendour; but there the Astrologer breaks the dream of bliss by demanding his price for the Golden Cockerel —nothing less than Queen Shemakha herself. Enraged, King Dodon strikes the Astrologer on the head and kills him. Then the Cockerel cries out shrilly, swoops down, and pierces the old man's skull with its beak. The King falls dead. In an enigmatic epilogue the Astrologer appears again to remind the audience that the play was nothing but a dream, and that perhaps he and the Queen were the only living persons in it.

Some of the allegorical details of the story are far from clear, but the main shaft of its satire strikes directly home and could not be mistaken by even the most obtuse public official. King Dodon personifies a desiccated aristocracy, with all its foolish vanity, its cupidity, its gullibility, and its passion for inaction.

Whether it was the scalding satire of the story which aroused his interest to its highest pitch or simply the delight of working again in the familiar field of fantasy, the fact remains that in *The Golden Cockerel* Rimsky-Korsakov produced a masterpiece, and one of the few successful operas of the twentieth century. His score is constructed on broad Wagnerian principles: a few leading motifs associated with the chief characters are developed symphonically into the fabric of the entire piece. The themes are among the best that Rimsky-Korsakov ever created, first for their aptness in character delineation, and second for their purely melodic interest. Melodic beauty, which had always been this composer's hardest problem, is present here almost in profusion.

In his previous operas Rimsky-Korsakov's muse was usually strongest when called upon to paint pictures, weakest when required to create human characters. In *The Golden Cockerel* there is no such unbalance. The scenic elements of the score are as we might expect—gorgeous, shimmering, and voluptuous; within these are placed a group of people who charm us continually with their witty and grotesquely vivid portraits. The fact that they are essentially caricatures does not detract from the deftness of Rimsky-Korsakov's themes. Underneath all caricature, whether in Daumier or Dickens, there is always real character.

It is not surprising that a man as paradoxically constituted as Rimsky-Korsakov should bequeath to Russian music a legacy which was many-sided and full of odd contradictions. There was first of all the sheer force of the man himself, the picture he presented of what a practising Russian musician could be—resolute and tireless in pursuit of knowledge and technical skill, serious in scholarship, a marvel of industry, the very antithesis of the dilettante. He educated not only himself but a whole generation of younger men, and he helped broaden and solidify the entire foundation of the music art in his country.

In spite of the fact that he broke with Balakirev, Rimsky-Korsakov actually did as much as any of the Five to shape the great movement of Russian nationalism. That he carried on and expanded the nationalist-eclecticism which Balakirev had inherited from Glinka is obvious on the one hand in the spate of original and imitation Russian folk and church themes which flood his works, and the Slavic subjects of his operas and songs; and on the other hand in his Oriental excursions, his use of Italian opera models, his debt to Liszt, Berlioz, Chopin, and in the latter part of his career to Wagner. All this, with his own masterly instrumental skill, he welded into a varied and highly colourful art which many of his music descendants were to admire and copy.

The weaknesses of Rimsky-Korsakov's music were obvious even in his own day, and often to the artist himself. It was ironical that this technician par excellence could never meet the highest technical test—the abstract forms of music. He loved humour and fantasy, but in these most difficult phases of art he was by turns brilliant and dull. Spontaneity is the keynote of both; and when a buoyant inspiration failed him Rimsky-Korsakov fell back, fatally, upon formulas. Then his work took on the methodical, almost mechanical aspects of a textbook. At the heart of his troubles was his shallow fund of original melodic ideas.

Excepting portions of his flawed masterpiece, *The Legend of the Invisible City of Kitezh*, Rimsky-Korsakov's music cannot be expected to move deeply. Its purpose is to entertain, to beguile, like so many delightful multi-coloured illustrations from the book of fable. Here this profoundly serious and sincere artist actually re-created in modern guise something of the rich legacy of ancient Russian minstrelsy.

IX

With *The Golden Cockerel* Rimsky-Korsakov brought to a close both his own life's work and the great era which he and his colleagues of the Five had begun fifty years before. Balakirev and Cui were to live on a few more years, but they added nothing to the main edifice. Any evaluation of the achievement of the Five must begin with the most obvious of truisms : that their work as a whole was greater than any of its parts. That five men of such talents should have been thrown together to begin with was wholly remarkable ; it was a phenomenon rare if not unique in the history of any art. Their unity (fragile and short-lived though it really was) gave their work a force and an importance in the public consciousness of the time which they could never have achieved singly. To this day their collective achievement remains a basis of comparison for all Russian music and for nationalist art in every other country.

Against that fortunate accident of their early association must be weighed the misfortune that the length of the careers of the Five was in the inverse ratio to their talents. Musorgsky, the most powerful and original creator, died first after barely two decades of work. Borodin had only a few years more. Rimsky-Korsakov's career was a long one, but he was outlived by both Balakirev and Cui. One may only speculate on the fruitfulness of their achievements had their life spans been reversed.

Viewing them in retrospect it is possible to see that the Five operated upon two main theoretical principles. On one of these they were united ; on the other they became sharply divided. The first was the principle of nationalism, the belief that the materials of folk-lore and folk song, all the primitivist art inheritance of a race, could be made the legitimate basis of a refined and highly-intellectual art. This meant (in Virgil Thomson's phrase) "bridging the gap that lay between the intellectual tradition of music and the folk-lore tradition". On this principle all Five were united, and that they established triumphantly the value of their creed is now beyond question. The second principle, on which they were divided, was of a more recondite nature and had to do with the connection between technique and inspiration. It was a declaration of artistic freedom, an insistence that the artist should be permitted to remain free and even ignorant of the technical rules, the academic restraints, and the traditional mores of music and instead to give rein to inspiration, imagination, and the natural inclination of talent. It was Balakirev, of course, who promulgated this doctrine, and it was Musorgsky who gave it a supreme validity. Borodin followed it to a lesser extent; but to Rimsky-Korsakov it became utterly abhorrent. When Rimsky-Korsakov broke away from the "free" teaching of Balakirev and began his long explorations of technique he helped change the entire course of Russian music history. Glinka and Balakirev, Musorgsky and Borodin were destined to be the last of the exploiters of purely natural talent as opposed to the highly-trained talent. The next generation of Russian composers and the present generation of Soviet composers have almost without exception followed the Rimsky-Korsakov line. Everyone of any consequence is a trained technician in the highest degree.

An examination of the collective work of the Five reveals that with relatively few exceptions their finest achievements were confined to the field of vocal music. They worked most naturally and with greatest power in the opera and the song. This was doubtless to be expected, considering the rigorous exclusion of musical instruments from Russian life for hundreds of years.

In the realm of opera the Five made two original contributions —the realistic opera of Musorgsky and the fantastic fairy-tale opera of Rimsky-Korsakov. Distinctive but less successful was the epical opera of Borodin. The force of Musorgsky's great piece of historical realism, *Boris Godunov*, did not make itself immediately felt, being retarded in part by the long delay in the acceptance of literary realism as a fertilizing agent for serious music.

Musorgsky's realistic songs remain almost in a class by them- selves—great works of art whose style has been imitated both inside and outside Russia but never equalled. The romantic songs of the Five have nationalist distinction which has given them charm and a beguiling flavour. They were something new in their field and they begat a progeny of nationalist art songs all over Western Europe.

In the orchestral field the music of the Five offers only a few outstanding successes. These are mostly picture or literary pieces in the romantic vein and most of them came from the pen of Rimsky-Korsakov. Symphonic literature finds the Five conspicuously weak : only Borodin's B Minor Symphony maintains a permanent though not a prominent place in the repertoire. Borodin, in fact, was the only one who was at home in the abstractions of the pure symphony, because it was his good fortune to possess along with a fecund gift for lyricism a rare sense of large proportion and of dynamic design.

Piano music was enriched only by Musorgsky with his single work, *Pictures at an Exhibition*. This composer also used the piano with real art in his songs. In part his method stemmed from Schumann : the instrument is not relegated to the role of accompaniment but performs a collaboration with the voice. Like Chopin and Debussy, Musorgsky explored the sonorities of the piano to find new avenues of expressiveness. Had Balakirev been endowed with a greater measure of creative power he might have composed with distinction for the piano. He was a superior pianist with discerning taste, but his output was too meagre to constitute more than a promise.

It was Borodin who saved the Five from registering a complete blank in the field of chamber music. His two string quartets have remained, until recently, the only worthy examples of Russian effort in this field. With the concerto form the failure is practically complete. Balakirev's late piano concerto is almost never heard, and Rimsky-Korsakov's seems hardly worth the effort.

CHAPTER IX

TCHAIKOVSKY

I

THE present chronicle has so far traced but one of the two main tributaries of Russian music in the nineteenth century, the strongly nationalist movement dominated by the Five. We have now to return to the formative period of the eighteen-sixties and explore the course of the opposing branch, that which owed its original impulse to Anton Rubinstein. It was Rubinstein's founding of the Petersburg Conservatory of Music in 1862 that aroused the antagonism of Balakirev and led to the latter's creation of the Free School of Music; and in the ensuing rivalry the issue was joined between Balakirev's nationalism, liberally conceived and free of pedantic restraints, and the conservative Western academicism of Rubinstein's group. It might seem from the immensely fruitful work of the Five and the comparatively sterile output of Rubinstein himself that the ultimate victory lay entirely with the nationalists. But that was by no means true. When the Petersburg Conservatory opened its doors in 1862 there appeared in the very first class a young student who was to become in later life the most renowned of all Russian composers, one whose work would gain an enormous international popularity. He was Peter Ilych Tchaikovsky.

So far as his origins were concerned Tchaikovsky could hardly have been distinguished from the members of the Five. His ancestors were middle class and fairly well-to-do, with only faint traces of those talents usually termed artistic. His father was a mining engineer. His mother bore the maiden name Assiere and was part French, her grandfather having been a Frenchman who emigrated to Russia after the Revolution. This French strain in the ancestry of the future Russian composer may have more than passing interest because of the strong affinity which he was to feel toward French music and the attractions which France held for him all through his life.

Tchaikovsky was born May 7, 1840, at Votinsk in the Viatka Government, where his father was an inspector of mines. The family was a large one (the elder Tchaikovsky married three times) and Peter Ilych had four brothers and two sisters. In his childhood

Peter Ilych was deeply devoted to his mother, and her death from cholera when he was fourteen left psychological scars which remained with him the rest of his life.

Tchaikovsky's education was typical of his class and time. As a child he was taught by a French governess, and when the family later moved to Petersburg he attended the School of Jurisprudence. At the age of nineteen he emerged with a loathing for the law and a diploma which carried with it the rights to a berth in the governmental bureaucracy. He became a first-class clerk in the Ministry of Justice. During childhood and adolescence he had shown talent for music, but had received only casual instruction. When he was twenty-one he made his first trip abroad (to Germany, France, Belgium and England) and soon after his return he began studying harmony with the theorist Zaremba, who in turn had studied in Berlin. The next year, when Zaremba became a member of the faculty of the newly-opened Conservatory of Music in Petersburg, his pupil Tchaikovsky followed him and became one of the first students to enrol in the historic institution.

From these details of his early life it seems fairly clear that Tchaikovsky had drifted by force of circumstance into the Conservatory and that his place on the Western side of Russian music circles rather than on the nationalist side was an accident. Although he remained a product of the academy and later became a teacher himself, Tchaikovsky had many of the progressive instincts which might have enlisted him with the Balakirev group. At the Conservatory he found himself antagonized by the extreme conservatism of Anton Rubinstein with whom he studied instrumentation. For Rubinstein the orchestral practices of Wagner, Liszt, and even Meyerbeer were perverse and damnable, but young Tchaikovsky risked the great man's temper by composing an overture to Ostrovsky's drama, *The Storm*, in which he employed the tuba, harp, and English horn—then instrumental symbols of a hare-brained ultramodernism. Aside from these mild indiscretions Tchaikovsky's student compositions seemed to contain few distinctions. His work was sufficiently good, however, to prompt Anton Rubinstein to recommend him for a post which was to change the entire course of his life. In 1866 Rubinstein's younger brother, Nicholas, opened the Moscow Conservatory which was to be the counterpart of the institution at Petersburg. At Anton's suggestion Tchaikovsky was offered, and accepted, the post of Professor of Harmony at the new school.

The decision was a crucial one for Tchaikovsky. Several years before he had resigned his clerkship in the Ministry of Justice, determined to become a composer; but the move to Moscow was a leap in the dark. Compared with the music life of Petersburg that of the older city was then provincial. Moreover, Tchaikovsky's separation from his family at Petersburg caused him agonies of homesickness and mental depression, aggravating the psychic unbalance and the neuroses which had been growing from early childhood.

The historical results of Tchaikovsky's move to Moscow were considerable. By his presence there and by the prestige which was later to attach to his name, Moscow itself would benefit and would soon begin to rival Petersburg as a capital of Russian music. The Moscow Conservatory would later have many distinguished pupils, some taught by Tchaikovsky himself. Less fortuitous was the antagonism which sprang up between Tchaikovsky and the Balakirev group at Petersburg. It is clear in retrospect that they had much in common. Tchaikovsky's contacts with Balakirev were to prove immensely valuable, and later he was drawn personally to Rimsky-Korsakov. Propinquity might have erased many of the artificial barriers raised by the issues of nationalism and Westernism, and the curious rivalry of cities; instead the two parties remained hostile, each viewing the other's work with suspicion. It should be noted that Cui, the master of unnecessary invective, often widened the breach with his criticisms of Tchaikovsky's music.

II

Tchaikovsky spent twelve years as a member of the faculty of the Moscow Conservatory, and in that time he passed from a young pedagogue of moderate ability and uncertain future to a composer of genius and one of the most brilliant creative talents of the later nineteenth century. It was also a time of enormous difficulty for Tchaikovsky. He was at first unhappy because he was shy and lonely, because his life with the hard-drinking, dissipating Nicholas Rubinstein repelled him, and because his income barely kept him alive. It soon transpired, however, that he was to be one of those creative artists whose chief obstacles come from within themselves. Tchaikovsky was neurotic to such an abnormal degree that an extreme pessimism and mental depression became almost the normal mood of his daily life. His art brought him equal measures of satisfaction and pain. He very soon developed such fluency at composition that he could turn out works of major proportions in a few months or even a few weeks; but with that fluency went unevenness of inspiration. The composer was only happy when working at tremendous speed and with a spate of ideas flowing from his brain; but later when he judged with cold reflection what he had done he was often appalled and maddened. The mediocre and the affected too often alloyed the gold of real genius.

The agonies of Tchaikovsky's early years and his morbid attitude toward his own art are plainly indicated in the history of his larger works. His First Symphony (1868) found him unequal to the task of maintaining a flow of interesting thematic ideas over a large area, or of solving the manifold intricacies of form. Before the work was completed the composer was so unstrung that he feared he would die or become insane. The same year he composed a Symphonic Fantasia, *Fatum* (Fate), which was played with fair success both in Moscow and Petersburg, but Tchaikovsky later destroyed the score.[1] His first opera, *The Voyevoda* (1868), suffered the same fate. It was produced at Moscow in 1869 but had only a mild success, and again Tchaikovsky destroyed the score.[2] He did the same with his second opera, *Undine* (1869), which was rejected by the committee of the Imperial Opera at Petersburg and never produced. A third opera, *Madragora* (1870), he left unfinished. *The Oprichnik* (1872), Tchaikovsky's fourth opera, had a brilliant première at Petersburg in 1874, but during the rehearsals the composer became convinced of the vapidity of his music and was so ashamed that three days after the first performance he fled to Italy.

Most of these early works were plainly inferior because they were written too hastily and because the composer had not achieved a balance between creative fervour and a sensible self-criticism. One work, however, must be set apart from these early failures. This is the Fantasy Overture *Romeo and Juliet*, which Tchaikovsky composed in 1870 and which was his first enduring masterpiece. This work had two significant advantages. It was composed with the advice and counsel of Mili Balakirev; it was also twice revised after careful study by the composer himself.

Tchaikovsky had met Balakirev and the other members of the Five in Petersburg in 1868. Balakirev had been eager to press a friendship which might yield a new disciple, and when he later

[1] It was afterward reconstructed and published as Opus 77.
[2] This opera, restored from rough drafts by Dr. Paul Lamm, was revived in a performance in Leningrad, September 28, 1949.

visited Moscow he told Tchaikovsky of his own Overture to *King Lear*, suggesting that his friend compose a similar work on the subject of *Romeo and Juliet*. The result was one of the rarest and happiest collaborations of two composers in music history. Tchaikovsky composed the piece alone, but every portion beginning from earliest sketches went to Balakirev for his detailed criticism. As might be expected, the latter responded with a multitude of instructions pertaining to style, form, tonalities, melodies, etc. Moreover, Balakirev had shrewdly suspected the lack of thoughtful preparation in much of Tchaikovsky's work for he prescribed a means of seeking music inspiration: "Arm yourself with overshoes and a cane and take a constitutional on the boulevards starting from Nikitsky. Allow yourself to be steeped in your plan, and I am certain that by the time you reach Sretensky Boulevard some melody or episode will have come to you." Meditation was the keynote of this advice—the carrying of a germ of an idea in the composer's head until something vital sprang from it. It was fortunate for Tchaikovsky and for *Romeo and Juliet* that he followed a great deal of Balakirev's advice, including a complete revision of the score some months after its first performance.

The various elements in Shakespeare's tragedy are condensed by Tchaikovsky into a brief but passionately expressive musical scenario. A sombre introduction suggests the figure of Friar Lawrence and leads to an Allegro, a scene depicting with fury and tumult the ancient quarrel between the two houses; the "star-cross'd lovers" are then described in two famous themes of lyric beauty and tenderness; a turbulent development section recalls the deadly feud during which Romeo and Juliet are again summoned, until their great love flares and dies; a mournful elegy concludes the work.

After Balakirev's direct help with *Romeo and Juliet* it seems that Tchaikovsky was most indebted to Liszt, for the piece follows both the general style and the mood of intensely passionate personal revelation which is the essence of Liszt's symphonic poems. Lisztian too is the sweet richness of many of Tchaikovsky's harmonies. There is also an operatic flair to this music, which more than suggests the Russian composer's interest in Italian and French opera. Admitting these influences and derivations, however, only serves to illustrate how completely Tchaikovsky had arrived at his own distinctive style. *Romeo and Juliet* contains most of the elements which were to give his music its astonishing vitality and its special colouring. Here, first of all, is his gift of melody—profuse, often touching, and evocative of romantic melancholy. At the same time there is great force and directness of presentation. The ideas are marshalled swiftly and with dramatic skill; the orchestration is a model of clarity and richness. The whole work exhibits Tchaikovsky's gift for establishing a personal mood or emotion, a vivid episode or scene, and then intensifying his conception on a canvas full of romantic colour and fire. In *Romeo and Juliet* he had, for him, the perfect subject—romantic passion and melancholia and the evocation of a tragedy that does not lie too deep for tears.

III

Five years were to elapse after the composition of *Romeo and Juliet* until Tchaikovsky could again write with such concentrated mastery. Meanwhile he composed steadily but with indifferent success—his fourth opera, *The Oprichnik*, his Second Symphony, two string quartets, the Symphonic Fantasy, *The Tempest*. The symphony is subtitled *Little Russian* for its use of folk themes, and was significant of a nationalist phase through which Tchaikovsky was passing. The piece shows a marked advance over the composer's First Symphony, but clings to the modern repertoire largely by reason of his later reputation.

The String Quartet No. 1, in D major, would probably be forgotten today were it not for its second movement, the famous Andante Cantabile. On a visit to his sister's home in Kamenka, Tchaikovsky chanced to hear a baker singing a tune whose opening words were "Vanya sat on the divan and smoked a pipe of tobacco". The composer transmuted this simple fragment of folk song into a movement of unusual lyric beauty and poignancy. It became the only movement in all string quartet literature to achieve what might be called, without prejudice, a popular success.

The Tempest was composed at Vladimir Stasov's suggestion. The critic had been delighted by Tchaikovsky's *Romeo and Juliet*, and had submitted a detailed scenario for a similar work based on Shakespeare's play.[1] Tchaikovsky completed the piece in 1873

[1] The published score gives the following programme: "The sea. Ariel, spirit of the air, raising a tempest at the bidding of the magician Prospero. Wreck of the ship bearing Ferdinand. The enchanted isle. Awakening of love between Ferdinand and Miranda. Ariel. Caliban. The amorous pair give themselves up to the magic of love. Prospero divests himself of his power of enchantment and leaves the island. The sea."

after only ten days of furious composition. It was unfortunate that *The Tempest* did not receive the thought and revision that had so benefited Tchaikovsky's first Shakespearean essay, for it contains many fanciful and distinctive ideas. What has driven it into comparative neglect is the noise and blatancy of its storm section, which now exhibits little more than Tchaikovsky's skill at generating kinetic energy and piling up wave after wave of orchestral excitement.

With his Piano Concerto No. 1, in B flat minor, composed in 1874, Tchaikovsky achieved another well-rounded and enduring masterpiece. Almost as well known as the piece itself is the story of the occasion when the composer first played this concerto privately for his friend Nicholas Rubinstein and the incredible scene that followed—Rubinstein's brutal denunciation of the entire work as inept, poorly constructed, derivative and vulgar; and Tchaikovsky's shocked amazement and resentment. The composer fortunately disregarded Rubinstein's advice to destroy or completely revise his piece, and within a few decades it had become the most popular of all piano concertos and had carried its composer's name all over the music world.

If one were to compile a Dictionary of Abuse as applied over the years to Tchaikovsky's music by its various detractors, one might well begin with the B flat minor Piano Concerto. It has called forth far worse epithets than Nicholas Rubinstein's. Its style is said to be pretentious and overweening, its moods obvious, its music substance shallow, its purpose vulgar. It is said to be lacking in dignity, taste, formal grace, and melodic purity. The list might go on endlessly but to no eventual purpose except to point up the confounding fact that the B flat minor Concerto is still beloved by millions of persons, both learned and unlearned in the art of music. The listener who can approach the work with an unprejudiced mind is likely to discover that for almost every weakness it has corresponding virtues that weigh heavily in its favour. It exemplifies, first of all, Tchaikovsky's peculiar mastery of dramatic effect, an element now fast receding from fashion in music composition but one which lies at the heart of much romantic music of the nineteenth century. Tchaikovsky knew how to make his music progress with a logic that anyone can understand; he knew how to contrast both mood and pace, and how to move from climax to climax toward one grand culmination. This was a dramatist's skill and Tchaikovsky used it intuitively.

Coexisting with effective construction in Tchaikovsky's concerto is a remarkable clarity. This applies not only to the lucidity of the piano and orchestral writing, but to the communicative quality of the music itself. Any dunce, it is said, may be oppressive, and any pedant may be prolix; but clarity is one of the marks of genius. In a music age that was fast running itself into a dead end of complexity, turgidity, and polyphonic complication, Tchaikovsky's best works are models of openness. His music always expresses itself surely and directly, and with the logic of a perfectly told story.

So far as invention is concerned Tchaikovsky did not add much to the concerto form itself; he did, however, display a considerable invention in piano figuration. Some of these figures it is true have to do largely with slashing octave passages designed to build up a roaring volume of sound against that of the heaving orchestra, but others show real ingenuity. Here Tchaikovsky displayed a creative imagination which is almost totally lacking in the mass of worthless "salon" material which he wrote for piano solo.

In the final test it is melody which makes this concerto impervious to the wear and tear of an incredible number of performances. From the majestic first movement with its grandiose opening and its lovely second theme, to the wild Russian dance of the finale, there is hardly a break in melodic interest. The second movement especially is a lyric delight. It is incongruous perhaps to pass through the giant portals of the massive first movement and into this inner chamber, and to find here enshrined a charming ballet in the French style; but Tchaikovsky usually found incongruity a minor obstacle, one which required only a beautiful melody to surmount.

IV

The insecurity of Tchaikovsky's creative powers even though he had reached the age of thirty-five is shown in the failure of his Third Symphony, composed in 1875. In this essay the composer abandoned the use of Russian folk song that had given his Second Symphony at least a stylistic cohesion, and bound together five totally unrelated movements, none of which had any mark of his genius. Another failure (and deservedly so from the haste with which it was composed) was his first version of the comic opera *Vakula the Smith*,[1] written just before the B flat minor Piano Concerto.

---

[1] In 1885 Tchaikovsky completely revised this opera. The later version was titled *Cherevichki* (*The Slippers*), or, outside Russia, *Oxana's Caprices*.

Early in 1876, in Paris, Tchaikovsky heard for the first time a performance of *Carmen,* and was intoxicated by the beauty of Bizet's score. In his search for a suitable libretto for another operatic attempt of his own he considered the subject of Francesca of Rimini; later he abandoned the opera idea and used the story as a basis for an overture-fantasy, the form that had yielded his *Romeo and Juliet.* The music was composed during the autumn of 1876, after the composer had attended the historic opening performance of Wagner's *The Ring of the Nibelung* at Bayreuth.

Tchaikovsky's *Francesca da Rimini* is based on the famous scene in Dante's *Inferno.* In the Fifth Canto the poet and Virgil arrive at the Second Circle of Hades, a region of furious and unceasing winds in which the souls of carnal sinners are blown about relentlessly. As the winds subside momentarily two figures move out of the darkness. They are Francesca of Rimini and her lover, Paolo. Dante listens as Francesca tells the story of the overpowering love which led her and Paolo to their deaths and to eternal damnation. One comfort remains for them: even in the Inferno they shall never be separated.

Tchaikovsky's orchestral fantasy falls into three main sections. The introductory measures, a grim portcullis, recall Dante's description of the entrance to Hades and the awful words inscribed: "All hope abandon, ye who enter here." Then follows the scene of the terrible winds. The second section is an Andante relating Francesca's story of her love for Paolo:

> "There is no greater grief than in a time of misery to remember vanished happiness. . . . One day for our delight we read of Lancelot, how him love enthralled. . . . When of that smile we read, the smile so rapturously kissed by one so deep in love, then he, who ne'er from me shall separate, at once my lips all trembling kissed. . . . That day we read no more."

In the closing section of the tone poem the lovers are again engulfed in the wind and darkness.

In quality *Francesca da Rimini* falls, as it does in popularity, below the composer's *Romeo and Juliet.* Its introduction is an impressive piece of scene painting and its love theme has those lyric qualities which were to become this composer's signature; but the infernal hurricane is again Tchaikovsky manufacturing emotional excitement by the more obvious means. The similarity between *Francesca da Rimini* and *Romeo and Juliet* does not end with the subject matter of two lovers destined for tragedy. The piece displays an even more fundamental pattern which Tchaikovsky was to use again and again. This was the simple and elemental clash of two opposing forces—the conflict between the good and evil, or of love and hatefulness, or the aspiring heroism of life and the ignominy of death.

V

In 1877 when he was thirty-seven years old Tchaikovsky's entire career was shaken and his sanity very nearly shattered by a series of events in his private life. For many years the more morbid details of this composer's personal affairs were suppressed by his biographers, which naturally served to inflame the general interest in their recent publication. Tchaikovsky was a homosexual, and his abnormality caused the unhappy man such agonies of frustration and fear throughout his life that one would prefer even now to respect his feelings and let that part of his story remain untold; but the fact remains that indirectly it affected his art. The emotional crisis which overtook him in 1877 left an impress upon his mind that could not help but be reflected in many of the larger works of his later years.

Nine years before, in 1868, it appeared that Tchaikovsky had hoped to marry an attractive French singer, Désirée Artôt, but she disappointed him by marrying a Spanish baritone. It is doubtful if the composer had ever really loved Artôt, but he lived in constant fear that his abnormality would be exposed and make him an object of scandalous ridicule. Marriage might be a subterfuge to remove all suspicion; moreover, he was lonely and depressed and he longed for the conviviality and the family companionship that had been denied him since he left Petersburg.

In the summer of 1877 while he was in an even more confused emotional state Tchaikovsky made an appalling mistake. He married a girl, Antonina Miliukov, whom he hardly knew and for whom he had not the slightest affection. The composer later revealed that she had threatened to kill herself if he rejected her proposal; also that he was deeply moved by the opera upon which he was then working, *Eugene Onegin*, and could not bear to play the role of the heartless Onegin who spurned the love of Tatiana. Whatever the true reasons for his action, the marriage very nearly drove Tchaikovsky insane.

The nightmare began the evening of the marriage, July 18, 1877, when he sat opposite his wife on a train, realized that he detested her, and wanted to scream like an animal caught in a trap; it ended not many weeks later when he tried by a devious method to kill himself. He stood up to his waist in the freezing waters of the Moskva River, hoping that death by pneumonia would conceal his suicide. He was a mental wreck when his brother Anatole finally took him to Switzerland and away from his wife forever. The girl herself was actually mentally unbalanced and spent the last decades of her life in an insane asylum.

If Tchaikovsky's marriage was like some dreadful chapter drawn from the chronicle of the Karamazov family, an even stranger though far different episode was already forming itself in the composer's life. Another woman had appeared who would rescue him from his despairs, sustain him like an angel of mercy for some fourteen years and then, incomprehensibly, dash him again to the ground. She was Madame Nadedja von Meck, the wealthy widow with whom Tchaikovsky carried on his famous correspondence. Mme. von Meck was herself the victim of an extreme emotional unbalance. While still middle-aged she walled herself up inside her palatial Moscow home, a recluse who dreaded contact with life, suffered neurotic tortures, and found solace only in music—Tchaikovsky's music. Very soon after she began corresponding with the composer whose work sent her into ecstasies she begged for his friendship; but at the same time she imposed the rigid condition that they should never meet.

And so for fourteen years they exchanged literally hundreds of letters until they were bound together by ties of the most devoted friendship, a paradoxical union of intimacy and remoteness through which the composer found one of the few happy outlets for his repressed nature. His letters to Mme. von Meck became the mirror of his mind, for they record many of the most intimate details of his life and the meanings which he read into his music; they record his gratitude when his "Beloved Friend" became also his patron by providing him with an annual income of $3,000 and when she paid for his numerous trips abroad; and they record too the cardinal and inexplicable fact of all—that not once did the two friends ever meet.

The emotional storm of the year 1877 had its inevitable effect upon Tchaikovsky's mind. His inability to take on the normal responsibilities of marriage, a home, and a family left him with an almost adolescent preoccupation with himself. It is hard to escape the conclusion that until the closing years of his life he never reached a balance of intellectual and emotional maturity. Being abnormally shy, neurotic, and repressed he found no outlet in his daily life for his enormous fund of emotional energy; he found it only in his music. It is surely not unusual for an artist to achieve such release in his art, but Tchaikovsky's case is one of the most potent examples on record.

VI

Tchaikovsky's sudden arrival at technical mastery is shown in the fact that in a single year—the terrible year 1877—he produced two large-scale masterpieces in forms which had heretofore found him uncertain and amateurish. These were the Fourth Symphony, in F minor, and the opera *Eugene Onegin*. Only two years had separated the composer's Fourth Symphony from his Third, yet in that time he had made one of those unexpected leaps which often mark the emergence of genius. The Fourth Symphony was the culmination of that period of the composer's growth that had begun with *Romeo and Juliet*. Here he is still youthful, full-blooded, eager and passionate; the emotional abnormalities brought on by the crisis of 1877 had not yet begun to affect his music. The Fourth Symphony is intense, darkly-coloured and at times melancholy, but never morbid. Like the B flat minor Piano Concerto it exhibits the composer's electric vitality, his mastery of sheer musical excitement, his ability to maintain melodic interest over a broad area, his genius for instrumental clarity and colour.

The famous brass fanfares which open the work and reappear at effectively-timed intervals are often cited as examples of a melodramatic quality in Tchaikovsky's music which place it, for some critics, on a lower scale of aesthetic values. Regardless of that judgement, the fanfares are also a clue to something quite original in the composer's conception of the symphony as a form. The whole piece contains such an enormous amount of drama (or melodrama) that it may very well be described as a "grand opera" symphony. It was thus something new of its kind. It is true that Tchaikovsky took a part of his pattern from Liszt's symphonic poems; but it appears that he drew most heavily, even if unconsciously, upon the Italian and French romantic opera which he so greatly enjoyed.

The Fourth Symphony is rich in grand opera effects—the

curtains parting to portentous fanfares, the establishment of emotional conflicts, the steady stream of song, the contrast of powerful chorus-like episodes, even the respite of a ballet movement. What composers like Rossini, Meyerbeer, and the younger Verdi had done to opera, Tchaikovsky was now doing to the symphony. He was giving it grandiloquence. He was making it a theatre piece. This meant shifting the interest away from the old German procedure of thematic contrast and development, and polyphonic complication, toward simpler and more strongly underlined melodies, greater dramatic drive, and an aura of theatrical brilliance over the whole work.

Tchaikovsky's own "programme" for his Fourth Symphony was contained in a letter written to Mme. von Meck after the first performance of the work, and invariably quoted since then by programme annotators. The composer described his introductory fanfare as "the germ of the entire symphony". . . "This is 'Fatum', the inexorable force that prevents our hopes of happiness from being realized . . . it is Damocles' sword, hanging over the head in constant, unremitting spiritual torment." The chief theme of the first movement depicted the "despair and discontent" of reality; the second theme was the respite of a sweet and tender dream. "So life itself is a persistent alternation of hard reality with evanescent dreams and clutchings at happiness." From this romantic and not-too-original allegory Tchaikovsky went on to similar descriptive matter for the rest of the symphony. It is not very convincing, and at the end of his letter he himself admitted that he had not succeeded in transposing his "musical ideas and images into words". His whole programme, in fact, sounds as if it had been read into the music after completion.

Programme music was at its flood-tide during Tchaikovsky's mature years. Romantic composers who took their cue from Berlioz and Liszt were expected to paint landscapes, character portraits, and dramatic situations in tone. Even the austere form of the symphony had developed a gallery of programme pieces, ranging from the *Fantastic* Symphony of Berlioz (or indeed the *Pastoral* Symphony of Beethoven) to the *Faust* and *Dante* Symphonies of Liszt, and the *Ocean* Symphony of Anton Rubinstein. It is probable that certain parts of Tchaikovsky's Fourth Symphony were linked in his mind with definite moods and emotions, but other vital parts (e.g. the entire third movement) do not fit into his "Fate versus Happiness" programme at all. We are left with the conclusion that the composer's programme was largely an afterthought aimed to place the work in a fashionable category.

VII

Tchaikovsky's symphonic works have so far overshadowed his efforts in all other forms that we are apt to forget the enormous labours which he expended in the field of opera. His eleven operas made him one of the most prolific of Russian composers for the lyric stage; indeed, there was hardly a time all through his career when he was not engaged in some phase of operatic creation. It is one of the curiosities of genius that so abundant a melodist as Tchaikovsky, who was also gifted with a passionate sense of the dramatic and sentimental, should have been a comparative failure when he tried to write for the opera house. The technique of operatic writing crops up continually all through his symphonic works, often giving them a unique brilliance and force; but only twice did he succeed in the old form itself. *Eugene Onegin* and *The Queen of Spades* bear the imprint of his mastery, but the nine other Tchaikovsky operas are either dubious ventures or flat failures.

Tchaikovsky's operatic standards were opposed to those of the Five at Petersburg. He had no interest in the Dargomyjskyan theories of realistic truth; instead he worked in the romantic traditions of the West. There his sympathies were narrowed still further, for it was primarily Italian and French opera which attracted him—Rossini, Donizetti, Bellini, Verdi, and Meyerbeer—while Wagner and the entire German school left him cold.

As for nationalism, the progress of Tchaikovsky's operatic style shows that he began by being as Russian as any of the Five in his use of folk music, but his interest gradually receded and after *Eugene Onegin* the nationalist element almost disappears from his operatic music. Thus, his first opera, *The Voyevoda*, is intensely national in flavour; his third completed opera, *The Oprichnik*, is also full of Russian folk melodies, but its general style so apes French grand opera that it has been called "Meyerbeer translated into Russian". *Vakula the Smith* makes copious use of Ukrainian folk music, and the entire work bears a close relationship to Glinka; but with *Eugene Onegin* Tchaikovsky's interest in the Russian national idiom begins to wane. After the folk music in Act I it disappears from the work and in no succeeding Tchaikovsky opera does it ever assume importance.

Pushkin's *Eugene Onegin* was not a drama but, in his own term, a "novel in verse", which satirized the provincial and city life of Russia in the 1820s. Onegin is a Byronic figure, a young romantic who is aloof and cynical beyond his years and who by his egotism and his absorption in the pose of worldliness destroys his own happiness. Onegin first repulses Tatiana, a shy and unsophisticated girl who had fallen in love with him; later, he again meets Tatiana who is now the wife of a prince and a poised and beautiful woman. Onegin realizes his desperate love for her but she, while admitting that she still loves him, sends him away forever.

Tchaikovsky fashioned his own libretto directly from Pushkin's verses, but because his sympathies were strongly aroused by Tatiana he made her and not Onegin the dominating character in the play. The unhappy, lovesick girl who is caught in a rush of passion she scarcely understands is Tchaikovsky's most touching operatic portrait, and the famous letter scene in which she writes to Onegin confessing her love is the composer's most celebrated scene for the lyric stage.

Until its true nature began to be better known *Eugene Onegin* was often a disappointment, especially in repertoires where it had to compete with lavishly-produced grand operas. Tchaikovsky himself knew that his opera was an intimate work which lacked dramatic action, and he deliberately gave it the sub-title, "lyric scenes". He refused to inflate it with big theatrical effects. The lovely melodies, so characteristic and abundant and sweetly mellifluous, would have been ruined by the magnifications of a Meyerbeer technique; instead the composer gave them the benefit of vocal settings of singular grace and reticence, and an orchestration of finely-wrought texture. Thus *Eugene Onegin* is best heard in small theatres. There it is like a fading, nostalgic picture of a vanished past which suddenly takes on the glow of life; the drama becomes real and moving as the music evokes the atmosphere of Pushkin's story—"young men with romantic, lofty ideas, hypersensitive, *schwärmerische* ladies; desperate passions and infinite longings".

The satire of Pushkin's original *Eugene Onegin* was essentially the poet's mocking comment upon the Europeanized Russian aristocrats of his day, who surrendered to the culture of the West even to the extent of apeing the fashionable *Weltschmerz* of romanticism. In Tchaikovsky's version the satire is abbreviated, and instead the centre of interest becomes the theme of romantic love. This is a typically Western theme, one vastly exploited in our literature and drama, but treated comparatively seldom in Russian art. Thus Tchaikovsky's opera is essentially a hybrid, a blending of Russian and Western materials. It gave evidence of his understanding of Western culture and his affinity for its romantic tradition. In Russia it also served to place him among the cosmopolitans, and open to the criticism of the more vehement nationalists.

Tchaikovsky's Violin Concerto, in D major, composed in 1878, was the last of the group of highly-successful works which he produced in his middle and late thirties. Like *Eugene Onegin* and the Fourth Symphony it exhibits some of his most endearing qualities as a composer, with few traces of the neurotic pessimism which was to darken the music of his later years. The Violin Concerto was to demonstrate, exactly as had the B flat minor Piano Concerto, the fact that virtuosi are often poor judges of new works in their own field. Tchaikovsky at first dedicated his Concerto to Leopold Auer, then a brilliant young concert violinist, who pronounced it unplayable. Three years went by before it was finally performed in Vienna. On that occasion Eduard Hanslick tore it apart with a foolish and vulgar diatribe.[1] It is not recorded that Hanslick ever changed his mind about Tchaikovsky's Concerto, but Leopold Auer did. He played it himself on many occasions, and later he taught it to a whole generation of violinists who made it one of the most popular and beloved works ever written for the instrument.

For many years critics continued to carp at the Violin Concerto, deploring its too-luscious melodies, its lack of formal perfection, or the fact that its difficulty made it a prancing ground for virtuosi with exhibitionist tendencies. The work has even been revised and rearranged by musicians who believed that they could cure what seemed to be a "lack of workmanship". Today, however, a growing respect for Tchaikovsky's music (resulting in part from the unfailing allegiance of the listening public) has brought a measure of tolerance for the Violin Concerto. Violinists of unimpeachable musicianship do not have to apologize for playing it, and musicologists of repute have pronounced it "very well organized".

After the composition of the Violin Concerto Tchaikovsky

---

[1] Hanslick wrote that the Finale "plunges us into the brutal, deplorable gaiety of a Russian holiday carouse. We see savages, vulgar faces, hear coarse oaths, and smell fusel oil." He went on to say :

"Friedrich Fischer, describing obscene painting, once said that there existed pictures one could see stink. Tchaikovsky's Violin Concerto brings us face to face for the first time with the revolting thought : may there not also exist musical compositions that we can hear stink ?"

entered upon a lean seven-year period during which he produced works of only moderate interest, when they were not out-and-out failures. His second Piano Concerto, in G major, falls far below the first. Though well made, it is often simply dull. The three orchestral Suites and the Serenade for Strings are good only in isolated movements, while the *Italian Caprice* and the *"1812" Overture* represent the "pop concert" Tchaikovsky, a composer who was enormously skilled at turning the symphonic orchestra into an electrical display. In the opera *Joan of Arc* (1879), Tchaikovsky tried to join Schiller's story of the Maid of Orleans with French grand opera music in the style of Meyerbeer; and in *Mazeppa* (1883), he returned to Russia and another poetic tale by Pushkin. For both efforts he wrote chiefly mediocre music—a depressing waste of a precious creative talent.

Many reasons have been offered for the wide gulf which separates the best and the worst of Tchaikovsky's work. Excessive haste was certainly one reason for his failures; lack of self-criticism was another. Increasing neurotic tension in his later years and the deepening spells of melancholia also affected his art. We are left with the suspicion that much of the time Tchaikovsky did not think clearly, so beset was he by the thousand gnawing afflictions of the world of hypersensitive nerves in which he lived. Often composition was simply a diversion that took him away momentarily from the private madhouse which was his conscious mind.

Outwardly, Tchaikovsky had achieved in his private life many of the requirements of comfort and happiness. In 1878 Mme. von Meck's pension had permitted him to resign his teaching job at the Conservatory, and at her expense he also made various sojourns in Western Europe. He was both financially independent and free of family obligations; yet his art, to which he could now devote all his time, seldom brought him happiness. His mental state is summed up in a passage from one of his letters: "To regret the past, and hope for the future, never satisfied with the present: that is how my life passes."

VIII

In 1885 Tchaikovsky, who hated cities, moved into a house at Klin, a short distance from Moscow. Here he lived a half-hermit existence, walking for hours in the countryside which he loved, studying English and philosophy, calming his nerves by drinking enormous quantities of liquor at night. It was at Klin that the composer took up a huge symphonic project which had been in his mind for several years. In 1882 he had renewed his correspondence with Balakirev, after the latter emerged from the silences of his mystical retreat. Characteristically, Balakirev had an idea which he pressed upon Tchaikovsky—a symphonic work to be based on Byron's dramatic poem, *Manfred*.

The fascination which the great English romantic held for a generation of European poets, novelists, and composers, from Ireland to the Carpathians, is nowhere better exemplified than in his enkindling effect upon the Russians. Musorgsky and Balakirev had read *Manfred* together in their early twenties and had gloried in it; in 1868 when Berlioz visited Russia Balakirev tried unsuccessfully to interest the Frenchman in Byron's hero as a symphonic subject; and now in the 1880s, more than half a century after the poet's death, the flaming verses still burned in Balakirev's mind. He wrote to Tchaikovsky: "Your *Francesca* gave me the idea that you could work out this subject brilliantly, provided you *took great pains*, subjected your work to stringent self-criticism, let your imagination ripen fully, and didn't hurry to finish anything." Two years later there came from Balakirev a detailed scenario of the various movements of the proposed symphony, a scheme of the tonalities to be employed, and the suggestion of a recurring theme, an *idée fixe*, in the manner of Berlioz' *Fantastic* Symphony.

At first Tchaikovsky was cold to the idea, and even when he began work he did so half-heartedly. He followed many of Balakirev's suggestions, but unfortunately not the most valuable advice of all—that he compose slowly and with extreme care. Tchaikovsky's *Manfred* Symphony is an enormous score, running more than an hour in performance, and its scheme is so ambitious that it deserved far more time and thought than the composer gave it. Once it was finished he thrust it away, later calling it "a repulsive work" whose last three movements he thought he might destroy. It must be accounted one of the tragedies of his creative life that he did not give *Manfred* the thoughtful revision that he gave *Romeo and Juliet*, for it contains some of the finest music he ever wrote.

In a preface to the score Tchaikovsky indicated the story of each movement: I. Manfred wanders in the Alps, "racked by remorse and despair . . . a prey to sufferings without a name. . . . The memory of the fair Astarte, whom he loved and lost, eats his heart." II. The Fairy of the Alps appears to Manfred beneath the rainbow of the waterfall. III. A Pastorale, depicting the life of the mountain folk. IV. The subterranean palace of Arimanes. "Manfred appears during an infernal bacchanale. Evocation of the spirit of Astarte. . . . Manfred's death." Like every other composer since Berlioz who has attempted a programme symphony, Tchaikovsky struggled with the task of reconciling two wholly disparate elements —the story he was trying to relate, with all its dramatic episodes, character studies, and fantastic landscapes; and the laws of form and thematic development which govern the classic symphony.

If the *Manfred* Symphony is a failure (except in the hands of the most able conductors) it is still a remarkable one. Although it is plainly overlong and marred by discursiveness and lack of co-hesion, it has both dignity and integrity. It generates passion, exquisite lyricism, and splendid romantic scene painting. Above all, Tchaikovsky succeeds in making both vivid and plausible the portrait of the tortured Manfred, a portrait that Byron himself could not always sustain. If that vision is one excessively romantic —with its wild and fire-streaked outlines of a soul racked by self-torment, wandering in the icy wilderness of the Alps—it is still a startling replica of an entire age in art, a great and passionate age now gone, but one which filled the lives of nineteenth-century men with magnificent spiritual adventure.

In spite of the fact that it holds its place among the most popular of all Tchaikovsky's works, the Fifth Symphony, composed in 1888, can only be described as a step downward from the *Manfred* and the Fourth Symphonies. If Tchaikovsky had composed the Fifth Symphony when he was still a young man he could be forgiven its aesthetic lapses, but it appeared when he was close to fifty and long after he should have outgrown such matters as Fate hanging like a Damocles' sword over a man's life—a sophomoric fancy at best. His mistake was to imitate, after eleven years, the motto theme idea of his Fourth Symphony; but while the ringing and oracular voice of Fate had served him well in the earlier work, he overdid it in the later one in a manner that disables some of his most enjoyable music.

Instead of having done with his sombre and distinctive E minor theme after his effective first movement, Tchaikovsky also dragged it into the three succeeding movements. The question here is one of propriety, effectiveness, and logic, and in no category does the composer succeed. Only in the third movement, the sombre Valse, does the theme seem appropriately recalled, when it is heard as a lugubrious echo at the close. When it twice erupts into the melancholy lyricism of the Andante cantabile it is merely a noisy distraction; but in the Finale it nearly causes the ruination of the entire work. When he transformed his sombre E minor theme into E major Tchaikovsky was led into a triumphal "happy ending" which exposes both the weaknesses of the theme and the shallowness of the composer's aims. This is once again Tchaikovsky's grand opera style of symphonic writing, but without the honest exuberance of the Fourth Symphony.

IX

All his life Tchaikovsky loved the ballet, and he never ceased to defend ballet music against critics who considered it too flimsy for serious consideration. When Sergei Taneyev once wrote him that parts of the Fourth Symphony sounded too much like ballet music, Tchaikovsky tartly replied: "I can never understand why 'ballet music' should be used as an epithet of contempt. The music of a ballet is not invariably bad, for there are good works of this class—Delibes's 'Sylvia', for example." It is one of the oddities of Tchaikovsky's career that he expended enormous amounts of time and energy on operas which rose but seldom above mediocrity; while for his three ballets which he turned out in a matter of weeks he created some of his most delightful and enduring music.

Tchaikovsky's first ballet, *The Swan Lake*, failed at its first performance in Moscow in 1877, largely due to a poor performance. It was revived successfully after the composer's death and since then has become one of the classics of the modern ballet theatre. Tchaikovsky's second ballet, *The Sleeping Beauty*, followed a dozen years later and was based on the famous fairy-tale by Perrault. Unlike its predecessor it was attended by a superlative and costly première at Petersburg, with choreography by the great ballet master, Marius Petipa. Sergei Diaghilev revived the work in 1921 in London, but again, in spite of a lavish expenditure of money and talent, the production did not prosper. Since then two smaller ballets, *Aurora's Wedding* and *Princess Aurora*, both derived from the score, have become international ballet successes, and so has the entire original. *The Nutcracker*, Tchaikovsky's third ballet, was based on a story by E. T. A. Hoffmann, *The Nutcracker and the King of the Mice*. Before its sumptuous first performance in 1892 (with the première of Tchaikovsky's final opera, the one-act *Iolanthe*) the composer had put together a Suite derived from the score. This so-called "Nutcracker" Suite has enjoyed a popularity that can only be described as fabulous. It is deserved, for the excerpts are little masterpieces of their kind. In recent years successful revivals have revealed the high quality of the complete score.

Tchaikovsky has been called "the greatest master of ballet music in the classic traditions". He is also the precursor of those modern composers (led by Igor Stravinsky) who have made the ballet a serious music art form, instead of a mere divertissement. *The Sleeping Beauty*, especially, indicates Tchaikovsky's attitude. Here he created a score containing a prologue and three acts, and comprising no less than thirty numbers. His music is symphonic in style and rich in elaboration; moreover, it all bears a close relation to the drama which is to be enacted by means of pantomime and dance.

Tchaikovsky was prodigally endowed with talent for creating ballet music, especially in the fairy-tale genre. He had first of all a fund of melody of a type which exudes both grace and charm; moreover, the splendid clarity of his music and its strong and simple rhythmic qualities made it ideally practical from the dancer's point of view. Most valuable of all was Tchaikovsky's highly-developed sense of humour, a delight in the whimsical, the exotic, and the bizarre, which fit perfectly into the world of the fairy-tale ballet. This was a side of Tchaikovsky's genius which one might never suspect from a man who had been so often preoccupied with the vast and gloomy themes of life, death, and Fate, and whose larger works were so often drenched with personal melancholia. Humour was, nevertheless, one of the strongest moods of his creative nature, and it appears with unexpected *naïveté* in some of his least humorous works. The most famous example is the Scherzo of the Fourth Symphony; another is the whimsical central portion of the slow movement of the B flat minor Piano Concerto. These and other expressions of musical grotesquerie were as much a part of Tchaikovsky's real artistic nature as were the broodings over the Fatum, or the hysterical outcries of his more neurotic moments.

X

In the year 1890 when he was fifty years old Tchaikovsky had reached a point of eminence never before achieved by a Russian composer. This was true not only in Russia, where heretofore the serious work of native composers had often met with indifference, but also in Western Europe and America where Tchaikovsky's music was creating the first of its sensational successes. In 1888 the composer had overcome his terror of conducting and had made the first of several international tours. His diaries of these years reveal, however, that he was still a morbidly unhappy man, whose abnormal shyness ruined what pleasure he might have derived from public adulation. As a young man he had often detested his life in Russia and had continually fled to Italy or France for a change of scene; now Western Europe only left him acutely homesick for his native land and its people.

It was late in 1890 that Tchaikovsky received a shock which totally unnerved him and from which he never recovered. While he was visiting in Tiflis a letter reached him from Mme. von Meck, who notified him that she was in serious financial difficulties and that his allowance must cease. The tone of the letter, moreover, was cold and distant and indicated that their correspondence too was at an end. Tchaikovsky's shock and bewilderment were soon to be aggravated by the discovery that Mme. von Meck had not been truthful with him and that her immense fortune was not seriously threatened. He never heard from her again. Had the composer been a more rational man he might have realized that Mme. von Meck was a prey to neurotic melancholia more desperate than his own; but he was beyond reasoning and rationalizing. By a single act his friend had destroyed a fourteen-year devotion that had been the prop and mainstay of the composer's life. She made him feel that he had been, all the while, no more than a pensioner.

Only three years of life remained for Tchaikovsky after the rupture of the Meck friendship, and they were years of unrelieved gloom and depression. Much of the time he travelled—to America in the spring of 1891 where he was honoured at the ceremonies marking the opening of Carnegie Hall; to Germany, France and Austria in 1892 for performances of his own works; and finally to England in 1893 to receive a doctor's degree at Cambridge. Meanwhile, his opera *The Queen of Spades*, composed in 1890 and based on Pushkin's story, had a brilliant première in Petersburg and was to become his most successful operatic work after *Eugene Onegin*. But the composer was morose and dejected. In 1892 he began work on a Symphony in E flat, but months later when the work was almost completed he abandoned the whole thing in a fit of despondency. He felt old and complained of being written out. Photographs taken of him at this time reveal that he had in fact aged greatly in appearance.

While on his way to Paris late in 1892 Tchaikovsky was seized with an idea for another symphony, and as its various details formed in his mind the composer was so moved that he repeatedly wept. When he returned to Russia and took up the task of writing he found to his delight that the ideas flowed again with all their accustomed abundance. He composed not only with furious haste but with the conviction that this Sixth Symphony, in B minor, was to be his finest work. After many interruptions the work was completed late in the summer, and it was performed for the first time on October 28, 1893, in Petersburg under the composer's direction.

Tchaikovsky was right in his estimate. The Sixth Symphony was his masterpiece, and after more than half a century it still has no peer in Russian music.

Everyone who has ever heard the Sixth Symphony must also have heard the endlessly recounted details of its origin, of the double mystery which for a time gave a melodramatic significance to the piece. The composer had written that this was to be "a symphony with a programme, but a programme that will remain an enigma to all. Let them guess for themselves. . . ." After its first performance he gave it the name *Pathetique*. Then, within a few days, there occurred the appalling event which added further mystery to the great symphony and its hidden meaning. On November 6, 1893, after a sudden illness from cholera, Tchaikovsky died. Because he had carelessly drunk a glass of unboiled water the rumour spread that he had in effect committed suicide, and that he had composed the *Pathetique* Symphony as his own requiem.

The suicide rumour has long since been disproved, but to this day no clue has ever been found to Tchaikovsky's programme for the *Pathetique* Symphony. Thus the work exemplifies the paradox which envelops all such music. Although it was created on the testimony of the composer himself to a definite programme, no one has any knowledge of what that programme might be; yet it would be inconceivable that such knowledge could now enhance the value or enrich our appreciation of the work. Tchaikovsky's programme was therefore not unlike some scaffolding which roughly contained the edifice during the course of construction, but which later could be stripped away and forgotten. One detail alone seems to force itself through the enigmatic mystery. It would seem to be inevitable that the symbolism of the final movement, the Adagio lamentoso, must be Death. Nothing else could befit, in majesty or in tragic finality, this sorrowful dirge.

One further mystery of art is contained in the measures of the *Pathetique* Symphony, and that is the transmutàtion of material which took place under the composer's hand. No one else could have created this work, so deeply cut are the indentations of Tchaikovsky's style. This means that it contains all the familiar Tchaikovsky mannerisms, the clichés, even, by which he had created emotional storm and stress, and which he had so often used for less lofty aims ; but now they seem to fall into their rightful places with logic and rectitude. Far from having lost his creative vigour, Tchaikovsky had at last reached his point of absolute mastery. The melodic ideas have all their accustomed richness but with a new distinction of treatment. Harmonies, without being saccharine, maintain a glow of colour over the whole work. As a piece of large-scale design the *Pathetique* Symphony is wholly unorthodox and yet structurally, dramatically, and aesthetically it triumphs over criticism.

In his first movement the composer establishes a mood of deep pathos. This is done with the conventional two themes of classic sonata procedure, which in the handling resemble the elements of emotional contrast in a tragic drama : the first theme creates and lets loose malignant forces in violent conflict, while the second is the means of surcease and resignation. The melodious second movement with its 5/4 rhythm, now only mildly exotic, is once again Tchaikovsky's tribute to the dance, but the mood is faintly grave as if the steps were to be ceremonious and stately. With the third movement the composer throws precedent to the wind, for he begins with a piquant and sharp-pointed scherzo which unexpectedly gathers force and momentum until it bursts into a prodigious march whose ending is one of shattering violence. To retreat from this pinnacle of excitement and still round off the symphonic design required nothing less than a master stroke, and this Tchaikovsky created in his incomparable Adagio. The problem of the triumphal ending which had troubled every symphonic composer since its creation by Beethoven, is evaded in the *Pathetique* Symphony with a slow descent into darkness and silence, achieved with such beauty of musical utterance that few listeners may leave this work without feelings of aesthetic satisfaction and emotional surfeit.

XI

Among Russian composers, as indeed among all composers of the late nineteenth century, Tchaikovsky remains a commanding figure. In the history of Russian music he is one of the greatest masters, whose eminence and influence may be challenged only by Musorgsky. In historical perspective we may see that he shares with Balakirev, Borodin, and Rimsky-Korsakov a pioneer place among Russian composers in the field of instrumental music. In the special field of the symphonic orchestra he remains pre-eminent, for with his symphonies and overtures he created almost single-handed a literature of Russian symphonic music.

In his own country and in his own day, Tchaikovsky's music was disdained by the nationalists as being too Western and eclectic. It is true that his training was in the German academic tradition, that he gradually lost interest in the use of the idioms of Russian folk music, and that he was heavily influenced by Italian and French opera and by Liszt ; even so his music retains a singular Russianness. Igor Stravinsky noted this quality in a tribute to his predecessor's art :

"Tchaikovsky's music, which does not appear specifically Russian to everybody, is often more profoundly Russian than music which has long since been awarded the facile label of Muscovite picturesqueness. This music is quite as Russian as Pushkin's verse or Glinka's song. Whilst not specially cultivating in his art the 'soul of the Russian peasant', Tchaikovsky drew unconsciously from the true, popular sources of our race."

It would be difficult to devise for any music a harder set of handicaps than those which have stood in the way of Tchaikovsky's. It has suffered from enormous popularity, from excessive sentimentalizing by interpreters, and from savage criticism. That it survives at all in the living literature of modern music should be proof enough of its vitality. So far as criticism is concerned it should be noted first that the most severe critic of Tchaikovsky's music was Tchaikovsky himself. Like all his worst detractors he knew its faults, but unlike them he sometimes recognized its virtues.

For many years it has been the fashion to dwell upon the lack of formal excellence in Tchaikovsky's music, its inability to develop properly, and the fact that his symphonies turned out to be, in the academic sense, mere suites; his melodies are dismissed as overly sentimental and too facile, his harmonies as all gilt and plush, his orchestration as blatant. His music is summed up as sensational and obvious when not actually hysterical, and thus fit only for the masses but not for the urbane and intelligent listener. Those who apply such epithets to Tchaikovsky's music are often reminiscent of the critics who could not abide the novels of Dickens because they were not written with the subtlety of Thackeray's, or the stories of Mark Twain because they could not compare in literary virtuosity with those of Henry James. The easiest way to damn any creative artist is to subject him to comparisons, especially in fields where he had no intention of going; the more honest way to appraise him is to seek the special merits of his finest, not his worst, works. Tchaikovsky is at home in the company of writers like Dickens, Twain, and Defoe because like them he is an exemplar of an art which is remarkable for its directness, its ability to reach swiftly and move deeply a wide audience. There is little of the recondite in this art, and little for the academician to ponder over or the student of classic procedure to imitate. But its great strength, and its great mystery, is the clarity of its thought and at the same time the abundance of the creative ideas which crowd into every line or every measure. Thus it is expressive and communicative in the highest degree. That it is also comparatively easy to absorb and appreciate should be accounted among its virtues instead of its faults.

It is beside the point to wish that Tchaikovsky had been less sentimental for he composed in a sentimental age, while we now listen in one which is increasingly hostile to sentiment in art. It is also fruitless to wish that he had worked with greater care, perhaps destroying as Brahms did far more than he ever published. Had he done so we would probably lack some singularly beautiful music, flawed though it may be. As for his temperament, it was unfortunate for his art that he did not mature more rapidly as a man, but it should be remembered that an emotional unbalance made much of his life a torment. It is safer and fairer to take Tchaikovsky's music exactly as it is, rejecting what is plainly inferior but being careful to give proper estimate to those works which continue to stand their ground among the masterpieces of the romantic age.

CHAPTER X

THE SECOND GENERATION

I

THE last three decades of the nineteenth century, those which had roughly spanned the creative careers of the Five and Tchaikovsky, saw a change in the entire Russian music scene. Anton Rubinstein had won his hard battle for the emancipation of musicians. Now an aristocrat or even a man of noble rank might be a composer or a pianist and still retain his social standing. With this imprimatur finally placed upon music, the art began to flourish in all directions.

The age represented the triumph of the two great conservatories founded by the Rubinstein brothers in Petersburg and Moscow. Sound music pedagogy had been established for the first time in Russia. The international reputations of men like Anton Rubinstein, Tchaikovsky, and Rimsky-Korsakov inevitably shed lustre on the two schools, and as the years went by lent them enormous prestige. A tradition of music teaching had begun.

Seen in retrospect, it was clearly an age of great pedagogues. Rimsky-Korsakov taught at Petersburg an entire generation of young composers, both in composition and in his special field of instrumentation; a group of efficient men under Nicholas Rubinstein did the same at Moscow. Instruction in the musical instruments was remarkable, and the rise of instrumental virtuosity spectacular. The Rubinsteins had done the spade work in implanting on Russian soil the traditions of piano playing in the grand style. Theodor Leschetizky, the most renowned of all modern teachers of the piano, was a professor at the Petersburg Conservatory from 1862 to 1878, when he laid the foundations of his own career and of the modern Russian school of piano virtuosity. Leopold Auer did the same for the violin. He was head of the violin department at the Petersburg Conservatory from 1868 to 1917, during which time he instructed an astonishing number of the most eminent modern violin virtuosi.

With the rise of the conservatories there came a corresponding activity in the field of music scholarship and research. In the historical background of Russian art music lay the vast fields of folk and church music, terra incognita for the most part, and penetrated but lightly by the composers. Into these fields the scholars began to move, armed with the modern tools of scientific research and documentation.

The collecting and classifying of Russian folk songs had begun in a primitive way in the late eighteenth and early nineteenth centuries. Balakirev's collection in 1866 was a pioneer work of value, even though his arrangements have been frowned upon by modern authorities. More astute in his realization of the peculiar characteristics of Russian folk music was J. N. Melgunov (1846–93), who had been a pianist and a pupil of the Rubinsteins. In 1879 and 1885 Melgunov published two important volumes of folk songs, with penetrating observations on their structure. Tchaikovsky's collection came in 1872, and Rimsky-Korsakov published two collections, in 1875 and 1877. Highly regarded by modern authorities for their intuitive handling of the folk songs and their harmonizations are the various collections made by the composer Anatole Liadov. In 1886 and 1893 the Imperial Geographical Society, under the aegis of Czar Alexander III, took an interest in the subject of native music, dispatching expeditions to the northern provinces. The resulting collections were edited by Istomin, Diutch, and the composer Liapunov. At the same time there appeared a notable collection of peasant songs by Palchikov.

With Palchikov there began a new attitude toward folk music. In essence this was the theory that these old songs should not be warped into modern or Western harmonizations or arrangements; that instead they should be kept scrupulously intact, and that the primitive polyphonic effects especially should not be "corrected" according to Western standards. This native polyphony was an integral part of the folk-song art, and had apparently developed independently of the growth of polyphonic music in Western Europe. None of the important nineteenth-century Russian composers had grasped fully this fundamental fact; Borodin, Musorgsky, and, later, Liadov are said to be the only ones whose music occasionally (and intuitively) takes on the true intonations of the folk song.[1] Alexander Kastalsky (1856–1926), who was a pupil of Tchaikovsky and Taneyev at the Moscow Conservatory, and who became one of the great modern authorities on the nature of the folk song and the old

---

[1] The Chorus of Peasants in the last act of Borodin's *Prince Igor* is said to be the nearest approach to a genuine Russian folk song in the works of the Five.

church chant, contributed much to the movement for their scrupulous preservation and treatment.

In the field of Russian church music the same movement toward scientific inquiry and documentation had begun in the mid-nineteenth century. The first professor of church music at the Moscow Conservatory (1866) was the priest D. V. Razumovsky (1818–89), who became expert in deciphering the old *znamenny* chants. Razumovsky was the author of many treatises on Greco-Roman church music. He was succeeded at the Conservatory by the most illustrious of all authorities on the ecclesiastical music of Russia—S. V. Smoliensky (1848–1909). This man's researches into the antique art were vast and exhaustive; he unearthed knowledge that had been lost for centuries. Smoliensky's successor in turn was the priest V. M. Metallov, who became a specialist in the *znamenny* chant of the sixteenth century, the golden age of Russian church music during the reign of Czar Ivan IV, when the art reached a point of rare beauty and variety.

In their labours these scholars were beset by difficulties which only the archaeologist may appreciate. They had to rescue the remains of an art which had been lost in the rubble of centuries, piecing it together from the relics of manuscripts whose notations had become all but meaningless. The *znamenny* chant, they were able to prove, had definitely derived almost a thousand years ago from the Byzantine chant (itself an art buried and rendered all but incomprehensible under the dust of time); it had become with the passage of centuries a thoroughly Russian art, the handmaiden to the beauty of the Russian church ceremonial; it had flourished luxuriantly, and then, in the great schism following Nikon's reforms, had all but met its death, either through disuse or the disfigurations of several centuries of Westernizing.

II

With the closing decades of the nineteenth century there began to appear the work of a new generation of Russian composers. In this second generation were the men who, being born in the eighteen-fifties and -sixties, followed immediately after the Five and Tchaikovsky. They were direct descendants, for most of them were personal friends, protégés, or at least pupils of the older composers. The younger group included Liadov, Liapunov, Arensky, Ippolitov-Ivanov, Taneyev, Glazunov, and Gretchaninov.

The work of this second generation reveals that even in the course of a few decades significant changes had already occurred in the directions of Russian music. One of the most noteworthy was the sharp decline of the Italian influence. The Italian operatic tradition which had held its place so long, exerting its powerful thrust upon Glinka and later on such widely diverse talents as Cui and Tchaikovsky, now remained only as a vestige. Replacing it was the force of German music. This was seen first of all in the conservatories, where the pedagogy was strongly German in character—thorough, scientific, and imbued with a reverence for the German classics. In the music of the Russian second generation we see the results. The interest is away from the restrictions of pure nationalism and toward the typically German forms and styles—the abstractions of the symphony and of chamber music, the picturesque tone poems of Liszt, the music dramas of Wagner.

Most of this second generation of Russians are eclectics and academicians, whose music shows their intellectual excursions into various fields. As a result their work is markedly synthetic in style and form. They are all skilled craftsmen whose training has fitted them for almost any task in the technical side of music. They compose in abundance, and in a great variety of forms. The academic bent is so strong in most of them that they become teachers in the conservatories, passing on the traditions of the first generation; at least one of them, Taneyev, becomes a theorist of international repute.

Inevitably, the strong academic influence brings with it a prevailing conservatism. And here we touch upon the weakness of all these composers. They lack the pioneering spirit, the urge toward enterprise which had set in motion Glinka, Balakirev, Musorgsky, Borodin, and Rimsky-Korsakov. They are competent but unadventurous.

With the second generation the long battle between the so-called nationalists of Petersburg and the eclectics of Moscow (i.e. Slavophiles *v.* Westernizers) comes virtually to an end. The issue had never been too clearly defined, and now the warriors all seem to be wearing the same uniform. What emerges is simply the old conflict between conservatives and liberals, and it is the conservatives who gain the victory.

In the music of the second generation is also written the defeat of Mili Balakirev, and it is possible that the stoic sadness of his final years came in part from his realization of this fact. Balakirev was the first great liberal in Russian music. He was not only an ultra-nationalist, but a champion of the romantic liberals of the West, and above all a believer in music freely taught and freely composed. He lived to see his nationalist idea triumph, but it soon became a diluted nationalism, watered down by conservative and synthetic practices. The real misfortune, perhaps, was the death of Balakirev's idea of free study and composition—his declaration of independence from the pedantry of academies. In the second generation there is no one remotely resembling Musorgsky; indeed his works were so completely ignored or even discredited that it is no wonder the liberal spirit which had engendered them fell into disrepute. Even Balakirev seems to have abandoned finally his ideal of free teaching and composition. In Russian circles it could never surmount the stigma of "dilettantism".

III

One of the finest natural talents among the second generation was that of Anatole Liadov (1855–1914). He was a pupil of Rimsky-Korsakov at the Petersburg Conservatory and later joined its faculty as a professor of harmony and counterpoint. Liadov's important work in collecting and editing folk songs has been noted. He was an excellent teacher who influenced Stravinsky, Prokofiev and many other modern Russian composers. But the creative side of the man's life was bottled up by curious quirks of personality.

Liadov was fantastically indolent, and in his youth had been expelled from the Conservatory by Rimsky-Korsakov for "incredible laziness". Teaching bored him so that he could scarcely drag himself to his classes; but once before his pupils, he imparted lucidly and with acid wit the wisdom of a remarkably keen mind. Aristocratic and sensitive, Liadov was also pathologically shy. He seldom appeared at public concerts. One of his pupils, Lazare Saminsky, recalls that "Liadov's timid form hiding behind some column at the première of his works, was unique and unforgettable. Of course, he *never* appeared in acknowledgment of plaudits." In 1913, at a milestone in his creative life, the musicians of Petersburg publicly honoured Liadov, but the composer remained away from the celebration.

"An artist scarcely exists," wrote Saminsky, "whose embodied creation is so mercilessly small a coefficient of great hidden gifts." Liadov's total output was only a moderate one, and it appears now that his best works were miniatures—the delightfully picturesque tone poems for orchestra, *Baba Yaga*, *The Enchanted Lake*, and *Kikimora*; the Eight Russian Folk Songs, arranged for orchestra; a group of beautiful children's songs, Opus 14 and 18; and a number of piano pieces (including the once-famous *Music Box*) in which field he was strongly influenced by Chopin.

Sergius Liapunov (1859–1924) attended the Moscow Conservatory where he studied under Tchaikovsky and Taneyev. He was a brilliant pupil, but he disliked the conservative standards of the Moscow school. He went to Petersburg and became a member of the second Balakirev coterie, that which formed around the archnationalist after his five-year retirement and the break in the unity of the original Five. Liapunov's devotion, both as friend and artist, remained firm until Balakirev's death in 1910. Meanwhile, he had held the post of Assistant Director of the Imperial Chapel, and later he taught at the Petersburg Conservatory. His researches in the field of Russian folk music yielded the publication of some 275 songs with piano accompaniment. The First World War and the Russian Revolution seemed to break the thread of Liapunov's creative life. He left the country and made his home in Paris, where he directed a music school for Russian exiles until his death in 1924.

Liapunov remained in spirit a nationalist and a close follower of Balakirev's creed, but like the other members of the second generation he was neither highly creative nor original. He wrote several symphonies, concertos, and tone poems, and many songs and piano pieces, in which mildly nationalistic idioms derived from Balakirev and Glinka were blended with ideas which stemmed from Liszt.

Anton Arensky (1861–1906) reversed, in a sense, the course that had been taken by Liapunov. He studied at the Petersburg Conservatory under Rimsky-Korsakov, but later became a professor of harmony and counterpoint at the Moscow Conservatory. The influence of Tchaikovsky pervaded much of Arensky's music, it being lyric in style and leaning toward eclecticism rather than a strong nationalism. His first opera, *A Dream on the Volga* (1892), was actually based on the same story by Ostrovsky which Tchaikovsky had used for his ill-fated first opera, *The Voyevoda*. Arensky composed in a variety of forms, including three operas, a piano concerto, two symphonies, two string quartets, a piano trio, much church music, and many songs. For the piano he composed nearly a hundred pieces, including three suites for two pianos. The charming Waltz from the Suite No. 1, Op. 15, has a special niche of its own in the restricted literature of music for two pianos; otherwise Arensky's name remains green in modern repertoires largely by virtue of his D minor piano Trio, and his Variations on a Theme of Tchaikovsky (originally a part of his String Quartet in A minor).

When Arensky died in 1906, Rimsky-Korsakov set down in his Chronicle a brief but sombre comment on the career of his former pupil. It appeared that Arensky had "run a dissipated course between wine and card-playing, yet his activity as a composer was most fertile". He had had the good fortune to receive a generous pension which left him free to compose, yet "he began to burn the candle at both ends. Revels, card-playing, health undermined by this mode of living, galloping consumption as the final result". . . . "In his youth Arensky had not escaped entirely from my own influence, later he fell under that of Tchaikovsky. He will be soon forgotten."

Michael Ippolitov-Ivanov (1859–1935) was another pupil of Rimsky-Korsakov and a product of the Petersburg Conservatory. After graduation he spent ten years at Tiflis, in the Caucasus, as director of the School of Music and the Opera. In 1893 he became a professor at the Moscow Conservatory, and a quarter of a century later, after the Revolution, he was made its director. In 1925 he became conductor of the Moscow Opera.

Like Liadov and Liapunov, Ippolitov-Ivanov was classed during his lifetime with the Moscow eclectics. His music appeared to be strongly influenced by Tchaikovsky, yet it was also coloured by the nationalist idiom. Crossed with this was a strain of Orientalism. During his ten years in the Caucasus the composer had steeped himself in Caucasian folk songs, and had made a study of ancient Hebrew melodies. His symphonic suite, *Caucasian Sketches*, was an immediate success on its first performance in Moscow in 1895 and soon earned the composer an international reputation. A minor *Scheherazade*, the piece remains one of the more popular specimens of Russo-Oriental music.

Ippolitov-Ivanov composed six operas, many orchestral works of a picturesque nature (employing variously Russian, Armenian, Turkish, and Oriental idioms), several cantatas and choruses, a few chamber works, and many songs. During the later years of his long life he contributed to the new literature of Soviet music with an opera on a revolutionary subject, *The Last Barricade* (1933–34), and songs and marches glorifying Soviet leaders. One of his last tasks was a completion of Musorgsky's unfinished opera, *The Marriage* (1931).

IV

Sergei Taneyev (1856–1915), one of Russia's greatest music scholars, became a pupil at the Moscow Conservatory at the age of ten, entered Tchaikovsky's class in harmony at thirteen, and Nicholas Rubinstein's piano class at fifteen. At nineteen he appeared as a piano virtuoso (playing no less formidable a work than Brahms' D minor Piano Concerto); he left the Conservatory loaded with honours, and already the composer of a symphony and part of a string quartet. In his mid-twenties Taneyev took Tchaikovsky's place on the faculty of the Moscow Conservatory; and there in the next quarter of a century he became an influential teacher and a scholar of massive erudition.

Taneyev's special field was theoretical counterpoint. He explored the music of Bach, Palestrina, and the old Netherland masters— Okeghem, Josquin des Prés, and Lassus—until he became one of the greatest of theoretical contrapuntists. After twenty years of labour he published his gigantic two-volume treatise, *Imitative Counterpoint in Strict Style*, in which the laws of counterpoint are expounded and brought into focus as a branch of pure mathematics. The mighty work bore an inscription taken from Leonardo da Vinci: "No branch of study can claim to be considered a true science unless it is capable of being demonstrated mathematically." An unfinished sequel on Canon and Fugue appeared after Taneyev's death. This terrifying erudition did not end with music. For diversion the composer relaxed in the study of natural and social science, history, mathematics, and the philosophy of Plato and Spinoza.

It would have been something close to a miracle had a strongly creative impulse been joined with those enormous sinews of learning. As a composer Taneyev has been called "the Russian Brahms", and a small but devoted cult maintains a deep admiration for his music; but not much of it is heard outside Russia. He composed several symphonies, a considerable body of chamber works, and—oddly enough—an opera. This last was *Orestes*, a representation of the Aeschylean tragedy that has been described as Wagnerian in style, although Taneyev hated Wagner's music until, late in life, he perused the score of *Parsifal*. His cantata, *John of Damascus*, is called a "curious hybrid, by Tchaikovsky out of Bach".

Except for the music of Tchaikovsky (his devoted master)

Taneyev seemed hostile to all that had happened after Mozart. His own approach to composition was coldly intellectual. As he himself described it, he first assembled his themes; then he wrote on them a series of contrapuntal exercises—"canons, imitations, etc."—until he had exhausted their polyphonic possibilities. Only then did he begin actual composition.

As a personality, Taneyev was one of the most interesting Russians of his time. Under the fortress of learning lay an odd whimsical strain. Says Gerald Abraham: "Taneyev had a dual nature rather like Lewis Carroll's, half mathematician, half humorist." Among his unpublished works are various parodies, including "Quartets of Government Officials", "humorous choruses, comic fugues and variations, toy symphonies, a mock ballet for Tchaikovsky's birthday with an absurd scenario and music which is an ingenious contrapuntal pot-pourri of themes from Tchaikovsky's works. . . ."

Taneyev was a man of complete intellectual honesty, fantastically honourable and truthful. He is said to have refused payment for the publication of the score of his *Orestes* and some of his string quartets because he deprecated their worth. His personal life was ascetic. He drank no liquor and was apparently a celibate, even though he was a handsome man possessed of great personal magnetism, and attractive to women. The wife of Leo Tolstoy was in love with him for years, but the composer gave no hint that he was even aware of her passion.

Alexander Gretchaninov was born in Moscow in 1864. He died more than ninety-one years later, on January 3, 1956, in New York City. His first important instruction came from Safonov at the Moscow Conservatory, but he moved to the Petersburg Conservatory so that he might study with Rimsky-Korsakov. In the long and productive life that followed, Gretchaninov composed an immense number of works in a wide gamut of the standard forms—operas, oratorios, cantatas, symphonies, chamber works, piano pieces, songs, choruses, and church music. Some of his songs, dramatic and highly romantic, are part of the standard Russian repertoire the world over. His first opera, *Dobrynya Nikititch*, had its première in 1903, in Moscow. Individual numbers from the piece remained popular in Russia for years, and the whole opera was revived and refurbished in recent times by the Soviets. A second opera, *Sister Beatrice*, after Maeterlinck, had less success (1912). Outside of Russia Gretchaninov is probably most admired for his choral works. He has been called "a master of religious choral writing". In general style his music stems noticeably from that of the Five. His serious scholarship is evident in his use of polpyhonic effects taken directly from Russian folk music, rather than from the polyphony of the West.

Gretchaninov left Russia in 1922 and resided for some time in Paris. From there he migrated to America, finally becoming an American citizen. In the new land he lived to be a kind of exiled patriarch of Russian music, practising his art in spite of venerable age. When well past eighty he finished an opera based on Gogol's *The Marriage*, part of which was performed at Tanglewood, Massachusetts, in 1948.

Alexander Glazunov (1865–1936) was the most prolific of the second generation of Russian composers, and for a time the most eminent. As a youngster in his teens he became Rimsky-Korsakov's pupil, so precocious and talented that Balakirev called him "the little Glinka". He wrote his first symphony at the age of sixteen, and when played under Balakirev's direction at a concert of the Free Music School it scored a triumph. From this moment Glazunov continued to win success and recognition both in Russia and abroad, his work becoming known in Western Europe almost as soon as did Borodin's and Rimsky-Korsakov's. Before he was twenty he had written two string quartets and half-a-dozen orchestral works, including his two overtures on Greek themes, and his tone poem, *Stenka Razin*. In 1899 the composer was appointed professor of instrumentation at the Petersburg Conservatory, and in 1905 he became its director.

Glazunov was the son of a successful book publisher, and he inherited both wealth and culture. His early career was uneventful; at first his music seemed to make its own way in the world without antagonism. He composed steadily and abundantly, and chiefly in the instrumental forms—eight symphonies, several concertos, four quartets and a quintet for strings, a number of orchestral tone poems.

After he had reached the age of forty the abundant stream of Glazunov's creative efforts stopped flowing. He composed comparatively little and then the coming of the First World War and the Revolution seemed to destroy his whole artistic life. H. G. Wells, who saw him in Petersburg in 1920, described the composer as a man once florid . . . "but now he is pallid and very much fallen away, so that his clothes hang loosely on him". He feared that he could compose no more because his stock of music paper was almost exhausted

PETER ILYCH TCHAIKOVSKY

ALEXANDER SCRIABIN
from a drawing by Sterl

and could not be replenished. Glazunov left Russia in 1928. He visited America the next year, and then returned to Paris where he remained until his death in 1936.

Glazunov was a musician of immense talent whose abilities astonished his contemporaries. In spite of expert workmanship, however, his music now sounds stereotyped, oscillating between a mild Russian nationalism, Lisztian romanticism, and a pale classicism. In his programme music Glazunov tried his hand at various idioms—Russian, Oriental, Greek, Finnish, old dance forms, and ecclesiastical modes; in his symphonies and string quartets he usually remained close to the standards of German classicism. Glazunov's powers of melodic invention were fluent but seldom distinguished; nor did he ever evolve a personal style. His best known work outside Russia remains the violin concerto, a sweetly melodious piece which shows off the violin tone beautifully, but hardly ever travels beyond the horizon of Mendelssohn. It remains in the old-fashioned romantic tradition, with only faint traces of its Russian origin.

V

Glazunov's music illustrates with reasonable accuracy what had happened to the entire second generation of Russian composers. Neither as a group nor individually were they genuinely creative. Instead they worked chiefly with formulas, which they evolved by imitating either the nationalist works of their great predecessors or the standard procedures of the West. The decline of the Russian nationalist impulse is, of course, most marked; but this was by no means restricted to the field of music. It was part of a movement that was affecting the whole intellectual life of Russia, and was a broad retreat from the upsurge of liberal-nationalism of the eighteen-sixties. The pendulum had swung sharply, and nationalism and realism in art, liberalism in politics, were losing ground. With the close of the eighteen-eighties Russia's literary giants, Turgenev and Dostoevsky, were dead; Tolstoy's greatest work had been done. In Russian music too we sense that a resplendent epoch had come to an end.

What remains of the second generation, besides their record of great pedagogy, is the memory of their picturesque personalities. All these men, if they did not inherit the creative spark of their predecessors, were yet loaded with unusual gifts. We are still struck by their enormous energies and their appetites, both for learning and for more earthly pleasures. All through this half century the pattern repeats itself: in one way or another these Russian musicians seem to have been cut from an outsize mould. They worked, studied, composed, practised, memorized in gargantuan measure.

The pattern began with Anton Rubinstein whose prowess at the piano was both intellectually and physically prodigious, as his famous series of historical recitals still bears witness. Rimsky-Korsakov had enormous capacities for work and concentration, while Taneyev's scholarship would have awed a mediaeval monastic. Borodin lived two entirely separate careers, and so did Cui. Glazunov, Ippolitov-Ivanov, and Gretchaninov composed floods of music, the last continuing undaunted past his eightieth year. Even when the energies of these men ran recklessly off the track and into sheer dissipation the results were spectacular: Tchaikovsky, Nicholas Rubinstein, Arensky, and Glazunov were Homeric drinkers, surpassed only by the unfortunate Musorgsky.

CHAPTER XI

SCRIABIN

I

THE history of music reveals no other personality, no phenomenon quite like Alexander Scriabin. He was a visionary who
deserted the world of normal experience for an occult world of the
spirit. Any attempt to probe the mind of such a man becomes
a fruitless task, for like many a religious fanatic Scriabin was so
dazzled by his divine hallucinations that he lost touch with reality.
He ceased to think and to act like normal men because his spiritual
aspirations were accompanied by an intense, an almost incredible
sense of joy. In this experience his art—music—played the dominating part, becoming the means of entry into the delights of his mystical
domain.

For a parallel to the case of Scriabin we must go to other fields
of art, perhaps to William Blake. Both men became absorbed in
a world of the spirit, and to both the mundane manifestation of this
mystical cosmos was art. But here the parallel must end. Scriabin
could not compare with Blake in intelligence, in prescience, or in his
ability to capture and to symbolize in his art his spiritual adventures.
Scriabin's case was tragic. He was an artist of rare talent; his tastes
were fine and his aspirations high; often he was boldly original.
Nevertheless, the spiritual significance which the composer attached
to his art is now all but meaningless. In the last years of his life many
who disliked his music and disbelieved in his mysticism decided that
he was insane. But madness, as Thomas Craven remarked, "is too
cheap an indictment to fling at the opaque side of genius".

Alexander Scriabin was born in Moscow on Christmas Day,
1871 O.S. (January 6, 1872). His family were intellectual, cultured,
and exceptionally musical. His father was a student of law and
Oriental languages; his mother was a concert pianist, a pupil of
Leschetizky at the Petersburg Conservatory. Only a year after the
child's birth his mother died of tuberculosis. His father entered the
consular service, which took him off to Turkey, Crete, and various
Near Eastern posts. The child remained in Moscow under the care

of his grandmother and a maiden aunt. The two women adored, pampered and sheltered him, thus helping to form certain eccentricities which later appeared in the character of the man. He became sensitive to the point of effeminacy, a hypochondriac, and an extreme egocentric.

Scriabin's early life resembled Glinka's, except that he was far more fortunate in his music education. When he began to show a precocious musical talent there awaited in Moscow music teachers of the first calibre. When he was ten years old he was taking piano instruction from N. S. Zverev, who taught at the Moscow Conservatory; at fourteen he began studying theory with Taneyev. One of young Scriabin's fellow pupils under Zverev was Sergei Rachmaninov, with whom he formed a life-long friendship. In 1888, when he was sixteen, Scriabin was enrolled in the Moscow Conservatory. He studied piano with Vassily Safonov (who later became an eminent conductor, leading the New York Philharmonic Society from 1906–09), counterpoint with Teneyev and fugue and composition with Arensky.

Scriabin displayed immense talent as a pianist, but was an indifferent student of theory. Arensky called him a "scatterbrain". Nevertheless, when he graduated from the Conservatory at the age of twenty he had already written a number of creditable works for the piano—preludes, impromptus, nocturnes and mazurkas—which were to be published in his Opp. 3, 5, 7, and 11. Scriabin's career as a pianist had almost ended in a disaster like that which overtook Robert Schumann. He became intensely jealous of the technique of Josef Lhevinne, his fellow student at the Conservatory, and by over-practising Balakirev's *Islamey* and Liszt's *Don Juan* Fantasia he badly lamed his right hand. While giving that hand a long period of rest he concentrated on the technique of the left, which is said to account for the unusually elaborate and difficult left-hand parts in his later piano works.

In 1894 Scriabin gave a piano recital in Petersburg, during which he played some of his own compositions. It was his good fortune to be heard by Belaiev, the wealthy publisher and music patron, who offered to publish the young man's works. More than that, he arranged the next year for a concert tour of Russia and Western Europe, with Belaiev himself accompanying the composer-pianist on his first travels abroad.

They were an odd pair: Belaiev, a great bear of a man, who sat upon the stage as his protégé performed; and Scriabin, small, delicate, with a kind of sickly fragility that must have reminded Paris audiences of Chopin. Wrote one French critic: "an exquisite nature equally great as composer and pianist, an enlightened philosopher, all nerve and holy flame". Chopinesque too was his music, an echo of his adoration of the great Pole.

In Russia Scriabin was welcomed into the Belaiev circle in Petersburg, but his personality was a problem. Some thought him supercilious and conceited. Rimsky-Korsakov noted in his Chronicle ". . . that star of first magnitude, newly risen in Moscow, the somewhat warped, posing, and self-opinionated A. N. Scriabin".

In 1897 the composer married Vera Ivanovna Isakovich, a graduate of the Moscow Conservatory and a brilliant pianist. The mercurial Scriabin was at times happy and exhilarated, or again depressed by neurasthenia; but meanwhile composition had proceeded with a flood of short piano works, his Piano Concerto, and his Third Sonata. It became necessary for the composer to find himself a job, so he accepted a professorship of piano at the Moscow Conservatory. Scriabin was an indifferent teacher, and after five troubled years at the Conservatory he resigned.

Meanwhile, the composer's mind and art were both in a period of turmoil. He began to desert Chopinism for the more grandiose style of Liszt. In 1900 he wrote his First Symphony, in E minor (Op. 26), a work in six movements with a choral finale. His Second Symphony, in C minor (Op. 29), appeared in 1903, a five-movement work in which the influence of Wagner makes its appearance. Thereafter, almost everything that Scriabin wrote was saturated with the potent Wagnerian chemical. But there were other outside influences which were carrying his susceptible, vibrating mind off into realms of mystical philosophy.

A detailed account of Scriabin's adventures in mysticism would be more pertinent to a study of abnormal psychology than to the present chronicle; nevertheless, certain events must be noted because of their interlocking action upon the man's art. Sometime near the turn of the century the composer became deeply enamoured of the teachings and writings of Prince S. N. Trubetskoy, a philosopher, mystic, and believer in the oneness of God and love. Trubetskoy's rather pallid concepts were churned in Scriabin's mind with his studies of Wagner, where he had imbibed the theory that music might not be solely an art form but an ethical and regenerating force for mankind. From Wagner he ascended to Nietzsche and *Also sprach Zarathustra*, and for several years the dazzling vision of the *Übermensch* held him. Scriabin, it appears, was following a course roughly parallel to that of a group of so-called "symbolists" who were then agitating the waters of Russian literature. In revolt against the age of realism, they had taken their leads from Baudelaire, Maeterlinck, and Nietzsche; decadent romantics, they drenched their poetic thought in philosophy, mysticism, and the occult.

Scriabin arrived at the principle that art was to be the "transformer of life". Art which takes for its materials the pain and ugliness of the world, the whole vast tragedy of man, and transmutes it into beauty, was to be the means of turning life itself into a "Kingdom of God on earth". The composer even conceived a super-artist, a messiah, who was to teach and redeem mankind through a vast synthesis of the arts; and in that ceremonial Scriabin himself became God. One of the first manifestations of this state of mind was his First Symphony, whose closing chorus with the composer's own words was a "Hymn to Art", embodying the idea of "art the transformer".

II

With his resignation from the Moscow Conservatory in 1903 Scriabin was seized with a desire to live in Switzerland. To earn the necessary money he composed in furious haste about thirty-five works for the piano, including the Fourth Sonata. This was the group of pieces between Op. 30 and Op. 42. At the same time he was composing his Third Symphony, known as *The Divine Poem*. With his wife and four children he made the trip to Switzerland and established a home on the shores of Lake Geneva. There the composer finished his *Divine Poem*; there he began preaching his new gospel of art to groups of wondering people (including a sympathetic fisherman) who apparently confused his doctrines with Socialism; and there too his marriage came to an unhappy end. Scriabin had already formed an attachment for a young Russian girl, Tatiana Fedorovna Schlözer, who had followed him to Switzerland. He explained the situation to his wife, Vera, whose last act of devotion was to copy out for him the entire score of *The Divine Poem*. Then the composer took himself off to France, again followed by Tatiana.

In the spring of 1905 *The Divine Poem* had its première per-formance in Paris, under Arthur Nikisch. The French city was at that time pregnant with artistic revolutionaries of varied species, and full of intellectual controversy; in another year the *fauves*, or "wild beasts", would produce their new modernist painting, to be followed by the Cubists, the Futurists, and the Expressionists. In this atmo-sphere of creative ferment *The Divine Poem* announced to the Western world the arrival of a new Russian music personality, one who appeared to be bold, vigorous, and properly revolutionary. It was during this period in Paris that Scriabin was introduced to the doctrines of theosophy which for a time deeply coloured his mystical thought.

After the premiere of *The Divine Poem* Scriabin and his mistress went to Italy, and in a charming little villa near Genoa they spent almost a year. There a daughter was born to Tatiana. The composer sat for hours in a sunlit garden surrounded by orange trees, pines and cacti, and overlooking the sea; he read *Das Kapital* by Karl Marx, planned his next large orchestral work, *The Poem of Ecstasy*, but otherwise composed very little. Financial troubles still pursued him, until he received a sudden offer for a visit to America. The invitation was from Modest Altschuler, who had recently formed the Russian Symphony Society in New York.

The American trip was a disaster for Scriabin. He arrived in New York late in November, 1906, and after Altschuler had given two successful concerts in Carnegie Hall, including the first American performance of *The Divine Poem*, Scriabin appeared in recitals in New York, Chicago, and Detroit. The conductor of the New York Philharmonic Society at that time was Safonov, Scriabin's old friend and instructor at the Moscow Conservatory. Scriabin's treat-ment of his wife, Vera, had a chilling effect on Safonov, who knew of the indignation felt in Russia at the composer's actions. Tatiana arrived in New York in January, 1907, to join Scriabin, and a few weeks later a storm broke.

Not long before the Russian novelist Maxim Gorky had visited America and the discovery that he was travelling with a woman not his wife had created a scandal which forced him out of the country. The episode was still vivid in the public consciousness when gossip began to circulate about Scriabin and Tatiana. At three o'clock one morning Altschuler appeared at their hotel to warn them that "serious unpleasantness" threatened the very next day. Within five hours the pair had packed and fled on a steamer bound for

Europe.[1] When they arrived in France Scriabin had left only thirty francs.

In Paris the composer's fortunes rose. Serge Diaghilev was giving the first of his historic concerts of Russian music, and he included two works by Scriabin—the Piano Concerto played by Josef Hofmann, and *The Divine Poem*, conducted by Nikisch. At a private gathering for a group of distinguished Russian musicians, including Rimsky-Korsakov, Scriabin expounded the meaning of his new *Poem of Ecstasy* and played excerpts at the piano. The older composer was left with "an impression of unhealthy eroticism", and the conviction that Scriabin was "half out of his mind already". Scriabin and Tatiana returned to Switzerland where he finished *The Poem of Ecstasy*. Shooting like a spark from the same creative furnace came the Fifth Sonata, supposedly composed in three or four days. Accompanying the *Poem of Ecstasy* was a long poem written by Scriabin in Russian. Bathed in a fog of allusion and symbolism, the poesy seemed to make plain not the substance of the music so much as the fact that the composer had ascended to a new and more frightening plane of mystical joy.

III

When Scriabin returned to Moscow early in 1909 after nearly five years' absence he found the music circles of Russia in a hurricane of controversy over himself and his music. At concerts devoted to his works there were "unrestrained scenes of agitation and enthusiasm". Meanwhile, the composer had gained a valuable friend in Serge Koussevitzky, who was then beginning his career as conductor and publisher of new Russian music. In the summer of 1910 the conductor made the first of his famous tours of the Volga. With a chartered steamer and a symphony orchestra, he gave concerts in towns and cities along the river. Scriabin accompanied the band as featured soloist in his own Piano Concerto.

---

[1] Nicholas Slonimsky, the Russian-American composer and musicologist, made an investigation at the Immigration Bureau in Washington which "failed to discover any proposed action of the authorities against the Scriabins, although technically they could be prosecuted for moral turpitude".

Scriabin himself was apparently not prejudiced against America by his experience. He wrote:

"I brought back with me an excellent impression of America. In my judgement, the customary opinions about that country are frequently immature and prejudiced. The Americans are not at all dull and artistically untalented, as is generally believed."

In March, 1911, in Moscow, Koussevitzky conducted the première of *Prometheus: The Poem of Fire*, Scriabin's last large work for orchestra. The performance was a disappointment. The composer's original score called for a colour-keyboard, which would project a correlated scheme of coloured lights to accompany the music. This feature had to be omitted for reasons that are not clear in the reports of the event; either the colour mechanism failed, or it did not yet exist outside the composer's imagination.

The appearance of the Fifth Sonata (1911) and the Sixth (1912) announced Scriabin's excursions into unexplored music domains, in particular the jungles of advanced harmony—the copious use of dissonance, chords built on superimposed fourths instead of thirds, new and arbitrarily constructed scales, the abandoning of key signatures and clearly defined tonalities, and finally the invention of the so-called "Mystic Chord". Over these innovations there raged a war of conflicting opinion all through Russian music circles and in Western Europe. But if the composer's music was causing disquiet to the conservative party, the reports of his mental state were nothing less than alarming. It was widely rumoured that he was insane.

For several years there had been growing in Scriabin's mind a plan of such cosmic vastness that he could find no word or title for its expression beyond simply, the "Mystery". What he foresaw was nothing less than the end of the world and the whole human race. From this cataclysm would arise a new race of men joined in mystical love to an all-pervading Spirit. The "embodiment of the world spirit" on earth Scriabin believed to be himself. The supreme moment of world doom would be signalled by a performance of his "Mystery". This was to be a grandiose ceremony blending music, dancing, poetry, colours, and scents; the celebrants would foregather in a temple in India, hemispherical in shape and reflected in the waters of a lake to form a perfect sphere. At the moment of supreme ecstasy the very walls of the universe would collapse and the souls of men would join at last with the Spirit.

The idea of the "Mystery" occupied Scriabin's mind for at least a decade, and in the closing years of his life it absorbed him utterly. Strangely enough, he set down no note of its music. As for the Indian temple (clearly Wagner's Bayreuth metamorphosed by mysticism) it is said that Scriabin did go so far as to make inquiries during a London visit about fares to India, and he bought himself a sun-helmet; otherwise the project made no visible progress.

During this London visit of 1914 *Prometheus* was performed, minus the colour organ. Sir Osbert Sitwell, who was present, describes in his resplendent memoirs the appearance of the composer :

> "To look at, he resembled a German professor, of the thin type, grey, careworn, fatigued by calculations. He received with equanimity the boos that greeted his work at the end, unmoved as his nephew, Monsieur Molotov, shows himself to be at the reception by foreign powers of his aggressive policy."

This same year, having postponed the composition of the "Mystery" because the time was not yet quite ripe, the composer wrote out an elaborate prose sketch for a "Preliminary Action", that is, an experiment or rehearsal for the divine event itself. This was to be a synthesis of various arts performed by some two thousand celebrants, possibly in London. Meanwhile Scriabin had composed his Eighth, Ninth and Tenth Sonatas, and various short piano pieces, all replete with advanced harmonies based on synthetic chords and other esoteric technical appurtenances, and supposedly full of occult allusion.

No part of the "Mystery" itself ever saw the light of creation. The composer had once said : "I shall not die. I shall suffocate in ecstasy after the 'Mystery' ". It was not an ecstasy that killed him, but a sudden and excruciatingly painful illness. A carbuncle developed on his upper lip ; blood poisoning spread quickly through his body, and on April 27, 1915, after hardly more than a week of illness, Scriabin died.

IV

After an exposure to the heat of Scriabin's own pronouncements about his music and to some of the claims that were made for it by his disciples, an attempt at sober evaluation becomes a chilling experience. The point should be made at once, however, that there is a limit to which deflation should go. Between the strange man's megalomaniacal estimates of his own works as mystico-religious art creations, and the appraisal put upon them today by honest critical opinion, lies a gap so vast as to seem either tragic or ludicrous, as the individual cares to consider it. But Scriabin's music cannot be written off as either tragically inadequate or a dull joke. It contains

SCRIABIN 219

too much of beauty, originality, style, and evocative power. Moreover, it has historical significance. That significance is of a three-fold
nature : in the development of Russian music, in the special field of
piano music, and in the large evolutionary movement that has been
taking place in the whole art of Western music with the slow decline
of nineteenth-century romanticism.

So far as Russian music is concerned Scriabin often appears to
be hardly a Russian composer at all, so strongly is his music turned
away from nationalism and toward the West. He had little affinity
for the nationalist movement, ignored almost totally the use of folk
song, and was at the opposite pole aesthetically from the concept of
realism in art. Scriabin sprang directly from the Western romantics
—Chopin, Liszt, Wagner, and Schumann. He later fell into the
company of the late romantics—Debussy, Richard Strauss, and
Mahler—in whose era the entire great movement came at last to
over-ripeness and decay. In his aesthetic Scriabin remained a
romantic to the day of his death ; but all through his mature years
he was also a revolutionary who contributed to the enormous
activity which was going on in the field of harmony and from which
would be born the technique of the new music of today. Thus, in
effect, his music personality was split. Had he lived longer he might
have resolved these differences and produced a more unified art with
more significance for the present era ; but that realization was denied
him.

In still another way Scriabin's art suffered from the pull of
opposing forces. Much of his best work was done in the smaller
forms. He had the delicate senses, the refined tastes, and the technical
mannerisms of a miniaturist, as a host of his smaller piano pieces
will testify. Yet the magnetic force of Wagner (coupled with the
grandiose concepts of his mystical philosophy) drew him into mag-
niloquence typical of German romanticism in its decline.

The restricted nature of this composer's creative thought is
clearly shown in the catalogue of his works. The great majority are
written for the piano where he was completely at home. The comparatively few works for orchestra were once regarded with awe, but
have long since shrunk. He composed no opera, almost nothing for
the voice, in fact,[1] and no chamber music.

It is usually the custom to fasten upon Scriabin's early piano

---

[1] A song dating from 1894 and published posthumously was composed to
Scriabin's own words and bears the title : "I wish I could spend a moment in your
soul as a beautiful dream."

music the label "imitation Chopin", and then dismiss it. Actually it proves quite plainly that this composer was remarkably precocious and that few artists have found in their youth a style so assured and even mature. The resemblances to Chopin's music are obvious. Outwardly the pianistic apparatus is all there, even down to the abstract titles—preludes, etudes, nocturnes, impromptus, mazurkas. That the Scriabin pieces are not first-rate Chopin goes without saying. The remarkable thing is that these dozens of short works were composed between his seventeenth and twenty-fifth years, yet hardly one could be called amateurish. Practically all are well made, and never is there a lack of taste. Scriabin, to his credit, produced no "salon" music of the type that Tchaikovsky and most of the second generation of Russian composers turned out with such easy facility. When hardly out of adolescence Scriabin had found and was using with remarkable sureness a singularly beautiful piano style.

Not many pianists outside Russia play Scriabin's music today; it went out of fashion almost as quickly as it came in. But many of these early short essays in the Chopin idiom could be a welcome relief from the overplaying of the standard favourites. Even such early works as the Etudes of Opus 8, and the Preludes of Opp. 11, 13, 15, 16, 17—all written before Scriabin was twenty-five—contain individual numbers of genuine beauty and distinction. The composer displays, first of all, his intuitive knowledge of piano sonorities. He is playing with the sheer beauty of piano sound, and the infinity of technical means which may be used for its exploitation. His musical ideas come to him in great profusion, both thematic and accompaniment schemes and figurations. Invariably, they are small ideas; after a few dozen measures their possibilities seem to be exhausted.

Any comparison with their Chopin prototypes reveals at once the weaknesses of Scriabin's imitations. There is a certain dryness to his melodic ideas; he seldom achieves a melodic line with the curve of pure lyric beauty. Nor can he approach the incredible range of the Polish master's moods and sentiments, which run (in Paul Henry Lang's words) "from light, almost ethereal melancholy to scintillating fireworks and hymnic exultations". The variety, the subtlety of Chopin's moods were among the most extraordinary phenomena in the growth of romantic music, but nothing so expressively pregnant is found in Scriabin's early Chopin imitations.

V

Scriabin's Fourth Sonata (Op. 30), composed in 1903, is one of those convenient works which help musicologists to establish "periods" in the life of a composer. With this unusual (and often beautiful) sonata the influence of Chopin has receded into the distance and the apparition of Wagner comes like a cloud over Scriabin's horizon. For the rest of his creative life his interest was to be centred in the development of new harmonies and harmonic systems.

The Fourth Sonata, though touched with originality as a piano work, is full of Wagnerian chromaticism, richness of key contrasts, and even melodic lines remindful of phrases from *Tristan and Isolde*. Wagnerian too are its erotic moods and its climaxes of soaring ecstasy. Through many of the piano works which followed directly after this sonata we find the same striving toward harmonic innovation, unusual modulations, and fluctuating tonalities in the manner of Wagner : e.g. in the Preludes Nos. 1 and 4 in Opus 51, the latter a curious echo of the "Wanderer" motif in *The Ring of the Nibelung* ; and the Prelude No. 2 in Opus 35, with its harmonies and melodic lines drawn from *Tristan and Isolde*.

Scriabin never fully escaped the Wagnerian influence, but after the Fourth Sonata his excursions into new harmonic territory often carried him considerably outside the Wagnerian orbit. Tonalities, which had heretofore been fairly well defined in his music, began to waver and loose their moorings ; dissonance appears in copious measure. Scriabin began to use chords of the ninth, eleventh, and thirteenth, often with intervals altered to form new and exotic scales. As early as the Prelude Opus 37, No. 2, there appears a chord built not upon customary thirds but upon superimposed fourths.

The climax of the Wagnerian influence on Scriabin appears in his large orchestral work, *The Poem of Ecstasy*. This piece is full of romantic sighings and heavings which became magnified in the process of music development into voluptuous ecstasies of sound, a procedure typical of late nineteenth-century attempts to outdo the Wagnerian aphrodisiacs. It makes copious use of mystical mood contrasts—between darkly mysterious or agitated cosmic rumblings, and the intoxicating joys of some unnamed triumph of the soul. Once a marvel of sensual excitement, of sheer exhibitionism in music, *The Poem of Ecstasy* seems now only an old volcano, smoking feebly.

The companion piece, the Fifth Sonata, is a more original work from which emerges Scriabin's later and most distinctive piano style. Like the four sonatas which were to follow, the piece is in one movement, but with wild fluctuations of tempo and mood. At one moment the piano works itself into paroxysms of exultation or fury, and then sinks as quickly into voluptuous languor. Scriabin made these convulsive, schizophrenic alternations his trade-mark. Remarkable too are the rhythmic complications of the piece, which, joined to radical harmonies, gave the sonata a shocking ultra-modernity in the year 1907.

Continuing his search for new harmonies Scriabin evolved what he termed a "mystic chord", which was destined to enjoy a considerable though short-lived notoriety in the music chronicles of the time. The chord was based on a series of intervals of the fourth, as follows: C, F sharp, B flat, E, A, D. From this succession of notes Scriabin built the entire score of his last orchestral work, *Prometheus : The Poem of Fire*. This work, composed in 1909–10, had various other unusual features. The symbolic basis of the score is a mystical variant of the ancient Prometheus myth which would require theosophical exegesis beyond the scope of the present volume. Complex, too, and large is the apparatus demanded for performance of the score—an enormous orchestra, including solo piano and organ; a chorus of mixed voices (singing notes without words); and finally, the instrument or machine known as the colour organ for which Scriabin composed a continuous "part" on the top staff of his score.

Before laughing off Scriabin's attempt to create a "dual symphony of sound and colour" as a ludicrous failure, we might remember that in the past the art of music has been joined to other arts with singular success. It was wedded with the drama to form opera, and with the dance to form the ballet. Scriabin's aim in *Prometheus* was to unite music with a dynamic form of elementary painting. It failed not only because the composer's own concept was vague and even crude, but because the machine itself, intended to project coloured lights upon a large surface, was hopelessly rudimentary. But it is by no means certain that in *Prometheus* Scriabin did not anticipate some future art form.

The musical style of *Prometheus* is the most original of all Scriabin's orchestral works. Wagnerian chromaticism no longer dominates the harmony; instead, the use of the mystic chord with its intervals of the fourth creates a new tonal hue with a strong resemblance to whole tone harmony. The mystic chord, when arranged to form a scale (C, D, E, F sharp, A, B flat), differs from the whole tone scale only in the fifth step—an A natural instead of G sharp. The chord also produces, like the protracted use of whole tones, a sense of monotony. Aside from this harmonic innovation the music of *Prometheus* offers little that is genuinely new. Its general plan is again the familiar contrast of romantic moods, ending in the expected triumph of light over darkness.

With his Sixth Sonata (composed after *Prometheus*) Scriabin abandoned key signatures entirely. He continued his use of synthetic chords based on intervals of the fourth, with the result that in practically all his later music the sense of tonality is either vague or lost. Familiar landmarks like the tonic-dominant relationship, and the contrast of major and minor modes also disappear. In employing his synthetic chords the composer was sometimes content with a single combination of notes for an entire piece; but more often he used two combinations for variety, with the first subject based on one group of tones and a second subject on another.

Regarding the Eighth Sonata, Katherine Ruth Heyman, one of the most gifted interpreters of Scriabin's music, wrote:

> "In Russia there has been since ancient times a sect called *Khlisti*, and they have invocational chants, series of notes that represent the elements. . . . Now whether Scriabin drew the motives that he used in his Eighth Sonata from the Russian sect *Khlisti*, or from other shrines in which they had been conserved, I have no means of knowing; but there are just five short motifs used as the basis of his Eighth Sonata, and some of them are familiar as nature motifs taught me by an initiate in London. . . ."

These five short motifs were the runes, apparently, of the five elements.

All the later works of Scriabin were wrapped in a fog of mysticism, and contemporary disciples found in them "terror, forebodings", and the "demoniacal howls" of dissonance; or a "Miltonic struggle between forces of good and evil. . . ." The Ninth Sonata was described as a veritable "Black Mass", a "Diabolical nightmare". From these satanic despairs Scriabin was happily able to extricate himself with the more "radiant" Tenth Sonata, whose trillings and flutterings still hold an odd fascination.

VI

More than any others of his mature works, the sonatas, beginning with the Fourth, display the finest things in Scriabin's music, as well as those elements which served most to weaken it. They show the warring factions of his art—the new and the old, the original and the reactionary. As examples of harmonic daring they are often engrossing. They place this composer among the real adventurers of his time, whose courage and integrity still deserve respect. It required no mean spirit to compose works of sonata proportions in an harmonic idiom so uncompromisingly "modern" and strange. We see today that Scriabin's harmonies (as they evolved after the Sixth Sonata) were less subtle than Debussy's, and comparatively lacking in variety, colour and evocative power ; they were less dogmatically severe than Schönberg's. Nevertheless, Scriabin stood with these men in their resolute march away from the old Wagnerian and pre-Wagnerian harmony and into the new fields of dissonance.

High in originality, too, is some of Scriabin's thematic material— the germinal ideas which carry his melodic thought. Writes Aaron Copland : "These are often magical in their effect—the best examples I know of 'pure' inspiration." This was another phase of Scriabin's music which began to take on a markedly modern sound, especially those themes of sharp contour, made up of leaping intervals that presage the angularity, the metallic ring of the new anti-romantic music. Rhythmic complication is still another mark of originality and modernity. In the last sonatas there is a continual shifting of accents and all manner of time values sounding against each other.

Emerging from these later works of Scriabin is a new and distinctive piano style. The composer, who had begun by working almost entirely in the pianistic idiom of Chopin (and occasionally in that of Liszt and Schumann), has at last invented a style that deserts the old nineteenth-century models. He opens up new means of technical display and puts new demands upon the pianist. The copious use of chords built upon fourths requires a new type of digital skill, while the rhythmic and chordal complexities demand a special degree of concentration. The dynamic range is enormous.

On the other side of the ledger we find those forces which drew Scriabin with irresistible attraction toward the past. The first was his complete satisfaction with the conventional forms. Although he

SERGE RACHMANINOV
The composer-pianist photographed during one of his last concert tours.
He wears evening clothes and a fur coat with his hands protected by
heavy gloves and an electric heating pad

AT THE HOME OF RIMSKY-KORSAKOV

Left to right: Igor Stravinsky, Rimsky-Korsakov; his daughter Nadya, with her husband, Maximilian Steinberg, and Mme Stravinsky

Sovfoto

came to write in his maturity in a tonal, harmonic, and rhythmic language that was startlingly new to music, the general construction of his pieces remained old-fashioned. Again, Aaron Copland: "The ten piano sonatas . . . present the incredible spectacle of musical ideas of genius being strait-jacketed in the old classical sonata form." Even the most "advanced" of these works remain in the familiar exposition-development-recapitulation matrix, just as the four-measure phrase remained the composer's chief building block. Scriabin never realized that his revolutionary themes based on insurgent harmonies deserved new forms of their own.

Even in his harmonies, which first gave his music its most original colour, Scriabin displayed a lack of truly creative power. Too often the progress of his harmonic thought is hardly more than a mathematical formula with one of his synthetic chords as the root. The result is as coldly calculated as some of Rimsky-Korsakov's harmonic series, and as lacking in growth, expressiveness, and evocative power. We miss the prevailing richness of harmonic invention which characterizes the music of Debussy and Wagner.

VII

In the history of Russian music Scriabin holds an important place, for with his contemporary, Sergei Rachmaninov, he gave Russia its first extensive literature of piano music. It is true that Scriabin is an anomaly as a Russian composer. He represents an extreme even for the Moscow group, being so completely Western that often all traces of his Russian origin are lost. Nevertheless, even though his star set rapidly in the music horizons of the West it has remained burning, and brightly, in Russia. His music moved powerfully a new generation of Russian composers, and we find it colouring the works of men like Gliere, Miaskovsky, and the youthful Stravinsky. It became a potent element in the earlier works of Serge Prokofiev and Dmitri Shostakovich. Today in Russia Scriabin is a classic, much performed and greatly revered. The non-Russian character of his work seems not to have outraged the nationalist ideology of the Soviet authorities.

Scriabin has also a significant place historically in the music of the West, where he was a key figure in the decline of romanticism. His music offers a perfect study in embryo of what happens when a romantic art declines and moves toward a classic art. As the romantic epoch reaches its apogee the artist works with ever-increasing licence to individuality of expression; the old technical restraints of the former classic epoch recede farther and farther into disuse. The point is reached where the artist may do, technically, almost anything that his own aesthetic judgements pronounce valid. But it is precisely at this point that the urge toward law and order which lies at the heart of all creative art begins to assert itself. The cycle moves, or the pendulum swings, toward the establishment of a new legal system which will be the basis of a newly-forming classic art. Thus, in the grand cycle, the romantic artist breaks rules and forms; the classic artist makes them.

Scriabin's place at the moment of transition between the two epochs is shown most clearly in his attempt to create a new harmonic system. His urge at first was to move beyond the horizon of Wagner into new fields of dissonance, abolishing the tyranny of key centres, the old major and minor modes, and the construction of chords based on thirds. But even as he shattered the old matrices he found it necessary to invent new ones to take their place, e.g. his pieces based on synthetic chords made up of intervals of the fourth, with procedure as rigidly prescribed as in a mathematical formula.

Thus Scriabin had a close affinity with Arnold Schönberg, who created the Viennese twelve-tone school. Although Scriabin did not carry his experiments as far, his experience often paralleled that of his Austrian contemporary. Both men, seeking ways of escape from the old fetters of technical practice, ended up by devising new systems. Moreover, there is a similar core of romantic sentiment, a nostalgic yearning for the past, in the works of both artists. The music of the Viennese twelve-tone school (Schönberg, Berg, Webern) is often drenched in the sentimental longing, the brooding introspections, and agonized passions of the nineteenth century, even though it is rigidly contained in the technical system of a new classicism.

CHAPTER XII

RACHMANINOV

I

FOR a study of contrasts in the field of human personality, there could be few richer subjects than Alexander Scriabin and Sergei Rachmaninov. The lives of these two artists, their works, their careers, and their temperaments present such astonishing differences that it is now almost impossible to realize that they came from the same music brood. They were born but a few years apart in roughly the same stratum of Russian society, they were fellow students and friends at the Moscow Conservatory, and they embarked on careers as piano virtuosi and composers. But from that point they moved in opposite directions. Scriabin's rise and fall were sensational; within a few brief years he was a burned-out rocket. Rachmaninov's progress was slow, careful, and steady, until at last he came to be one of the most eminent composers of his time, and finally an elder statesman of Russian music.

Compared with his friend, Rachmaninov seems like a practical and balanced man to whom Scriabin's mystical flights were sheer insanity. Rachmaninov had an acute sense of his own limitations, always proceeding cautiously, whether as a composer, conductor, or pianist. Thus he remained always a conservative. During his lifetime the entire art of music moved through an astonishing metamorphosis. In the year of his birth Wagner was completing *Die Götterdämmerung*, and when he died Stravinsky was approaching his Symphony in Three Movements. Of the aesthetic light years which lay between these works one could find no hint in Rachmaninov's music. From first to last it remained in the nineteenth-century romantic tradition. It remained, too, a typical product of a conservative Russian eclecticism.

Sergei Vassilievitch Rachmaninov was born April 2, 1873, at Oneg, in the province of Novgorod. He was descended on his father's side from an ancient and aristocratic family. His grandfather, Arkadi Rachmaninov, had been an army officer in the Russo-Turkish War, but greatly preferred music to military science. Arkadi had studied the piano with John Field during the Irish composer's

227

long stay in Russia, and after his early retirement from the army became a brilliant amateur pianist. Arkadi's son Vassili (the composer's father) was an irresponsible and profligate man who begat six children and then by speculation, gambling, and fast living proceeded to dissipate the family fortune, including the estate at Oneg. The family moved to Petersburg in 1882.

Sergei Rachmaninov's mother, a woman of character and cultural attainment, gave him his first piano lessons at the age of four. The child displayed such talent (including absolute pitch) that at the age of nine he was entered in the children's classes at the Petersburg Conservatory. Several years later the boy's mother heeded the advice of her nephew, Alexander Siloti. This young man was a brilliant pianist who had studied at the Moscow Conservatory with Sverev, Tchaikovsky, and Nicholas Rubinstein, and later at Weimar with Liszt. Siloti strongly urged that his cousin Sergei be sent to Moscow and placed under the tutelage of Sverev; and this was done in 1885.

Sverev was one of the best piano teachers in Russia. It was his custom to select a small group of his young pupils to live and study in his home, and Sergei Rachmaninov was one of three chosen for this honour. The youngsters lived like Spartans. They arose at six to spend long hours at practice, memory training and theory—all rigorously supervised. This was in the Rubinstein tradition and it aimed to develop pianists with prodigious technical skill, huge repertoires, and powers of memorizing that approached the metaphysical. Rachmaninov once learned to play Brahms' Variations on a Theme by Handel in three days.

From Sverev, Rachmaninov passed on to Arensky's classes in advanced harmony and composition at the Conservatory. Later he studied composition with Taneyev and piano with his cousin Siloti. But the central sun of his young life was Tchaikovsky. The composer's influence at that time in Moscow was enormous; on Rachmaninov the effect of his music was almost hypnotic. Tchaikovsky went out of his way to encourage the young student and to praise his early efforts at composition, thus forming an artistic kinship that lasted through Rachmaninov's entire creative career.

Rachmaninov was one of the most brilliant students ever to attend the Moscow Conservatory. In 1891, in his eighteenth year, he won highest honours for piano playing; and in 1892 he was awarded the gold medal of honour for composition, graduating a year ahead of his class. Part of his task for the final examinations was the composition of a short opera. In a few weeks Rachmaninov wrote his one-act *Aleko*, based on Pushkin's poem, *The Gypsies*; and the following year it was produced with considerable success in Moscow. Meanwhile the young man had also impressed Moscow audiences as a piano virtuoso. Thus, at the age of twenty, he was already one of the most promising figures in Russian music circles.

It was at this moment that Rachmaninov had the remarkable fortune to compose the most famous piano piece of modern times— the C sharp minor Prelude. The popularity of this work, which began with a performance by Siloti in London and spread to every corner of the music world, might well be a starting point for an inquiry into the mass psychology of music. So incredibly large has been the number of its performances in the past half century, both in private and at music events of every nature, that few persons contemporary with the piece could give an unbiased estimate of its intrinsic worth. But the truth remains that whether it was played by kings of the piano like Rachmaninov himself and Josef Hofmann, or vaudeville performers, the C sharp minor Prelude seldom failed to make an effect. Early publicists sometimes endowed the piece with a lurid programme, "The Burning of Moscow in 1812"; but it needed no literary assistance. Its chief virtue is its remarkable sonority, an expert deployment of chordal structures that permits a minimum of technical skill to produce a maximum of melodramatic sound. The fact also remains that the C sharp minor Prelude was a benefit to Rachmaninov in his early career, both as pianist and composer. Modern publicity has its advantages, even to those most scrupulously opposed to it.

II

Success went straight to the young composer's head. Years later he recalled a scene at one of Balakirev's soireés in Petersburg when all the music élite of the town were present. Rachmaninov played his first Suite, and Rimsky-Korsakov, noticeably pleased, offered a mild suggestion about the handling of one of the themes. Recalled Rachmaninov: "I was silly and stuck on myself in those days. I was only twenty-one—so I shrugged my shoulders and said: 'And why?' . . . and never changed a note. Only later did I realize how just Rimsky-Korsakov's criticism had been. The true greatness of Rimsky-Korsakov dawned on me gradually, and I was very sorry that I never got to be his pupil."

Rachmaninov was to learn the lesson of humility in the cruellest possible way for a young artist. For several years he had been working on his First Symphony, in D minor, and in 1897 came its première under brilliant auspices when Glazunov conducted it in Petersburg. To the amazement of the young composer the first performance was a fiasco. The orchestra played execrably, and Glazunov conducted so badly that it was believed that he was drunk. Rachmaninov finally fled from the hall. Later the Petersburg critics took delight in mangling the work of a young Moscow hopeful. Wrote Cui: "If there were a conservatory in hell Rachmaninov would get first prize for his Symphony, so devilish are the discords he places before us."

Rachmaninov was shocked almost to the point of insanity. The First Symphony was never performed again during his lifetime, for in his shame he withheld the score from publication. After his death, almost half a century later, however, the orchestral parts were discovered in the archives of the Petersburg (now Leningrad) Conservatory, and in 1945 the work was performed in Moscow. On March 19, 1948, the Philadelphia Orchestra gave the first American performance, under Eugene Ormandy. Eagerly awaited because of its curious history, the work proved to be no mislaid masterpiece; but it did reveal that the disgrace of the Petersburg première was no fault of the composer.

In spite of Rachmaninov's youth the First Symphony is neither amateurish, clumsy, nor blatant. It was based on themes taken from the *Oktoedos*, the choir book of hymns used daily in the Russian Church service. It was carefully designed with a motto theme as its central stem. The work shows strongly the influence of Tchaikovsky, and at times of Borodin; but even the borrowings are significant. Rachmaninov had taste. When he took from Tchaikovsky it was usually a good idea, seldom a meretricious one. Thus the symphony usually strives for fine workmanship rather than theatrical display, and the result is a competent piece in the Russian eclectic style.

As for the critics who damned Rachmaninov's First Symphony, their error was not the familiar one of underrating a work of art at first hearing, but one equally bad. They had simply failed to consider the most obvious facts of all about the work: that the composer was a young man only twenty-four years old; that he had unusual talent, technical skill, and serious intentions; and that he deserved therefore both respect and encouragement instead of ridicule.

There is some mystery about the psychological shock which Rachmaninov suffered with the failure of his First Symphony. Several other disappointments including a broken love affair seem to have struck him at the same moment. Whatever the real cause of the crisis, Rachmaninov was never again the same man. To the end of his life he suffered from melancholia and from doubts about his own talents.

While he was trying to pull himself out of his mental depression the composer was offered the post of assistant conductor at a Moscow opera house. He learned quickly the rudiments of an art he was later to master, but the rough fighting of the opera house and its rowdy personalities did not help the sensitive young man, and he soon resigned. In 1898 he went to London at the invitation of the Philharmonic Society. He conducted and played with such success that he was invited to return the following season; but he went back to Russia in a worse mental state than ever. He had promised to compose a new concerto, but at this his sick mind rebelled. The spectre of the First Symphony stood between him and all creative endeavour, virtually paralysing his will.

Fortunately, the science of psychiatry, then in its infancy, came forth with a dramatic rescue. The composer's family persuaded him to consult a psychologist in Moscow, a Dr. Nicolay Dahl, who was experimenting with auto-suggestion and hypnotism. Every day for three months Rachmaninov sat in a darkened room while Dr. Dahl repeated again and again the words: "You will begin to write your concerto. You will work with great facility. The concerto will be of excellent quality."

The effect was magical. Rachmaninov set to work, and in the summer and early autumn of 1900 he completed the slow movement and Finale of his Second Piano Concerto, in C minor. These he played at a concert in Moscow under Siloti, with immense success; and the following spring he composed the first movement. Dr. Dahl had spoken not only with singular persuasion but with prophecy, for the C minor Concerto is one of Rachmaninov's best works, and one of the most successful pieces of its kind in Russian piano literature.

After Dr. Dahl, the composer owed his greatest debt to Tchaikovsky. The C minor Piano Concerto is a child of the celebrated B flat minor, with similar flower-laden and highly-scented melodies, and a technical display almost as theatrical. The piece resembles a romantic costume drama of the late nineteenth century, with a leading role that is an actor's dream. The pianist, like the actor, enjoys all the choice scenes designed for melancholy brooding, impassioned love-making, furious conflict, and final triumph. The lights play constantly upon all the facets of his heroic conduct and all his changes of costume.

Whatever else Dr. Dahl had done for Rachmaninov, in the C minor Concerto he certainly set free the young composer's lyric gifts. The melodies are among Rachmaninov's most effective and they are set forth with fine variety in the Tchaikovsky manner. Whether they are proclaimed boldly in octaves, embroidered with piano tracery, sweetly sung by solo woodwinds, embedded in the soft velvet of the strings, or shouted by full orchestra and solo instrument—always the melodies are given preferred treatment.[1]

One of the early advantages of the C minor Concerto, oddly enough, was its lugubrious mood. To audiences of Western Europe and America this had been one of the more fascinating aspects of Tchaikovsky's music—an art in tonal purples and blacks. Tchaikovsky had established a tradition that Russian music should wear the mask of tragedy. Doubtless the idea derived from the great Russian novelists of the nineteenth century, especially Tolstoy and Dostoevsky, who had made the Western world aware of the deep wells of Slavic psychology from which they drew their studies of human pathos. Now it appeared that Rachmaninov, like Tchaikovsky before him, must be exploring those same depths.

III

In the next phase of his career Rachmaninov returned to the opera house, both as conductor and composer. In 1904–05 he worked on two operas, *The Miser Knight*, after Pushkin, and *Francesca da Rimini*, to a libretto by Modest Tchaikovsky, brother of Peter Ilych. Composition was interrupted, however, by Rachmaninov's agreement to conduct at the Imperial Theatre in Moscow. In the next two seasons he established himself as one of the ablest opera conductors in Russia, and a notable interpreter of the standard Russian works. Rachmaninov produced both his new operas at the Grand Theatre, but neither met with the success of his student piece, *Aleko*. At least ten other operatic subjects occupied his mind at one time or another,

[1] In recent years several of the themes of this concerto have met the hardest test of all. Flattened out of shape and joined to words by various Broadway poets they appeared as popular songs, scoring notable successes on the "Hit Parade".

including Boris Godunov, Salammbô, and Uncle Vanya; but he never completed another work for the stage.

Rachmaninov's two seasons at the Grand Theatre were an unsettling time in his life. Revolution was in the air, and even the opera company felt the growing tension. The singers, the orchestra, the ballet, and the stage hands were all embroiled in hot issues of social reform. One of the spokesmen was Serge Koussevitzky, then a young member of the double bass section, who wrote an inflammatory article in the press denouncing the working conditions in the theatre.

Many of the theatres closed down for fear of revolutionists' bombs; the opera house dared not perform Glinka's *A Life for the Czar* because the gallery hooted Susanin's aria declaiming his act of self-sacrifice for his ruler. Writes Victor I. Seroff, Rachmaninov's biographer:

> "It was sufficient for someone during a performance to shout, 'Down with the monarchy!' to make the whole theatre become a battlefield where hats, coats, umbrellas, and galoshes flew through the air. . . ."

Amid these ominous scenes Rachmaninov remained frigidly aloof. For him the opera house had become a "backstage tavern", and "a brothel". He finally resigned with a vow never to return. Several years before he had married and now had an infant daughter, so with his small family he left Russia in the spring of 1906 and went to Italy.

Rachmaninov's retreat from Russia at a critical moment is a clue to a curious paradox in the man's character. Those who did not know him intimately seldom guessed the truth. To the public he seemed a man of massive reserve, as sure of himself as anyone could be. Few artists in the concert hall ever matched him for sheer dignity. His commanding figure, and deliberate walk; his head with its heavily chiselled features, the close-cropped hair, the coldly melancholy eyes whose shape suggested some remote Mongolian strain—this was the familiar portrait of Rachmaninov and it bespoke a character of granite. Not many guessed that it was a mask. Dr. Dahl's cure had been only a partial one; Rachmaninov never regained complete self-confidence. Indecision tortured him. He would brood for days over details of his music, or the course his life should take.

While in Italy Rachmaninov received an offer for an American concert tour. To a friend he wrote: "you . . . could not possibly understand what tortures I live through when I realize that this question has to be decided by me and me alone. The trouble is that I am just incapable of making any decision by myself. My hands tremble!"

IV

Rachmaninov met his problem by moving obliquely. Late in 1906 he took his family to Dresden, where he remained for the better part of three years. This was one of the most fortunate decisions of his life, for in the German city he found both the intellectual stimulus and the isolation he needed for creative work. The Dresden period yielded a number of large-scale works—the Second Symphony, the First Piano Sonata, the symphonic poem *The Isle of the Dead*, and the Third Piano Concerto.

Rachmaninov's Second Symphony, in E minor, was originally a mammoth work running an hour in performance. The composer later sanctioned various cuts which are generally observed today. The piece shows Rachmaninov's rapid rise to mastery of technique. Themes are manipulated and integrated with ingenuity; contrapuntal skills are present everywhere; the use of the instruments is brilliant. The composer relied strongly on what he must now have realized was his most precious asset—the richly mellow, long-flowing themes that he could stretch into a kind of endless melody. Yet the symphony misses fire. It is still too long and it lacks variety, the thing that helps move the composer's more successful piano concertos. Nor is there much of originality. Rachmaninov repeated himself and he repeated Tchaikovsky. The symphony's chief fault, besides its now old-fashioned style, is the familiar one of size without significant content.

The symphonic poem, *The Isle of the Dead*, bears the sub-title "To a Picture by A. Böcklin". Arnold Böcklin (1827–1901) was a Swiss painter who achieved a considerable academic fame in his day, and an enormous popular success with this picture. A volcanic island north of the Gulf of Naples became under the painter's brush a romantic vision of nature's receiving vault for the dead—whitened cliffs, shrouding cypress trees, a lifeless sea, and a boat approaching with a cargo of death.

For this sepulchral scene Rachmaninov wrote some of his most characteristic music. He evoked perfectly the chill landscape and the funereal mood. His piece has a solemn dignity, conveyed with the composer's unusual feeling for the darker orchestral colours. Effective allusion is made to the notes of *Dies Irae* which were to haunt Rachmaninov all the days of his life. If the piece suffers it is from excessive length, being too long a meditation on a single gloomy theme. The picture, moreover, no longer enriches the music. Böcklin's canvas has become little more than a chromo which most listeners would prefer to forget.

The Isle of the Dead shows clearly that with Rachmaninov's residence in Dresden a familiar pattern had begun to form itself once more. The powerful influences of the West were crowding in upon the consciousness of this Russian artist. In Germany he also experienced for the first time the mighty ground swell of the Wagnerian music dramas. Thus *The Isle of the Dead* mixes Rachmaninov with Tchaikovsky and Wagner—long lyric phrases, impassioned climaxes, melting harmonies, all in the familiar mood of Russian melancholy.

V

In 1908, after much soul-searching, Rachmaninov finally agreed to make an American concert tour. He had little faith and no interest in America, and he undertook the venture partly because he wanted to earn enough money to buy an automobile. In preparation for these appearances he composed especially his Third Piano Concerto, in D minor.

On November 4, 1909, at Smith College in Northampton, Rachmaninov gave a piano recital—his first appearance in the country which was later to become his home and which he would grow to love. From the beginning the American public received him with enthusiasm. Within a few weeks he played the Third Piano Concerto with two New York orchestras, the Symphony Society under Walter Damrosch, and the Philharmonic under Gustav Mahler. In Philadelphia he conducted the first American performance of his Second Symphony, while in Boston his success was so extraordinary that he was offered the conductorship of the Boston Symphony Orchestra. Rachmaninov declined the post, but the man and his works had made a lasting impression upon American music life.

The D minor Piano Concerto was the last of Rachmaninov's larger Dresden works. It represented a climax in his career, for many years would pass before he would again create anything for the piano of comparable power. The Concerto is also a monument to the composer's own mastery of the instrument. It is one of the most difficult pieces of its kind, and in the concert hall he met its challenge with thrilling command of every technical resource.

This Concerto has been called "a fitting epilogue to the era of the romantic piano concerto", and indeed it practically brings to an end the concerto of the Lisztian type, that which blends primarily the lyric and the theatrical. Sonorous and impassioned, it generates emotional excitement in a series of waves. The piece also shows the composer's development as a craftsman. It is long and intricate, but it hangs together.

Lyrically the D minor Concerto is not quite as successful as the C minor, which was in reality a group of extended melodic passages rather loosely put together but with an immediate appeal for the tender-minded. The melodies of the later work are more sombre and at times drier. The opening theme shows the change which had come over the composer. It strongly resembles some simple Russian folk song, but this soon dissolves as the piece moves on its complex course, a synthesis of styles and idioms. All through his early writing Rachmaninov had made use of native Russian themes, especially those of the church; but with the Dresden period he began to move farther and farther away from the old materials. Most of his melodies are now originally conceived. Often they bear only a distant family resemblance to their nationalist ancestors.

In the spring of 1910, after the successful American tour, Rachmaninov returned to Russia and was later appointed conductor of the Moscow Philharmonic Concerts. He quickly became the most powerful personality in the Moscow music scene, and his conducting aroused immense enthusiasm. But at that moment there appeared upon the stage a rival faction, led by the ambitious and resourceful Serge Koussevitzky.

Koussevitzky operated in the triple role of conductor, music publisher, and patron of new Russian composers. He began sponsoring the brilliant Alexander Scriabin. Around the exponent of mysticism and modernism there rallied all Moscow's music radicals; against them were the conservatives like Taneyev and, inevitably, Rachmaninov. In the rivalry which followed Rachmaninov tried to remain aloof, even going so far as to perform his friend Scriabin's music at his concerts; but the public wanted, and got, a battle—full of personal heat and acrimony.

It was during these days that Rachmaninov carried on his curious correspondence with a young girl of twenty-four, Marietta Shaginian, who became in later years a noted Soviet authoress. At his concerts Marietta had fallen in love with the austere conductor-composer, and had written him a fan letter. The friendship which followed was never publicly revealed until after Rachmaninov's death, when Marietta Shaginian published some of his letters to her. They reveal the rift in the man's character—his strange indecision and lack of self-confidence, his yearning for praise and sympathy, his resigned melancholy: "I am a most ordinary and uninteresting man" . . . "there is no critic in the world who is more doubtful about me than myself." "If ever I had faith in myself, that was a long time ago, in my youth!" "I am mentally sick." In the early stages of his correspondence he asked the young girl for help in finding suitable texts for songs. "The mood," he wrote, "should be rather sad than gay. The light, gay colours do not come easy for me." "I love your letters because I find in them your faith, love and hope in me—the balm with which I cure my wounds."

In a letter written in 1912 we find: "I am afraid of everything—mice, rats, beetles, oxen, murderers. I am frightened when a strong wind blows and howls in the chimney, when I hear raindrops on the window pane; I am afraid of the darkness. . . ."

VI

During his years of his conductorship of the Moscow Philharmonic, Rachmaninov sacrificed time which might have gone to composition. His only large work was composed in 1910—a group of twenty Russian Orthodox hymns for mixed chorus, based on the Liturgy of St. John Chrysostom. The work was performed by the Synodical Choir but was quickly suppressed by the church authorities for its dangerous "spirit of modernism". Otherwise Rachmaninov composed chiefly short pieces—thirteen piano Preludes (Op. 32), six Etudes-Tableaux (Op. 33), and fourteen songs (Op. 34).

Rachmaninov's importance as a composer for the piano is magnified when viewed in the special field of Russian music. With his contemporary, Scriabin, he practically created a literature of Russian piano music, which heretofore had contained only a few isolated specimens of value. It does not detract from Rachmaninov's achievement to point out that the nationalist flavour of his work varies greatly, and that often all traces of Russianness is lost.

Rachmaninov's piano style stemmed directly from the romantic masters of the West, especially Chopin and Liszt, with occasional passing reference to Schumann, and even Brahms. It is interesting to note that the Russian composer must have observed, but almost totally disregarded, Debussy's revolutionary treatment of the piano. Instead he concentrated on the Chopin-Liszt framework of singing melodies and rich sonorities, decorated by elaborate technical embellishments. Though the formula was old he yet contrived to use it with individuality.

In Rachmaninov's piano pieces, large and small, there is nearly always a portrait of Rachmaninov the pianist. Anyone who tries to play these works instantly becomes conscious of his great hands with their immense spread (a twelfth), his incredibly dexterous fingers of steel and velvet. The average hand has difficulty fitting itself into the huge chordal structures that sprout with notes, the arpeggios made up of giant intervals and sweeping octaves wide, the swarms of double note figurations. All this is Rachmaninov's piano style— massive, florid, a colossal baroque oddly placed against an eclectic Russian background.

The best of Rachmaninov's piano art is epitomized in his Preludes. Following Chopin, he wrote twenty-four essays in this form, one in each of the major and minor keys. The famous C sharp minor began the set, and was composed in 1892; then came the ten Preludes of Opus 23, composed in 1904; and finally the thirteen Preludes of Opus 32, composed in 1910 following the fertile Dresden period.

In miniature these pieces trace the growth of Rachmaninov as an artist. The C sharp minor Prelude is a brilliant flash of talent; though hackneyed almost to oblivion, it is still a remarkable success for a young man not yet out of his teens. In the ten Preludes of Opus 23 Rachmaninov had matured, but was still strongly under the influence of Chopin. The moods are impassioned, declamatory, meditative, or dreamy; the harmonies shift with vivid chromatic colours; lovely melodies ride above waves of arpeggios or from a welter of swirling figurations. All is beautifully pianistic, perfectly written for the instrument. The melodies have not the distinction of Chopin's; they resemble more often Tchaikovsky's. But they have, too, the peculiar touch of Rachmaninov himself, especially in their ability to extend at great length without loss of motion.

In the final thirteen Preludes of Opus 32 Rachmaninov reached a climax. Imaginative, varied, often daring, these pieces represent one of his chief contributions to the piano music of his age. A few of them (e.g. the serenely beautiful G major) are restrained and express a reserved sentiment, but most of the others are powerfully built, full of declamations and dramas, demanding prodigious technical skill and a bravura style. Under the composer's own hands they made a carillon of gorgeous piano sound. Many of these Preludes are like Chopin's Etudes, in that they give the pianist a knotty technical problem to solve, one which then becomes a brilliant sidelight on his art as performer.

The fifteen Etudes-Tableaux were composed in two sets—six in Op. 33 (1911), and nine in Op. 39 (1917). The title was intended to indicate that each piece grew from the composer's contemplation of some picture. The various canvases were never fully identified, but most of then are said to be by Böcklin. The lack of knowledge is not vital, for in Rachmaninov's pieces the etude far outweighs the picture interest. The pieces are closely related to the final set of Preludes, being massive in style and difficulty. Musically they do not quite attain the interest of the finer Preludes.

VII

It almost goes without saying that as a composer of songs Rachmaninov remained firmly in the romantic tradition, and that the realism of Musorgsky left no impression on him. He was again a son of Tchaikovsky, and his songs breathe only the romantic airs. Most of them are hymns of passionate longing or desire, or lovely landscapes.

Rachmaninov's first published songs, the six of Op. 4, were composed before he had even come of age. The third of this set, *In the Silent Night*, is still one of his most popular pieces, whose passionate melody and darkly purple harmonies might have been written by Tchaikovsky. The fifth, *O Thou Billowy Harvest Field!* is another famous essay, which derives from Dargomyjsky's *Heavenly Clouds*, being the same type of early nineteenth-century romanza, with its mixture of Russian folk song and Italian opera lyricism. The finest song of the group is the fourth, *The Songs of Grusia* (after

Pushkin), which is a small masterpiece. Strongly remindful of Borodin, it blends a Russian folk style with a suggestion of the exotic East.

After these early imitations Rachmaninov began to go very much his own way. He never ventured into realism, and he exploited the folk-song idioms only moderately, but he enriched the Russian repertoire with many interesting examples. Some of his more florid pieces, like the dramatic *Floods of Spring* (Op. 14, No. 11), have been the most popular, but they are not always the best. There is a far purer and more subtle strain in works like *The Little Isle* (Op. 14, No. 2), *Lilacs* (Op. 21, No. 5), *How Fair this Place* (Op. 21, No. 7), and *Before My Window* (Op. 26, No. 10).

There is also a deeper note of human pathos in *The Soldier's Wife* (Op. 8, No. 4), *By a Grave* (Op. 21, No. 2), and *All Things Depart* (Op. 26, No. 15). *To the Children* (Op. 26, No. 7) stands by itself. Rachmaninov never again matched its tenderness and restraint, its poignant evocation of an unhackneyed idea.

The composer reached a point of sustained inspiration with the fourteen songs of his Op. 34, composed in 1912. Here the quality is high and the workmanship skilled. *Vocalise*, which ends the set, is one of his most admired lyric flights, and has found its way by transcription into violin and orchestral repertoires.

Rachmaninov's approach to the song was similar in many respects to Schumann's. He was primarily a pianist, and the accompaniment in his songs is seldom a mere prop or a means of underlining the vocal line. By going along on a contrapuntal track of its own the piano collaborates with the voice in stating the poetic thought. In Rachmaninov's earlier songs the piano parts are often overwhelmingly dramatic or even flamboyant; but in the more mature pieces they are far more laconic, spare, subtly understated.

VIII

With the year 1913 Rachmaninov had had enough of conducting, and more than enough of the hubbub over his own and Scriabin's music. In the fight he was being praised as a conductor but damned as a reactionary composer, so he solved his problem, characteristically, by retreating from the field. For the second time he left Russia, moving with his family to Switzerland and then to Rome. In the Italian capital he found a small apartment where Tchaikovsky had once lived. Here he found too the solitude he craved : "All day long I spent at the piano or the writing table and not until the sinking sun gilded the pines of the Monte Pincio did I put away my pen." Thus Rachmaninov composed his largest single instrumental work, his choral symphony, *The Bells*, after the poem by Edgar Allan Poe.

The choice of the verses by the American poet was the result of a curious incident. The composer had received an anonymous letter which suggested a composition based on a Russian translation of *The Bells* by Constantin Balmont. Rachmaninov seized upon the idea, but never learned who wrote the letter. According to Seroff it was a young Moscow girl, Maria Danilova, a student of the 'cello. She was an ardent admirer of Rachmaninov's music, but was too shy ever to reveal her identity to him.

Rachmaninov's *The Bells* is written for orchestra, mixed chorus, and three solo voices. It is one of those grandiose hybrids, part choral symphony and part dramatic cantata, which stem from Beethoven's Ninth Symphony. A form of this kind is essentially a romantic conception, as shown by the number of romantic composers (including Berlioz, Liszt, Mahler, and the youthful Schönberg) who have tried their hand at it. In all such attempts the basic aim has been the same : to achieve majesty of utterance by employing vast orchestral and vocal masses.

One of the chief stumbling-blocks in most of these works has been the text. Only thought of monumental poetic dignity or philosophical depth can justify the use of such forces. Rachmaninov handicapped himself by building his huge work upon a poem which might have been exploited by far simpler means. Poe's verses are basically a study in onomatopoeia, in the music latent in English words, and do not pretend to lofty spiritual significance. The most they do is to symbolize in picturesque fashion four successive phases of human life.

Rachmaninov built his score like a symphony in four movements. Each exploits a separate mood and a special bell tone. The first movement, an Allegro, recalls the sledge bells and their silvery sound. The second movement, Lento, evokes the wedding bells whose sound is golden. The third movement, a tremendous scherzo, sounds out the brazen voices of the alarum bells ; while the close, Lento lugubre, is a second slow movement depicting the tolling bells of iron.

One might anticipate from the title that *The Bells* would be one of Rachmaninov's most strongly Russian works, possibly seeking to capture something of the grandeur of the bell sounds that once pervaded the life of old Russia. But the Russian origin of the work only occasionally breaks through the surface. The piece is a hybrid in every way. Rachmaninov went to the West not only for its text but for its general form, and much of its music style. *The Bells* is strongly Wagnerian, with many passages resembling *Parsifal*. It is thus a giant synthesis, and it remains not much more than a curiosity.

After the composition of *The Bells* Rachmaninov returned to Russia. He could not know it, but all around him his world was crumbling to ruin. The first shock came in 1914 with the outbreak of World War I, and even before that the composer had been suffering from morbid fears of his own sudden death. But it was Scriabin who was carried off, and with his friend passed something of Rachmaninov's own lost youth and the spirited battles of his early manhood.

During the winter of 1914–15 Rachmaninov composed his Vesper Mass, Opus 37. This work, one of the most extraordinary in modern Russian liturgical music, is also unique in Rachmaninov's catalogue. He was not outwardly a religious man, yet this liturgical setting came from an artist deeply moved by every phrase, every word of the exalted text. Its mood is unmatched elsewhere in the composer's music, and so is its style. Rachmaninov was so much an eclectic that a large part of his work bears no nationalist trace; but the Vesper Mass, reaching to the heart of the ancient church chants, seems a complete spiritual evocation of this archaic Russian art.

The work consists of fifteen hymns on texts taken from the Russian Orthodox liturgy, and is written for men's and boy's voices *a capella*. Six of the hymns are based on ancient *znamenny* chants, two on Kiev chants, and two on Grecian chants, while five are on themes of Rachmaninov's invention. The music style of the work is austere, but with a cumulative richness that is remindful of Byzantine art. The composer uses a mixture: first, the old unison chants, either in their stark simplicity or supported by an archaic modal harmony; second, polyphony reminiscent of the eighteenth century; and third, a free modern harmony.

Rachmaninov's extraordinary use of the ancient ecclesiastical idiom was in part the result of special study. He acknowledged his debt to Alexander Kastalsky, the noted composer of liturgical music, who was at that time director of the Synodical School in Moscow. Rachmaninov learned much from conversations with Kastalsky and a study of his works, calling him "the Rimsky-Korsakov of choral music". Rachmaninov had also studied briefly the neume notations of the ancient chants under the great authority, Stephen Smoliensky, to whom the Vesper Mass is dedicated.

Scholarship alone could not have produced a work as inspired as the Vesper Mass. From the days of his childhood Rachmaninov had loved the Russian Church chants, and the thought of transmuting them into a modern work of art must have lain in his mind for years. Intuitively he had absorbed the archaic style—in Riesemann's description,

> "the peculiar dynamics of Russian chanting with its sudden swell and diminuendo, its expiring pianissimos and sharp accentuations . . . the perfect chastity and austerity of the phrasing . . . the touching simplicity and purity of sound and an absolutely unconditional subjection to a style which does not allow even one sweetly-seasoned harmony to intrude".

Rachmaninov stripped from these hymns all trace of the lachrymose sentiment that had dampened so much of his other music. He worked instead with utmost restraint, to achieve a spare and ascetic spirituality. Although the homogeneity and sustained inspiration of the Vesper Mass are noteworthy, certain of the hymns stand above the rest. Few would quarrel with the composer's own choice of the fifth, Nunc Dimittis, "Lord, now lettest Thou Thy servant depart in peace" (Luke ii, 29), a brief and poignant hymn which he had once hoped would be his own funeral music.

IX

When the Revolution finally descended upon Russia in 1917 Rachmaninov tried to remain aloof, as he had so often in times of crisis. He cared little for politics; but as the storm broke, piling up into wreckage a rotted, thousand-year-old social structure, he soon realized what was to follow. "Almost from the beginning of the Revolution," he said later, "I realized that it was mishandled." But at his country place at Ivanovka and at Moscow he tried to shut out the roar of the tempest by working at a revision of his First Piano Concerto.

He became, he said,

> "so engrossed with my work that I did not notice what went on around me. Consequently, life during the anarchistic upheaval,

which turned the existence of a non-proletarian into hell on earth, was comparatively easy for me. I sat at a writing table or the piano all day without troubling about the rattle of machine guns and rifle shots. I would have greeted any intruder with the answer Archimedes gave the conquerors of Syracuse."

It was not long, however, before he sensed danger. The composer and his wife were aristocrats from an ancient family of land-owners, and their peril increased by the hour. But at first he saw no way of escape.

Rachmaninov's First Piano Concerto, in F sharp minor, was his Opus 1, a student-work originally composed when he was eighteen years old. He revised it, making it a respectable and playable work. This Concerto is, naturally, the simplest of Rachmaninov's larger piano works, both in style and structure. It again recalls Tchaikovsky, being dramatic, passionately lyrical, darkly colourful in the orchestra, and brilliant in the piano part. What the piece lacks is thematic material of immediate interest—the composer's golden touch in his later works.

Late in 1917, as Rachmaninov tried to concentrate on the task of a fourth piano concerto, his increasing fear for his wife and children made his life intolerable. Then came a sudden deliverance. He received an offer for a concert tour of Scandinavia. The composer was able to secure a passport for himself and his family, but he could give no hint of his real plans. He left his home in Moscow carrying a small suitcase with a few personal belongings ; otherwise everything that he and his wife owned, including many of his music manuscripts, he abandoned.

At the Finnish border the Rachmaninovs crossed in a sleigh through a furious snowstorm. If the composer looked back through the curtain of white at the country he loved, he may have sensed dimly the full meaning of his parting. He never saw Russia again.

Swiftly decisions seemed to make themselves for Rachmaninov. Europe was still ablaze with war and could offer him no home. America was the only haven. While in Scandinavia he began to receive offers for recital tours and conductorships of American orchestras. On November 10, 1918, Rachmaninov and his family arrived in New York after a voyage on a small Norwegian ship. Before him lay a new world and a new life, all profoundly different from the old.

X

During the first half of Rachmaninov's adult career, roughly the twenty-five years prior to his departure from Russia, it appeared that three individualities had struggled for ascendancy—the conductor, the composer, the pianist. Now, in the final quarter century, Rachmaninov made his decisive choice. He thrust conducting almost completely out of his life. Composition dwindled to a few works over a long period of years. Rachmaninov became Rachmaninov the virtuoso pianist.

Few artists in modern times have equalled his success on the concert platform, for at the height of his career he held secure both the acclaim of critics and the enthusiasm of enormous audiences in America and Europe. Many considered him the first pianist of his age. Rachmaninov came perfectly equipped for the role. He had had superb training to which he brought great physical stamina, a capacious music mind, intuitive understanding of the instrument, and a magnetic personality.

Rachmaninov soon became a fixture in the music life of America. Every year he made a long transcontinental tour, giving recitals in scores of cities. His appearances with orchestras were especially memorable. The pianist was soon drawn to the Philadelphia Orchestra, which in the nineteen-twenties was at its first peak of virtuosity. With Leopold Stokowski, who created and maintained the exquisitely tempered instrument, Rachmaninov began to preserve on phonograph records his performances of his own works. They remain today among the peerless examples of piano and orchestral playing in the grand romantic manner.

Rachmaninov became one of the highest paid musicians of his time, but he had to work hard and long at his virtuoso career. Usually he found time for relaxation in the summer, which he spent with his family in Europe. In 1931 he bought a home in Switzerland, on the shores of Lake Lucerne. His hobbies were gardening, motor-boating, and driving his car; but above all he enjoyed a simple family life with his wife, his two daughters, and his grandchildren. His closest friends were mostly Russians, expatriates like himself.

The few Americans who knew him well remember him as a man of great personal magnetism, who could be as charming and affable at close range as he appeared forbidding on the concert platform.

When he visited friends it was not unusual for him to arrive at the wheel of his latest expensive car, and then spend hours with the hood up, delving into the mechanism which he loved with a passion, until his hands and his magic fingers were black with engine grease.

The reasons why Rachmaninov, a gifted and successful composer, could virtually abandon his art for the career of a pianist, is still a matter of mystery. The surface explanation—that he did it for money—will hardly suffice. He himself hinted that exile from Russia had damaged his inspiration, and this was no doubt true. When his friend Nicolas Medtner asked him why he had stopped composing, Rachmaninov replied: "The melody has gone, I can no longer compose. If it returns, then I shall write again." His separation from his native land and his people was a wound that never healed; he suffered nostalgia to the end of his life.

For almost a decade after the beginning of his exile Rachmaninov the composer remained silent. Then in the summer of 1926, in France, he finished his Fourth Piano Concerto, in G minor, Op. 40. The work was performed for the first time on March 18, 1927, in Baltimore, with the composer at the piano and the Philadelphia Orchestra under Stokowski. Those who were present at that event, or its repetition four days later in New York, remember the chill of disappointment. This Concerto seemed like a pale ghost of its clanging and colourful predecessors. The slow movement presented a problem: its first theme had a disconcerting resemblance to the nursery tune, "Three Blind Mice".[1] The entire piece seemed a reworking of old ideas. The composer realized that it was wanting, and he tried three years later to rescue it from failure. There are signs in the Fourth Concerto that Rachmaninov was trying deliberately to avoid his old formulas, successful though they had been. There is an astringent quality to this music, at times a grey bitterness that suggests the composer's disillusion. The harsh, unyielding present was crowding in upon him, blotting out the romantic past. The glint of steely dissonance and a certain abruptness of utterance more than once suggest that Rachmaninov the conservative was aware of the presence of a new age in music.

There was to be one magnificent revival of the composer's creative vigour, and it came in the summer of 1934. At his Lake

[1] This theme also recalled a song then popular in America, *Nobody but You*, written by George Gershwin, but doubtless never heard by Rachmaninov. In later years when Gershwin began composing in more serious forms his piano writing was strongly influenced by that of the Russian composer.

Lucerne home he wrote his Rhapsody on a Theme of Paganini, for Piano and Orchestra (Op. 43). On November 7 of that year, in Baltimore, he played it for the first time, with Stokowski and the Philadelphia Orchestra, and the result was a dazzling success.

The Rhapsody is a series of twenty-four variations. The theme itself was already famous as a vehicle for variations, having been used by Paganini himself, Liszt, and Brahms. The Russian composer's work is concerto-like in size, brilliance, and difficulty; from deceptively simple beginnings it grows steadily more complex and ingenious, with the pianist exhibiting one diamond after another in his blazing virtuoso's crown.

In one respect the Rhapsody is strikingly different from the composer's previous large works. Its mood is ironic. Gone is the old Rachmaninov of the brooding and the repining; here the composer is sardonic without ever being morbid. There are moments of lyric passion, notably the famous Variation XVIII, a lovely cantilena in D flat major; but chiefly the flavour of the music is one of sharpness and tang, as if the composer, a conservative romantic all his life, had taken note at last of this new anti-romantic age. Emphasizing the ironic quality of the piece is Rachmaninov's use of his curious *idée fixe*, the theme of the *Dies Irae*. Ominously it appears in the seventh variation and again in the tenth, while at the close of the work it rises like a death's head with a diabolic proclamation of the brass.

That Rachmaninov felt the macabre quality of this music is shown by the suggestion he made several years later to the famous choreographer, Michael Fokine, who wanted to create a ballet based on the Rhapsody. Wrote the composer: "Why not resurrect the legend about Paganini, who, for perfection in his art and for a woman, sold his soul to an evil spirt?" Fokine seized Rachmaninov's suggested scenario and in 1939 created from the Rhapsody his superlative *Paganini*, a fantastic ballet in three scenes.

Two years before the composition of the Rhapsody Rachmaninov had produced a work in the same general form for solo piano, which was the real beginning of his brief period of renascent creative strength. This was his Variations on a Theme by Corelli, Op. 42 (1932). The theme, derived from Corelli's Twelfth Violin Sonata, was actually an ancient dance melody and a favourite variation vehicle for composers through several centuries. Rachmaninov's comments take the form of twenty short variations, and he wrote as in the later Paganini Rhapsody with skill and conviction. From the simple stem the ideas proliferate into attractive pianistic blooms, with ingenious contrasts of mood, texture, design, and melodic and rhythmic metamorphosis.

The excellent results which Rachmaninov obtained with his Corelli Variations must have heartened him after the long barren period, inspiring him to attempt the brilliant complexities of his Paganini Rhapsody. The two works together gave promise that the once-gifted composer of years long past was to live again; but the promise was never fulfilled. The Corelli Variations were his last work for solo piano.

An enormous span of almost thirty years separated Rachmaninov's Second Symphony from his Third, in A minor. The latter work was composed in Switzerland in the summers of 1935 and 1936, and was first performed by Stokowski and the Philadelphia Orchestra on November 6, 1936. "It was played wonderfully," wrote Rachmaninov to a friend, adding ruefully that "the reception by the public and the critics was . . . sour. . . ." The symphony has not yet been able to reverse that early decision. Even less interesting were the *Symphonic Dances*, for Orchestra, Opus 45, written in 1940–41. After that, Rachmaninov composed no more.

With the coming of World War II the composer could no longer continue his yearly sojourns to Europe, so he bought a home in Beverly Hills, California. Rachmaninov was now close to seventy. He was ailing and weary, but at the piano he still played with magnificent skill and authority, giving no hint of his failing strength. While on tour early in 1943 he became ill in New Orleans and had to be taken home to California. He died at his Beverly Hills home on March 28. His burial place is in the Kensico Cemetery, near the Kensico dam, in New York State.

XI

Like Tchaikovsky's music, Rachmaninov's has attracted the admiration of the general public and the hostility of many critics. It is true that his music has much more of emotional than intellectual substance; it often seems extravagantly sentimental, almost too poetical and sweet for this age of steel and blood. It was written in an idiom of the past, always an easier method than to write in the ingenious, daring, and intricate idiom of the future, where the standards are not yet established and the boundaries are not fixed.

Thus Rachmaninov's music seems old-fashioned, even soft, especially when compared with the art of such hardy adventurers as Stravinsky, Prokofiev, Schönberg, or Bartok. We know now that Rachmaninov was a troubled, sensitive man, for whom the time was out of joint. He longed to live in an age and in a country which had vanished into the past. For all its softness, however, and its anachronistic sentiments, his best music has vitality. It continues to live. Most of its strength came from the composer's lyric gift, on which he leaned heavily. When this natural outpouring of melodic ideas failed him, he had the good sense to stop composing.

It might be said of Rachmaninov that he was a typical Russian composer because he seemed able to write on two planes—as a nationalist who could project much of the spirit of his country, and as an eclectic who had assimilated widely from Western music. His achievement in the field of piano music was considerable. Russian music in the nineteenth century had grown rich in operas, art songs, and pieces for symphonic orchestra; but the composers had done comparatively little for the piano. Tchaikovsky's B flat minor Concerto and Musorgsky's *Pictures at an Exhibition* could hardly constitute a literature of Russian piano music. Rachmaninov was the first composer to start filling out the room. His Preludes, Etudes-tableaux, Concertos, and the Paganini Variations make up a solid body of fine music, no less worthy of respect because it is related to the nineteenth rather than the twentieth century. Rachmaninov must share some honours with his contemporary Scriabin, whose art was bolder and more experimental; but there can be little doubt whose music is the more durable.

As an expatriate who had expressed himself bluntly about the Soviet authorities Rachmaninov incurred the enmity of these new masters of the Russian people. In 1931 the men of the Kremlin spoke through the oracular voice of *Pravda*, the official news organ, and pronounced on the composer a wrathful excommunication. His music, it appeared, "is that of an insignificant imitator and reactionary: a former estate owner, who, as recently as 1918, burned with a hatred of Russia when the peasants took away his land— a sworn and active enemy of the Soviet Government". To this blast and a subsequent boycott of his music in his native land Rachmaninov replied only, "I am quite indifferent". But the attack hurt him more than he would say.

The boycott did not effectively blot out from Russia the memory of the man or his music. With the passing years Rachmaninov often received letters from composers there who had been his friends; his music continued to be heard at least privately. Finally, after his death, there came one of those enigmatic changes in the direction of the Soviet party line which confound even the most faithful. The new directives indicate that Rachmaninov's departure from Russia is now viewed as a sad mistake, and that he had paid dearly in loss of creative vigour for his life in America, "surrounded by feverish business and cultural decadence". Purged of their composer's heresy, Rachmaninov's works may now be played again, and Soviet musicologists are busy collecting manuscripts, letters, and other documentary evidence of his life in Russia.

CHAPTER XIII

STRAVINSKY

I

THE present chronicle has so far traced, as part of its purpose, the multifarious ways in which the music of the West has affected the composers of Russia, to bring into being a Russian nationalist music. Little has been said of the reverse, i.e. the impact which this Russian music has had upon the Western art. The most immediate effect was a sudden awakening of interest in folk music in a number of European countries and the Americas; nationalism began to be cultivated. At the same time there was some outright imitation of the Russians by important Western composers. But in the closing years of the nineteenth century German music still enjoyed the prestige of an established religion, finally challenged after the turn of the century by the new French impressionism of Debussy. Very soon after the close of World War I, however, the world of art witnessed an exhilarating phenomenon. For the first time in history a Russian composer became the most powerful single force in modern music. With Igor Stravinsky the tide of Russian art music began to flow strongly in the opposite direction, so to speak, giving a new and pungent colour to the stream of Western music from which it had sprung.

Stravinsky had music and the theatre in his blood, but he almost missed being a composer. He was born at Oranienbaum (a suburb of Petersburg) June 17, 1882, the son of F. I. Stravinsky, who had been for years a leading bass singer at the Imperial Opera, and had sung the role of Boris Godunov in early productions of the opera during Musorgsky's lifetime. As a child Igor Stravinsky was intensely interested in music but not at all precocious, so his family decided that he should become a lawyer. He entered the University of Petersburg, where he soon lost interest in legal matters and began taking lessons in harmony. When he was eighteen the world of counterpoint, which he had been exploring on his own, suddenly opened before him like a thrilling adventure.

One of Stravinsky's fellow students at the university was Andrey

Rimsky-Korsakov, a son of the composer. Through Andrey, Stravinsky met the famous man (at Heidelberg, in 1902) and had the temerity to play his first attempts at composition. Rimsky-Korsakov's advice was kindly but wise: Stravinsky should continue with his music but not leave the law school. The young man took lessons in harmony and counterpoint from one of Rimsky-Korsakov's pupils; but three years later he finally got what he wanted—private instruction from the master himself. These studies in composition and instrumentation continued for three years.

Unlike practically all the other important Russian composers of his generation, Stravinsky had no formal education in music. He had no conservatory background, but had to dig out for himself the first principles of music technique. He is thus in many respects a true descendant of the early Petersburg group, the famous Five. He came to a music career indirectly; until he approached Rimsky-Korsakov he had little training and his real talents lay undeveloped. He was moved chiefly by instinct, love, and determination, the same motives that had impelled Musorgsky, Borodin, Rimsky-Korsakov, and Balakirev.

It was inevitable that the prime influence in Stravinsky's early career should be his mentor, Rimsky-Korsakov. He also greatly admired Glazunov and Tchaikovsky. But at this time a group of modern French composers, whose work was little known in Petersburg, began to attract him—Franck, d'Indy, Faure, Dukas, and especially Chabrier and Debussy.

Stravinsky's own compositions during these early years show clearly his inclinations. He composed a symphony (in E flat major, his Opus 1), a piano sonata, and his *Scherzo Fantastique*, a symphonic poem reflecting his study of the life of the bees. The symphony (by his own candid appraisal) was an imitation of Glazunov; the *Scherzo* had a then-fashionable chromatic colour with glints of Dukas and Chabrier, and something of Rimsky-Korsakov's orchestration.

Real mastery began to appear in Stravinsky's first work for the theatre, *Le Rossignol* (The Nightingale), based on Hans Christian Andersen's famous story of the Chinese emperor. This opera was begun in 1908, but was not completed until 1914. Later the composer made it into a ballet for production by Diaghilev.

In the spring of 1908 Stravinsky composed a short piece for orchestra, *Fireworks*, which he intended as a wedding present for one of Rimsky-Korsakov's daughters. It was never heard by Rimsky-

Korsakov himself because the old man died before the manuscript could be delivered. Doubtless the little piece would have delighted him, for it is a vivid fragment of artful artificiality—pinwheels gaily whirling, rockets streaming into the sky, sparks falling in cascades, and a final bomb shaking the heavens. *Fireworks* was a tiny key which opened for Stravinsky the doors of fortune. It was played, with his *Scherzo Fantastique*, at a concert in Petersburg attended by Serge Diaghilev. The impresario was then preparing his programme for his first season of Russian ballet in Paris the following spring, and he asked Stravinsky to orchestrate two of the Chopin pieces in the ballet *Sylphides*—the opening "Nocturne" and the closing "Valse brillante".

The success of Diaghilev's Russian ballet, which began with those Paris performances of 1909, is a phenomenon never duplicated in the history of the theatre. The story cannot be related here, for it had ramifications all through the evolution of the modern ballet, the theatre, music, painting, and stage design; it was a sudden flowering of aural and visual beauty which stunned a generation of Western Europeans and Americans. It was a story of fabulous creative talents and personalities—of Diaghilev himself, the man of imperial tastes and ambitions, from whose imagination the visions sprang to life; of Michael Fokine, the choreographer who created the first classics of the modern ballet; of Leon Bakst, the brilliant scene and costume designer; of Nijinsky, the dancer, for a few brief seasons an almost supernatural apparition of beauty; and Igor Stravinsky, whose scores would change the face of twentieth-century music.

II

Exhilarated by the success of his first Paris season, Diaghilev planned for months a series of new productions for his season of 1910. His choreographer, Fokine, had in mind a ballet based on the ancient Russian legends of the Zhar-Ptitsa, the marvellous bird with wings of golden flame. Anatole Liadov agreed to compose a score, but being a born procrastinator he let precious weeks slip by without setting down a note. Diaghilev finally sent a telegram to young Igor Stravinsky offering him the job.

Fokine devised the scenario of *The Firebird*, using three favourite figures of ancient Russian mythology—Ivan Czarevich, the legendary hero-prince; Zhar-Ptitsa, the bird of fire; and Kashchey, an ogre or wizard. In his *Russian Folk Tales*, W. R. S. Ralston describes radiantly the Zhar-Ptitsa :

> "Its feathers blaze with golden or silvery sheen, its eyes shine like crystal, it dwells in a golden cage. In the depths of night it flies into a garden and lights it up as brilliantly as could a thousand burning fires. A single feather from its tail illuminates a dark room. It feeds upon golden apples, which have the power of bestowing youth and beauty—or according to a Croatian version, on magic grasses."

The monster Kashchey was in league with the powers of darkness, and one of his specialities was turning people into stone. Rimsky-Korsakov had made the wicked wizard the chief character in his opera, *Kashchey the Immortal*, and before that had used him as a "man-skeleton" among the odd assortment of characters in the opera-ballet, *Mlada*. In Fokine's ballet version Prince Ivan, with the aid of the Firebird, escapes petrification and instead kills Kashchey by smashing an egg which contains the evil one's life.

The Firebird was first produced by Diaghilev at the Paris Opera, on June 25, 1910. Stravinsky's music, Fokine's choreography, and settings and costumes by Golovin and Bakst, all contributed to an immense success. Within a few years an orchestral suite drawn from the score was in repertoires of symphonic orchestras the world over, and Igor Stravinsky's international fame had begun.

After almost half a century the lovely music still retains its opalescent, shimmering colours and its naïve charm. So far as derivations are concerned, the familiar remark that *The Firebird* hatched from an egg found in the nest of Rimsky-Korsakov's *Golden Cockerel* is only a partial truth. The score sums up in one brilliant flash the whole apparatus which Rimsky-Korsakov had evolved for his series of fantastic fairy-tale operas—*The Golden Cockerel*, *Kashchey the Immortal*, *Czar Saltan*, *Sadko*, *Christmas Eve*, and *Mlada*. In *The Firebird* there are echoes from all these sources—the lavish colour, the grotesque, infernal element, the iridescent orchestration which sets off the music's gorgeous substance. The chromatic harmonies go considerably beyond Rimsky-Korsakov's in complexity, while certain uses of whole tone scales and chords recall Scriabin (of the middle period) and, at times, Debussy.

The origin of Stravinsky's second Diaghilev ballet, *Petrouchka*, was the composer's rather casual idea of writing a short orchestral piece with an important piano part—"a sort of *Konzertstück*," he termed it. "I had in mind a distinct picture of a puppet, suddenly endowed with life, exasperating the patience of the orchestra with diabolical cascades of arpeggios. The orchestra in turn retaliates with menacing trumpet blasts." When Diaghilev heard the piece he saw possibilities of something far more elaborate. Again he called in Fokine, and with Alexander Benois, the costume and scene designer, they devised a scenario for an entire ballet. The original *Konzertstück* became the second scene of *Petrouchka*.

Like *The Firebird*, *Petrouchka* is a story ballet, but its fantasy has a realistic setting. The scene is a Petersburg square, about the year 1830. A street carnival is in progress and an old charlatan sets up a puppet show with three stuffed dolls—a dancing girl, a blackamoor, and Petrouchka, a clown. The charlatan exhibits his legerdemain: when he plays on his flute the puppets come to life and dance for the crowd. But when the scene shifts to the inside of his booth a sinister reality is revealed behind the curtain of burlesque. The clown Petrouchka is a pitiful figure. His master beats him brutally; the dancing girl laughs at his ugly, clumsy body, and spurns him for the blackamoor, who finally kills him.

Musically, *The Firebird* was imitation. *Petrouchka* is creation. The score teems with new ideas and new treatments—polyrhythms, polyharmony, polytonality, a radical orchestral style. The harmonies are bolder than any in Russian music since Musorgsky. Some of them derive from Debussy's impressionism, but there is a fundamental difference from the Frenchman's misty, purposely-softened fluctuations of keys and chords. In Stravinsky's score every effect is stamped out with the cleanness of a steel die. Typical are the famous bi-tonal passages in the second scene, with their arpeggios combining the keys of C major and F sharp major. The instrumentation, in carrying this concept of clean openness, establishes a new kind of orchestral sonority. The old nineteenth-century orchestration has been likened to "organ playing", that is, a rich and unguentary blending of timbres, with the various tonal tints melting one into the other. *Petrouchka* departs radically from that practice. Instead, the choirs or the individual instruments are heard in the open, in sharp clean blocks of sound, unmixed and unsoftened, like powerful primary colours juxtaposed.

III

Petrouchka at first shocked many listeners, but the composer had even more startling ideas in reserve. Two years later, again under the aegis of Diaghilev, Stravinsky brought forth his masterpiece *Le Sacre du printemps* (The Rite of Spring), one of the most controversial works of art of modern times. Its première on May 29, 1913, at the Théâtre des Champs-Elysées, in Paris, was an historic scandal. The French audience, expert at creating scenes in the theatre, outdid itself with the gaudiest demonstration since the Paris première of *Tannhäuser*. During the next decade, as Stravinsky's enormously difficult score slowly found its way into orchestral repertoires, the music inspired, shocked, or repelled a whole post-war generation.

The subject matter is indicated in the sub-title: "Pictures of Pagan Russia". The germinating idea had been in Stravinsky's mind even before he began work on *Petrouchka*.

> "I had a fleeting vision which came to me as a complete surprise, my mind at the moment being full of other things. I saw in imagination a solemn pagan rite: sage elders, seated in a circle, watching a young girl dance herself to death. They were sacrificing her to propitiate the god of spring."

Le Sacre du printemps is in two parts. Part I is called "The Adoration of the Earth", and its sections (joined without pause) depict the Harbingers of Spring, Dances of Adolescent Boys and Girls, a Mock Abduction, Spring Rounds, Games of the Rival Tribes, a Procession of the Tribal Sage, and a Dance of the Earth. Part II is titled "The Sacrifice". After an Introduction (said to depict the "Pagan Night"), the sections describe the Mysterious Circles of the Adolescents, Glorification of the Chosen One, the Evocation and Ritual of the Ancestors, and finally the Chosen One's Dance of Death.

The music which Stravinsky composed for these pictures of pre-Christian Russian life was so brutally realistic in style, so violent in mood and raw in colour, that many listeners could hear nothing but an insane cacophony calculated to induce nervous shock. Even those who realized the originality of the work and were deeply moved by it, often understood but vaguely its real significance. What

Stravinsky had done was to enter a new domain of pure realism in music, where no vestige of the old romanticism remained.

Realism, the portrayal of human life in terms devoid of the sentiment of romance, had been a force in Western and Russian literature for more than half a century. Yet in all that time only one composer, Musorgsky, had made use of a true realistic impulse in music. The prevailing fashion continued to be the motifs of the long overripe romantic era.

Partly in *Petrouchka*, and now wholly in *Le Sacre du printemps*, Stravinsky became an artist of a new realism in music, a descendant after many years of Modest Musorgsky. If there could be a counterpart to *Le Sacre du printemps* in literature it would be Zola's *La Terre*, the novel that had horrified France a generation before. Zola's theme and Stravinsky's are basically the same : the human animal and his dependence upon the soil. The more primitive the man, the more fierce becomes his struggle to live, to reproduce, to scratch and tear the means of living from a fecund but unheeding earth. Frankness was essential to such a theme, and both artists met it manfully ; but in so doing each shocked a generation which still clung to the sentimental illusions of romance.

As a piece of Russian music, Stravinsky's score represents a new extreme in the use of nationalist idioms. The themes are either Russian folk melodies or Stravinsky's close imitation, and they are carried to an ultimate in stylization. This is the far outpost in that march which had begun with Glinka, and which was (in Stravinsky's own phrase) "the introduction of the 'popular' melos into 'scientific' music". The science employed by Stravinsky is highly complex, especially in the departments of harmony and rhythm.

In the entire score there is hardly a conventional chord. The use of tonalities in counterpoint, so to speak, the one sounding over the other, appeared at intervals in *Petrouchka* ; in *Le Sacre du printemps* polytonality dominates the entire work and is employed with great expressive power. The effect is to destroy the last remnants of the silken fabric of romanticism, and to leave instead the raw colours, the saline freshness, the earthiness of a realistic, naked primitivism.

The rhythmic scheme of Stravinsky's work is a systematic complication without parallel in music before its time. The score is a mass of metric irregularities, including polyrhythmic effects. As in *Petrouchka*, the old-fashioned instrumental blending into organ-like sonorities is wholly abandoned. The instruments and the choirs stand out in high, razor-sharp relief ; mellifluous beauty is shunned ; the sounds are raucous, strident, hysterical, as if the orchestral pressures were strained to the highest pitch.

More than a third of a century has now passed since Stravinsky's score first struck its blows upon the art consciousness of its age. Within a decade it had become the scripture of modernist procedure, creating a new tonal language and a literature of imitations remarkable chiefly for their ugliness. Today, *Le Sacre du printemps* shows little sign of wear. Now that the novelty and the shock have worn off sheer beauty remains, especially the expressivity of its melodic material. The score has lost almost nothing of its power to inflame the imagination. It holds the mirror up to nature, and the animalistic sights and sounds spring forth—the obscene gestures, the bestial rutting, the sweating gyrations of primitive man, his mind beclouded with fearsome superstitions, performing his act of obeisance to an all-powerful earth. Here, in Jean Cocteau's words, is

> "a symphony impregnated with a wild pathos, with earth in the throes of birth, noises of farm and camp, little melodies that come to us out of the depths of the centuries, the panting of cattle, profound convulsions of nature, prehistoric georgics".

Standing in close relationship to *Le Sacre du printemps* is *Les Noces* (The Wedding), which Stravinsky composed chiefly between 1914 and 1917. The work was not produced until June 13, 1923, when Diaghilev mounted it in Paris. Meanwhile, it had undergone a considerable metamorphosis as the composer experimented with the instrumentation. In final form *The Wedding* calls for an unusual ensemble: four solo voices, a mixed chorus of twenty-four voices, four pianos, and a large group of percussion instruments. The pianos are actually treated as part of the percussion group. The piece has been called " a cantata with dances", or a "ballet cantata".

The first scene of *The Wedding* takes place in the bride's home, and depicts the ceremony of the plaiting of her hair. In scene two, at the bridegroom's home, the groom receives the blessing of his father and mother. Scene three depicts the departure of the bride from her home, and scene four is the wedding feast.

Stravinsky had never seen a Russian peasant wedding and he did not intend to reproduce his subject literally. His purpose, he said, was to use "as I liked those ritualistic elements so abundantly provided by village customs which had been established for centuries in the celebration of Russian marriages. I took my inspiration from these customs, but reserved to myself the right to use them with absolute freedom." His evocation, in short, was to be realistic but not photographic.

The realistic nature of *The Wedding* is even more pronounced than that of *Le Sacre du printemps*. The scenario is a lifelike approximation, highly stylized, of the folk ceremonies, reproducing the various customs and ceremonies, and using not the Russian literary language but a local peasant dialect. Stravinsky employed in his score only one folk melody (a factory song); the rest of the melodic material was his own invention. He succeeded in creating what Russian critics have called the most perfect evocation of the genuine Russian folk life and folk music. The Russian musicologist, Victor Belaiev, reveals in his study of *The Wedding* that Stravinsky evolved practically all his melodic material from a single thematic germ which is presented in the opening measures.

The disposition of the music ideas between voices and orchestra is wholly individual. For the most part, the voices carry the main thematism, usually creating a sense of tonality. The orchestra sustains rhythm and harmony, the latter usually in a tonality different from that of the voices. Even when the orchestra does not establish a contrasting tonality it will often move "heterophonously" in relation to the vocal parts, that is, in exactly parallel intervals of the third, fourth, fifth, sixth, etc. The result is dissonance, even more pronounced than that of *Le Sacre du printemps*.

The Wedding exhibits three remarkable phases of Stravinsky's genius: first, his pure intuition as a Russian artist, able to create a work saturated with a nationalist spirit; second, his equipment as a music scientist and scholar, a knowledge acquired by deep study of the technical side of the folk idioms; and third, his art as music stylist, applying to the pure Russian folk materials the most advanced Western techniques and still weaving a cloth which bears his own stylistic pattern.

The Wedding has not achieved wide popularity among Stravinsky's stage pieces, possibly because it is one of the most strident works in modern music. Its brutal, insistent rhythms flail the nervous system; the voices, with their shouting and screaming, at times torment the ear. But that is inevitable by the very nature of the work. *The Wedding* is a study in the primitive, the half-barbaric, and all barbarisms have the same effect upon civilized man. At one and the same time they seem repellent and fascinating.

IV

Very soon after the composition of *Le Sacre du printemps* signs of a deep-seated metamorphosis began to appear in the music of Stravinsky. During the next decade his three ballets piled up for the composer an enormous international reputation; at the same time his newer works created a sense of disquiet, even of anti-climax. It was apparent that he was seeking some new music domain, but for a time his real directions were not easily charted.

What finally came to light was the fact that Stravinsky was not simply attempting to create a new personal style, or to exploit some new technical system. He was seeking to change the very spirit of modern music. He was reversing its polarity, turning it completely away from romanticism into a new domain of classicism. More than a century before him the first romantics had turned the wheel of the classic-romantic cycle until the classic eighteenth-century Age of Enlightenment had descended into the discard; now, in the second decade of the twentieth century, he appeared as a neo-classicist to bring the wheel full circle.

If his progress from the romantic to the classic phase of the art cycle had been the only cause of the change in Stravinsky's music, his aims would have been understood much more quickly. We may now see that what has made his art so controversial and to some so opaque has been the sheer number of movements going on within it. Thus it is not possible to trace in a single straight line the progress of an art like Stravinsky's. Rather it is a complex series of evolutions which all progress according to logical principles, but which, in their overlapping and intermingling, have given his music a highly-individual character and often made it difficult to grasp at first hearings.

Stravinsky's main evolution, as we have noted, has been along the grand elliptical curve of the romantic-classic cycle; another has been his progress from a strongly nationalist artist to one cosmopolitan and eclectic. He has also carried on a continual experimentation in harmony and rhythm, and a long series of studies in instrumentation; he has made various attempts to evolve new dramatic forms which, when wedded to music, create new experiences in the theatre. Finally, in a series of special technical expeditions, he has devised his now famous stylistic evocations, by which he recreates in his own modern terms the mannerisms and spirit of other artists or other ages.

There was still another factor, and a powerful one, which partly accounted for the protean nature of Stravinsky's music. This was the sudden transplanting of the artist himself from his Russian homeland to a new life in the centre of Western culture. Stravinsky happened to be in Switzerland at the outbreak of World War I, and this accident changed the entire course of his life. After the Russian Revolution the rupture with his native land became complete and final. He never returned to Russia.

The war years were difficult ones for the composer. He had a wife and four young children to support, but was cut off from his Russian income. Diaghilev's enterprise was shattered by the general disruption of Europe, but later the impresario regrouped his forces and made tours of South America and the United States. There was no place for Stravinsky so the composer remained in Switzerland. At times his financial situation grew desperate; but he found congenial, intellectual friends, and he was able to make several visits to Italy and to Spain. The attractions of Western culture cut a deep impress upon his mind, and so upon his art.

Up to that time no other Russian composer of importance, not even Tchaikovsky, had ever spent so much of his life in Western Europe. The longer Stravinsky remained away from his native background the more he absorbed of the stream of culture around him. In part this was the result of his association with Diaghilev. The original Russian ballet had ceased to be wholly Russian as the impresario, eager to sample fresh experiences, sought out the most original creative talents in Europe—Debussy, Ravel, Falla, Tommasini, Poulenc, Auric, and Milhaud; Picasso, Matisse, Derain, Braque, Sert, and many others. Stravinsky came to know many of these men; with some he formed important friendships. As his viewpoint on life became more cosmopolitan, his art became nonnational and classical.

In 1920 Stravinsky left Switzerland and took up residence in France. During the busy years which followed he travelled all over Europe for performances of his works. Life in France especially appealed to him, and he became a leader in the development of her post-war art. Many expatriate Russians, notably Rachmaninov, seemed never to get over a nostalgic longing for their native land; but Stravinsky never permitted either his art or his life to be ruled by excess of sentiment. He grew to admire deeply the French way of life. In 1934 he became a French citizen.

V

The first signs of the fundamental change in Stravinsky's music began to appear in a series of works which he composed in the decade after *Le Sacre du printemps*. These include *Renard* (1916–17), *Histoire du soldat* (1918), *Pulcinella* (1919), Symphonies of Wind Instruments (1920), *The Wedding* (1914–17), and the Wind Octet (1923). In following his new aesthetic Stravinsky began, first of all, to scale down the physical size of his works. All these pieces are comparatively short. The enormous orchestras of his three big ballets have given way to intimate chamber ensembles. With smaller size has also come a lowering of the emotional pressure. These pieces are all notable for the way they avoid romantic sentiment. Some are passionless, even deliberately cold. Inevitably these changes demanded a new conception of craftsmanship, one based primarily on discipline. All these attributes—modest size, emotional restraint, delicacy of workmanship—bespeak the classic art; and accompanying them in Stravinsky's scores was the most revealing clue of all—a mood of urbane and satirical humour.

Renard was written at a time when Stravinsky's interest in Russian folk legend and folk song was at its height. It shows the composer testing out a new type of instrumentation, and a new dramatic form. The piece is scored for a chamber orchestra of eighteen instruments, including a cymbalon. The four singers (two tenors and two basses) are placed in the orchestra. The composer himself arranged the text from Russian folk tales. He described his piece as a "burlesque story sung and played, conceived for the stage . . . The piece is to be played by clowns, dancers and acrobats, preferably on a trestle-stage, it must be played before the curtain . . . The roles are mute." The little score is satirical and highly animated, with the flavour of a child's fairy-tale.

Histoire du soldat is another miniature theatre piece, full of experiments. It had a curious history. The composer and several of his friends in Switzerland, all desperately hard up for money, got the idea of creating a small travelling theatre which could be moved easily from town to town. The miniature play would require but three elements: a little movable stage set up on saw horses with a barrel on either side, a reader who sat on one of the barrels, and a tiny orchestra seated on the opposite side of the stage.

The scenario for the play (written by Stravinsky's friend, C. F. Ramuz) was based on Russian folk tales. Says the composer:

". . . we were particularly drawn to the cycle of legends dealing with the adventures of the soldier who deserted and the Devil who inexorably comes to carry off his soul. This cycle was based on folk stories of a cruel period of enforced recruitment under Nicholas I. . . ."

Stravinsky chose his orchestra with shrewd economy: a violin, a double bass, a clarinet, a bassoon, a trumpet, a trombone, and percussion—a total of seven players. They play in full view of the audience; indeed, their visual performance was deemed by the composer a vital part of the show itself. The elaborate battery of percussion instruments, all handled by one player, sprang from Stravinsky's sudden awareness of the American jazz of that era. Eric Walter White notes "how closely the instrumentation . . . resembles that of the 1916 New Orleans Dixieland Jazzband with its clarinet, trumpet, trombone, piano and drums . . ." and that the composer "not only included a ragtime in his set of dances, but also built up his percussion on jazzband lines".

Histoire du soldat blends the realistic and the classic. It satirizes the common music of the dance hall and the vaudeville show; at the same time it has the precision and terseness of an eighteenth-century chamber work. Played alone the music becomes repetitious; it needs the stage and its picturesque action. In the theatre the vigorous and pungent little score has a peculiar fascination, a flavour as original as the tang of a strange new vintage.

Stravinsky's one-act "ballet with song", *Pulcinella*, was composed at the behest of Diaghilev, who had collected certain unfinished manuscripts of the eighteenth-century Italian master, Pergolesi. Diaghilev's success with the ballet *The Good Humoured Ladies*, with Scarlatti's music arranged by Tommasini, led him to suggest a similar task for Stravinsky, who greatly admired the art of Pergolesi. The resulting ballet, scored for chamber orchestra and three singers, with scenery and costumes by Picasso, was first performed in Paris in the spring of 1920.

It was not at first realized that *Pulcinella* was a key work in the progress of Stravinsky's art. He had not merely touched up and modernized a few pieces by an old master. He had had to work from mere themes, unfinished pieces, fragments. These he built into an entirely new score which is practically an original work. *Pulcinella* has been termed "in effect a portrait of Pergolesi and his period, painted by Stravinsky". The forms and mannerisms of the period, the stylistic elegance, he evoked with delicate perception. If *Pulcinella* seems pallid among its lusty Stravinskian predecessors, it nevertheless exerted a powerful influence upon the composer himself. For him it opened a window upon a new horizon, that is, the modern evocation of some phase of music's past.

The experiments with miniature orchestras in *Renard* and *Histoire du soldat* had meanwhile led Stravinsky into still another bypath—an absorbing interest in the special field of wind instruments. This can be traced, perhaps, to a night in Rome, in 1917, when for Diaghilev's ballet season Stravinsky dashed off in a single night an orchestration of the famous Russian folk song, *The Song of the Volga Boatmen*. He used only the wind instruments of the orchestra, plus three percussion instruments.

Three years later, to pay homage to the memory of Claude Debussy, Stravinsky produced a far more startling study in sonorities, his Symphonies of Wind Instruments, scored for a wind orchestra of twenty players. The work made a negative impression at its first performances. The sound patterns, rasping with dissonance, were a shock to listeners expecting the velvet organ tones of the romantic wind choir ; moreover, the austere spirit of the work and the mechanical rigidity of its motion repelled any hint of sentiment ; while the complex design stood in the way of any quick assimilation. This was a new classicism, which posed not easy enjoyment but an intellectual challenge.

Even more recondite was the real core of Stravinsky's homage to Debussy. The Russian composer's earlier works had shown many derivations from the French master, most obvious perhaps in the little-known cantata, *The King of the Stars* (1911). The Symphonies of Wind Instruments is actually a subtle evocation, under Stravinsky's sharp personal style, of some of Debussy's mannerisms—the curviform melodic lines, the complex chord formations, the sense of fastidiousness, even a hint of the great impressionist's own scheme of mediaeval evocation. One thing alone is conspicuously lacking—the sensuous quality of Debussy's music. This was a deliberate elision. Wrote Stravinsky of his score : "It would be futile to look in it for any passionate impulse or dynamic brilliance. It is an austere ritual which is unfolded in terms of short litanies between different groups of homogeneous instruments."

VI

It was not long before another stylistic evocation appeared on Stravinsky's agenda. His one-act opera, *Mavra*, produced by Diaghilev in Paris, in 1922, was a re-creation of the Russian opera of the nineteenth century, and it paid homage to three great figures— Pushkin, Glinka, and Tchaikovsky. The story is taken from Pushkin's humorous tale in verse, *The Little House in Kolomna*. A young girl, Parasha, lives in a suburban town with her widowed mother. She is in love with a handsome Hussar, and she succeeds in getting her sweetheart into her mother's house disguised as a female cook named Mavra. The masquerade succeeds until the mother discovers the new "cook" in the act of shaving.

In his autobiography Stravinsky explains his evocation of the nineteenth-century Russian opera style. He was at pains to point out that it was the "cosmopolitan" and not the "nationalist" Russian school on which he based his *Mavra*, that is, the frank blending of Russian materials with the Italian operatic models, as typified by the works of Glinka, Dargomyjsky, and Tchaikovsky. Stravinsky's re-creation is a satire that approaches an exaggerated burlesque, in which the whole apparatus of the original is lustily parodied—the typical Russian melodies with their bright harmonies, the Italian singing style, and even some gypsy music.

Mavra is far more highly stylized than *Pulcinella*, that is it indulges in rhythmic and harmonic complications to give it a contemporary flavour and avoid mere imitation. What Stravinsky chiefly displays in this little opera buffa (as in *Pulcinella*) is his profoundly analytical mind, which works not merely on the surface, but rather ferrets out from under a music structure its entire system of roots.

Mavra was the last of Stravinsky's works to be based on a Russian literary subject, and the statement is commonly made that from this point on he ceased to be a Russian composer. This is an over-statement which misses a significant point. It is true that in his comments on *Mavra* Stravinsky stated emphatically his own ideas on the nationalist question, allying himself with "that wonderful line which began with Peter the Great and which, by a fortunate alloy, has united the most characteristically Russian elements with the spiritual riches of the West". He was opposed to the narrow nationalist concept, which was for him a "doctrinaire catechism". But even though Stravinsky preferred to be a cosmopolitan and ceased to write music with a special nationalist flavour, he has never, in a larger sense, ceased to be a Russian composer. Rather he has remained as typically Russian as Pushkin or Glinka, Tchaikovsky or Diaghilev, in exhibiting once again the peculiar Slavic genius for a penetrating eclecticism on a broad gauge cosmopolitan scale.

With Stravinsky, nationalism and eclecticism were not intermingled as they were in the careers of Glinka or Borodin or Rimsky-Korsakov. Stravinsky's nationalism came first, and only after he had exhausted his own interest in that phase did he turn to the other hemisphere. Eclecticism with this composer began to take a highly-specialized form, that of stylistic evocation, which became the axis around which his whole art would revolve. The actual beginnings of this procedure are not easy to discern, but certainly the references to American jazz in *Histoire du soldat*, *Ragtime* for eleven instruments (1918), and *Piano Rag Music* (1919) are among the pioneer examples. After that new specimens follow rapidly: *Pulcinella* evokes the style of Pergolesi, the Symphonies of Wind Instruments that of Debussy; *Mavra* recalls the nineteenth-century Russian opera style, and *The Wedding* the Russian folk style. In the next two decades the composer carried the process to a high state of refinement and efficiency.

Much has been written about Stravinsky's penchant for stylistic evocation, and the simple explanation is usually befogged by technicalities. Actually we need go no farther than the fact that he has been running true to form as a Russian composer exercising his natural eclectic gifts. The difference between Stravinsky's procedure and that of his predecessors is largely one of approach. The nineteenth-century Russian composers, being romantics, used the music idioms of other times and places for purposes of colour, or for magnification of exotic charms; moreover, they often went for their sources to the folk music. Stravinsky, being by nature and practice a classicist, uses an opposite approach. He avoids colour for its own sake, wants no part of exotic passion; instead he evokes the spirit and the technical mannerisms. Some of his earlier evocations (ending with *The Wedding*) were based on folk music; those which came later are nearly all based on examples already in a high state of technical refinement.

Following *Mavra*, which he said "marked a turning point in the evolution of my musical thought", Stravinsky plunged into the crystal waters of the new classicism. During 1922–23 he wrote his Octet for Wind Instruments—flute, clarinet, two bassoons, two trumpets, and two trombones. Absorbed in classic abstraction, the composer finished the first movement before he was aware of what instrumental garb the piece should take. The wind choir performs in the eighteenth-century manner, with fleet gracefulness, but with a wholly modern and delightful pungency. The dry, crackling wind tones, blended by beautifully detailed counterpoint, leave an impression still farther removed from the romantic than the Symphonies of Wind Instruments.

For his next classic adventure Stravinsky again used evocation, this time turning to Bach. In his Piano Concerto (1923–24) he recalled the florid keyboard style of the baroque era. The composer brought this piece with him on the occasion of his first visit to America early in 1925, and he performed the solo part with various orchestras. Interest in Stravinsky's music at that time was intense, due chiefly to the successes of his three large ballets. But few of his smaller evolutionary works of the intervening decade had been heard in America. The Piano Concerto, therefore, dashed like cold water over a bewildered public.

Stravinsky had cleverly paraphrased the keyboard figurations found in Bach's organ and clavier works. These were coupled with modern dissonant harmony; rhythms were broken up jaggedly in a way that suggested to American ears the jazz idioms of the period; the piano part was dry and percussive. The effect posed an aesthetic problem for audiences of that time. Moreover, the instrumentation seemed perversely strange. Stravinsky was then at the peak of his interest in wind instruments and his disdain of the strings. He insisted that piano tone and string tone do not blend well. He therefore scored the concerto for what he called the "harmonic orchestra", i.e. wind instruments and tympani, with double basses the only strings permitted.

The Piano Concerto has never been a popular work, even though its strangeness has long-since departed. The harmonic orchestra now sounds normal; indeed, it is part of the proof that Stravinsky has been one of the most original orchestral thinkers since Berlioz. The Concerto has its moments of dynamic power, of lightning brilliance, and in its slow movement a depth of feeling rare with this composer. Its limited success with audiences cannot rob the work of its place as the most original of modern concertos.

A companion work which also suffered neglect is the Sonata for piano, composed in 1924. The second movement, Adagietto, strongly recalls the highly-embellished lyricism of the early Beethoven piano sonatas, which were themselves more grandiose versions of the slow movements of Mozart. In his closing movement, a kind of two-part invention, Stravinsky returns with obvious relish to the keyboard style of Bach.

In his autobiography Stravinsky reveals that while composing this Sonata he had been restudying and rediscovering the piano sonatas of Beethoven. He confessed to having been alienated from Beethoven for many years, disgusted by the "sentimental attitude" toward his works, "his famous *Weltschmerz*", his "tragedy", indeed, "all the commonplace utterances voiced for more than a century about this composer . . ." Stravinsky would sweep away this clutter of "extra-musical elements". "It is in the quality of the musical material and not in the nature of his ideas that his true greatness lies."

VII

In 1926 Stravinsky felt the need to plan some homage to Diaghilev whose twentieth anniversary as an impresario was to occur the following year. The composer accordingly broke a long interval of thirteen years during which he had composed no large-scale works for the stage. He chose as his subject the *Œdipus Rex* of Sophocles. His friend Jean Cocteau compressed the story into a short libretto, which in turn was translated into Latin. This was Stravinsky's wish —to cast his work in an ancient tongue, "so monumentalized," he said, "as to have become immune from all risk of vulgarizations".

Stravinsky's version is a form of his own invention, an "opera-oratorio" in two acts, for large orchestra, chorus, six solo voices and a reader. At the premiere in Paris a sombre stage-set provided a scenic background ; the chorus remained stationary as in the Greek drama (or the oratorio) ; several of the singing characters appeared in costumes and masks, but moved only their arms and heads ; only two characters made entrances and exits. The reader, in modern evening dress and speaking in modern French, delivered short explanatory comments on the plot.

Stravinsky's music for *Œdipus Rex* is built, in the main, along the lines of an eighteenth-century oratorio and was at first thought to be an evocation of the style of Handel. The sources are in fact much more varied. Consciously or unconsciously, Stravinsky had availed himself of the practice of a nineteenth-century Russian composer with whom he had often allied himself—namely Glinka. The precedent for *Œdipus Rex* is, oddly enough, a work like *Ruslan and Ludmila* in which a diversity of music idioms welds into an artistic whole. Glinka's procedure was naïve; Stravinsky's is artful. The various elements in *Œdipus Rex* are first of all the eighteenth-century opera-oratorio framework, with powerful choruses, florid arias, and recitative-like declamations. But in certain numbers there are strong suggestions of ancient church chant, or plainsong, contained in melodic lines of stark simplicity. There are also references to the lyric style of the nineteenth-century Italian opera, and even a few hints of Russian folk music.

In Stravinsky's scheme the ancient liturgical style has the solemnity and tragic dignity necessary to the theme. The eighteenth-century oratorio style lends dramatic passion to the story, and at the same time avoids any taint of the contemporary. The Italian lyricism gives life and warmth to the characters lest they petrify amid the surrounding stone. Finally, the entire work is unified by Stravinsky's own personal style. In this case he uses no rhythmic complication whatever, but relies instead on his special harmonic colours. Tonalities are strongly defined, but are made rugged and angular by an abrasive dissonance.

Œdipus Rex was at first received with disappointment. It has not since prospered, possibly because as a work of stylistic synthesis it was never wholly successful. The juxtapositions of enormously contrasting styles at times approaches the ludicrous; even Stravinsky's genius could not bring them into focus. What remains is a work of majesty, grandly conceived and often powerfully executed, expecially in its choral passages; an original but not a consistent work of art.

Remaining for a time in the classic Greek vales Stravinsky next produced his wholly contrasting ballet, *Apollo Musagetes*. This piece was commissioned by the noted American patroness of music, Elizabeth Sprague Coolidge, and was first performed on April 29, 1928, at one of Mrs. Coolidge's chamber music festivals in the Library of Congress, Washington, D.C. Scored for strings only, *Apollo Musagetes* marked a sudden reversal of Stravinsky's long prejudice in favour of wind instruments. There was no relaxing, however, against romantic sentiment or emotional excess. This score is one of the composer's most severely classical.

The scenario of the ballet is brief. Scene one describes the legend of the birth of Apollo. Scene two is a series of allegorical dances in which Apollo inspires three of the Muses—Calliope, Polyhymnia, and Terpsichore. In a final apotheosis the god leads the Muses to Parnassus. Stravinsky revealed that he had in mind a "white ballet" of the classic school, purely conceived and devoid of excessive colour effects, but of a "wonderful freshness". He cast his music accordingly. His orchestra of strings alone projects an instrumental monochrome, a study in white, with everything revolving, according to the composer, "about the melodic principle". The major mode prevails almost continuously, as does a mood of serenity.

Like most of Stravinsky's stage works after *Le Sacre du printemps*, *Apollo Musagetes* needs its visual counterpart for its realization. As a ballet it has engendered some of the most exquisite dancing of this age; as music, it added to a rising chorus of doubts about Stravinsky's future as a composer. By this time, indeed, his entire classic aesthetic was under loud critical attack in many quarters.

Stravinsky had again become a storm centre in modern music. It began to be said that neo-classicism had robbed him of his virility, that he was written out. Works like *Apollo Musagetes* were described as melodically sterile, sweetly enervated, and bloodless. In this critical warfare a dwindling but loyal faction, including Diaghilev, defended the composer; but this time the general public did not take sides. It largely remained indifferent.

Stravinsky's next ballet, *The Fairy's Kiss* (1928), was based on a story by Hans Christian Andersen, but the music evoked was none other than Tchaikovsky's. People who had been bewildered by Stravinsky's adventures in neo-classicism were long recovering from the shock of discovery that he professed profound admiration for the art of the most romantic of all Russian composers. But it was Tchaikovsky the master of classic ballet music whom Stravinsky admired, and to prove his point he concocted a score which paraphrased a number of Tchaikovsky's more popular (and even hackneyed) melodies. In *The Fairy's Kiss* he avoided the modernist stylizing process which he had used in *Mavra*. Instead he remained almost completely in the melodic, harmonic, and orchestral style of Tchaikovsky himself.

The next year, 1929, Stravinsky quickly confounded his critics by composing one of his most successful instrumental works, the dashingly brilliant *Capriccio* for piano and orchestra. In three movements and of concerto proportions, this work was a kind of *Konzertstück* in the style of Carl Maria von Weber. "That prince of music," was Stravinsky's term for this composer who, he said, dominated his thoughts as he composed his *Capriccio*. The piece has been called "a grandiose parlour ornament", and "the happiest of Stravinsky's eclectic compositions". Certainly it proved that the composer had suffered no loss of masculine vitality, and that he could still strike off a scintillating show-piece full of brash, sardonic humour.

VIII

In the *Symphony of Psalms* (1930), for mixed chorus and orchestra, the unpredictable composer suddenly revealed a wholly-contrasting phase of his art. Heretofore, Stravinsky's catalogue had contained but a single short work (*Paternoster*, for mixed choir, 1926) of a religious type; nothing else had even hinted at the deeply spiritual side of the composer's nature. Now he produced a work which, though not for the church, was a powerful meditation on a liturgical theme.

Characteristically, Stravinsky disclaimed any religious "inspiration" for this work. Its genesis was simply a request by Serge Koussevitzky that he compose a symphony to commemorate the fiftieth anniversary of the Boston Symphony Orchestra in 1930. The composer decided first that his piece would bear no relation to the nineteenth-century romantic symphony, but instead would be "a work of great contrapuntal development". He chose a choral and instrumental ensemble "in which the two elements should be on equal footing, neither of them outweighing the other". Since he would need words, he sought words which had already been written for singing. "And quite naturally my first idea was to have recourse to the Psalms."

However coldly calculated the composer's description of his method might sound, the music shows the deep devotion and the reverence with which he approached his subject. The *Symphony of Psalms* is one of the few commanding religious works in modern music. It seems to bear no direct relationship to Russian church music; rather it invokes a freer, a more universal faith. In a mysterious way its austere quality is at once more modern and more ancient. The first movement with its stark chanting by the chorus over stiff, dissonant harmonies might be the church music of tomorrow; the dense polyphony of the double fugue of the second movement recalls the weighty chorale preludes of Bach's last years; but with the close of the third movement we seem to sink far into antiquity, to the earliest Christian centuries. Short, constantly-repeated melodic figures over a three-note ground bass have recalled "the mosaics in a Byzantine church"; the cumulative effect is one of solemn and ancient grandeur, an echo of some long-forgotten chant composed by a hymnwright of a thousand years ago for the ceremonial mysteries under the great dome of St. Sophia.

For five years after *The Fairy's Kiss*, which failed at its première, Stravinsky did no work for the theatre. Diaghilev had meanwhile died, and with him an epoch both in Russian and Western art had come to an end. Stravinsky felt the loss keenly, but more as friend than artist. The impresario had long since ceased to influence the composer's creative life. Stravinsky's return to the theatre followed a request by Ida Rubinstein that he create a stage work from a poem by André Gide, which was based on the Homeric Hymn of Demeter. The result was *Persephone*, composed chiefly in 1933. This work, termed a "melodrama", is scored for orchestra, chorus, and soloists, and requires singing, recitation, miming and dancing. Its three parts depict: 1. The Abduction of Persephone, 2. Persephone in the Underworld, and 3. The Rebirth of Persephone.

Persephone is an exquisite score which stands high among Stravinsky's works after *Le Sacre du printemps*. It weds a classically-restrained style and an almost romantic richness of feeling. The colours of this canvas never flash or flow; rather they are soft pastels in the delicate pinks and greens of early spring, cool with morning freshness.

Persephone represents the acme of French influence on Stravinsky's art, the final flowering of his years spent absorbing Gallic culture. There is no doubt that he reacted powerfully to the poetry of Gide, and in so doing he seemed to evoke in his music the art of the French composers around him. *Persephone* is never a copy of French music, but the spirit pervades the work. Often we sense the style of Debussy, but more often that of Ravel, with its clean, elegant workmanship, its obedience to discipline and design. Subtly evoked are not only the melodic lines which French composers have joined to their language, but their idiosyncrasies of harmony, rhythm, and form.

Infinitely remote from the mood of *Persephone* was Stravinsky's next stage work, *A Card Game*, composed in 1936 for an American ballet company and first performed at the Metropolitan Opera House in New York. The scene is a gambling house, and the action describes three deals in a game of poker. The characters are cards in the pack. Light and frivolous, this "adroit sherry trifle of music" has no more serious purpose, presumably, than that of a card game itself. Its music substance is a blend of Rossini, Delibes, Johann Strauss, Tchaikovsky, and perhaps others.

IX

In the years immediately preceding the composition of *Persephone* Stravinsky had composed two works for the violin—the Concerto in D, for violin and orchestra (1931); and the Duo Concertante, for violin and piano (1932). Few modern violinists have accepted the challenge of Stravinsky's concerto, and it remains comparatively neglected like the Piano Concerto. What the two violin pieces really signalled was the beginning of a whole series of abstract works in the old classic forms which would fall from Stravinsky's pen during the next fifteen years. These would include the Concerto for two solo pianos, the Concerto in E flat for chamber orchestra, the Symphony in C, the Sonata for two pianos, the Symphony in Three Movements, and the Concerto in D for orchestra. Here Stravinsky would fill out into a massive structure his work as a classic artist. Here he would establish with finality the arrival of a new classic age in music.

The big and vital Concerto for two solo pianos (without orchestra) was composed in 1936, and its first performances were by the composer and his second son, Sviatoslav. This is Stravinsky again writing for the instrument he obviously loves, and the results are brilliant and satisfying. In its four concise movements the concerto seems to sum up an entire age in piano progress. Its vigorous first movement has something of the dynamic quality of Beethoven's piano sonatas, mixed with the dry, rippling scale passages and the sharp, jolting accents typical of Stravinsky's own piano idiom. The second movement, Nocturne, is rich in ornamentation and cantilena strongly recalling Chopin, but with startling effects possibly derived from modern jazz pianists. The third movement consists of four variations, all ingeniously constructed and climaxed with technical diablerie remindful of Liszt. The final movement, Prelude and Fugue, closes the circle by returning to the derivation of the first—a massive contrapuntal effort, in the style of Beethoven.

In the Concerto for two pianos Stravinsky shows what a master can do with this difficult instrumental combination. Where other composers and arrangers fall into turgidity and bombast he has maintained fluency, crystalline clarity, and a steady flow of new pianistic effects.

The Concerto in E flat (called *Dumbarton Oaks* from the estate of the American music patron who commissioned it) was composed in 1938, and is scored for a chamber orchestra of fifteen instruments. The brisk, exuberant opening movement instantly recalls the style of Bach's Brandenburg Concertos. But as with all Stravinsky's evocations, the old baroque concerto style is used as a kind of cantus firmus, over which is reared the modern composer's personal idiom—his rhythmic dislocations, tart dissonances, distinctive instrumental colours, and a complex rather than a straightforward statement of thematic ideas.

The Symphony in C was composed for the Chicago Symphony Orchestra, which gave its premiere performance on November 7, 1940. It is a four-movement work, a neo-classic example which evokes the golden Viennese age of the symphony—that of Haydn, Mozart, and the early Beethoven. It proved to be one of the least admired of all Stravinsky's larger instrumental works, and has had few performances in recent years. The prevailing impression has been one of dryness, and a forbidding lack of thematic warmth.

Stravinsky introduced his Symphony in Three Movements on January 24, 1946, when he conducted it with the Philharmonic Symphony Society of New York. Compared with the frigid reception of the Symphony in C, this work has enjoyed a considerable success. Freed of some of the severities which bound the former work, it indulges in a virile, an almost romantic display of energy. Portions of it so strongly resemble *Le Sacre du printemps* that it has been called Stravinsky's *Heldenleben*. The moods too are often so powerfully stated and vividly contrasted as to suggest a programme. This the composer has denied, but he has hinted that World War II which raged while he composed the symphony may have left its marks upon his music. Others have hinted a parallel with Picasso's "Guernica".

X

In 1939, for the second time in Stravinsky's life, the crash of a world catastrophe broke the whole order of his existence. It happened that he had accepted the Charles Eliot Norton chair of poetry at Harvard University, and his lectures (on music) required his presence in Cambridge during the academic year 1939–40. The composer was fortunately still in America in the spring of 1940 when the Nazi armies overwhelmed the nations of Western Europe. He had no wish to subject himself again to the sufferings of Europe at war so he remained permanently in the United States, becoming an American citizen in 1945. He established a home in Hollywood, California, and for the second time began to adapt himself to the ways of a strange country.

It is said that Stravinsky has grown to enjoy his life in America. Here he has found peace of mind, financial security, and a place where he may practise his art undisturbed. In the past decade he has become a familiar figure in American concert halls, as conductor and piano soloist in performances of his own works.

As might be expected, Stravinsky is a personality study of uncommon interest. On the podium or at the piano he appears as a small man, quick and vital of mannerism, slender and agile as an athlete. He is intent, disciplined, precise, with great powers of concentration. Order, it is said, is the keynote of his life; there is a scrupulous neatness to his workroom and desk, his manuscripts in multi-coloured inks, and the methodical regularity of his daily habits. Stravinsky's mind is capacious. He has studied exhaustively in music and many related fields; those subjects which especially attract him he scrutinizes with an astounding perspicacity, forming his own bold opinions and filing them in the recesses of a memory that any scientist might envy. Friends of the composer find him the most stimulating of companions, whose conversations (in several languages) are enlivened by a corrosive sense of humour.

During the years when Stravinsky's later classic works were coming to flower the composer had settled himself into his new life in America. Except for jazz, his adopted country has made little indent upon his art, certainly nothing comparable with the previous French influence. Nevertheless, a few smaller works composed during these years do owe their existence to the American scene, having been commissioned by various producers in the entertainment field.

Dances Concertantes (1942), Stravinsky's first work composed in America, was commissioned by Werner Janssen, conductor of the Janssen Symphony Orchestra of Los Angeles. In five short movements and scored for chamber orchestra, it is an essay in the classic ballet style. All the delicate refinements of the classic dance are present—sprightly, lilting rhythms, bantering interplay of instruments and tone colours, themes of supple grace or leaping agility. A wedding of this score with the ballet itself was inevitable, and it was later produced for the stage with brilliant choreography by George Balanchine.

The *Circus Polka* was written in 1942 for Ringling Brothers and Barnum and Bailey's Circus. It is a short piece scored for band, and accompanied a ballet of the elephants. *Four Norwegian Moods* (1942) are orchestral pieces in the style of Grieg, and are said to have been planned originally for a Broadway revue. *Scherzo à la Russe* was composed in 1944 for Paul Whiteman's Band, and was first performed on a programme broadcast over the Blue Network. It might have been an unused fragment from *Petrouchka*.

Considerably larger in scope is the *Ballet Scenes* (1944). This work was commissioned by the Broadway producer, Billy Rose, for his musical show, "The Seven Lively Arts". Only portions of the work were actually used in the revue. This is another of Stravinsky's scores for the purely classical ballet. It is based on no literary or dramatic programme but uses the old classic ballet forms like the Variation, Pantomime, and Pas de Deux.

The Ebony Concerto, another short work, was composed in 1945 for Woody Herman's Orchestra. This was Stravinsky's first essay in American jazz in a quarter of a century. Wrote Virgil Thomson: "It is not a solo concerto of any kind, nor does it use only the black keys, nor has it anything to do with Negroes; it is rather a sinfonietta in four movements." The piece is interesting in the light of the change that has taken place since Stravinsky's early ragtime experiments. Both the composer's art and the character of American dance music have undergone a burgeoning change.

The ballet *Orpheus* (1947) was Stravinsky's most extensive stage work after *Persephone*. The scenario, devised by the composer and Balanchine, describes the lament of Orpheus over the loss of Eurydice, his descent into the Underworld and his rescue of his beloved, the return and death of Eurydice, the Furies tearing

Orpheus to pieces, and an apotheosis as Apollo raises the lyre of Orpheus to the heavens.

With *Apollo Musagetes* and *Persephone*, *Orpheus* might be said to complete a trilogy of stage works based on Greek mythology. Though the music forces of the three works differ (*Orpheus* employs a symphonic orchestra but no voices) all are pervaded by the same spirit of calm and understatement. Except for the few measures when the Furies perform their violent act, the orchestra of *Orpheus* is used with the refinements of a chamber group. An extraordinary atmosphere suffuses the work. Pale, cool, washed clean of passion or sensuality, this music seems to evoke the beauty of idealistic art concepts rather than the warmth of human life. Its moods are distant and withdrawn, grave and unsmiling. In every measure of the score Stravinsky surrenders to a severe discipline, with the result that the music seems almost naked when performed alone. Joined with Balanchine's exquisite choreography, however, it has become one of the masterpieces of the modern ballet.

Like many another devoutly religious man who is also an artist, Stravinsky has been aware of the serious decline in modern church art, especially liturgical music. "In Los Angeles," remarked the composer, "one hears anything in church, Rachmaninov and *Tristan and Isolde*." In 1948 he made a move to revivify an ancient tradition by composing a Mass. Although the composer himself is of the Russian Orthodox faith, this work is intended for use in the Roman Catholic Church. It follows the five sections of the liturgy—Kyrie, Gloria, Credo, Sanctus, and Agnus Dei—and is scored for a small chorus of men's and boys' voices, and ten wind instruments.

Stravinsky strips from his Mass all the grandiloquent vestments of the romantic or the baroque, and returns to far more ancient models. It is said that he has evoked the style of the Flemish contrapuntists of the fifteenth century; but there are also uses of organum, effects that recall plainsong, and even "a distant Byzantine strain". Every measure may yield some allusion of technique or method to delight the music antiquarian.

The Mass is a work of utmost austerity. It is spare, ritualistic, evoking no more passion than the voice of a priest intoning the words of the liturgy. Yet the gentle, cantabile style has warmth, like that of soft sunlight on ancient stone.

In the autumn of 1951 Stravinsky produced what might well be the capstone of his career, his first and only full-length opera, *The*

Rake's Progress. The composer whose music forty years before had seemed to exemplify Russian nationalism in its very essence, now gave the world fresh evidence that he is also a supreme eclectic whose perceptions acknowledge few limits of time or place. The mere statistics of the work and its première show the astonishing range of the composer's cultural orbit. The first performance, reported at length in the world's press as the outstanding music event of the year, took place on September 11th at the historic Teatro La Fenice in Venice, before a brilliant audience drawn from the entire Western Hemisphere. Stravinsky himself conducted the performance, which was prepared by the La Scala Opera Company of Milan with an international company of singers. The libretto derived from the famous series of engravings by which William Hogarth had poured the acid of realistic social satire on the scene of eighteenth-century England. The text, in English, was prepared by the poet, W. H. Auden, in collaboration with Chester Kallman, an American.

Divided into three acts and nine scenes, the story recounts Tom Rakewell's progress, which is in fact the moral degeneration of the young spendthrift as he deserts his provincial home and the virtuous Ann Trulove to follow the evil Nick Shadow into the licentious life of London. He revels in brothels and gin houses, marries a bearded lady from a circus, cheats Shadow in a match for his soul, but meets his death, wide-eyed and mad, in Bedlam.

The music of *The Rake's Progress*, the longest work ever composed by Stravinsky, is based on the matrix of eighteenth-century opera—arias, concerted numbers, ensembles, with recitative both accompanied and secco. It evokes a variety of sources—Italian opera and opera buffa, the tragi-comedy of Mozart's *Don Giovanni*. Melody prevails, a lyricism which is said to "awaken memories" not alone of Mozart but of Handel, Bellini, Gounod, and even Tchaikovsky. Harmonies recall eighteenth-century practice, but are stylized subtly by a hand that knows every ramification of mid-twentieth-century technique. Elegance is everywhere in this score —in its perfect craftsmanship, its mannered style, its urbane and satirical wit, its moments of restrained poignancy, its total allegiance with the finest traditions of Western art, poesy, music, and the drama. These are matters of intention, and few critics of the première performance denied Stravinsky's triumphant achievement. Those who filed dissenting opinions did so in familiar terms: that this was a desiccated neo-classicism, a pale replica of Mozart without his humanity, a collection of dry melodies intellectually induced, a theatre piece devoid of theatrical passion, an ornament too fragile to endure in the opera house. Doubtless the final judge, the public, will be slow in evaluating Stravinsky's work; but music so consummately wrought can usually afford to wait.

Two shorter pieces followed the opera in Stravinsky's catalogue. "After finishing *The Rake's Progress*," he said, "I was persuaded by a strong desire to compose another work in which the problems of setting English words to music would reappear, but this time in purer, non-dramatic form." During 1951–52 he composed a secular Cantata, for solo soprano, solo tenor, female chorus, and an instrumental quintet of two flutes, two oboes (the second interchangeable with English horn), and 'cello. The words are anonymous fifteenth- and sixteenth-century English lyrics. A Septet appeared in 1953, and seemed to be a neo-classical evocation somewhat like the earlier Octet. It is a three-movement piece in the general contrapuntal style of the early eighteenth century, and is scored for violin, viola, 'cello, clarinet, bassoon, horn, and piano.

XI

In the course of his long creative life Stravinsky has composed music on an astonishing variety of subjects and in many forms. He has worked as a romantic, a realist, and a classicist. Few composers ever pass through so great an art cycle, much less compose significant examples in every phase as Stravinsky has done. It is also a gauge of his strength that he has always managed to impress upon his music the stamp of his personal style. The Stravinsky style, moreover, is no simple trick or mannerism. It is a whole complex of procedures which the composer invented over a long span of years.

In Stravinsky's earlier scores, culminating in *The Wedding*, his stylistic labels were more obvious—complex, dynamic rhythms which drove his music with furious vitality; a strong sense of dissonance which often resulted from polytonality. The Stravinsky style of the later neo-classic music is much more subtly achieved, but certain features stand out. Always first to be noted is the classic mood of restraint which sets it apart from romantic models. After that the listener is conscious of polyphonic texture and dissonant harmony. Stravinsky's music is not atonal, nor is it chromatic; it gives the impression of being diatonic, but with dissonance derived from what has been called "secundal" counterpoint, that is, counterpoint based not on thirds and sixths but on seconds and sevenths.

The peculiar continuity of Stravinsky's later music is another stylistic label. At first hearings there might seem to be a lack of continuity; it has been said that the composer "picks up one musical idea, puts it down and picks up another". Short phrases may be repeated, but seldom long ones. The result is a series of mosaics—short, irregular ideas pressed together to form a large design. This method was original not with Stravinsky but with Debussy, who used it in certain later works, notably *La Mer* and *Jeux*. It avoids the old standard technique of repetition and development, the "dynamic continuity" which reached its apex with Beethoven. Only after repeated hearings or careful scrutiny of the score are the recondite relationships of the various elements revealed.

One of the most characteristic of all Stravinsky's devices is the minute pause. Nearly all music utilizes moments of silence, by means of pauses and rests. With Stravinsky the pause has a characteristic irregularity, a ricochet which suddenly halts the continuity of the music, and carries on a second later. The instant of silence is not used to create repose, but to sharpen attention and interest.

Stravinsky has been the most powerful assailant of the music of the romantic age. It would be hard to say whether it was the example of his own music or his written and spoken words which have struck the heaviest blows. In the composer's autobiography (written in 1935), in his lectures at Harvard, and in many didactic pronouncements about his works, he has carried on a hammering assault against the crumbling fortress of romanticism—against virtuoso performers (especially conductors) who personalize and "interpret" music; against "orchestral opulence" which has "corrupted the judgement of the public"; against the idea that music may "express" anything; against the excess baggage of day-dreams and sentimentality, of programmes read into music; and above all against Wagner—that Lucifer who dragged down with him in his great fall the whole proud art of music.

In their way Stravinsky's opinions have often been as dogmatic as Wagner's. Inevitably he had invited counterattack, as for example the remarks of the noted composer and exponent of the twelve-tone school, Ernst Krenek, who wrote in 1938 of Stravinsky's "comedy masquerade in which he hides behind Pergolesi, Bach, Weber, and Tchaikovsky for so long that when he finally emerges again as Stravinsky one does not recognize him for himself. His individuality can always be identified in the unmistakable gestures with which his genius animates his figures, but no one knows what has become of the real personality—perhaps he does not know himself, possibly he does not want to know. In his autobiography, written so coolly and with such conscious detachment, Stravinsky speaks of many people and things, but is silent about the only cardinal fact of his mysterious career: namely, how he journeyed from the 'Sacre du printemps' to 'A Card Game'."

Stravinsky's is the most intellectual music of our time, and its influence on the technique of other composers has been great. But technique, it must be noted for the thousandth time, is the science of art, the machinery. It has nothing whatever to do with creative power. Nor has intellectual capacity, nor learning. In Stravinsky's music there is always at work a powerful creative force, but because art is a mysterious and paradoxical business, works of satisfying beauty have not always emerged. Possibly the answer lies wrapped within the supreme enigma of music—the power of melody. "My music aims only at being melody," said Debussy in answer to those who accused him of trying to destroy melody. Much of the music which Stravinsky composed after *Le Sacre du printemps* and which often seems so lean of melodic idea, will have to satisfy that criterion some time in the future, as Debussy's music did a generation ago.

As for the emotional restraints of Stravinsky's art, there is something to be said on both sides. Someone had to put up the dikes against a swollen romanticism, and this composer deserves credit for his courageous stand. At the same time there is a paradox in the fact that, while so much of Stravinsky's work is for the theatre where art can come closest to life, it yet remains so passionless and cold. It is remarkable how seldom in his long stage career he has worked with living human feelings, and how instead the common emotions are screened by elaborate devices of fantasy or legend or literary allusion, or are completely ignored. What was said of Shaw, the greatest dramatist of this age, can also be said of Stravinsky the theatre composer: that he has given the stage of his time the keenest intellectual satisfaction and the meagrest emotional satisfaction.

Parallels have also been drawn between the art of Stravinsky and that of his contemporary among poets, T. S. Eliot. The object of both men has been much the same : to erect a new classic order from the wreckage of the old romanticism. Their equipment as artists has many points in common. With both the intellect leashes the emotions ; both are armed with great technical skill and informed by redoubtable learning. Similar technical devices run through their works : concentration of idea, understatement, economy of means. Both like to use the shock of incongruity, the placing together of ridiculously contrasted ideas, and not always for the purpose of humour. Most curious of all, both artists have relied extensively on a system of allusion, a display of erudition which they have been prone to use (as was said specifically of Eliot) "not quite without ostentation".

For musicians there is a more revealing analogy to be drawn between Stravinsky and (of all men) Berlioz. Fantastically contrasted in personality and in their immediate aims as artists, these two nevertheless performed exactly similar functions. Both undertook the task of reversing the polarity of the art cycle of their day— Berlioz from classic to romantic, Stravinsky from romantic back to classic. Thus *Apollo Musagetes* is no less revolutionary (to use a word which Stravinsky detests) than was the *Symphonie Fantastique*. Both composers were inventors, explorers. Both greatly influenced other composers of their time, in their larger aims and in innumerable technical details. It is a curious fact that, with both artists, certain brilliant works of their comparative youth have remained the more vigorously alive, appealing to the wide audience. These are the sheer explosions of genius. The more mature works, the products of reflection and experience, will always delight technicians even if their audience appeal should remain small.

There remains to be summed up the position of Stravinsky in the field of Russian music. Here his historical significance becomes very great. Only a century has passed since Glinka made his first attempts at a nationalist art music, which then seemed to many Western European composers to be hardly more than a minor experiment. Now, with Stravinsky, a Russian composer has for the first time assumed in influence and range the position held for centuries by German, Italian, or French composers. He has become one of the two or three dominating figures in the entire international music scene, and his hand will help direct the course of this art for some years to come.

Remembering the ironies of history, it is not surprising that one of Russia's greatest creative artists should now be bereft of influence in his own land. Here one must speak with caution, since no one outside the Iron Curtain can know for certain what goes on within. Specifically we cannot be sure to what extent the music of Stravinsky is disseminated privately among present-day Russian students and composers, and how much of it may be dispassionately studied. But it is certain that this man, one of the prophets of modern art, has been without honour among the masters of the Russian state. In the Kremlin there is no relaxing against him as there was against Rachmaninov, whose music was found to have virtue popular enough to counteract the composer's political heresy. Stravinsky's offence is rank. Not only has he hated the Soviet dictatorship and expressed his contempt for it; his music has become, to them, appallingly un-Russian.

If Stravinsky's work is not one of the chief adornments of Russian music, indeed of all modern Russian art, then there are no longer any sane criteria by which art in that country may be judged. For this man has combined in overwhelming measure those talents which are intensely and typically Russian: he has been both an ultra-nationalist and an eclectic on a cosmic scale. As the composer of *Petrouchka*, *Le Sacre du printemps*, and *The Wedding*, he is a pure Russian, hardly second to Musorgsky himself; elsewhere he has surpassed any of his countrymen, except possibly Pushkin, in powers of assimilation. He has absorbed an amazing range of music styles, techniques, and schools—near and far, ancient and modern. He is a time-traveller par excellence in art, a student of traditions, an explorer of cultures.

CHAPTER XIV

MUSIC IN THE COMMUNIST STATE

I

SINCE the revolution of 1917 profound changes have occurred in the course of Russian music. What has happened to this art and to the men who create and practise it is almost incomprehensible without some knowledge of the accompanying political drama. In a totalitarian state as despotically controlled as the Soviet Union not only every man in every walk of life, but every science, every philosophy, every art ceases to enjoy freedom of growth. Instead, growth may be shaped, guided, warped, stimulated, or extinguished by government order. The recent history of Russian music is thus a mere reflection on a miniature scale of another and far more complex history—that of the Soviet state itself.

In 1917 the overwhelming majority of the Russian people were at heart revolutionists who longed for an end of the Czardom and all it stood for. When at last the old regime fell under the weight of World War I and its own decay, there existed in Russia a number of rival political parties, both open and secret, but only one strongly organized revolutionary faction—the Bolsheviks. Led by Vladimir Ilych Ouilanov, who operated under the pseudonym of Lenin, they gained control of the national government by a *coup d'état* which grew out of their own shrewd organization, calculation, and energy, the disorganization of their rivals, and the unaccountable accidents of history.

The Bolsheviks were part of the general socialist movement which had been growing in Europe since the mid-nineteenth century. Among Marxian theorists they were an extreme radical wing who would abolish private property as well as the capitalist profit system. Soon after 1917 they dropped the name Bolshevik and called themselves Communists. It is important to note that the Russian communist government has never ceased to reflect the peculiar mentality of the men who created it. Lenin, Trotsky, Stalin, *et al*, were, even by Russian standards of political thought in 1917, not simply revolutionists but fanatics. The intellectual classes and the broad middle classes of Russia were almost wholly against them, and at first

284

believed that they would soon be ousted by some more rational faction.

The government which the Bolsheviks set up was supposed to be based on the tenets of Marxian socialism. The reader of the present volume can hardly fail to note the familiar force which was at work here. This was another instance of the Russians seizing upon Western ideas and transmuting them with Slavic ingenuity to their own purposes. But a process which in the field of art is benign, can become in the field of politics, malignant. To the mind of the Bolshevik leader, government meant only one thing. It was an instrument of suppression. It was the tyranny by which the Czars had stunted the social and intellectual growth of the Russian people for generations, and had herded them into isolation from the free peoples of the world; it made conspirators of any opposition, to be hunted down with cold ferocity. The Bolsheviks understood no other concept of government; and so in their new state they proceeded to graft a form of radical Marxian socialism on to the old tree of Russian despotism.

From the first moment it was a government as ruthless as that of any czar, a dictatorship ostensibly of the proletariat but actually of a few men who controlled the Communist Party. No hint of freedom of speech or of the press has ever been permitted. All religions were suppressed and the power of the old Russian Orthodox Church destroyed. All classes of persons, from peasants and factory workers to artists and intellectuals, have had their lives ordered by government fiat.

Students of the art of mass propaganda find a sobering lesson in the fact that this gigantic operation in human suppression, one of the most reactionary known in modern times, can still be trumpeted by Soviet ideologists in and out of Russia as a forward march of social progress.

II

The first stage of the Soviet era in Russia lasted roughly from 1917 to 1921. This blood-red dawn of the communist state was actually a prolongation of the revolution itself during which the Bolsheviks seized the government, put down a long series of civil wars and peasant uprisings, and then by means of the army and a terrorist secret police set about exterminating the old aristocrats and the so-called bourgeoisie. The Russian people were already exhausted from the vast casualties of World War I; now they went through bloodshed, famine, and terror on an even greater scale. Not since the Thirty Years' War had a nation endured such physical and spiritual haemorrhage.

The intellectual classes of Russia were decimated. Hundreds of thousands of scientists, scholars, teachers, and artists fled the country; many more died in prisons and concentration camps, or starved in the great famine of 1920–21. For those who remained, life was profoundly different, but it went on. Artists, like all other men, had to adjust themselves to the new dictatorship of the proletariat or die. In the vast confusion musicians were too unimportant to warrant the close attention of the authorities. The music conservatories went on as before, but with a new class of proletarian students who, it was expected, would create the new music and culture of the proletarian society. At first the restrictions on music were not many, and they were chiefly unofficial. For public performance words of certain songs and librettos of operas had to be purged of any flattering references to the old order. Banned completely were works of a religious nature, like Handel's oratorios, and the Masses of Bach, Beethoven, and Mozart. Karl Marx had called religion "opium for the people", so the communist leaders were all militant atheists, determined to uproot religion from Russian society.

Out of the confusion of the first stage there came a certain amount of experimentation in the arts, especially among the young Russian painters and architects. A flurry of futurism in pictures and building designs showed that these men were eager to make the art of the new *proletkult* revolutionary in every sense, free of the academism of the past. A typical manifestation of the times was the formation in 1922 of the famous Moscow Persimfans Orchestra, which operated without a conductor.

It was in the theatre that the most spectacular changes took place. To indoctrinate the masses with the new communist ideology a *proletkult* theatre was formed, headed by the brilliant stage director, Vsevolod Meyerhold. This man was the most radical and controversial figure in the Russian theatre, whose futuristic conceptions included "constructions" of wood or iron to replace scenery, and all manner of audacious lighting, acting, and musical effects. For the government Meyerhold created a host of "flying theatres", productions sent out from Moscow and set up on temporary stages in small cities and towns to entertain and indoctrinate the peasants. At Leningrad and Moscow he produced gigantic open-air spectacles intended to glorify the Bolshevik "liberation" of the peoples of the world.[1]

In another department of the *proletkult* theatre the communist theorists went off on a different tack. Believing that the old Russian circus with its buffoons and acrobats was closer to the hearts of the people than the theatre, which was a Western importation, they produced a form of circus-in-the-theatre, which included hours on end of gymnastics, running, jumping, juggling, rope dancing, and clowning.[2] The *proletkult* theatre, with its attempt to indoctrinate the masses by means of entertainment, ranging from mass spectacles to circus acrobatics and clowning, was to leave its mark in curious ways upon the music of a generation of Russian composers, including some of the most eminent.

Between 1921 and 1927 there came a second stage in the life of the U.S.S.R., ushered in by the so-called New Economic Policy, or N.E.P. After four years of communism the country had reached a point of crisis and the economy was falling apart. Lenin realized that he would have to compromise. Over bitter opposition within the Party he promulgated the N.E.P. to permit the resumption of a certain amount of private ownership and operation, both in industry and agriculture. Thus, for a time, the U.S.S.R. was a combination of communism and capitalism.

The N.E.P. had a buoying effect on the economy of the nation. The government began to relax many of its controls, and even some of its intolerant attitude toward the capitalist countries. During this period the theatres of Russia resumed performances of Western dramas, both classic and modern. The art galleries exhibited pictures by Picasso, Matisse and other *avant garde* painters. Much new foreign music was performed in the concert halls and opera houses, including works of the Central European modernists—Schönberg, Berg, Krenek, and Hindemith—and of the new French school. From America came the first importations of jazz, which would later sweep the Soviet Union like a public craze.

[1] Meyerhold's supreme effort was a colossal re-creation of *The Storming of the Winter Palace*, performed at Leningrad. One hundred thousand persons took part, including regiments of soldiers—to the sound of rifles, machine-guns, rockets, and a bombardment from a battleship in the Neva River. These vast "dramatic eruptions" recalled to theorists of the drama the mass festivals of the ancient Greek theatre, the Roman Circus, and the mediaeval mystery plays.

[2] Sergei Eisenstein, the celebrated film producer, was a pioneer director of the *proletkult* theatre and one of the first to use the apparatus of the circus in the theatre. He also experimented with machine effects, producing one of his plays in a large factory in Moscow with factory workers as actors.

III

On January 21, 1924, amid the tolerant period of the N.E.P.,
Lenin died, and instantly a battle for power gripped the inner circle
of the Kremlin. For a time Russia was ruled by a triumvirate
—Stalin, Kamenev, and Zinoviev—with the ultra-communistic
Trotsky a disrupting force between them. It was not long before
Stalin was ranged alone against the three other men, he favouring
the N.E.P. as against a return to dogmatic communism. The fierce
hierarchical struggle came to a climax in 1927 when Stalin was able
to purge his rivals out of the Party.

Stalin's strength had come from his insistence on placing the
reconstruction of Russia before its complete communization; but
once he had the reins of power firmly in his hands he set about
combining the two objectives. Thus came the third stage of the
Soviet era, the period of the First Five Year Plan, beginning in
1928. The heart of this plan was the gigantic expansion of Russia's
weak industrial plant, especially her heavy industries. It also called
for the beginning of the collectivization of the farms and the liquida-
tion of a growing class of kulaks, or "rich" peasants, by wholesale
killings, mass deportations, and imprisonment.

This was one of the darkest periods in Russian life since the
revolution, with the whole populace burdened by the gigantic costs
of the First Five Year Plan, the terrible casualties in the agrarian
districts, and finally the famine of 1930–31. To counteract the
general unrest the government tried to whip up enthusiasm for its
Plan, and for the "classless" society it was trying to build.

During this period a special campaign aroused the writers and
artists of Russia to redouble their efforts in glorifying the new
proletkult and damning the "degenerate" capitalist West. In the
field of music this had important repercussions. Western music in
general was played down; performances of contemporary works
were stopped. Jazz music was heard no more. This was the heyday
of the so-called proletarian composers. All the large music schools
and conservatories had groups of proletarian students whose studies
were in sharp contrast to the regular curriculum. They were Communist Party members of impeccable proletarian ancestry, and their
function was to provide a new music for the masses. This people's
art had to be simple—songs, marches, and dance tunes—for the

edification of the factory workers and the farmers. Russian folk music held an exalted place in this scheme, while the music of the West, especially in its complex modern forms, was excoriated. The spearhead of this movement was the Association of Proletarian Musicians, known as the R.A.P.M., which had been founded in 1924.

In 1929 the proletarian groups, encouraged by the government's class campaign, began to reach for power in Russia's music affairs. For a time they controlled the Moscow Conservatory, changed its name, drove out all students with the least class taint, and tried to bend the curriculum in the direction of simple music for the masses. In their lexicon not only the old "bourgeois" art music of the West was degenerate, but even Russian composers like Tchaikovsky were considered no more than panderers to the old aristocratic regime. Only Musorgsky was valued a revolutionary worthy of notice.

Fortunately, this incredible experiment in bigotry came to a halt in 1932, when the government suddenly abolished all proletarian art groups.

In 1933 Stalin inaugurated his Second Five Year Plan, in effect a continuation of the First. But so depressed were the Russian people that the government relaxed some of its iron commandments. Stalin himself coined the slogan: "Life is Better, Life is Happier." Less was heard of class distinctions and the new dictatorship of the proletariat. The old spirit of Russian nationalism (as opposed to the international communist dogma) was revived; Soviet writers, teachers, and scholars were urged to glorify Russia's great historic heritage—except, of course, the Czarist regime and its bourgeois parasites.

One of the odd by-products of the Second Five Year Plan was the jazz mania of the nineteen-thirties. To help prove that life was better and happier, American popular music was permitted to raise its head. Jazz struck the Russian people with even wilder impact than the similar craze in Western Europe. All over the U.S.S.R. jazz bands and jazz clubs sprang up. Government officials were not immune and it is said that even Molotov, that redoubtable statesman, took lessons in the tango and the rhumba. Inevitably, the government sought a way to turn the popularity of jazz to its own uses by forming a State Jazz Band. But the people did not take to it, possibly because its repertoire contained little real American jazz but instead much music of the Soviet proletarian type.

IV

One reason for the abolition of the proletarian art groups in 1932 was their complete ineptitude as instruments of propaganda. The new government policy which followed was an attempt to force all the artists of Russia—her finest creative talents in art, literature, the films, the theatre, and music—into large unions so their efforts could be channelled directly into the service of the state.

At the First Convention of the Soviet Literary Union, in 1934, the writers of the U.S.S.R. forgathered to learn their new duties. One of the speakers was the eminent writer, Maxim Gorky, who was then a close personal friend of Stalin. He expounded a new doctrine, called "socialist realism", which was to play an enormous part in the future of all Soviet art.

According to the Soviet ideologists the old bourgeois concept of realism in art was essentially negative, critical, destructive, exposing the ugliness of life. Socialist realism was to be the antithesis —soundly constructive, optimistic, with emphasis only on the health, security, and beauty of socialist proletarian existence. The term socialist realism was thus a convenient catch-phrase to summarize what the government wanted its writers to write, i.e. only pieces which idealized the manifold phases of life under a communist regime.

In the various directives outlining the duties of the Soviet artist another catch-word began to appear, one which conveniently summarized all which was bad and to be avoided. This was "formalism". The word covered a multitude of sins. Formalism meant art for art's sake, as opposed to art with a message. It meant art for the few, instead of for the many. Any extreme of individualism, sophistication, or experimentation was formalism, and so was excessive use of abstraction. Art too concerned with esoterica, too refined technically, or too complex for easy consumption by the masses, was formalism. Formalism was usually described as a manifestation of decadence, and was therefore continually linked up with Western art which was supposed to be in an advanced state of putrefaction.

Formalism became a particularly handy club for use in the field of music, where it could be made to strike at a large and varied assortment of culpabilities.

In the midst of the Second Five Year Plan Stalin's dictatorship was imperilled by the assassination of his right-hand man, S. M. Kirov. There followed another violent period of mass arrests and purges, and finally, in 1936, the sensational trials of Stalin's old enemies, Kamenev and Zinoviev, and eleven other conspirators. All were executed, supposedly for having plotted the murder of Stalin and a return to capitalist practices.

Early in 1936, during the worst of this turbulent period, the small world of Soviet music was suddenly shaken as if by a blast. The official newspaper *Pravda* issued the famous criticism of the opera *Lady Macbeth of Mzensk* and its composer, Dmitri Shostakovich. The work was driven from the stage because of its flood of "formalist errors", and Shostakovich, then the most eminent composer in the Soviet Union, was publicly ostracized.

In the government's effort to make all creative artists active state propagandists the writers had been quickly brought to heel; so had the makers of films, and the producers and directors of the great art theatres, like the Moscow Art Theatre, the Vakhtangov Theatre, and the Kamerni Theatre. All had come under a despotic control, never since relaxed. But composers of the eminence of Shostakovich, Prokofiev, and Miaskovsky still enjoyed a certain artistic freedom. The *Pravda* article served them with notice that their period of liberty was ended. Hereafter they would be expected to follow closely the directives of the state.

If any composer, writer, dramatist, or other creative artist felt the urge to declare his independence of the government's wishes, he might ponder an episode which occurred a few years later. The theatrical director, Vsevolod Meyerhold, finally made a public protest against the government's policy, declaring in a moment of desperation that it was achieving nothing more than the destruction of Russian art and culture. Meyerhold was immediately arrested, and was never seen or heard of again. A few weeks later his wife was brutally murdered.

No other eminent Soviet artist followed the unfortunate Meyerhold's action. The more progressively-minded composers could only try to decontaminate themselves of formalist influences; Shostakovich declared his allegiance to the new order by composing his popular Fifth Symphony. The coming of World War II, however, caused an interregnum in the progress of socialist realism in Soviet art. The country was fighting for its life against Hitler's Nazi armies, and the composers almost without exception patriotically enlisted their talents. The next few years brought a spate of propaganda pieces, ranging from simple songs and marches to gigantic symphonies and choral works, describing the heroism of the Russian people and their cause. The arch example of this genre was the *Leningrad* Symphony of Shostakovich.

During the war less was heard of socialist realism. Composers like Shostakovich, Prokofiev, and Miaskovsky began to take liberties again. Among their patriotic tracts we find other scores obviously written without reference to government standards. Some of the most important Russian music of the present generation was produced during this period.

V

With the end of the war in 1945 the Soviet government performed another of its wrenching changes of direction to swing the entire nation back into the grooves of communist ideology. The Iron Curtain was lowered ; the nations of the West which had helped save Russia were assailed by a barrage of vilifying propaganda ; the international communist parties resumed their sapping at the foundations of existing governments everywhere. The period of the Cold War had begun. Inside Russia the despotic controls were tightened as never before.

In 1946 Stalin announced that the nation would be put through at least three more Five Year Plans, with vast sums of money to be poured into the heavy industries instead of into consumer goods. To counteract this discouraging news it became necessary to harness every possible source of propaganda to the service of the regime, and also to stamp out heretical thinking, especially among the intellectual classes. Scientists, artists, writers, musicians, playwrights, teachers, historians, and philosophers all came under a heavy fire of government criticism, intended to force them into the role of active propagandists for the communist ideology and against the influences of the West.

For the composers, the epoch of war freedom lasted until 1948. Then the axe fell. On February 10th the Central Committee of the Communist Party published its Decree on Music, one of the most extraordinary documents in the history of Russian music. Harking back to the *Pravda* criticism of *Lady Macbeth* in 1936, the decree stated that in spite of repeated warnings many eminent composers had "persistently adhered to formalist and anti-people" practices. Singled out were Shostakovich, Prokofiev, Khachaturyan, Shebalin, Popov, and Miaskovsky, whose music was found to be "marked by formalist perversions, anti-democratic tendencies which are alien to the Soviet people and their artistic tastes". These faults included "atonalism, dissonance, and disharmony; the rejection of . . . melody; and a striving after chaotic and neuropathic discords . . ." "This music savours of present-day modernist bourgeois culture." The Decree bluntly warned the composers of the Soviet Union to "liquidate the faults", and to "become more conscious of their duties to the Soviet people".

The publication of the Decree had been preceded by a remarkable three-day conference of Russia's leading musicians, presided over by the late Andrei Alexandrovich Zhdanov, one of Stalin's lieutenants in the Politburo. Zhdanov was a man of steel, whose great achievement was his fanatical defence of Leningrad in 1941. He was Chief of the Communist Party in Leningrad, and was widely regarded as a possible heir to Stalin's dictatorship. Zhdanov was no musician, but to the assembled Soviet musicians at the 1948 conference he was a sinister personification of the sword-blade that now hung over their heads.

Zhdanov proceeded to tell the conference, which included nearly all the most eminent composers, exactly what he thought of them. He found them guilty of formalist errors, and classed some of their most admired music with the "degenerate" art of the West. Even works which had once gained honours like the Stalin Prize did not escape wholesale condemnation.

No one dared to raise a voice to contradict Zhdanov. Shostakovich and Khachaturyan, among others, spoke, but made no real defence of artistic principles; the former admitted his "errors" and promised to "do better" in the future. Contempt for the proceedings was shown indirectly only by Miaskovsky, who refused to attend the conference. A story circulated in Russia that Prokofiev had deliberately sat with his back to Zhdanov; but in a letter made public later the composer praised the Decree, apologized for his own past errors, and blamed "infection" in his music to "contact with certain Western currents".

Remembering the fate of the stage director, Meyerhold, it is palpably unfair to judge any of these men by standards of artistic integrity that are common in a free democracy.

VI

In the present chapter an attempt has been made to chart in outline those political manœuvres of the Soviet government that have had a direct bearing on the course of Russian music since the revolution. In the following chapters we shall observe the effects on the lives and the art of a number of eminent Russian composers, at close range and in detail.

CHAPTER XV

PROKOFIEV

I

"WHEN I was three years old," wrote Serge Prokofiev in his autobiography, "I bumped my forehead against an iron trunk, and the bump stayed for something like twenty-five years. A painter who did my portrait used to touch the bump and say, 'Well, perhaps your talent is in this bump.'"

Whatever the mystery of its powers, the bump went to work quickly and well for Prokofiev. He became one of the most precocious musicians since Mozart. He improvised at the age of five and a half; at six he was composing short pieces for the piano, and at nine he completed a rudimentary opera. Like Glinka, Prokofiev had a rich music-loving uncle, at whose estate the child's opera (written for voices and piano) was actually performed. When he entered the Petersburg Conservatory in 1904 at the age of thirteen, young Prokofiev had already composed four such operas (one based on Pushkin's *A Feast in the Time of Plague*), two sonatas, a symphony, and a large number of piano pieces.

So far as the bump on his forehead is concerned, we may note that it carried Prokofiev through a distinguished career at the Petersburg Conservatory, and that when it deserted him in manhood it left with him one of the great music talents of this age. Thus Prokofiev's experience contrasts happily with that of the legendary wizard Kashchey, whose life was contained in, but expired with, an egg.

Prokofiev was also fortunate with his family and his early music education. He was born on April 23 (11, O.S.), 1891, in the Ukrainian village of Sontsovka, in the Ekaterinoslav government (now the Dniepropetrov district). "My father," he wrote, "was director of the estate of the Sontzovs. This estate comprised large expanses of the steppe, and the owners never lived there. My mother played the piano rather well, chiefly Beethoven and Chopin, and this gave me a taste for serious music from my youngest years."

The list of Prokofiev's teachers reads like a galaxy of famous names. First was Reinhold Gliere, who took him in hand at the age of eleven. When he entered the Conservatory Prokofiev studied harmony and counterpoint with Liadov, and orchestration with Rimsky-Korsakov. Later he studied conducting with Tcherepnin, and piano with Annette Essipova, a noted teacher who had been a pupil as well as the wife of Leschetizky. Prokofiev graduated with highest honours in 1914. At the commencement exercises he won a grand piano for his performance of his First Piano Concerto.

Even as a young student Prokofiev was a belligerent leftist. In 1908 he joined a society in Petersburg dedicated to the performance of new and controversial works by Debussy, Dukas, Faure, Schönberg, Reger, Richard Strauss, Hugo Wolf, Scriabin, and Stravinsky. At one of these evenings, in December, 1908, Prokofiev made his first appearance at a public concert. When he played his *Diabolic Suggestions* from his Op. 4 he stunned his listeners. In 1911 he gave the first performance in Russia of Schönberg's *Klavierstücke*, Op. 11. The next year when he played his own First Piano Concerto in Petersburg and Moscow, Prokofiev had become the "enfant terrible" of Russian music, a title which would take him many years to live down.

Few composers have had a greater natural aptitude for the gentle art of making enemies. Prokofiev's fault (or perhaps virtue) was his inability to speak with anything but utter frankness on any subject. He was gruff, outspoken, loudly sarcastic, sparing nobody's feelings and nobody's ideas. To some he was a porcupine personality, all spines and quills. At the Conservatory he caused untold anguish to the conservative professors by his reckless opinions and his radical music.

The First Piano Concerto, which he practically forced down the throats of the unwilling professors, was composed in 1911 when Prokofiev was twenty years old. From some highly-unpromising thematic material he constructed a long one-movement piece that is actually an extended scherzo, with contrasting passages either lyric or bombastic. The scherzo qualities have nothing to do with Mendelssohnian grace or delicacy. This is the modern scherzo, with the steely glint and the persistent rhythm of a machine, and the brutal drive of an athletic contest. In fact, the Russian critics called it "football music", and the term stuck. Like Prokofiev's first shocker, *Diabolic Suggestions*, it is a show-piece for the athletic pianist. Its toccata-like figurations and its dynamic drive forecast the mechanistic style that was later to become the composer's badge of identification.

II

In the next seven years a spate of brilliant works came from young Prokofiev's pen. These included an opera, *The Gambler*, a ballet, *The Buffoon* ("Chout"), his Second and Third Piano Concertos, three Piano Sonatas, his First Violin Concerto, the *Scythian Suite*, various short pieces for piano and for voice, the Classical Symphony, and the cantata, *Seven, They Are Seven !* In this remarkable group of works, Prokofiev quickly established himself in the forefront of Russian composers of that time, rivalled in eminence only by Stravinsky.

The *Scythian Suite* was the result of a commission by Diaghilev. When Prokofiev graduated from the Conservatory in 1914 his mother rewarded him with a trip to London, where he saw the Russian Ballet in its last brilliant season before the outbreak of World War I. A friend introduced him to Diaghilev. The impresario listened to the young composer play his Second Piano Concerto and straightway gave him an order to write music for a ballet.

Following Diaghilev's suggestion that he go for a subject to Russian fairy tales or prehistoric themes, Prokofiev chose certain legends of the ancient Scythians. But early in 1915 when he brought his sketches to Diaghilev in Italy, the impresario rejected the whole thing as too close to the subject of Stravinsky's *Le Sacre du printemps*. Fortunately, the young composer was already sufficiently sure of himself not to be crushed by the great man's dictum. He later recast his ballet score (called *Ala and Lolli*) into the *Scythian Suite* for orchestra, Op. 20.

The Scythians were a wild, nomadic race, a mixture of Aryan and Mongol, who once roamed the steppe lands above the Black Sea. A century before the birth of Christ they had disappeared from history.[1] In their pantheon of barbaric gods the Scythians

[1] There still exist at least two vivid sources of information about the Scythians. The first is the account of Herodotus, who described them as a fat, flabby race who lived on boiled horse meat and mare's milk, avoided washing, practised polygamy, and were ruled by despotic kings and harsh gods. The second source, which is the famous Kerch collection in the Hermitage Museum in Leningrad, reveals that with all their barbarisms the Scythians were among the most artistic of all ancient peoples. The collection is one of the richest treasures of antique art in the world, containing thousands of specimens of Scythian handiwork—helmets, scabbards, vases, urns, bracelets, necklaces, diadems, and innumerable other objects of adornment, both for persons and horses—all magnificently designed, many of them delicately carved, in gold, silver, and electrum.

revered chiefly the sun, which they named Veles. The daughter of
the sun was Ala. Prokofiev built his ballet story around episodes
in the Scythian mythology which describe the sun worship, the
injury of Ala by evil spirits, and her rescue by Lolli, a legendary
hero. The four sections of the Suite are titled: (I) Invocation to
Veles and Ala. (II) The Evil-God and dance of the pagan monsters.
(III) Night. (IV) Lolli's pursuit of the Evil-God, and sunrise.

Prokofiev's *Scythian Suite* has been compared with Stravinsky's
Le Sacre du printemps, since both scores are pictures of pagan
Russia, and both composers employed primitivist techniques and
a brutalized style. Prokofiev's music is considerably less original
than Stravinsky's, but it was shocking when first performed in
1916, being full of clashing dissonance, thunderous climaxes, and
aboriginal rhythms, all streaked with violent orchestral colours.

This work shows the diverse influences which were at work on
the young Russian composer, and the way he was already welding
them into a style of his own. His music stems in part from the
fantasy of Rimsky-Korsakov's fairy-tale pieces, and from the
grotesquerie of Musorgsky's *Bald Mountain*; but under Prokofiev's
hand the old romantic picture pieces are sharpened, painted over,
hardened into a glaring and powerful realism. Crossed with these
Russianisms is a strong flavour of French impressionism. Debussy's
orchestral style had obviously impressed young Prokofiev—the
blurred harmonies, the delicate effects of woodwinds, harp, and
muted strings. These he used as a contrast to the raw barbarisms.

When Diaghilev rejected Prokofiev's Scythian ballet, the impresario had softened the blow by offering the young composer another
chance. Together they devised an idea for a ballet called *The Tale
of the Buffoon Who Outwitted Seven Buffoons*, derived from A. N.
Afanasyev's collection of Russian folk tales. A Buffoon plays a
trick on seven other buffoons. Conniving with his wife who is also
a buffoon, he pretends to beat her to death, and then brings her back
to life by means of a whip. The seven other buffoons try the same
trick on their wives, but cannot whip them back to life. To escape
their wrath the Buffoon disguises himself as a woman cook, only
to fall into worse predicaments.

Prokofiev composed his score in 1915, but the ballet was not
produced by Diaghilev until 1921. The music stylizes Russian folk
song in a manner that resembles Stravinsky's *Petrouchka*. The
orchestration is full of ingenious effects to set off the eccentric
action and jagged caricature. The score also owes something to

Musorgsky. It recalls the mood of the older composer's satires and comic songs, except that with Prokofiev the comedy is carried to the heights of savage burlesque.

Prokofiev went to a totally different Russian source for his opera, *The Gambler*, composed in 1915–16 and revised in 1927. The libretto is based on Dostoevsky's story, which was an auto-biographical account of the novelist's love affair with a young university student, and his adventures in the gambling houses of Western Europe. Prokofiev's treatment of the story shows clearly his anti-romantic bent. He rejected the whole scheme of romantic opera and used instead the methods of Musorgsky's pioneer work of realism, *The Marriage*. Prokofiev devised his own libretto, employing actual dialogues from Dostoevsky's story. The characters and stage action are wholly lifelike; the texture of the score is a continuous dramatic declamation following closely the spoken inflections of the words, with an orchestral part also following the words obediently.

In 1916 *The Gambler* was scheduled for performance at the Marinsky Theatre in Petersburg, but was later removed from the repertoire when the performers were floored by its difficult style.

III

Prokofiev had shown himself a formidable anti-romantic, adept at the uses of satire and realism to upset the old order. His next step was logical, even inevitable. Late in 1916 he conceived the idea of composing a symphony in the classic manner of the late eighteenth century. The Classical Symphony (Op. 25) was completed in the summer of 1917, and within a decade it had become the most widely performed and admired of all Prokofiev's works.

It has been said that the composer's thoughts had been turned toward classicism when he re-entered the Petersburg Conservatory for a post-graduate course in organ playing. But his friend and fellow composer, Nicolas Nabokov, writes that Prokofiev used to laugh at the wise, critical discussions of his "neo-classic style" in his little symphony. It appears that the piece had a much more practical reason for being. Prokofiev always composed at a piano, so he decided to test the accuracy of his hearing. "He therefore decided to write a piece without the help of any instrument, but in order to hear the harmonies well and to be sure of what he was doing, he adopted a simplified, conventional, so-called classical style! Thus he limited himself to the use of conventional chords."

Even if the classicism of this symphony did spring from reasons more practical than esoteric, the fact remains that the work was one of the first, and is still one of the most successful, examples of a new genre. It antedated even Stravinsky's new classicism. Prokofiev's procedure, the evocation in modern terms of another age and place in music, is accomplished with a mastery typically Russian. His symphony sums up to perfection the classic elements: formal balance and constraint, crystalline style, an urbane point of view. It does not grow from the joining of romantic melodies; it develops from themes. None of the burlesquing, sarcastic Prokofiev, or the mechanistic Prokofiev, disturbs the exquisite, rippling progress of this music. Only a touch of satirical smiling crops out now and then, when the composer uses his favourite device of strolling innocently away from a conventional harmonic scheme into all sorts of distant keys, and then turning a sudden corner back into the home tonality.

In the summer of 1917 Russia was aflame with revolution, but the industrious Prokofiev spent his time calmly and profitably. He composed his Third Piano Sonata, planned a new piano concerto and a string quartet; he finished his First Violin Concerto and the Classical Symphony. Finally, he started work on the Cantata (or Incantation) for tenor solo, chorus and orchestra, *Seven, They Are Seven!*

Prokofiev's text for the Cantata was one of three poems by the Russian poet Constantin Balmont, which derived from inscriptions found on the walls of an ancient Akkadian temple in central Mesopotamia. Balmont's poem represents an Akkadian priest conjuring, while a crowd of worshippers is whipped to a frenzy of fear and supplication. These are the tenor soloist and the chorus of Prokofiev's score. The words are a kind of litany, an incantation against seven fearful demons who, in the Akkadian mythology, were a source of all human woe.[1]

---

[1] "Seven, they are seven! Seven, they are seven!
Telai! Telai! Telai! Telai!

In the deep abyss
Their number is seven . . .
They are neither male nor female!
No union, no begetting!
The winds are, as they, wanderers . . .

Serge Koussevitzky conducted the first performance of Prokofiev's score in Paris, in 1924, and two years later played it with the Boston Symphony Orchestra. Those who heard it then are not likely to forget *Seven, They Are Seven !*, even though in the interval of a third of a century it has been revived but seldom. The outcries of the chorus, the shrieking exhortations of the tenor, the din of the orchestra all revived for the moment the savage grandeur of an ancient race and its terrible demonology. The work is painted with the same brush that had coloured the *Scythian Suite*, but here the effects are even more brutal, the cumulative dissonance more violent. With *Seven, They Are Seven !* Prokofiev had reached the end of one phase of his growth as an artist, and he was soon to realize that he could go no farther.

IV

When the Russian Revolution finally broke Prokofiev brooded upon the idea of joining the thousands of intellectuals who were trying to escape the Bolshevik dictatorship of the proletariat. In the spring of 1918, and shortly after the highly-successful first performance of his Classical Symphony in Petrograd, the composer applied for permission to leave the country. "You are a revolutionary in music," remarked the People's Commissar pointedly, "we are revolutionists in life"—but permission was granted. Thus Prokofiev got one of the first passports issued by the Soviet Government.

On May 7, 1918, the composer left Petrograd for Vladivostok. His goal was America, and he chose the long way round to avoid the war dangers of Western Europe. Instead he ran into great peril on the trans-Siberian railway. It happened that in the wild confusion of the time, the railway line was crowded with troop trains

> They know not goodness nor kindness,
> They are without regret, remorse,
> They are deaf to prayers and entreaties
> Everywhere by force they open doors !
> They grind men as men grind grain.
>   Seven, they are seven ! . . .
>
> Winds of storm, disastrous winds !
> Deadly lightnings, deluge of fire !
> Behold the ordeal, behold the torment,
> See the heralds of terror arriving—
> Seven spirits of the infinite heaven,
> Seven spirits of the infinite earth ! . . .
>   Seven, they are seven !"

of Czech soldiers who were freed prisoners of war. When the Bolsheviks suddenly ordered the Czechs interned again, war between Czechs and Bolsheviks broke out like a sputtering fuse, all the way from the Volga to Vladivostok. Fortunately for Prokofiev, his train got through safely to the Pacific.

The composer stayed two months in Japan, giving recitals in Tokio and Yokohama. Then he set out across the Pacific to San Francisco, and finally to New York where he arrived in September, 1918. On the long journey he had not been idle. He worked on an opera, *The Love For Three Oranges*, the idea of which had been suggested to him in Russia by the stage director, Vsevolod Meyerhold.

Prokofiev's first public appearance in America was a piano recital in New York's Aeolian Hall, on November 20, 1918. The following month he played his First Piano Concerto with Modest Altschuler's Russian Symphony Orchestra. The New York critics, then on one of their downswings into reaction, found his music alarmingly ultra-modern, an anarchy of noise and steel; confusing somewhat the order of historical events they labelled him an exponent of "Bolshevism in art", and a "representative of Godless Russia".

In Chicago the composer had better luck, and the Chicago Opera Company contracted to perform his opera, *The Love For Three Oranges*, the following season. In spite of a serious illness in which he came down with both scarlet fever and diphtheria, Prokofiev completed the score in October, 1919. When the opera company found it necessary to postpone the production, the composer was so furious that he started a lawsuit. He tried giving piano lessons to make a living, but with little success. In a mood of despair he began work on another opera. This was *The Flaming Angel*, based on a story by the Russian poet Valery Bryusov, a luridly melodramatic tale of sixteenth-century Germany and the religious fanaticism which swept the land in the wake of the Counter Reformation.

Prokofiev long remembered those first disheartening months in America:

"I wandered through the enormous park in the centre of New York and, looking up at the skyscrapers bordering it, thought with cold fury of the marvellous American orchestras that cared nothing for my music and of the critics who reiterated what had been said a hundred times before . . . and who balked so violently at anything new, and of the managers who arranged long tours of artists playing the same hackneyed programmes fifty times over."

During the next few years he made several trips between America and Europe, trying to find a place for himself and his music. He gave a series of concerts in California, but that pleasant experience was offset by long wrangling with the Chicago Opera Company over their failure to produce *The Love For Three Oranges*. In the spring of 1921 he was in Paris for the première of *The Buffoon*. The eccentric and dissonant style of the piece delighted the Parisians but later stung the London critics into loud alarums. The composer meanwhile had retired to the coast of Brittany, where he worked on his Third Piano Concerto.

Prokofiev returned to Chicago late in 1921 for a crucial event in his career—the première of *The Love For Three Oranges*. The Chicago Opera Company gave the work a splendid production, and the first performance (December 30, 1921) was a great success with both audience and critics. But when the company brought the work to New York two months later it fell flat and the critical faculty damned it. Thereafter the opera had occasional performances in Western Europe and Russia, some with success; but it seemed that the piece was kept alive only by a few popular orchestral excerpts, notably the scintillating March.[1] After remaining unheard in America for almost three decades, *The Love For Three Oranges* was revived in 1949 by the New York City Opera Company with astonishing success. Overnight it became a box-office attraction.

For his libretto Prokofiev had gone to one of the classics of the eighteenth-century Italian drama, a satirical comedy by Count Carlo Gozzi. In his *Fiaba dell' amore delle tre melarancie* (produced in Venice in 1761) Gozzi had parodied with deadly effect the works of two rival dramatists, Chiari and Goldoni. The personal issues originally involved in the satire mean little or nothing today. In writing his own libretto from Gozzi's play Prokofiev simply created an extravaganza of Commedia dell' Arte characters, and a vastly amusing caricature of grand opera itself.

The scene is a mythical kingdom ruled over by King Silvio,

---

[1] The March was long familiar to the American radio audience as the opening and closing theme of the programme, "The F.B.I. in Peace and War", advertising Lava Soap.

whose son, Prince Tartaly, has been ill for ten years with insomnia, and various imaginary maladies of the heart, liver, kidneys, and bladder. The physicians prescribe laughter as his only hope. All efforts fail until the Prince observes the malignant old witch, Fata Morgana, slip and fall into a somersault. The Prince roars with laughter, and the enraged witch puts a curse upon him: He shall fall in love with three oranges and he must travel night and day for three thousand miles to find them. After many adventures the Prince finds the oranges and sets free three beautiful princesses who have been magically ensnared therein. The most beautiful princess eventually becomes his bride.

Part of the comical apparatus of the opera is a mock audience, seated in boxes on either side of the stage. These ladies and gentlemen, partisans of various types of drama, make loud comments about the story and at times try to take part in it.

There is not much room for vocal display in *The Love For Three Oranges*. It is primarily a piece for jesters, who take over the stage with a fast-moving succession of choruses, solos, duets, dances, comical exits, and fantastic interludes. With farceurs who know their business the results are riotous. The drollest of the comedy comes from the orchestra where the instruments carry on a continual smirking commentary on the wild buffoonery going on upon the stage. The instrumental colours are garishly brilliant in the Russian manner, deriving from the style of Rimsky-Korsakov's fairy-tale operas, especially *The Golden Cockerel*.

Prokofiev's Third Piano Concerto, in C major (Op. 26), though begun in 1917, was not actually completed until the Autumn of 1921, when the composer was in Chicago for the première of *The Love For Three Oranges*. The first performance occurred on December 16, with the composer at the piano and the Chicago Symphony Orchestra under Frederick Stock. Prokofiev played the work many times thereafter both in America and Europe, but it found its way only slowly into the repertoires of enterprising pianists. Today, it is by common acclaim one of the ornaments of modern music; it has been called "the finest piano concerto of our century".

The eclectic genius of the Russian composer, the ability to assimilate ideas from a dozen different sources, was never better exemplified than in Prokofiev's masterful concerto. Everything is poured into the brimming bowl, but what comes out is always Prokofiev's own. This is a modern piano concerto in every sense: it utilizes the piano as an instrument of speed and percussive force.

It is neo-romantic; it is also coloured with Russianisms, even hints of Tchaikovsky and Rachmaninov. Conspicuously absent is the romantic melancholy of the older Russian music; instead the prevailing mood, in the composer's own words, is one of "caustic humour".

The modern note is struck soon after the opening measures when the pianist sprints into toccata-like figurations that roll with the speed of a racing machine. All is vigour, power, excitement, verve. The percussive sonorities prevail. The piano speaks with a brittle, glassy sound, or the dry clatter of a xylophone. Tonalities are often vague, blurred by dissonant notes, or based on chords that are indeterminate, poised between keys.

The second movement is a theme with five variations. The theme itself, stately and rather plaintive, has an almost Tchaikovskian sound; but the variations are wholly modern. The movement alternates between a soft, mellow lyricism and diamond-hard brilliance, between graceful daintiness and demoniacal speed and grotesquerie.

In the closing movement there crops up among the steely ironies another lovely lyric theme, soaring on such romantic wings that one might almost suspect the hand of Rachmaninov. But the piece never falls into sentimentality. The end is no romantic peroration, but a volley of artillery.

The early reception of Prokofiev's Third Piano Concerto followed that of *The Love For Three Oranges*. The Chicago critics praised it; the New York critics detested it. A few months later the disheartened composer left America, convinced that his music would have to make headway elsewhere. He spent the next year and a half in the Bavarian village of Ettal, not far from Oberammergau.[1] Late in 1923 he moved to Paris, and for the next ten years the French capital became his home and the axis around which his artistic life would revolve.

v

It was inevitable that Prokofiev should gravitate to Paris in the post-War years. Many Russian emigrants of his own class,

---

[1] At Ettal, Prokofiev worked hard on his opera, *The Flaming Angel*, but he was never to hear it performed. It was not produced until 1955, when it received a successful première in Venice. At that time the story was given out that in the ensuing years the score had been lost, and was finally found after World War II in a box of old papers in a basement in Paris.

including Stravinsky, were there; Diaghilev had made the French capital his headquarters, and so had Serge Koussevitzky who would later publish and widely perform a number of Prokofiev's works. The great city itself was in one of its periods of teeming fruitfulness. In every field the artists were working with incredible industry. Head and shoulders over the painters, then as now, stood Picasso, a marvel of creative energy, imagination and daring. In his wake came many men and many movements, large and small. The early Cubism of Picasso and Braque had given way to the Purist movement of Ozenfant, an attempt to transform Cubism into an art based on classic principles. From that impulse sprang Purist-Functionalism in architecture, initiated by the architect-painter Le Corbusier, a movement that would change the face of modern building, interior decoration and equipment. The *style mécanique* was born.

Surrealism had registered the first resounding impact of Freud's theories of dreams and the subconscious upon the pre-War painters; now in the nineteen-twenties came Neo-Surrealism, partly sired by the nihilistic and anarchistic Dadaism. The dream, the nightmare, the hallucination, the sex-ridden world of the subconscious—all the apparatus of Freudian psychiatry formed the shock technique of the new art. The German Dadaist, Max Ernst, came forth with Neo-Surrealist *collage* (derived from the literary *collage* of the French Dadaist, André Breton), which involved the haphazard technique of the scrap-book paste-up; later Ernst moved on to Neo-Surrealist *frottage*, the production of significant blots, smears, and rubbings upon a medium, with the artist's hand uninhibited as in the operation of a ouija board. Among the Neo-Surrealists there appeared in 1929 the young Catalan, Salvador Dali, whose pictures seemed to spring from the dreams recorded in a psychiatrist's case histories.

With the new art there came a new music. Stravinsky, the leading anti-romantic, stood like Picasso above the rest; following him was a virile new generation of French composers. When the critic Henri Collet, writing in 1921 in *Comoedia*, grouped together Milhaud, Honegger, Poulenc, Auric, Durey, and Tailleferre, and christened them "The Six", he crystallized with a stroke of journalistic nomenclature a new force in modern music. These French composers, like Stravinsky in his younger days, were all nationalists, and they were also anti-romantics. They attacked the excesses of the old German romanticism with the familiar weapon of satire.

Following their elder compatriot, Eric Satie, they created a new technique of musical parody. Satie had used typewriters and sirens in his score of *Parade* (which Diaghilev produced in 1917); so Milhaud used whips, whistles, and hammers in his *Les Choéphores*; the vocal text of his *Machines agricoles* (1919) was not poetry but words taken from a manufacturer's catalogue of farm implements, and his *Catalogue des fleurs* (1920) used a seed catalogue. Poulenc, immensely gifted as a writer of songs, used many of the comical street songs of Paris as his points of departure. Honegger showed that romantic picture-painting was a dead issue. The new vogue would be descriptive realism—a locomotive in *Pacific 231*, a game of football in *Rugby*.

It was one of Serge Diaghilev's greatest achievements that he brought together in a series of collaborations many of the significant painters and composers of that exciting decade. His productions had ceased to be simply "Russian" ballet. In one brilliant stage piece after another he fused the new art and the new music of Europe.[1]

So far as the Russians were concerned, two composers contributed most to this later phase of Diaghilev's enterprise. They were Stravinsky and Prokofiev. It seemed that Prokofiev had found his ideal environment. His ballet, *The Buffoon*, had already shown Paris the stuff he was made of. He was strongly anti-romantic, a satirist with a scalding sense of humour; he had also classic leanings; the harmonic colour of his music was properly dissonant; and he had created his own powerful *style mécanique*.

In 1925 Diaghilev approached Prokofiev with a remarkable idea—the creation of a ballet which would depict the new life in Soviet Russia. This was during the tolerant N.E.P. period when the

---

[1] Diaghilev's productions included the already-noted *Pulcinella*, with the Stravinsky-Pergolesi music and designs by Picasso (1920). Picasso also designed Satie's *Parade* (1917), Falla's *Three-Cornered Hat* (1919), Milhaud's *Le Train bleu* (1924), and Satie's *Mercury* (1924). In 1920 Matisse designed the scenery and costumes for Stravinsky's *Le Chant du rossignol*. In 1924 Braque designed *Les Facheux*, music by Auric; Marie Laurençin designed *Les Biches*, music by Poulenc. In 1925 Braque designed *Zéphyr et Flore*, music by Vladimir Dukelsky; Utrillo designed *Barabau*, music by Vittorio Rieti; the Spaniard, Pruna, designed *Les Matelots* and *Pastorale*, music by Auric. In 1926 Derain designed *Jack-in-the-Box*, music by Satie (orchestrated by Milhaud); Ernst and Miro provided paintings for *Romeo and Juliet*, music by Constant Lambert. In 1927 the Russian Purist-Constructivists Gabo and Pevsner designed geometric scenery in transparent celluloid for *La Chatte*, music by Henri Sauguet; Yacoulov designed costumes and construction for *Le Pas d'acier*, music by Prokofiev. In 1928 Tchelitchev designed *Ode*, music by Nicolas Nabokov; Bauchant designed Stravinsky's *Apollo Musagetes*. In 1929 Chirico designed *Le Bal*, music by Rieti; Rouault designed *The Prodigal Son*, music by Prokofiev.

U.S.S.R. was importing some Western art and music, and exporting much propaganda about the way Russia was being modernized. Aided by Georgi Yakoulov, a Russian stage designer of the radical constructivist school, Prokofiev devised a libretto which would show the transition from the old regime in Russia to the new age of mechanized industrialism. The composer, artist, and impresario, working in faraway France, were not daunted by the fact that the mechanization of their native land was still a dream in the minds of the men in the Kremlin. What they created in their ballet, called *Le Pas d'acier* ("The Progress of Steel"), was not a picture of modern Russia but rather a record of the impact of machinery upon modern stage design, ballet, and music—an impact already recorded through the *style mécanique* in painting and architecture.

The first scene of the ballet represents a railway station; the second is a steel mill working at full blast. In and around these two giant manifestations of the steel age swarm the workers and other inhabitants, finding a busy and not too unhappy life amid the hum, roar, and violence of the machines.

Le Pas d'acier was produced by Diaghilev in Paris in 1927, but it had no lasting success. As a piece of descriptive realism the score is vivid and exciting, but no more successful than its predecessor, Honegger's *Pacific 231*. Among Prokofiev's own works it represents the apex of his mechanistic style. Blended with the tonal steel are various themes in the Russian folk manner, given jagged edges by means of dissonant counterpoint.[1]

During the years of his residence in Paris, Prokofiev appeared as pianist and composer-conductor in various European cities. In the winter of 1925–26 he made another concert tour of America, this time with much success. In 1926 he was in Italy where he had a significant meeting with Maxim Gorky. It was said that the Russian novelist and inventor of socialist realism "carried the composer off with him to his villa in Sorrento for a long, heart-to-heart talk lasting far into the night". The next year Prokofiev returned to the U.S.S.R. for a three months' tour. The Russians gave him a tumultuous welcome. His *Love For Three Oranges* had been produced the year before in Leningrad, and Moscow had heard his Third Piano Concerto, First Violin Concerto, and his *Scythian Suite*. The

[1] When this ballet (under the title *The Age of Steel*) was first performed in America, by the League of Composers and the Philadelphia Orchestra (1931), the Russian element was ignored. Lee Simonson, the designer, created an entirely new scenario which transplanted the scene to America and made the work "a satire on the machine era, on the irony of 'speeding up'."

composer went back to Paris, but the sojourn in his native land after nine years of exile had left a deep impression.

The year 1928 saw the composition of Prokofiev's music for the ballet *The Prodigal Son* which Diaghilev mounted in Paris the following spring, and which happened to be the great impresario's last production. The scenario is an abbreviated version of the episode in the fifteenth chapter of the Gospel according to St. Luke. Recent revivals of the work, with Rouault's glowing designs and Balanchine's moving choreography, prove that Prokofiev had created one of the masterpieces of the modern ballet.

The Prodigal Son offers evidence that Prokofiev's art was in a state of transition. From realism and neo-classicism the composer had swung sharply toward a neo-romanticism, composing with great depth of feeling. A steady outpouring of lyric beauty illuminates this drama. The closing scene, with the broken and humiliated son crawling on his knees to the arms of his father, is a moment of pathos seldom matched in the music of the modern theatre. The influence of Prokofiev's French contemporaries is also evident in this score. Gallic restraint and elegance had clearly impressed him. There are subtle references to the general style of Ravel's music, and that composer's method of combining classic lucidity with romantic expressiveness.

Several other large-scale works belong to Prokofiev's Paris period. His Second Symphony, in D minor (Op. 40), had its première in Paris in 1925, was coldly received and had few performances elsewhere. Employing a vast orchestra to travel through a jungle of dissonance, it represented an extreme in Prokofiev's development. The Third Symphony (Op. 44) was composed in 1928, and was based on themes from the opera *The Flaming Angel*. It was played a number of times by the Philadelphia Orchestra under Stokowski, and is remembered as a work of power—grim of mood, the colour of blue-grey steel, discordant and unyieldingly severe in its music language. In 1931 after another American tour Prokofiev was commissioned to compose his Fourth Symphony (Op. 47) commemorating the fiftieth anniversary of the Boston Symphony Orchestra. The second and third movements of this work are taken almost bodily from the ballet score *The Prodigal Son*, while the first and fourth are newly developed from its themes. The Quartet in B minor (Op. 50) was commissioned by the Library of Congress in Washington. The Fourth Piano Concerto (for the left hand) was composed in 1931 for the one-armed pianist Paul Wittgenstein, who found the piece so difficult that he refused to play it. Late in 1932 Prokofiev's ballet *Sur le Borysthène* (On the Dnieper) failed at its première at the Paris Opera and was dropped from the repertoire. The Fifth Piano Concerto in G minor (Op. 55) was one of the last of the composer's Paris works. It was also a final bow to his most acidulous style of piano writing. Prokofiev himself said that each of the five short movements contains at least four themes or melodies, and that the developments of these themes "are as compressed and condensed as it is possible to make them". Most of this thematic material is remarkable for its angularity and the width of its intervals, so that the piano part often becomes a study in sheer acrobatics for the fingers, hands, and arms.

During the Paris years it might have seemed that Prokofiev had fitted his life perfectly into his new environment. He lived happily with his wife Lina, a Cuban by birth, "very beautiful and strong-minded", and their two children. His wife was an accomplished singer who often appeared with him in recitals. But for the composer there were inner dissatisfactions. For one thing, his music was meeting with varying success. For the prestige that comes from sheer radicalism it could no longer compete with the well-advertised scores of Stravinsky, or the unplayed but influential twelve-tone pieces of Schönberg. Prokofiev had fallen into the unhappy role of a conservative among radicals and a radical among conservatives. He visited Russia again in 1929, and was moved again by the familiar sights of his homeland and the sound of the old language in his ears. Three years later he reached his moment of decision. He returned to Soviet Russia, to make his home once again in his native land.

Prokofiev told a friend in Paris: "Foreign air does not suit my inspiration, because I'm a Russian, and that is to say the least suited of men to be an exile, to remain myself in a psychological climate that isn't of my race. My compatriots and I carry our country about with us. . . . Here I'm getting enervated. I risk dying of academism."

VI

Prokofiev was a profoundly self-knowing artist. This is to be expected of a mind so obviously well ordered, disciplined, and integrated to the functions of his craft. No better example of the lucidity of his thought could be asked than his own analysis of his music, as contained in his autobiography. Here the composer outlined the five principal elements which have dominated his art.

First is the classical element. Prokofiev traced its origin to childhood when he heard his mother play Beethoven sonatas. After that there was hardly a year in his creative life during which some one of the classic forms did not engage his interest. The second element is that of innovation. "At first," says the composer, "this innovation consisted in the search for an individual harmonic language, but later was transformed into a desire to find a medium for the expression of strong emotions. . . ." The third element, which he calls "the toccata, or motor element", he traced to his youth, when Schumann's *Toccata* greatly impressed him. This element he considers the least important. Fourth is the lyric element, which lay for a long time in comparative obscurity in his work, but grew gradually to a place of first importance. Lastly, there is the element of the grotesque, which the composer prefers to call "scherzoness", or "jest", "laughter", "mockery".

Until he reached a jumping-off place in his career, shortly before his return to Soviet Russia, the element which seemed to dominate Prokofiev's music was that of innovation. This was most noticeable in his harmony, where he relied strongly on dissonance. He mixed the simple, basic chords with others of great complexity. A favourite Prokofiev device was to dart off continually into remote tonalities while seeming to remain within the confines of a conventional tonal scheme. Innovation in melody meant chiefly angularity. The contours of Prokofiev's themes were often distorted by means of wide gaps between notes or by sudden landings on unexpected tones. Here again he used a mixture : the angular contours alternated with others of classic smoothness. In rhythm, innovation consisted not in complexity, but rather in the sheer mechanical persistence of a single basic pulse.

The dividing point in Prokofiev's outward life, his return to Russia in 1932, was actually preceded by a crisis in his art. He had been weighing his own music and that of his Western contemporaries and had found it in need of overhauling. In a newspaper interview with Olin Downes of the *New York Times* (February 2, 1930) Prokofiev outlined his new creed :

"I strive for greater simplicity" (he said), "and more melody. Of course I have used dissonance in my time, but there has been too much dissonance. . . . We want a simpler and more melodic style for music, a simpler, less-complicated emotional state, and dissonance once again relegated to its proper place as one element in music, contingent principally upon the meeting of melodic lines."

The composer went on to say that counterpoint was bound by the fact that "three melodies remain about the limit that the average ear can grasp and follow at one time. I think we have gone as far as we are likely to go in the direction of size, or dissonance, or complexity in music." Prokofiev had thus come to conclusions about modern music which had been reached by many other contemporary composers, including such exemplars as Stravinsky, Schönberg, Hindemith, and Bartok.

As for melody, the new focal point in Prokofiev's music, he would insist that he had always been a melodist.

"I am always on the lookout for new melodic themes" (he revealed to a Boston interviewer). "These I write in a notebook, as they come to me, for future use. All my work is founded on melodies. When I begin a work of major proportions I usually have accumulated enough themes to make half-a-dozen symphonies. Then the work of selection and arrangement begins. . . ."

VII

In the two decades which followed after Prokofiev ended his exile in the West and returned to Russia he composed in greater abundance than ever. The same five elements still dominated his art; at the same time there were significant changes. Most noticeably, there was less of innovation and instead "greater simplicity and more melody". Prokofiev's sense of humour and his ability to give it vent in his music was still one of his greatest assets as a creative artist, but his comedy became less violent. The former creator of musical gargoyles and griffins had mellowed. There was also a new element of nationalism and of political propaganda in Prokofiev's music, a reflection of the Soviet environment in which he was living and working.

Prokofiev returned to Russia just before Stalin's promulgation of the Second Five Year Plan. Soon afterwards came the first announcements of the new doctrine of socialist realism as a guide for the country's writers, followed by the long campaign (interrupted by the war) to make all creative artists propagandists for the state. For a time Prokofiev seemed to enjoy a privileged position among Soviet composers, due partly to his international reputation, and in part to influence which he was said to have somewhere in high government circles. He appeared to work very much as he pleased. An examination of his catalogue, however, reveals that his Soviet music fell roughly into three periods. For the first few years he composed a great deal for the theatre—ballets, films, incidental music for plays. After 1936 (and *Pravda's* attack on Shostakovich) he began to contribute his share of propaganda pieces of various species, and later a series of war tracts. During the war itself he began a third period, in which the works which predominate are in the old abstract forms—symphonies and chamber works.

Among Prokofiev's works for the theatre are the ballet scores *Romeo and Juliet* (1935) and *Cinderella* (1941–44), from which the composer later drew orchestral suites. These scores rank with the most successful creations of the Soviet ballet theatre, where both have been given sumptuous productions. A London correspondent wrote that the performance of *Romeo and Juliet* in Moscow, in 1947, was "so stuffed with colour and violence and emotion and swordplay that some people can't take more than one act of it per night. . . . As art it seems to be a new form. There is very little real dancing. It is rather an elaborate mime or an opera without words. . . . The production is really stupendous."

Both *Romeo and Juliet* and *Cinderella* are ballets in the Tchaikovsky tradition, that is, they are long works requiring a full evening performance. Both are said to benefit from Prokofiev's expert knowledge of the classic ballet technique. *Romeo and Juliet* seems the richer of the two works, both in melody and drama. *Cinderella* by comparison is rather thin. These ballet scores contain little of Prokofiev's early radicalisms, but rely mainly on old-fashioned models of melody, harmony, and rhythm.

Among Prokofiev's various film scores are the satirical *Lieutenant Kije* (known in the West through the charming orchestral suite), and the two productions of Sergei Eisenstein, *Alexander Nevsky* and *Ivan the Terrible*. Prokofiev composed his score for *Alexander Nevsky* in 1938. Earlier that year he had made a long concert tour of Europe and America, and while in Hollywood had studied the

American methods of producing music backgrounds for sound films. From his music for *Alexander Nevsky* he later selected portions to be published as a cantata (Op. 78) for chorus, orchestra, and soloist.

The story of the *Alexander Nevsky* film was based on an episode in mediaeval Russian history. When an army of Teutonic Knights invaded Russia in the year 1242 they were repulsed by the heroic Prince Alexander Nevsky, after a violent battle on the ice of Lake Peipus. Eisenstein's film was a masterpiece of historical evocation and dramatic power, and as a background Prokofiev's music served admirably. Standing alone as a cantata, however, it is less successful. Its best pages are contained in the poignant lament "Field of the Dead" for the mezzo-soprano and orchestra, in the brief opening orchestral picture of Russia under the Tartar yoke, and in some of the Battle on the Ice. Long sections of the score lose the stylistic imprint of Prokofiev and sound instead like a pastiche of nineteenth-century Russian music. Imitations of Borodin, Musorgsky, and Rimsky-Korsakov haunt these measures. Some are as simple as Glinka, but not so good. Much is saved only by the power of Prokofiev's expert orchestration.

What considerations persuaded the composer to adopt a music idiom other than his own is not known. The film itself was partly intended as a propaganda piece to arouse the Russian people to an appreciation of their historical heritage, and Prokofiev may have felt that the masses would understand the language of Glinka and the Five better than his own sharp, modern tongue. There is no doubt that this was the view of the government officials. At this time they were putting pressure on all creative artists, urging them to gear their work to the intellectual level of the broad masses. Creating enduring art works within the comprehension of the masses is actually a task of enormous uncertainty, not to say difficulty. To some artists it is an impossibility. In his various Soviet scores Prokofiev appears to have struggled with the problem of excessive simplification, but only in one category did it come naturally to him—when he wrote for children. He composed many charming children's songs and piano pieces, and the immensely successful *Peter and the Wolf* for orchestra and narrator (1936).

The text of *Peter and the Wolf* is by the composer. Both in the little tale and in his music Prokofiev proved that his humorous gift was by no means limited to the cynical or satirical, but had a side of tenderness perfectly suited to the world of childhood. The themes of *Peter and the Wolf* are full of life, both as melodies and as vivid little pictures of persons and animals. Outwardly simple, the score bears in every measure the craftsmanship of a master.

Soviet ideology began to permeate Prokofiev's music soon after 1936. His catalogue shows a number of works which contribute to those forms of propaganda demanded by the Soviet government—political tracts, glorification pieces, and war propaganda pieces. Among them are the Russian Overture, for orchestra (Op. 72); Songs of Our Days (Op. 76), for chorus and orchestra; Seven Songs of the Masses (Op. 79), for voice and piano; the cantata *Zdravitsa* (Toast to Stalin) (Op. 85), for chorus and orchestra, a tribute to the Soviet leader on his sixtieth birthday; and the Cantata for the Twentieth Anniversary of the October Revolution, to words by Marx, Lenin, and Stalin—as yet unperformed and unpublished. An opera, *Simeon Kotko* (first produced in Moscow in 1940), was based on a novel by Valentin Katayev, *I, Son of the Working People*, and relates the struggle of the Ukrainians against the German invaders in 1918. The Suite for Orchestra, *1941*, and *The Ballade of an Unknown Boy*, for chorus and orchestra, both celebrate the defence of Russia against the Germans in World War II. *Ode to the End of the War*, for orchestra (Op. 105), appeared in 1945.

During the war years Prokofiev composed two operas, *The Duenna* (1940–41) and *War and Peace* (1941–42). The first was based on Richard Brinsley Sheridan's eighteenth-century comedy, and for it the Russian composer became once more a cosmopolitan-eclectic. The piece is a modern opera buffa, a situation comedy whose general form mixes lyric recitative and concerted numbers. Prokofiev made his music conservatively melodic, with lively witticisms for singers and orchestra. *The Duenna* has been produced with success in the West.

War and Peace is Prokofiev's largest work of a nationalist nature. From the panorama of Tolstoy's novel he composed a huge two-part score, which has been called by Russian critics a "monumental historical narrative" of the type of Musorgsky's *Khovanshchina*. Its style is part realistic, part romantic. It blends dramatic declamation based on the prose of Tolstoy's story with elaborate choral episodes and symphonic scene painting, all bound together by a complex system of leit-motifs. In spite of an impressive production in Leningrad in 1945, *War and Peace* was a failure. A considerably shortened version of the score had more success on its first performance outside the Iron Curtain, in 1953, at Florence.

In the first busy years of his residence in the Soviet Union Prokofiev seemed to have little time for the classic forms, so occupied was he with the theatre, films, and propaganda. Exceptional was his Second Violin Concerto, in G minor (Op. 63), composed in 1935. This exquisitely written work shows clearly the new direction in which the composer was steering, away from complication and towards the pole of melody. The Concerto is one of the most lyrical of all Prokofiev's works, and its slow movement has been called Mozartean in its clarity and structural unity. In 1938 Prokofiev began sketching his First Violin Sonata; and then, all through the nineteen-forties and into the fifties, he produced a long series of classic abstractions—his Sixth, Seventh, Eighth and Ninth Piano Sonatas, his Second String Quartet, a Flute Sonata, his Second Violin Sonata, his Fifth, Sixth, and Seventh Symphonies, a 'Cello Sonata, and a Sonata for an unaccompanied violin. In these pieces, devoid of either pictures or political editorials, the composer showed that his art was still a flourishing organism.

Years before, Prokofiev had begun his career as one of the comrades of Stravinsky, i.e. as an anti-romantic rebel. Slowly their directions diverged. Stravinsky became the first neo-classicist of this age; Prokofiev became a neo-romantic with a fondness for the classic forms, a twentieth-century counterpart of Brahms and César Franck.

The First Violin Sonata (F minor, Op. 80), not completed until 1946, is one of the most successful of these later works. Many measures have a Brahmsian solidity and logic. The Andante is romance in full flower, rich in refinements of violin and piano sound, and in fragile, soft-spoken melodies that are sheer poetry. The Second Violin Sonata (D major, Op. 94) was completed in 1944. Like its predecessor it blends thematic manipulation with romantic ardour. The Scherzo is dance-like, almost salon music, though sophisticated in melody and harmony—another example of the resounding impact of Western ballet music on a Russian composer.

Prokofiev's Second String Quartet (F major, Op. 92) was composed in 1941, under unusual circumstances. When the Soviet Union came under violent attack by the Germans, Prokofiev was among the many prominent artists who were evacuated to sections remote from the war. He spent some time in the Caucasus, mainly at a retreat at Nalchik, in the Kabardino-Balkarian Republic. There the little-known folk songs of the region caught the composer's fancy. He conceived a work which would be, he said, a "combination of one of the least-known varieties of folk song with the most classical form of the quartet".

In the first movement the Caucasian folk themes are plainly visible, but they are harmonized dissonantly so that we feel (says Prokofiev's Soviet biographer, Israel Nestyev) "the stern, warlike, vengeful Caucasus. The poetry of the Caucasian love songs is subtly reproduced in the slow second movement, with its flowery, ornate violin grace-notes, so characteristic of Oriental music. The flexible syncopated rhythms of mountain dances dominate in the rhapsodic finale of the quartet."

Prokofiev's Fifth Symphony (Op. 100) was composed in 1944, and within a few years it became his most popular orchestral work since the Classical Symphony. The earlier piece was a modern composer's discourse in the manner of the eighteenth century; the Fifth Symphony is neo-romantic, a harking back to the Brahms-Tchaikovsky era of the symphony. In the first movement and the slow third movement the resemblances to Brahms's procedures are striking— the polyphonic texture, the closely-integrated thematism, the general mood of restraint, even the subdued orchestration. The scherzo and the finale are brilliant, but less interesting from the point of view of craftsmanship. There is much reliance on typically Russian tramping rhythms which never seem to get very far melodically, but do have bounce and a dashing style. Occasionally, amid the whirl of Slavic gusto, we catch glimpses of an odd character—Strauss's Till Eulenspiegel. Viewed as a whole the Fifth Symphony undoubtedly deserves its success, for it is attractive even though not deeply-moving music. It exhibits the familiar fabric of Russian eclecticism, done by an expert weaver.

Prokofiev's Sixth Symphony (1946) did not achieve the immediate popular success of the Fifth. An austere, even a dour work, it contains little of its predecessor's bland melodiousness. Its careful craftsmanship and restrained lyricism again strongly resemble Brahms; while in the second movement, Largo, the incredible happens as the shade of Richard Wagner (that ghost despised by all modernists) rises from the past. Long lyric lines meet to form rich chromatic harmonies which more than faintly recall *Parsifal*.

Prokofiev began his career as a virtuoso pianist, and in his later life he seldom strayed away from that instrument. His is one of the largest and most important contributions to the literature of Russian piano music. In this field he remained very much in character : he was primarily a stylist. From his earliest writings for the piano Prokofiev had tried to free himself of the outworn, "arpeggio-ridden" techniques of the nineteenth century, with their indulgence in sensual sonorities. Thus he was led to his most striking invention as a composer—his *style mécanique*. He gave the piano a new lease on life, making it almost an instrument of percussion and an important medium in producing the dry, dynamic sounds of the realistic and neo-classic music of the new age. Because of the progressive nature of his thought Prokofiev's piano music has never enjoyed a popular success like Rachmaninov's. A few of his shorter pieces and his Third Piano Concerto are fairly well known to modern audiences, but his sonatas are making their way but slowly.

The shorter piano works number more than a hundred— études, preludes, pieces in various dance forms, mood pieces (individually and in cycles), and pieces for children (both for amusement and instruction). They range in size from epigrams to long essays ; their moods run from impish humour to Slavic brooding ; their individual styles touch scores of sources. Their quality, too, is varied.

The Sixth, Seventh, Eighth, and Ninth Sonatas (composed between 1939 and 1947) contain some of Prokofiev's best work for the instrument. The Seventh Sonata (Op. 83) sums up the essentials of his mature piano style—the dry mechanistic mingled with the soaringly lyrical. The opening movement exhibits a leanness of treatment, with compact ideas economically handled. The slow movement, Andante doloroso, relates to Chopin's songful essays— a rich, baritone cantilena sings from the piano's middle register. The last movement, Precipitato, is one of Prokofiev's malignantly powerful toccatas, which mesmerize the listener. The peculiar 7/8 rhythm holds unrelentingly from first note to last like a tribal drumbeat.

IX

Prokofiev was not seen in the West after 1938, when he made his last trip outside the Iron Curtain. His name continued to appear in the press, but personal reports about him were meagre. It would seem that his private life had been far from happy. In 1940 his home was disrupted when he left his wife and two children. Later he married a young woman who was a militant Communist, with personal connections at the very top of the Kremlin hierarchy. His new wife became his collaborator in the libretto of *War and Peace*. In 1944 the composer almost died from a fall down a flight of stairs, after a sudden heart attack. It was rumoured that later Stalin himself had German specialists brought in to treat the eminent composer, who remained incapacitated for many months. Still later Prokofiev had at least two similar attacks, each time returning with courage and fortitude to the practice of his art.

For a long time Prokofiev's international reputation and his political connections had kept him free from assaults like the *Pravda* attack on Shostakovich, but the Soviet ideologists were not happy about his music. Even his later simplified style they considered too difficult for the broad masses to assimilate. Inevitably, he began to come under the range of the ideologists' guns. Works like *War and Peace* and the Sixth Symphony, as well as many of his older masterpieces, were stamped in the Soviet press with the awful, black-plague label—"formalistic".

At Zhdanov's conference with the Soviet musicians in 1948 and in the ensuing Decree on Music, when the most celebrated composers of the country received a verbal horsewhipping, Prokofiev took some of the worst punishment. He later went through the accepted ritual of acknowledging his "errors" and trying to clear himself of sin. He composed an opera, *The Story of a Real Man*, with a libretto (written by his second wife, Mira Mendelssohn) based on a popular war novel about a Soviet airman who lost both legs in battle. The opera was not produced. After a hearing in concert form in Leningrad it was denounced as a complete failure—full of "formalism", "Western modernism", and "anti-melodiousness".

In the Spring of 1951 as Prokofiev approached his sixtieth birthday word came through the press that he had not only redeemed himself but had been named for a signal honour. The Stalin Prize had been bestowed upon two new works—*Winter Holiday*, a suite for young listeners, scored for children's chorus and orchestra; and an oratorio, *On Guard for Peace*. The former work is simplicity itself; its eight parts illustrate in rather pallid music sections of a long poem by the noted Soviet poet, S. Marshak, in which a group of boys is taken on a winter sojourn in the country. A genuinely powerful work is *On Guard for Peace* (Op. 124), composed in 1950 and scored for children's choir, mixed choir, soloists, and orchestra. Its theme is, in a sense, pure propaganda: The horrors brought upon the Russian people by World War II, their victory over the enemy, their resulting joy in "creative labour", and the happiness of the children. Prokofiev himself noted that in his music he tried to express his ideas about peace and war . . . "my firm belief that war shall not be, that the nations of the world will safeguard the peace, save civilization, our children, our future". The guardians of Soviet art policy would have been foolish indeed if they had tried to ban this work on the ground that the composer did not stick to their canons of technical simplicity. In grand outline it follows everything that they could ask for in a patriotic work, for it is big, solemn, and stirring. In this field in which dozens of other harassed Soviet composers have failed to produce anything genuinely inspiring, Prokofiev managed to work with much of his unique mastery—his fund of original ideas, his ability to avoid the commonplace and the expected, his distinctive ideas of melody and harmony, and his powerful dramatic sense—e.g. the use of a speaking voice for certain declamations that become as moving as music itself.

Prokofiev's last ballet, *The Stone Flower* (Op. 126), was composed during 1949–50. It is based on a story, *The Malachite Box*, from a book of folk legends by Bazhof, and was given a sumptuous première at the Bolshoi Theatre in Moscow, in 1954, a year after the composer's death. Excerpts from the score reveal Prokofiev's fulsome melodic gifts at work for the last time, with much that is charming and fanciful.

In 1952 the composer completed his Seventh Symphony, his last work in the form. On its première performance in Moscow early in 1953, *Pravda* gave a beaming benediction. The reasons were plain. Prokofiev had obviously avoided all problems, not alone political but musical, and had composed hardly more than a suite-like collection of simple movements. Blandly lyrical and sentimental, uncomplex, reminiscent (but not of its own composer's great past), the piece seemed to indicate the final peaceful ebbing of a once-vital force in modern music.

On March 8, 1953, dispatches from Moscow announced the death of Serge Prokofiev. The composer had actually died four days before, but the news was held up while world communications were glutted with accounts of the death-struggle of Josef Stalin, who died on March 5. The composer succumbed to a cerebral haemorrhage following a stroke, the same illness that killed the great tyrant.

On the occasion of his sixtieth birthday Prokofiev had been

SERGE PROKOFIEV

DMITRI SHOSTAKOVICH

publicly honoured by his friends and colleagues and by thousands of music-lovers all over the Soviet Union. Had the composer been permitted to know what goes on outside the Iron Curtain he might have been further gladdened by expressions of homage from all over the Western world. In those countries where neither artists nor works of art can be proscribed by government fiat Prokofiev is revered as a master, as the greatest composer of the Soviet Union, one who has advanced notably the tradition which makes Russian music an art both pungently national and richly cosmopolitan.

CHAPTER XVI

SHOSTAKOVICH

I

THE grim shadow of Siberia lies over the ancestry of Dmitri Shostakovich. Both the composer's parents were born there, although their families had come to the vast penal colony under differing circumstances. The paternal grandfather had been a revolutionist, banished to the Siberian town of Narim for implication in the Polish insurrection of 1863 and the assassination of Czar Alexander II. The maternal grandfather of the composer, Vassily Jakovlevich Kokaoulin, was a native of Kirensk, in south-central Siberia, and spent many years as manager and operator of various mining projects. Kokaoulin was remembered for his comparatively humane treatment of the mine workers whose lives were a purgatory of cold, hunger, and overwork.

The composer's mother, Sonya Kokaoulin, attended an exclusive school for children of the privileged classes at Irkutsk. Later she entered the Petersburg Conservatory where she studied the piano. She met a young university student of engineering, Dmitri Boleslavovich Shostakovich, and married him in 1903. Their son Dmitri was born in Petersburg on September 25, 1906.

The future composer was eleven years old at the outbreak of the revolution. He was attending a private school; his mother was giving him his first piano lessons, and his life in general was that of a well-cared-for child of cultured intellectuals. He said later that he "met the revolution in the street", for he saw at first hand the milling crowds of rioters, police, Cossacks, soldiers, and sailors. One incident he would never forget: a small boy killed in the street by a policeman.

When he was thirteen years old Dmitri Shostakovich entered the children's classes of the Petersburg Conservatory. He had already composed a number of little pieces which impressed Glazunov, then head of the school. The boy was entered immediately in the composition classes of Professor Maximilian Steinberg.

The life of the Shostakovich family during the post-revolution years was one of continuous misfortune, illness, and privation. In

1922 the father died suddenly of a heart ailment. Dmitri later developed tuberculosis in a gland of the neck. Much of the time he and his two sisters were ill from undernourishment and cold. In the city around them life was a chaos of inflated money, overcrowded houses and apartments, and cruel lacks of clothing, fuel, and food. The composer's mother worked as a typist to hold her family together and keep them alive, and above all to see that her son's music education should not suffer. She was a woman of iron courage and resolve, who exhausted herself to protect her children.

At the Conservatory young Dmitri made remarkable progress both as a pianist and in composition, but in the summer of 1924 when he was eighteen years old he was so ill and emaciated that he had to go to a sanatorium in the Crimea to rest. He earned the money by giving a private recital. Later his mother wrote a heart-breaking letter to his aunt who had gone to America: "Our greatest misery is that Mitya (Dmitri) is going to play in a movie house."

These hard adolescent years are told in detail in Victor I. Seroff's biography of the composer. Seroff describes the movie theatre—

> "old, draughty, and smelly, it had not seen fresh paint or a scrubbing brush for years. . . . Down in front below the screen sat Mitya, his back soaked with perspiration, his near-sighted eyes in their horn-rimmed glasses peering upwards to follow the story, his fingers pounding away on the raucous upright piano. Late at night he trudged home in a thin coat and summer cap, with no warm gloves or galoshes, and arrived exhausted around one o'clock in the morning. . . .
>
> "It was in the midst of this that Mitya began composing his First Symphony."

Those who are on the lookout for prophetic moments in the early lives of artists may find one of singular significance in this pathetic picture of the young music student drudging away at a piano in a decaying old movie house. It is not generally realized that Shosta-kovich the composer is a child of the theatre, and that one of the most pressing influences upon his art would be the Russian theatrical world as it unfolded around him in the nineteen-twenties and -thirties, with all its odd mixture of Russian nationalism and realism, cosmopolitanism, and communist proletarian propaganda.

II

Shostakovich was only nineteen years old when he completed his First Symphony (Op. 10). It was actually a student work, the last of a series of pieces which he composed for his classes at the Conservatory. The success of the First Symphony was astonishing. After the première performance, in 1926, by the Leningrad Philharmonic, Shostakovich was compared with Glazunov (the "little Glinka"). Bruno Walter played the symphony in Berlin. Leopold Stokowski performed it in 1928 with the Philadelphia Orchestra and later recorded it, and America, like Western Europe, took to the music of the strange new Soviet composer.

In the quarter century which has passed since then, Shostakovich has achieved world renown, and has become the most successful of all Soviet composers both inside and outside Russia. He is one of those personalities who seem to kindle the magic fires of publicity. Again and again he has been news in the world press, often front-page news. His music, meanwhile, has had its vicissitudes.

Shostakovich's student symphony proves again that the child is the father of the man, for the piece forecasts almost everything that the young composer would later become. It displays its creator's origins and his bent : he is Russian, and an eclectic, with modernist leanings ; he has a strong sense of humour, and a broad strain of romantic sentiment. The neat, compact workmanship, moreover, shows clearly the high quality of his schooling.

The work begins with charming bits of fanciful, grotesque comedy, in the manner of Prokofiev ; but soon come echoes of Tchaikovsky, Borodin, and Rimsky-Korsakov ; a lyric theme reminds us again of the enormous influence of nineteenth-century French ballet music on Russian composers from Glinka to the present. For a contrast to the impish humour and the incisive rhythms, Shostakovich presents the other side of his palette of moods —a broodingly sorrowful meditation which finds expression in long-drawn lyric passages, developing at times into passionate declamations. All this is in the tradition of nineteenth-century Russian romanticism, as is the fateful (and rather naive) "motto" which sounds through the gloom of the slow movement. But withal this is a modern symphony. The mildly dissonant harmonies and the angular edge to some of the themes give it a contemporary sound. Moreover, these harmonies and melodies (and a peculiar plaintive "falling" interval in some of the themes) bear Shostakovich's own signature, which would be recognized in much of his work of the future.

Even though Shostakovich's First Symphony is not one of the greatly significant works of its time or of the composer's country, it has charm, and a freshness of idea that has not yet let it grow stale. The piece shows the composer's enormous natural talent, his facility, his imagination and, most of all, his ability to arrange a group of musical ideas with dramatic effectiveness and to infuse them with nervous intensity. He has the gift of narration.

Immediately after completing his First Symphony, and not unlike any young graduate eager to celebrate his freedom from the professors, Shostakovich began to run after the new crowd of Western modernists. This was during the NEP period when the barriers of Soviet ideology were temporarily down, and works by such Western radicals as Schönberg, Berg, Stravinsky, Hindemith, and Krenek were heard in the land. Their impact on Shostakovich is recorded in his Piano Sonata No. 1, Op. 12 (1926). This gratingly dissonant work was most obviously influenced by Prokofiev's piano style, but it also has quotations from Stravinsky, and the dry, linear counterpoint of Hindemith. There is even some Scriabin—moods of mysterious brooding contrasted with wild hysterics, and many chords built on intervals of the fourth. The piece is continuously dissonant, with flashes of tonality. It bears almost no trace of the old Russian nationalism. For this sonata Shostakovich invented little, but imitated much.

With his Second Symphony, Op. 14 (1927), a new and highly-significant element makes its appearance in the work of Shostakovich, that of political ideology. The Soviet authorities commissioned him to write a symphony in commemoration of the coming tenth anniversary of the October revolution, and the composer responded with an imposing one-movement work for large orchestra and mixed chorus, subtitled "To October". At the top of his score he inscribed the words, "Proletarians of the World, Unite!"

It was said that in this symphony Shostakovich aimed to draw at the outset a picture of anarchy, of political chaos, from which a guiding revolutionary force slowly establishes order, then moves on to a massive, rallying climax of triumphant success. To achieve this grand panorama the composer spared no expense in utilizing the most advanced music techniques. His score is a mass of dissonance, intricate polyphony, and complicated rhythms. Nicolas Slonimsky noted "such formal patterns as a nine-part canon on a chromatic theme, in which different instruments enter at the interval of a sixteenth note, so that, in the end, chords of nine chromatics move in parallel blocks". Said one Soviet writer, "Minor seconds leaping through nearly entire octaves tear the ear like a saw." Taking note of the new *style mécanique* of the West, the composer introduced a factory whistle in the instrumentation.

Lenin himself had once said that "music is a means of unifying the broad masses of the people". But if music is of a kind which is incomprehensible to the masses it obviously loses that part of its point. Clearly, in Shostakovich's Second Symphony the Soviet authorities had made a bad bargain. The work fell flat, both with any of the broad masses who might have heard it and with the more musically cultured who had greatly enjoyed the composer's First Symphony. It was later proscribed by the Soviet music censorship.

Shostakovich had meanwhile gone on to his Third (or *May Day*) Symphony, Op. 20. This work is also in one movement, with a choral ending which describes the glories of the Russian revolution and extends a cordial invitation to other workers of the world to a similar uprising. The composer termed it "a proletarian tract in tones".

Although the *May Day* Symphony caused no little bewilderment (at least outside the U.S.S.R.) we may now discern the reasons for its peculiar content. Russia was then in the midst of the First Five Year Plan, when the government was urging its creative artists to join in raising the dejected spirits of the people by glorifying the communist order. The proletarian art groups were thriving. In his *May Day* Symphony Shostakovich was following the government's wishes by creating a tonal hymn to the new *proletkult*, and at the same time fashioning his musical material out of the songs, marches, and dance tunes of the masses. The technical apparatus of the piece, however, is like that of the Second Symphony—dissonant, complex, and generally incomprehensible to the masses. Shostakovich tried out one of the newer schemes of organization which he had noted in recent Western music. There is no conventional thematic development, in fact, no re-use of any theme either in its original or varied form; instead, the fabric is a profusion of individual themes.

The Third Symphony had its première in Leningrad in 1930, but like the Second it did not prosper. It had a few performances in

America, where it is now scarcely remembered except as a singularly raucous and blatant score.

III

So far, it is clear that two main influences were at work in shaping the major part of Shostakovich's music. One of these was the external force of communist proletarian propaganda.[1] The other was internal and purely technical—the strong natural attraction which the young artist felt for the most advanced contemporary music of the West. The wedding of these two influences is most obvious in pieces like the Second and Third Symphonies. But there was still another and very powerful force at work on Shostakovich, one which added a variety of odd and bewildering facets to his music and which has never been fully perceived outside his own country. That force was the Russian theatre.

Shostakovich grew to manhood during the days of the propaganda theatre, with its gigantic mass entertainments conceived by Meyerhold on the scale of the Roman Colosseum, and the circus-theatre with its blend of acrobatics and buffoonery. Later the composer entered the far more sophisticated world of the Russian art theatres, like the Vakhtangov Theatre, in which he would create incidental music for classics of the Russian and Western drama. During this period he would also compose music for a number of Soviet motion pictures. Upon the susceptible mind of Shostakovich, as upon a photographic film, were recorded a multiplicity of these theatre experiences, ranging from the sheer vulgarity of the mass festival and the circus clowning to the urbane refinements of the most advanced drama. And in his music they would all reappear, often in disarming juxtaposition, not alone in his stage works but in the pure abstractions of his symphonies.

Shostakovich composed his first opera, *The Nose*, in 1927–28. The libretto was pieced together from several stories by Gogol, but

---

[1] It is said that in his earlier years Shostakovich was not a member of the Communist Party in Russia, but he appears to have accepted its dogma. He found occasion to emphasize in various public statements the connection he found between music and the so-called "class struggle", for example :

"Music cannot help having a political basis—an idea that the bourgeoisie are slow to comprehend. There can be no music without ideology. The old composers, whether they knew it or not, were upholding a political theory. Most of them, of course, were bolstering the rule of the upper classes. Only Beethoven was a forerunner of the revolutionary movement."

chiefly it utilized the tale of the nose which was separated from its owner's face in a barber's chair and later became a government official. Shostakovich parodied opera, particularly Italian opera, in a rowdy burlesque. The score is an instrumental vaudeville, with all manner of sounds—horses' hooves, drunken hiccups, and the scrape of a razor blade—realistically simulated.

There followed two full-length ballets, *The Golden Age* (1928) and *The Bolt* (1930), both produced in Leningrad and both failures. In the former work the action takes place in a large capitalist city which is visited during an industrial exposition by a Soviet football team. The ensuing clash between the Soviets and the wicked Fascists has an outcome not unexpected. Both ballets explored the circus type of humour which obviously delighted the composer; he later explained these pieces as simply attempts "to write good entertaining music which would be pleasant and even amusing".

Shostakovich's first film score was for the picture *New Babylon*, produced in 1928–29. In the next decade he scored more than a dozen films, composing as many as four in a single year. In these same years, until the outbreak of World War II, he also composed incidental music to eight stage works, including productions of Shakespeare's *Hamlet*, and a play derived from Balzac's *The Human Comedy*.

IV

Toward the close of 1930 Shostakovich began composing his second opera, *Lady Macbeth of Mzensk*, which was destined in more ways than one to be the pivotal work of his entire career. He based his libretto on a famous story by the novelist Nicolas Leskov, which had been published originally in 1864. The book was a work of unrelenting realism, a character study of the young wife of a wealthy merchant in a small provincial town in the 1840's. The terrible boredom and discontent of her life unleash in Ekaterina Izmailova the twin passions of greed and sensuality. She falls in love with a young clerk, then poisons her brutal father-in-law who discovers her adultery. With her lover she strangles her husband, and also murders his little nephew. Her wedding to the clerk is interrupted when the husband's body is found buried in the cellar. On her way to Siberia with a group of convicts Ekaterina drowns herself in a river, pulling in with her a prostitute for whom her lover had deserted her.

In contriving his scenario from this sordid story Shostakovich attempted an important alteration. He tried to make Ekaterina not the incredibly vicious woman of the novel, but a heroine, "lovable and worthy of pardon", the victim of her social and psychological environment. This transformation stemmed from the composer's larger plan to make his *Lady Macbeth* the first of a tetralogy of operas. The basic theme would be woman, the Russian woman, depicted as the victim of her decadent surroundings through the past century, and emerging in the fourth opera as "the Soviet heroine of today". The plan was never carried beyond the first opera.

The political ideology of *Lady Macbeth* was actually less important than the fact that Shostakovich had here picked up the thread of realism in Russian opera where Musorgsky had left off half a century before. The most immediate stimulus to *Lady Macbeth*, however, was undoubtedly Alban Berg's *Wozzeck*. Shostakovich was greatly impressed by this wholly modern treatment of a group of human creatures drawn up from the lower depths and magnified under the glass of psychology, which alternately exposed the tragedy and the comedy of their sordid lives and their twisted, tortured souls. *Wozzeck* was related to the "intensified reality" of German expressionism. *Lady Macbeth* was pure Russian realism and was one of the works which has helped bring the modern opera story up to date in terms of literature and the drama. Shostakovich spared nothing of naturalism. The vileness, the sensuality of his characters, their hypocrisy, vulgarity, and appalling cruelty, even their gross acts of fornication are all illustrated in his music.

For his music pattern Shostakovich went to Musorgsky. *Lady Macbeth* is built, not like the old opera of arias, choruses, and recitatives, but of music symphonically conceived and obedient to the dialogue and the action. The libretto is not poetry, but simple (and often vulgar) speech. The music has a strong Russian flavour, gained chiefly through the use or imitation of Russian folk song. The techniques employed are varied; the harmonies, for example, range from the simplest diatonic procedures to the extreme dissonances of polytonality and atonality.

As for the quality of the music of *Lady Macbeth*, the criticism which applies to so much of Shostakovich's work is valid here. It is erratically uneven. At its best it contains moments of great dramatic effectiveness, of vivid (though often uglified) characterization. At its worst it descends to the level of musical comedy, especially in those scenes where the composer for reasons of political necessity applied the rasp of social caricature.

Shostakovich had completed his opera in 1932, and it was first performed on January 22, 1934, in Leningrad. Its success was enormous. It was later mounted in Moscow and in various cities in Western Europe. In 1935 it was introduced to America by Artur Rodzinski and the Cleveland Orchestra. In Leningrad it continued its phenomenal run to packed houses for more than two years.

With the completion of his *Lady Macbeth* in 1932 the art of Shostakovich began to undergo a series of highly critical transformations. For one of these the composer himself was responsible. He had a change of heart about his music, one which corresponded to the experience of Prokofiev, Stravinsky, and many other composers of that era. It was a revulsion against the extremes of dissonance, complication, mechanism, and eccentricity. Shostakovich began to evolve a much more simple, open style, with more easily recognizable melodies ; he began experimenting with neo-classicism.

Two works for the piano show these tendencies very clearly— the Twenty-four Preludes (Op. 34), composed during 1932–33, and the Piano Concerto (Op. 35), composed in 1933. The dates are important. They prove that Shostakovich himself had begun renovating his musical thinking several years before the Soviet authorities issued the first of their various directives aimed at coercing and intimidating the composer.

The Piano Preludes superficially resemble Chopin's, in their number, their variety, and in the fact that each one develops briefly a single music idea and projects a single mood. But Shostakovich also uses the typically Russian device of making each work a small commentary on some other composer's style. We hear paraphrases of Chopin, Bach, Prokofiev, Scriabin, Tchaikovsky, and Richard Strauss. Others of the Preludes sound like parodies (possibly intentional) of old salon pieces from the *Albumblat* era of Russian piano music—the Songs Without Words, Reveries, Consolations, Tender Reproaches, and other pressed violets from the pens of Arensky, Cui, Karganov, Pachulski, *et al.*

The Piano Concerto is an excursion into neo-classicism. The instrumentation is novel, solo piano and solo trumpet supported by a body of strings, and is remindful of the old classical concerto. The work is pumped dry of the rich tonal juices that made the romantic concerto overflow with sentiment ; instead this piece is steely and spare, and has the nature of a parody. The bugle call motif in the first movement and the gallop finale do have a certain humour; but the listener is reminded again that good comedy is the hardest thing to create in any medium, and that comedy lacking in subtlety is no more than burlesque.

On January 26, 1936, two years after the première of *Lady Macbeth of Mzensk* and while audiences were still crowding its performances, there appeared in the official newspaper *Pravda* an historic article, under the title "A Muddle Instead of Music". It damned the opera on every count. The sounds (said *Pravda*) were not musical, but a grinding and squealing roar; the piece could not be followed, much less remembered. Singing was replaced by shrieks; classical opera had been turned inside out. This was Leftist confusion, infecting the masses with petty-bourgeois, formalist clowning. The opera had borrowed the nervous, convulsive, spasmodic idiom of jazz. It had perverted Leskov's story. It was coarse, primitive, vulgar, the music of quacks, grunts, and growls, scribbled down to reach only the effete formalists. Its success abroad was explained by the fact that it tickled the perverted tastes of the bourgeoisie with its fidgety, screaming, neurotic music.

Hardly resting from the fury of his efforts, the *Pravda* critic (said to be A. A. Zhdanov) only a week later went to work in like terms on the ballet *The Limpid Stream*, also by the unhappy Shostakovich.

Had a similar blast appeared in the Western press aimed at some composer of eminence, it would have been relished by music reactionaries, deplored as a piece of bigotry by liberals, and probably ignored by the composer himself. It would have been forgotten long since. But in Soviet Russia it had enormous consequences. The country at the time was in the midst of the Second Five Year Plan and Stalin's purge of his political rivals. Two years before, the country's writers had been taught the lesson of socialist realism, and with the artists of the stage and films were also being made into active propagandists for the state. Meanwhile, the composers of serious music had been enjoying a period of comparative freedom. But now, with *Pravda's* attack on Shostakovich, they too were being bluntly informed that they would have to buckle down to the business of writing propaganda music; moreover, it would have to be in a style that the masses could understand. Modernism, in Russian music, was dead.

The shock to an artist like Shostakovich must have been profound. For a decade he had been the most illustrious composer of the Soviet Union and had repeatedly received its highest honours. Now it appeared that even his most ambitious propaganda pieces, like the *October* Symphony and the *May Day* Symphony, were falsely conceived. Their propaganda value was nullified, in the government's view, by their too advanced music style. The issue was plain: if Shostakovich (or any other serious composer) was to continue living and working in the U.S.S.R. he would have to revise drastically his technique of composition.

At the moment of publication of *Pravda's* article, Shostakovich's Fourth Symphony, on which he had worked during 1935–36, was being rehearsed by the Leningrad Philharmonic Orchestra. The composer withdrew the work, and it was never performed or published. Possibly he destroyed it. In the months that followed Shostakovich suffered a kind of public ostracism. When his name did appear in the press he and his music were excoriated. The composer himself remained silent; but after a difficult period of almost two years he announced his new position in a most dramatic way—with the presentation of his Fifth Symphony.

v

The Fifth Symphony was first performed in Leningrad, late in 1937. Its success was magical. The audience acclaimed the composer in a wild demonstration, and soon the word went round the music world that the "composer laureate" of the Soviet Union was once again in good grace. There is little doubt that part of the enthusiasm of Russian audiences was a personal demonstration of sympathy for the composer, with whom they sided against the government. But on the other hand the Soviet ideologists could have found little to arouse their fears of "formalistic" heresy. Shostakovich's Fifth Symphony is as safely old-fashioned in this day as were the symphonies of Anton Rubinstein in the age of Wagner.

The model of the Fifth Symphony is obviously the familiar grand opera symphony of Tchaikovsky; it is a large theatre piece full of dramatic thrills, and compounded musically of many sources. The first movement surges with Slavic *sturm und drang* in the Tchaikovsky manner, coloured by moderate dissonance. For variety, a long-drawn, sentimental melody sings over a throbbing accompaniment; only the spread of the melody and its widely-spaced intervals save it from banality. The second movement is a dance-scherzo which veers from grotesque mockeries (after Prokofiev) to old-fashioned ballet music—spirited and full of orchestral colour. The slow movement is an outburst of romantic *weltschmerz*. The symphony closes with a rousing finale. The substance of this movement may be gauged from the fact that it begins with a typical Russian march infernal, and closes with a long build-up from soft mutterings to an exultant major mode pronouncement in the brass, with tonic-dominant hammer strokes of the tympani to ring down the curtain.

It would be unfair to say that the Fifth Symphony is wholly wanting. It is a good grand-opera symphony, but one which shows its weaknesses when compared with a masterly example like Tchaikovsky's Fourth. Shostakovich has something of Tchaikovsky's sense of dramatic organization ; he projects great nervous intensity ; he communicates his moods as readily as if they lay on the surface of his thought. But as a melodist he is never in Tchaikovsky's class. If this symphony had been Shostakovich's second work in the form instead of his fifth, and if it had been separated from his student First Symphony by two years instead of twelve, it would engender less of a sense of disappointment. Coming from a composer so profusely endowed with technical skills and so strong an interest in the progress of twentieth-century music, it only made plain the tragic dilemma in which all Soviet artists now found themselves.

Shostakovich's Sixth Symphony (Op. 54) followed in 1939. The composer had meanwhile announced his plan to write a symphony dedicated to the memory of Lenin—a gigantic tonal monument for orchestra, chorus, and soloists. Shostakovich prepared himself by a careful study of the poetry, literature, "folk tales and folk music" devoted to the Russian revolutionary ; but when the Sixth Symphony appeared it was simply an abstract work in three movements devoid of personal portrait or political message.

The form of the piece is curiously lopsided. By opening with a slow movement the composer had to place the two following rapid movements together. The music content is even more incongruous. The opening Largo has it moments of grave beauty. It is in the nature of an elegy, with sweeping cantilena passages in the strings and plaintive woodwind solos, heavy with Slavic melancholy ; a sighing motto theme recalls some enigmatic sorrow ; long trilling pedal points in the middle strings drone ominously. The second movement, an Allegro, breaks in upon the gloom by reintroducing the satirical, smirking Shostakovich of an earlier day. This is no light-footed scherzo but a buffoon's dance. The orchestration is mainly ponderous, though there is some of the composer's favourite piping, whistling, and shrieking from solo woodwinds. In the third movement, a Presto, all pretence of seriousness vanishes. This is proletarian music, the Soviet gallop which Shostakovich has relished from boyhood. The jolly march with which the symphony ends would be used in capitalist countries in a musical comedy or a circus.

For a brief moment Shostakovich's Seventh Symphony (Op. 59) was the most famous symphony of modern times. Many still remember vividly its inspiring history. When the Nazis began the siege of Leningrad in 1941 Shostakovich at first refused to leave the city. He became a fire-warden at the Conservatory (to which he had returned as a professor of composition), and as he saw at first hand the long agony and the courage of the people he was inspired to write a giant symphony which would be "an emotional image of the war". He worked on at such speed day and night and with such powers of concentration (it is said that, like Glinka, he can work no matter what goes on around him) that the enormous symphony was completed in five months.

With the première performance (in Kuibyshev) in the Spring of 1942 the *Leningrad* Symphony became a national symbol of the defence of Russia, and was played all over the Soviet Union as a tonic to morale. Well publicized was the dramatic flight of a microfilm copy of the score, rushed by plane and automobile to Teheran, Cairo, across the Sahara and the Atlantic to America, where several of the world's most eminent conductors engaged in a public quarrel for the right to give the first American performance. The prize fell to Arturo Toscanini and the NBC Symphony Orchestra, who broadcast the symphony on July 19, 1942. The name of Shostakovich blazed on the front pages of the world's press.

The subsequent history of the *Leningrad* Symphony is as sobering as its conception and birth were inspiring. Once the war had ended few conductors of any eminence wanted to perform it again, for no amount of admiration for the composer's heroic theme could counteract the reactionary quality of the music itself. Shostakovich had borrowed wholesale from both local and foreign music sources, of which the most obvious was the repetition device of Ravel's *Bolero* in the appallingly long first movement. In its swollen proportions the piece was a throw-back to the epical symphonies of Mahler (which Shostakovich greatly admired); but it also related to a type of tonal monolith which had become fashionable among Soviet composers. Urged by the government to write music which would glorify Soviet heroes and revolutionary episodes and prove that socialist realism was greater than anything ever produced in the West, the composers were responding with mammoth symphonies and choral works which were related to the grandiose mass entertainments of the propaganda theatre, and which were at least the acme of size, loudness, and stupefying length.

The Eighth Symphony (Op. 65), another essay in the monumental, followed in 1943. Shostakovich had meanwhile left Leningrad and was living in a rest home for Soviet composers near the city of Ivanovo. Like the Seventh Symphony, the Eighth was a tonal recreation of the war and its dreadful impact on the Russian people. The immense five-movement work requires more than an hour to perform, and much of it is unrelieved gloom. The pessimistic, even neurotic, quality of the music apparently displeased the Soviet authorities who wanted at that time pieces to cheer the war-weary people; so the symphony had few performances. It is not much praise of the Eighth Symphony to say that it is better than the Seventh, though still uneven. Its first, third, and fourth movements maintain the composer's best standard of lyric inventiveness, intensity of expression, and even stylistic distinction.

While composing his Seventh and Eighth Symphonies, Shostakovich had indicated that he was planning a war trilogy, and that his Ninth Symphony would be a concluding paean of victory. When this last work appeared in 1945, however, the composer had returned to a mood of bantering exuberance with no visible programme, martial or other.

The first of the five movements of the Ninth Symphony begins by suggesting a neo-classic paraphrase of Haydn; but soon the face of the Russian satirist peers out from behind the eighteenth-century façade. A piccolo does a mosquito dance (or perhaps another "March of the Wooden Soldiers"), introduced each time by loud trombone blasts; and we know that Shostakovich the comedian is himself again. A serious second movement has long lyric lines characteristic of this composer; the scherzo oddly blends Tchaikovsky and Beethoven. In the short fourth movement, Largo, a bassoon sings over a background of sustained chords, as if the shade of Borodin were brooding over the tonal landscape. The final movement is fast and furious, and not a little comical. Taken from its symphonic surroundings it might provide music for acrobats.

VI

The chamber works of Shostakovich are not nearly as well known as his symphonies, but they contain many of his best pages. Several are remarkable for their consistently high quality, without the alloy of either questionable humour or political propaganda. They display, too, a more consistent personal style, with less of the obvious borrowing which is often so disturbing in his more popular scores. Here Shostakovich seems to work with greater care and for the quiet joy of exercising his great skill in the purely technical side of music.

The composer's first important chamber work was the excellent Sonata for 'Cello, Op. 40 (1934). His first String Quartet (Op. 49) appeared in 1938, after his Fifth Symphony; his Second String Quartet (Op. 69) came in 1944. In the interim Shostakovich composed a Quintet for Piano and Strings, Op. 57 (1940), which was so well received that it won the Stalin Prize, First Class, amounting to one hundred thousand roubles. During these years the composer was regaining something of his self-assurance after the *Pravda* episode. While none of these works is markedly radical, all nevertheless show that Shostakovich was daring to glance over the fence into the forbidden pastures of formalism. During the War he, like other composers, took advantage of the government's relaxed attitude. Both his Trio in E minor, Op. 67 (1944), and his Third String Quartet, Op. 73 (1946), would probably have been damned had they appeared in 1936.

The Trio in E minor for piano, violin, and 'cello was composed in memory of Shostakovich's friend of many years, Ivan Soller-tinsky, a writer and music critic who had recently died. This accounts for the elegiac mood of many of the Trio's pages, especially the slow movement, which is a dirge-like passacaglia (or chaconne) based on a series of eight sombre chords declaimed by the piano. Over these the violin and 'cello sing their mournful lament. The closing movement is equally striking though wholly contrasting—a kind of *danse macabre* with themes of an Hebraic or near-eastern flavour. The movement is long, persistent, even vehement in the working out of its curiously fascinating melodies.

The Third String Quartet was composed during the summer of 1946. There is nothing spectacular about the work; it is discreet

NICHOLAS MIASKOVSKY

ARAM KHACHATURYAN

and even modest in tone, but with expert writing for the instruments. At the outset the listener is alerted to Shostakovich's habit of borrowing when the opening theme turns out to be a transformation of one of Rimsky-Korsakov's. The first ten notes of the B minor melody which begins the second movement of *Scheherazade* are transposed (without the grace notes) down a half tone to sound in F major. After that, and except for certain resemblances to Prokofiev, the quartet moves on its own way. The harmonic colour is contemporary, a mixture of consonance and bitter dissonance. Nowhere in this quartet does Shostakovich interpolate any of his proletarian marches, factory songs, or the more obvious Russian peasant dance rhythms; burlesque humour is also conspicuously absent. The composer maintains his highest standard in the fourth movement, an impressive Adagio.

VII

Since the end of World War II and the lowering of the Iron Curtain interest in Shostakovich and his music has greatly waned in Western Europe and America. In part this has been due to the difficulty which Western correspondents encountered in trying to gain first-hand information about anything happening in Russia. Only occasional brief newspaper dispatches announced the première of some new work by Shostakovich and its approval or disapproval by the Soviet authorities. The composer himself was permitted to leave Russia for a visit to Prague in 1947, and in 1949 he was brought to New York for a personal appearance at a so-called Congress in Defence of Peace. The crudely disguised nature of the gathering as an instrument for communist propaganda aroused such general public resentment that the American government was obliged to curtail the length of the composer's visit. After a few days he was taken home.

Persons who saw Shostakovich on that occasion remember him as a slightly built, rather frail man who appeared much younger than his years, his round, thick-framed glasses giving him the air of a serious, unsmiling student. Intense, nervous, and very shy, he read his prepared statements mechanically and in a low voice. The few who were able to reach brief personal contact with the composer found him a highly sensitive and reticent man, under the tensions of strained embarrassment in the presence of strangers.

Following the verbal castigation which Shostakovich received in the Decree on Music of 1948 and from A. A. Zhdanov, it appears that the composer made a major effort to get himself back into the strait-jacket of socialist realism. In 1949 he composed a six-part oratorio, *The Song of the Forests*, Op. 81, for children's choir, mixed choir, soloists and orchestra. The libretto would have defeated an artist of lesser stamina. Its subject matter was a glorification of Stalin's fifteen-year plan for the reforestation and reclamation of large drought-ridden areas of the Soviet Union. The quality of the work may be judged by the fact that it won a Stalin Prize in 1949 and the fulsome praise of the Soviet press. Its musical style is so old-fashioned that a conservative of the eighteen-sixties could have filed few objections. Aesthetically it seldom rises above the level of motion-picture mood music, except that today Hollywood's composers are technically more daring.

Another product of apparently similar vintage appeared in 1953. At a concert in Moscow at which the Composers' Union presented new works, Prokofiev's Seventh Symphony received its première along with a cantata by Shostakovich called *The Sun is Shining Over Our Homeland*. *Pravda* described the piece as "beautiful, emotional music, majestically orchestrated"; and went on to extol as further virtues its "energetic revolutionary" spirit "glorifying homeland and glorifying party".

If Shostakovich had wanted deliberately to prove to the rest of the world that the writing of political pot-boilers had not damaged his immense skill as a serious composer, he could not have done so more pointedly than in the two chamber works which he produced during this very period. His String Quartet No. 4, Op. 83, dates from 1949, when he was working on *The Song of the Forests*; the String Quartet No. 5, Op. 92, came a few years later. Both are works of distinguished quality, in which the composer maintains a high level of technical virtuosity and creative vigour. It should be noted that most of the hated devices of abstract "formalism" beginning with acidulous dissonance are here in abundance.

Similarly abstract are the Twenty-four Preludes and Fugues for piano, Op. 87, completed in 1951. These are varied modern treatments of the old forms, in which Shostakovich displays both his fluent technical skill and his intuitive knowledge of the piano and its sonorities. We do not know if these piano pieces and the string quartets were in any way a courageous defiance on the composer's part, or if he had received some private dispensation by which he was partly freed of censorship. At any rate, a few years after 1948 he was obviously working on two separate planes, on the one producing propaganda pieces and on the other works of serious artistic purpose.

Shostakovich's Tenth Symphony, in E minor, Op. 93, appeared in 1955, his first work in the large form in ten years. It was received in and outside Russia with reserve. That the symphony is expertly made and brilliantly playable goes almost without saying. Except in a short second movement, an Allegro which is chiefly sound and fury, the mood is prevailingly lugubrious, the familiar Slavic melancholy; the orchestral hues are sombre or dark. Harmonies are mainly conservative; there is little or no rhythmic or contrapuntal complication. Absent too are the composer's former lapses into proletarian march effects, or contrasts of orchestral clowning. The entire work is seriously conceived and soberly presented. But in general Shostakovich has said very little that he (and many others including Tchaikovsky and Rachmaninov) has not said before.

Another large-scale, seriously-wrought work appeared late in 1955 when David Oistrakh, the noted Russian virtuoso, introduced Shostakovich's Concerto for Violin and Orchestra, in A minor, Op. 99, playing it in Leningrad on October 29 and in New York on December 29. The composer had not touched the concerto form in more than twenty years, since his Piano Concerto of 1933, but in the new work he sought no startlingly new deviations either from his own stylistic language or from established conceptions of the form as a brilliant show-piece. Although the four movements of the work are not over-long the solo part is formidable. The violin plays almost continuously, seldom leaving the centre of the musical stage. The soloist who can meet the relentless test of endurance and skill is likely to gain entrance to the Paganini circle.

Any attempt to summarize the art of Dmitri Shostakovich should begin with the remarkable fact that, when hardly more than a school-boy, he had already found his way with sureness in the intricate domain of the symphony, a place where even the most mature composers have walked with worried insecurity. He had not only rare talent but intuition, and a natural spontaneity. With these went the good fortune of first-rate academic training.

What happened to Shostakovich in the next quarter of a century may long be a matter of debate, the question being whether the un-fulfilled promise of the First Symphony should be blamed on weaknesses in the composer's own armour or on the peculiar social conditions which have surrounded him since childhood. Whatever the cause, the results can be simply stated: as an artist he did not grow up. Manifestations of immaturity are everywhere in his music. He has lacked soundness of taste and sureness of judgment. He arrived quickly at an individual style, but has seldom been able to comb out of it a thousand and one derivations from other composers' styles. His sense of humour is keen but crude. Real humour is one of the richest gifts ever vouchsafed to an artist, and the comedy of composers like Musorgsky, Rimsky-Korsakov, Stravinsky, and Prokofiev is one of the treasurable elements of Russian music. Shostakovich has been slow in learning that the sign of a matured master of comedy is subtlety.

The music of Shostakovich remains for the most part in what is now the classic Russian tradition, with obvious strong links to the works of Borodin, Musorgsky, Tchaikovsky, and Glinka. To these he has added personal mannerisms which derive from the sharp contours of contemporary Western music and from the symphonies of Mahler. Shostakovich has a recognizable style of his own, but it is not as original or as pervading as either Prokofiev's or Stravinsky's. Nor has Shostakovich succeeded, as many other Russian artists have done, in making an eclectic bent work for him instead of against him. Often he imitates facilely but does not absorb; he reproduces but does not recreate.

We return to the conviction that Shostakovich is by nature a theatre composer, a dramatic illustrator. Like one who excels at writing incidental music his technical skills are great, his adaptability even greater; he can produce effective passages in a dozen different styles; he can score a film or work up a gargantuan political symphony; he can write a beautiful string quartet; he can simulate the more obvious moods as easily as putting on so many masks, from romantic pathos to ribald clowning. He is, in short, an artist of superb natural talents. He is also a weather vane, shifting obligingly with the winds of either political or musical ideology.

CHAPTER XVII

OTHER CONTEMPORARY SOVIET COMPOSERS

I

BEFORE passing to a discussion of other eminent Soviet composers we must take note that Russian music, as a matter of strict historical fact, has split into two separate parts. A small faction, a kind of lost battalion, became separated from the main body after the revolution of 1917. These were the expatriate musicians who among hundreds of thousands of intellectuals fled from their country and the dictatorship of the proletariat. For a generation or more after World War I many of these men clung together in the big Western capitals—chiefly Paris, London, and New York. Gradually they became a part of the music life of Europe and America, and in the concert halls, opera houses, and music schools they brought Russian music more closely than ever to the attention of the West.

The most famous and influential of the expatriate Russian composers were of course Stravinsky and Rachmaninov, but there were many others—Glazunov, Liapunov, Gretchaninov, Nicolas Medtner, Nicolas Tcherepnin and his son Alexander, Nicolas Obukhov, Igor Markevich, Nicolas Nabokov, Arthur Lourie, and Vladimir Dukelsky (who writes American popular music under the name of Vernon Duke).

Never a brilliant composer but widely respected was Nicolas Medtner. He was born in Moscow in 1880, studied at the Moscow Conservatory with Arensky, Taneyev, and Safonov, and soon proved his worth as a virtuoso pianist. He later became a member of the faculty of the Conservatory, but as an artist he settled down to a life devoted mainly to composition for the piano. In 1921 Medtner left Russia never to return. He appeared as a concert pianist in many European cities, and in 1924 made his first tour of America. He lived for a time in Germany and France, and in 1936 settled in England.

Medtner's departure from Russia separated him completely from the influences of the Soviet state. His catalogue contains no propaganda music, political tract, or proletarian specimen. His art is instead a recollection of the late nineteenth century, specifically of

341

that age which produced a harvest of Russian piano music and piano virtuosi. Medtner's music offers another illustration of the great variety of ways in which Russian composers have reacted to the music of the West. The foundations of Rachmaninov's style and of Scriabin's were chiefly Chopin and Liszt. Medtner descended from Brahms and Schumann. In the West itself not many late romantics had followed the two German masters of classic-romanticism; fewer still followed them in Russia. Taneyev was the outstanding exception, until Medtner's extensive body of piano works helped establish a slender Brahmsian tradition in Russian music.

Even the statistics of Medtner's work suggest Brahms. He moved so cautiously that for almost twenty years he composed chiefly for the piano and the voice. His first large work was his Piano Concerto in C minor (Op. 33), composed in 1918 when he was approaching his fortieth year. At no time in his career was he ever seduced into writing for the lyric theatre or the ballet.

In Medtner's piano music the Brahms technical mannerisms rise instantly to the surface: the same close-knit contrapuntal style that seldom spreads out into rich sonorities or becomes indulgently lyrical; a similar deployment of chords, with close, heavy clusters of notes for the left hand. Medtner's harmony, though at times ornamented with chromaticisms, is mainly conservative. The tonal adventures of the twentieth century were not for him.

The piano works are about equally divided between the large forms (many sonatas and three concertos) and a host of small pieces of which the delightful *Fairy Tales* are most widely known and played. The sonatas show that this composer was not always a rigid classicist. He tried to vary the form, moderately, with experiments like the Sonata-Trilogy (Op. 11), Sonata-Ballade (Op. 27), Sonata Romantica (Op. 53a), Sonata Minacciosa (Op. 53b), and Sonata-Vocalise (Op. 41a), the last being written for piano with a voice part which is partly wordless.

Medtner (who had in fact German blood) was at times completely indifferent to his Russian heritage, and composed as if he were a nineteenth-century German. But just as often he made the Russian folk-song idiom the basis of his thoughtful craftsmanship, especially in the *Fairy Tales*. Here he showed too that he had (like Schumann) a mind that loved the airily poetic, the slyly mysterious. That he also felt a kinship with the wider heritage of Russian music is proved by a work like the Sonata Romantica. The first movement, cast in the richly-coloured key of B flat minor, at first suggests a lyric flight in the Tchaikovsky manner; but Medtner's thoughts had run deeper. He had gone rather to Tchaikovsky's sources—the earlier nineteenth-century romanzas in which Glinka and Dargomyjsky had woven their Russian threads on the loom of the Italian operatic aria. Medtner died in London in 1951. His last years must have been brightened by the formation of a Medtner Society for the propagation of his works. Chief among the sponsors was the enormously wealthy Maharajah of Mysore. This enlightened potentate later expanded the foundation to include music by other composers, among them Balakirev and Liapunov.

II

The composers who have created the music of the Soviet Union during the first third of a century of its existence fall roughly into two classes. First are the men who, being born well before the close of the nineteenth century, were already mature artists with the coming of the communist era, but succeeded in adapting themselves to the new life. Second are those who were born in or near the present century and whose entire artistic careers are bound up in communist politics. To the first group belong men like Ippolitov-Ivanov, Gliere, Miaskovsky, Steinberg, Alexander Krein, Michael Gnessin, Shaporin, Prokofiev, Boris Assafiev, Alexandrov, and Vassilyenko. In the second group are found Shostakovich, Khachaturyan, Kabalevsky, Knipper, Shebalin, Dzerzhinsky, Khrennıkov, and many others who are hardly more than names to the Western world.

Nicholas Yakovlevich Miaskovsky (1881—1950) enjoyed for many years a place of high distinction among Soviet composers, usually ranking with Prokofiev and Shostakovich. His international reputation is a curious one. It rests almost entirely on his enormous output of symphonies. He wrote twenty-seven works in this form, and was thus the most prolific symphonist since the eighteenth century. Even more curious is the fact that in the West these pieces, though famous collectively, remain obscure as individual works. Only the Twenty-First Symphony, a work of singular beauty, has had widespread performance.

Miaskovsky was a very shy man and something of a recluse. He never sought a reputation abroad but remained in Russia, hard at work at the two-fold task of composition and teaching. Of his private life and personality not much is known even in Russia.

Alexander Werth described him as a "little man, whose neat grey beard and fine features made him look like one of the more lovable characters in a Chekhov play". At performances of his own works he appeared to suffer agonies of shyness, and like Liadov preferred to escape from the hall unseen rather than face an ovation.

Miaskovsky was born in the fortress town of Novogeorgievsk, near Warsaw, the son of an army engineer. As a boy of twelve he entered the Cadet College in Nijni-Novgorod to follow obediently the family tradition of a military career. The next dozen years were a struggle, not so much to acquire knowledge of military science which he detested, but to find time on the side to study music which he adored. In 1902 he graduated from the School of Military Engineers, entered a sappers' battalion, and was soon transferred to Moscow. There he began studying music with Reinhold Gliere, who had recently graduated from the Moscow Conservatory. Transferred to Petersburg, he studied for three years with one of Rimsky-Korsakov's pupils, I. I. Kryzhanovsky. Miaskovsky was intensely interested in the newest trends in the art and music of the day. He composed abundantly, including many songs to words by the Russian symbolist poets. In 1907 he was released from military service, but the year before he had already made his great decision: music, not the army, would be his life. He enrolled in the Petersburg Conservatory.

Miaskovsky's first teachers were Liadov and Rimsky-Korsakov, and one of his fellow pupils was Serge Prokofiev, with whom he formed a life-long friendship. Together they explored the new music of the West and the latest Russian scores. At one of the "Evenings of Modern Music" at which Prokofiev made his first public appearance, shocking the audience with his *Diabolic Suggestions*, Miaskovsky also made his début, with a group of songs to words by the Russian poet Gippius. After graduation from the conservatory Miaskovsky contributed critical articles to a progressive musical journal, in which he took every occasion to praise his friend Prokofiev's then-controversial works and to force their performance in public.

When he left the conservatory Miaskovsky was thirty years old. By enormous industry he seemed to have made up the time lost to music by his service in the army. Already his predilection was plain for by 1914 he had composed three symphonies. But with the outbreak of World War I he was called to front-line positions in Galicia, near Lvov and Przemysl, and into the first tremendous battles of the Eastern theatre. He spent three years at the front, and was seriously wounded and shell-shocked. In December, 1917, the ill soldier-composer returned to Petersburg. Neither war nor revolution could shake his resolve to compose. Instantly he began work on his Fourth Symphony, which he finished three months later. In 1919 Miaskovsky was transferred to Moscow, where in the next thirty years his life and art would find their fulfilment.

The next phase of Miaskovsky's career resembles Rimsky-Korsakov's. He became a composer-teacher. It is said that he composed steadily, day-by-day, and with methodical exactitude. The immense labour which Rimsky-Korsakov expended on his fifteen operas is matched by Miaskovsky's twenty-seven symphonies; and just as the older composer taught a whole generation of Russian composers at the Petersburg Conservatory, so did Miaskovsky emulate this feat at the Moscow Conservatory where he became a professor of composition in 1921. In the ensuing years his pupils included Khachaturyan, Shebalin, Muradeli, Starokadomsky, and Kabalevsky.

Miaskovsky's music is not easy to classify or describe, largely because it exhibits neither a high degree of originality nor a quickly recognizable personal style. Some of its more salient features can be revealed by comparisons, chiefly with the music of the composer's friend and contemporary, Prokofiev. As young men they were both music radicals, but their wholly different natures took them off on diverging tangents. Prokofiev was strongly anti-romantic, unsentimental; he hated Scriabin's music, and was already sharpening up the tools of his *style mécanique*. Miaskovsky remained in the romantic tradition and most of his music was strongly coloured by sentiment; he was carried away by the powerful currents of Scriabin's style. In his Second and Third Symphonies there is much Scriabin, and still more in the Second, Third, and Fourth Piano Sonatas. Here the harmony is often highly dissonant, and based on intervals of the fourth and the augmented fourth. Tempos, following moods, fluctuate wildly.

In another respect Miaskovsky differed from both Prokofiev and Scriabin, that is, in the mood of deep sadness which saturates much of his music. Eighteen of his twenty-seven symphonies and eight of his nine string quartets are in minor keys. Over the earlier works especially there hangs a pall of heavy, oppressive gloom. Russian critics were quick to compare Miaskovsky with Tchaikovsky and Dostoevsky, travellers in "the realm of mental darkness". They saw his lugubrious tone poems, *Silence* after Poe and *Alastor* after

Shelley, as studies painted in solemn greys and blacks ; his symphonies seemed like tonal landscapes through whose troubled, mysterious twilight a funeral cortège might pass, or the notes of the *Dies Irae* sound their knell; visions of Russia's ancient fanatics of death, the Old Believers, sprang forth as from sinister flashes of sheet lightning.

Little of Miaskovsky's better music is written for quick, easy consumption. It always shows technical skill and often remarkable contrapuntal ingenuity. The composer's Soviet biographer, Alexandrei Ikonnikov, has noted the peculiar "close-grained" and "dense" quality of his scores, especially in the earlier works. The harmonies are usually intricate ; the chords occur "only rarely in their pure form (irrespective of whether they are formed by thirds or by fourths). There are nearly always extraneous elements in them. Furthermore, the voices are usually crowded together. . . ." In Miaskovsky's tonal world harmony is subordinate to polyphony. Thus his music often has a disciplined austerity, even a harshness. His orchestration too is sombre, almost Brahmsian, with little brilliance or startling colour.

The Russian folk idiom germinated much of Miaskovsky's melodic thought, but he seldom used it for a sweet, lyric effect. Even with this outward nationalist costume, the composer's basic structures and his procedures came from the classic technicians of the West. It is no exaggeration to say that his life work was a long meditation on the principles of the sonata-allegro form.

In the latter half of his career Miaskovsky's music began to show the heavy marks of political ideology. His first important work with a political message was his Sixth Symphony, in E flat minor (Op. 23), composed during 1922–23. Scored for large orchestra and chorus this was one of the first of the monumental type of symphony which Soviet composers began to turn out whenever called upon for a big propaganda effort. Its subject was the war and the revolution—a grand panorama of strife and suffering, culminating in the apotheosis of a dead hero.

A more specific propaganda piece is Miaskovsky's Twelfth or "Collective Farm" Symphony (Op. 35), composed in 1931 to celebrate the fifteenth anniversary of the revolution. At that time the country was in the midst of the First Five Year Plan and the revolt of the "rich" peasants against collectivization. The government was demanding that every shoulder press against the wheel of propaganda. Miaskovsky's Twelfth Symphony was described by the composer as "about the countryside, showing it before the new life (i.e. collectivization), in the struggle for this new life, and during the new life". The biographer, Ikonnikov, in a guarded remark states that "the musical themes of the symphony fell short of its subject".

During the next few years the Soviet government was working hard to promote proletarian art, and was urging all composers to create works in the idiom of the folk song, the factory song, and the worker's march. Miaskovsky's Twelfth, Fourteenth, Fifteenth, Sixteenth, Seventeenth, and Eighteenth Symphonies, composed between 1931 and 1936, contain many such simple themes which might appeal to the masses. The finale of the Sixteenth Symphony is based on a popular aviators' song, *Planes are Flying*. The Nineteenth Symphony was composed in 1939 to celebrate the twenty-first anniversary of the Red Army. It is scored not for orchestra but for brass band. During this period Miaskovsky also composed many short works of a proletarian nature—choruses, songs, and marches on such Soviet themes as Lenin, Karl Marx, the Russian Air Force, the collective farmers, and the Arctic explorers. The Violin Concerto, Op. 44 (1938), however, appears to be abstract.

After Russia's entry into World War II Miaskovsky was evacuated with many of his fellow artists to the government retreat at Nalchik, in the Caucasus; later he moved to Tbilisi (Tiflis), the capital of Georgia. He worked with patriotic fervour on a variety of propaganda works—not only overtures, choruses, songs and marches, but three symphonies and three string quartets, which he related to the war effort. The Twenty-Second Symphony, in B minor (Op. 54), called a "Symphony-Ballad", was composed in 1941 and was a companion to Shostakovich's Seventh Symphony. The Twenty-Third Symphony (Op. 56) was composed the same year, and was based on Kabardino-Balkarian folk melodies. A mammoth cantata, *Kirov Is With Us* (1942), for orchestra, chorus, and soloists, is Miaskovsky's largest effort in the Soviet epic style. Like Shostakovich's Seventh Symphony, it celebrated the heroic defence of Leningrad. Among the composer's last works were the *Pathetic Overture*, and a cantata, *Kremlin by Night*. These disquieted the Soviet critics, who feared that Miaskovsky had not done full justice to his subject matter but had strayed into the bog of formalism.

The serenely beautiful Twenty-First Symphony, in F sharp minor, (Op. 51), is the best known of Miaskovsky's larger scores. It was composed in 1940 (in a space of only twelve days, says Ikonnikov), and is a compact, single-movement treatment of symphonic principles. Its form and workmanship are classic, almost Brahmsian;

it is expressive in a restrained romantic manner. Miaskovsky uses something of the familiar Tchaikovsky-Rachmaninov overcast of personal melancholia, which gives his music a characteristic Russian flavour; but he avoids the blatant or the hysterical. The work has lyric beauty, which arises from polyphonic rather than openly melodic patterns. So far as we know the Twenty-First Symphony is an abstraction. Even without benefit of propaganda inspiration or political editorial it remains one of the finest works of the Soviet era.

III

One of the chief problems confronting the communist ideologists has been the welding into one tight federation the amorphous mass of races, nations, and even tribes which make up the Soviet Union. For many years the Russian communists have wooed in various ways the good will and co-operation of all the various "republics". The task is a formidable one because ethnographers can distinguish more than two hundred distinct nationalities living in the vast land area which stretches over two continents. All manner of men are found within this giant orbit—White Russians and Ukrainians in Eastern and South-eastern Europe; Laplanders in Karelia; Georgians, Armenians, and Azerbaijans between the Black and Caspian Seas; Uzbeks, Turkmen, and Tadjiks near the borders of Afghanistan; Kirghiz and Kazakh peoples in Central Asia; Buryat-Mongols in South-east Siberia; Yakutians in the Siberian lands around the Arctic Circle; Yamals, Oyrots, Tartars, Kalmuks, Mordvinians— the list is endless.

While the ultimate aim of the Russian communists is to fuse these peoples into what Stalin called "one General Culture, socialist as to form and substance, and expressed in one general language", many of the non-Russians in the Union are fiercely race-proud. For at time at least it was the government's policy that each nationality should not only preserve but even stimulate its own cultural individuality. Scientists, scholars, and artists were encouraged to dig into each people's past, to study and record its history, native customs, folk art, and music.

In the field of music some of the results of this policy have been interesting. Music schools have been established in the various republics, even some of the most remote; musicologists are at work collecting and publishing obscure folk music, and expounding its ancient and distinctive scales, melodies, and rhythms; composers are encouraged to blend these materials with local folk legends and epics for the creation of operas, symphonic works, and songs. Each republic is supposed ultimately to have its own national theatre, with orchestral, choral, and ballet organizations, trained to perform with proper colour and individuality the products of its local artists. One of the earliest projects of this kind was the opera *Katchkyn* (The Fugitive), by a Tartar composer with the formidable name of Nazyb Djyganov. It was written in the Tartar language and on the basis of Tartar folk music, and was performed in Kazan, the capital of the Tartar Republic. Its subject was the uprising of the Volga people under Pugachev.

The challenge of creating modern art works out of these native music systems—some of great antiquity and with peculiarities far removed from Western music, some crudely primitive, some with remnants of what was once a subtle and highly-organized art—presents difficulties often greater than those which faced the nineteenth-century composers in their first experiments with Russian folk song. Even though much of this movement must still be in the experimental stage (and little can be evaluated beyond the tightly-closed borders of the Soviet Union) its effects are visible in the works of a number of Soviet composers of eminence.

One of the first Soviet composers to interest himself in exploiting the native music of the outlying republics was Reinhold Moritzovich Gliere. Born of Belgian ancestry in Kiev, in 1875, Gliere is almost old enough to be classed with the second generation of composers who were the immediate successors of Tchaikovsky and the Five. At least half his creative career, however, belongs to the Communist era.

Gliere's father was a maker of wind instruments, but the son learned to play the violin. When he was nineteen he entered the Moscow Conservatory, studying under Taneyev, Arensky, and Ippolitov-Ivanov. In 1913 Gliere returned to Kiev where he became a professor of composition and later director of the Kiev Conservatory. In 1920 he was again in Moscow, and for years thereafter was a member of the faculty of the Moscow Conservatory. In the course of his long career he has taught some of the most eminent composers of present-day Russia, including Prokofiev, Miaskovsky, and Khachaturyan.

Gliere has taken a prominent part in the development of Soviet music. His ballet *The Red Poppy* (1926–27) was one of the earliest stage works glorifying the revolution. The Sailors' Dance from this work is the composer's most popular work. In the era of the proletarian art groups Gliere was active in organizing concerts for workers' clubs. During World War II he composed many patriotic songs, marches, and overtures and even an opera, *Rachel*, after Maupassant's story, *Mademoiselle Fifi*, as an illustration of the hatred felt by the French people for the German invaders of 1870. Gliere has been an avid student of the folklore and folksong of the outlying Soviet republics. Early in the Soviet era he was sent to Baku, the capital of Azerbaijan, to help in a modern development of the music of this ancient country on the shores of the Caspian Sea. A store of exotic folk music lies in the Azerbaijanian epics, called *Mugamat*. These elaborate rhapsodic song-legends, for which there was no musical notation, were sung by the native bards, or *ashugs*. Poet-songsters akin to the troubadours of mediaeval Europe, the *ashugs* roamed at one time over much of Central Asia, especially Azerbaijan, Uzbekistan, Turkmenistan, Armenia, and Georgia. They created an improvised poetry and song; they sang to the accompaniment of native stringed instruments ; some danced and operated puppet shows. In many of the ancient folk epics the *ashugs* were themselves the heroes, for they were beloved by the Eastern peoples.

One purpose of Gliere's studies in Azerbaijan was to teach the younger music students of that republic how to exploit their native folk art. Accordingly during 1924–25 he composed an opera, *Shah Senem* (revised 1933–34), based on a famed legend of Azerbaijan which recounts the love of Shah Senem, the fair daughter of a Persian potentate of the sixteenth century, for the poor but noble *ashug* Kerib. Gliere based his music on pure Azerbaijan themes, and on Iranian music with which many of the *ashug* songs were inextricably mixed. He tried to preserve native rhythms, and to imitate the sound of folk instruments. The task was a formidable one, for the ancient and distinctive melodies, scales, and rhythms often defied warping into the matrices of Western music. It is said that Gliere's score is scholarly, but rather conventional and lacking in imaginative treatment.

In 1936 Gliere performed a similar service for Uzbekistan with his opera *Gulsara* (described in some catalogues as incidental music to a play). This piece and the later opera *Leili and Majnun* (1940) are based on native Uzbek music.

Gliere has composed more than five hundred works in a wide variety of the standard forms. For his efforts as composer, educator, and propagandist he has received many of the highest awards of the Soviet state ; he has also been one of the chief figures in the Union of Soviet Composers. Although he has long been a popular composer in his native country comparatively little of his work is known in the outside world. He is usually regarded as a competent but conservative artist, who has seldom ventured beyond the horizon of the nineteenth-century Russian classics.

In the West Gliere's best known large work is his Third Symphony, in B minor, *Ilya Murometz* (Op. 42), composed during 1909–11. Ilya Murometz was one of the most resplendent figures in the whole galaxy of Slavic folk legend. The tales of this hero are part of the epic known as the *Cycle of Vladimir*, named from Prince Vladimir of Kiev who introduced Christianity to Russia. Ilya was a peasant of the primeval forest of Murom. For the first thirty years of his life he lay paralysed ; then, commanded by two holy wanderers to arise, he set forth on a life of heroic adventure, apparently an intermingling of history and legend. Ilya has been called a "mediaeval Slavic Paul Bunyan"—a figure of gigantic strength and stature whose very footfall shook the earth, and whose great horse "galloped as the falcon flies, bestrode lakes and streams, while his tail swept away cities". He was part legendary hero and part saint. A portrait of him published in the seventeenth century in a book of Kievan holy men made him appear as "a gaunt ascetic, with masses of hair and beard, barely covered with his mantle, and with hands outstretched". Ilya finally died in a weird battle, and his body turned to stone.

The four parts of Gliere's symphony each describe a phase of Ilya's dazzling career, and the huge musical pictures are painted with immense gusto and with scintillating orchestral colours. But Gliere was not a great enough artist to treat this wildly fantastic, ultra-Russian subject with the originality it deserved. Mixed in fairly equal parts in his symphony are drafts of Borodin's bardic style, Rimsky-Korsakov's fairy-tale apparatus, Wagner's sensuous chromaticism, and Scriabin's ecstasies. The second movement of *Ilya Murometz* might well mark the high tide of Wagnerism in Russian music. The gorgeously fantastic tale of Ilya's capture of Solovei the Brigand, a malignant creature of the dark forest who sings like a nightingale, reverberates in Gliere's score with echoes from the Venusberg and the night-shrouded garden of King Mark's castle.

IV

Aram Ilich Khachaturyan was born in Tiflis in 1904, the son of a bookbinder. At the age of nineteen when he enrolled at the Gnessin school in Moscow he was almost completely ignorant of the technique and the literature of music, but was already fanatically sure that music was to be his life. The young man learned rapidly. For two years he studied the 'cello, and then composition. It is said that some of his student songs are remarkable examples of the Armenian, Turkoman, and Turkish folk idioms. In 1926 Khachaturyan entered the Moscow Conservatory where Miaskovsky became his principal teacher. He graduated with highest honours in 1934, and has since become one of the few Soviet composers to gain an international reputation.

Khachaturyan's works include a Trio for clarinet, violin, and piano (1932), a String Quartet (1932), the First Symphony (1934), a Piano Concerto (1936), a Violin Concerto (1940), the Symphonic Poem, *Poem About Stalin* (1938) for mixed chorus and orchestra, the ballets *Happiness* (1938) and *Gayane* (1942), the Second Symphony (1943), a 'Cello Concerto (1946), a *Symphony-Poem* for orchestra, brass instruments, and organ (1947), incidental music to various films and to stage productions of the Moscow Art Theatre, the Vakhtangov Theatre, and the Armenian State Theatre. The composer has also written many simple pieces of a propaganda nature for the entertainment of the masses, and a number of marching songs for the Red Army.

Khachaturyan's works are saturated with genuine and imitation folk idioms, not only Armenian but Georgian, Ukrainian, Azerbaijan, Uzbek, and Russian. These he uses with intuitive skill, and with appreciation of their exotic harmonies and rhythms, and the distinctive sounds of native folk instruments. He is able to impart, too, much of the spirit of this music, for his own product has great vitality, rhapsodic freedom of expression, vivid colouring, and a pervading lyricism.

The early Trio for clarinet, violin, and piano, composed while Khachaturyan was still at the Conservatory, was his first work to bring him fame outside the Soviet Union. Based on folk music of Transcaucasian peoples, it is also related to the art of the Armenian *ashugs*. In the first part the piano lays out a heavily-chorded structure against which the clarinet and violin sing a rhapsodic duet—"winding ornamental melodic phrases" said to be typically Transcaucasian. The second part conveys "the whirlwind velocity of Eastern dancing"; while the finale is based on a genuine Uzbek folk song. While writing this work young Khachaturyan was strongly under the influence of Ravel's music, and he delighted in mixing modal folk harmonies with the complex chromaticism of the French impressionists. At times he aimed to suggest the peculiar sonorities of stringed folk instruments.

The Piano Concerto, now familiar and even popular in the West, is based in part on Armenian folk songs and also imitates Armenian folk instruments. For all its folk ornamentation, however, this piece remains closely linked with the standard Russian classics—a *mélange* of Tchaikovsky's brilliant dramatics, the heroic style of Borodin, and Rachmaninov's personal melancholia. In the scintillating finale there appear to be conversations with Prokofiev. Thus Khachaturyan's use of folk idioms never results like Bartok's in a complex, intellectual product; his music is more conservative technically, easier to assimilate, more reliant upon the charm of exotic and sentimental melody, and gaudy colour. This accounts for the quick popular success of the Piano Concerto and of the excerpts from the ballet scores.

The Khachaturyan Violin Concerto is a show-piece, extremely difficult but rewarding the virtuoso who masters it with brilliant technical effects and voluptuous melodies. In 1941 it won one of the Stalin prizes, amounting to 50,000 roubles. *Poem About Stalin* is a symphonic poem for orchestra and mixed chorus, with words by the *ashug*, Mirza Bayramov, a noted poet of the Azerbaijan Republic. It is said that Khachaturyan here blended some of the finest Transcaucasian folk tunes—Azerbaijan, Armenian, and Georgian.

Khachaturyan's Second Symphony (with Bell Effects) was composed during World War II, and was a large-scale, propaganda piece intended to bolster mass morale. It did not find popular favour. Nor has the 'Cello Concerto achieved the success of those for piano and violin, in spite of expert writing by a composer who is also a 'cellist. The *Symphony-Poem*, for orchestra, brass instruments, and organ, was composed to celebrate the Thirtieth Anniversary of the October Revolution. According to the Soviet writer, Rena Moisenko, it pleased nobody: "Throughout its performances, the audience sat in stunned silence." For the first time the dread word "formalistic" appeared in criticisms of Khachaturyan's work.

Khachaturyan was by no means the first composer to exploit the Armenian folk idioms. A vigorous Armenian school of composers antedated the Russian Revolution. These pioneers included Christopher Kara-Murza (1854–1902), Makar Ekmalian (1855–1909), and Nikolai Tigranian (1856–1936), who studied, arranged, and published Armenian folk tunes, and also Iranian, Turkish, and Kurdish music. Outstanding was the work of Komitas Kervorkian (1869–1935), a composer, teacher, and scholar. Said to be the first to decipher the intricate Armenian neumes, this man greatly stimulated the study of his nation's music by his teachings and publications. His career ended tragically in 1916, when he became insane and destroyed the manuscripts of most of his own compositions.

Later composers of the Armenian school include Spiridion Melikyan (1880–1933), a pupil of Kervorkian; Romanos Melikyan (1882–1935); and Alexander Spendiarov (1871–1928), a pupil of Rimsky-Korsakov, who became a specialist in Armenian folk song and the *ashug* art. Early in the century Spendiarov met the great Armenian *ashug*, Dzhivani, who had begun life as a shepherd and rose to fame singing and improvising hundreds of his own poems. Spendiarov wrote down some of the old and dying bard's songs. In 1917 he began work on an Armenian national opera, *Almast*, which was produced in Moscow in 1939, more than a decade after his own death. In his later years Spendiarov headed a group of scholars who compiled the enormous, thousand-year-old Armenian epic, *David of Sassun*.

v

Dmitry Kabalevsky was born in Petersburg in 1904, but when he was fourteen his family moved to Moscow. There he began serious study of the piano and composition. In 1925 he entered the Moscow Conservatory where Miaskovsky was one of his teachers. A brilliant student, Kabalevsky graduated in 1930, and became a professor of composition at the Conservatory. He has since devoted much time to music criticism and musicology, has edited the review *Soviet Music*, and has been a prominent figure in the Union of Soviet Composers.

Kabalevsky is a prolific composer in many forms—operas, symphonies, concertos, ballets, chamber works, songs, theatre and film scores, a number of pieces for children, and the usual spate of simple pieces for the proletariat. Several of his larger works are based on propaganda subjects, e.g. *Poem of Struggle*, for mixed chorus and orchestra (1930); the First Symphony (1932), commemorating the fifteenth anniversary of the October Revolution; the Third, or *Requiem* Symphony (1933), a tribute to Lenin, for chorus and orchestra; the Fourth Symphony, for chorus and orchestra, a tribute to the Red Army leader, Shchors; and *Our Great Fatherland*, a cantata for mixed chorus and orchestra (1942). Two of Kabalevsky's ballets glorify life on a Soviet collective farm.

In the West Kabalevsky is known chiefly by his Second Symphony, in C minor (1934), and the Second Piano Concerto, in G minor (1936). While neither of these works shows any great distinction of style or thought, both do indicate an expert craftsman who can create attractive if not profound music. Like so many Soviet composers Kabalevsky borrows much from the Russians of the past— Borodin, Tchaikovsky, Rachmaninov, and Scriabin; like some he borrows from the present, chiefly from Prokofiev. It is said that during his formative years in the nineteen-twenties Kabalevsky studied closely the music of Stravinsky and of the *avant-garde* composers of France and Germany; but none of these exerted any significant influence on his work. He has the good fortune to own a decided lyric gift, which is responsible for much of the success of his music both in and out of Russia. This composer has so far shown only a mild interest in the subject of exotic folk music. His ballet, *The Golden Spikes* (1940), is related to Byelorussian folk-lore; while *People's Avengers*, a suite for mixed chorus and orchestra (1942), is said to show the influence of Ukrainian popular music.

Kabalevsky's most important score is his opera, *The Master of Clamency*, completed in 1937 and based on Romain Rolland's story *Colas Brugnon*. This tale of a Burgundian master-craftsman of the sixteenth century would seem an odd subject for a composer of twentieth-century Soviet Russia, but Rolland's book had enjoyed great popularity in the U.S.S.R. and the Soviet ideologists were able to find in it traces of "social significance". The overture to the opera, a brisk and dynamic piece, has been well liked in the West. The opera itself was at first damned by Soviet critics, but succeeded largely because of its graceful lyricism.

Friends of Kabalevsky invariably speak of him as a man of unusually attractive personality and gifts—modest, intelligent, cultured, utterly absorbed in the world of music. Juri Jelagin, in his study of music and the theatre under the Soviets, describes him as "tall and gawky", with "very long arms and legs and an unusually narrow face". At the piano in his small Moscow apartment, and surrounded by piles of music, he would play insatiably for hours at a time, his cosmopolitan tastes ranging from Borodin, whom he holds one of Russia's greatest masters, to the object of his profound veneration, Bach.

Like Khachaturyan, Lev (or Leo) Knipper is a native of Tiflis, where he was born in 1898. He studied at the Gnessin school in Moscow, and also went abroad for a time and studied in Berlin. Knipper's Opus 1 was the dance suite (intended for ballet performance), *The Legend of a Plaster God*, composed in 1924. It was performed in America four years later by the Philadelphia Orchestra under Stokowski, and is remembered as a grotesque and satirical piece which showed the young composer's early anti-romantic bent. His opera, *North Wind*, was produced in Moscow, in 1930. Its almost continuous recitative was called dry and intellectual, an experiment in the *sprechgesang* technique of the Middle European composers. Knipper was for a time under the spell of Stravinsky and certain Western radicals.

In 1931 Knipper spent some time in the mountains of Tadjikistan. His studies of the national folk music resulted in a series of orchestral and piano works on Tadjik themes. Writes Gerald Abraham:

> "Knipper's approach to his Tadjik themes is quite different from that of nineteenth-century Russian composers to Oriental material. There is no picturesque Russification but a serious attempt to evolve a more highly-organized work of art from the essence of the themes themselves. . . ."

Knipper has composed two other operas, *Candide* (1926–27) and *Maria*, several ballets, various songs, a violin concerto, and an extensive body of works for symphonic orchestra. Of these last the most important are his seven symphonies, which have led Abraham to call him "the Mahler of Soviet Russia". The Third Symphony is an ideological work, dedicated "To the Far Eastern Army", and composed in 1932–33 after Knipper had spent some time with units of the Red Army on the Manchurian front, as music instructor and conductor of army choirs. This *Far Eastern* Symphony is a five-movement work, for orchestra, military band, male choir, and soloists—one of the earliest of the mammoth, Communist-glorification type. It contains picturesque scene painting, a battle, a funeral march saluting fallen comrades, and a gigantic finale with a proletariat marching song in which the audience is invited to join. Abraham describes the work as uneven but powerful; the mass marching song he terms "incredibly banal".

Subsequent symphonies showed Knipper alternating between what seemed to be his own sophisticated interests in modern music techniques and the demands of Communist ideology. His Fourth Symphony (1933) blended unorthodox instrumental experiments with melodic material in the manner of Tchaikovsky. The Fifth Symphony (1933–34), with choral ending, has the sub-title "Komsomol Fighters", and is another big propaganda piece glorifying the Union of Communist Youth. The Sixth Symphony (1936) was devoid of programme or ideology, and its dry, unromantic writing called forth the wrath of the Soviet critics who showered on the composer all the familiar epithets denoting formalistic heresy. Knipper recanted with his Seventh Symphony (1942), in which he came up with propaganda on an unimpeachable subject—the defence of the Soviet fatherland and the final triumph of the Red Army.

VI

Vissarion Shebalin was born in 1902 in the Siberian city of Omsk. In 1923 he came to Moscow and entered the Conservatory, studying under Miaskovsky. Like his mentor he made teaching part of his career; on graduation he became an instructor at the Conservatory and in later years its director. Symphonies and chamber works form the bulk of Shebalin's compositions, although he has also written for the stage and the films.

Shebalin's earlier works appear to typify the kind of music which the younger and more progressive Russians were composing in the early nineteen-twenties, before the hand of Soviet direction began to bear down upon them. Their interest at that time was strong in instrumental works and away from the old Russian traditions of vocal music; operatic writing had little attraction for them. They studied closely and at times imitated everything that the more-advanced Western composers were doing. Shebalin's earlier symphonies and string quartets are said to show that he was first of all a descendant and devoted student of the older classic Russians, especially Borodin; he also coloured his work mildly with harmonies based on unusual scales, and mixtures of modal, chromatic, and even atonal harmonies. His early piano music employed some of the Scriabin apparatus. He was scholarly and skilful; Abraham describes his music as "lyrical, technically fluent, individual but not startlingly so".

In the nineteen-thirties Shebalin's work began to reflect the new political climate. His symphonic poem, *Lenin* (catalogued, apparently, by some as his Third Symphony), for orchestra, mixed chorus, and soloists, is based on a eulogy to the Soviet leader by the poet Mayakovsky. As originally planned this vast work would have run two hours, for its four movements depicted crucial political events beginning with the 1905 uprising and continuing through World War I and the October Revolution and ending with Lenin's death. The piece was curtailed somewhat and reduced to three movements. Another propaganda piece is Shebalin's Fourth Symphony (1935), a two-movement work celebrating the heroes of the Perekop campaign in the civil war of 1920.

Shebalin's interest in the nineteenth-century Russian classics is shown in his reconstruction (1933) of Musorgsky's *The Fair at Sorochintzi*, which he completed and filled out with music of his own. In 1938 he completed a Symphony-Overture which Glinka had begun in Berlin in 1834. More recent works by Shebalin include a cantata, *Moscow*, a string quartet (his Fifth) on Slavonic themes, a violin concerto, a 'cello concerto, and a comic opera, *The Embassy Bridegroom*, based on a story of the period of Catherine II.

Shebalin's place in the hierarchy of Soviet musicians has been a high one both as composer and pedagogue. In the famous Decree on Music in 1948 and in Zhdanov's previous meeting he was singled out with Shostakovich, Prokofiev, Khachaturyan, and Miaskovsky as one whose work was marked by "formalist perversions", and "anti-democratic tendencies". As director of the Moscow Conservatory he was held responsible for what was called a hotbed of formalism. Shebalin could not dare to reply directly to Zhdanov's castigations; he could only defend himself and his students against those musicians present who chorused praise of the party line. His remarks about the Conservatory contained the plea that "the building and the two concert halls are in very bad condition. The roof is leaking all the time. In the hostels, the students live like sardines in a tin. . . . There aren't enough instruments for teaching the students."

Yury Alexandrovich Shaporin was born in 1889 in the small Ukrainian town of Glukhov. Like Stravinsky he studied the law before he decided on a music career, entering the Petersburg Conservatory in 1913 when he was twenty-four years old and with a degree in jurisprudence. When he graduated five years later he began his long association with various Russian theatres, both as conductor and composer. Shaporin's scores for plays by Schiller, Shakespeare, Molière, Beaumarchais, Pushkin, and Turgenev were highly regarded. They also indicate the state of the great Russian art theatres in the nineteen-twenties and -thirties, when the productions were still of high artistic integrity and cosmopolitan interest, and before the Soviet authorities closed or disrupted them, or made them into dull propaganda machines.

Outside the theatre Shaporin has worked with extreme deliberation and care, sometimes requiring years for a single large work. His catalogue is therefore small. Besides his theatre and film scores he has written two piano sonatas, a symphony, a symphonic cantata, an oratorio, several song cycles, and a single opera, *The Decembrists*.

Shaporin has been called "the chronicler of past and present glories of Russia", for his larger works all have an historical if not a modern political background. His First Symphony, in E minor, (begun in 1926 and not finished until 1932) is a mammoth work for chorus, orchestra, and brass band. Its main theme, says Rena Moisenko, is "Revolution and Intelligentsia ; it is full of intonations, reminiscent of national songs and dances". The composer himself acknowledged his debt to his close friend, Maxim Gorky, who gave him inspiration and help in the uses of Russian folk-lore. The symphony, Shaporin said, was an attempt "to show the development of the fate of a human being in a great historical upheaval. It portrays the gradual transformation of individual consciousness in the progress of acceptance of the Revolution." The final movement of the symphony is a vast thunder of choruses, antiphonal effects between orchestra and brass band, and a concluding "mass song" which was actually a popular army marching tune. It appears that in spite of its revolutionary theme the music of Shaporin's symphony is reactionary. Soviet critics found it a compound of Borodin, Musorgsky, and Rachmaninov, with some of Rimsky-Korsakov's orchestral apparatus.

The symphonic cantata, *On the Field of Kulikovo*, for orchestra, chorus, and soloists, is another giant. It was composed in 1938, at a time when the government was playing down the international aspects of communism and seeking to glorify Russia's past. Shaporin's piece is based on a cycle of verses written in 1908 by the poet Alexander Blok, and describing the great mediaeval battle of

Kulikovo in the year 1380 when the Russians under Dmitry Donskoy threw back the Tartar hordes. At the top of his score Shaporin wrote: "The Russians, by halting the invasion of the Mongols, saved European civilization." The huge work is in eight parts, a blend of orchestral scene painting, operatic choruses, and aria-like solos. It has been highly praised by Soviet critics, possibly because its music style ventures hardly at all beyond the borders of the nineteenth century. In 1941 it won a Stalin prize of 100,000 roubles.

Even the mammoth proportions of the symphonic cantata were surpassed by Shaporin's oratorio,[1] *The Lay of the Battle for the Russian Land*—a two-part colossus which requires three hours to perform. Its subject is the defence of Stalingrad, and in 1946 it won for the composer another Stalin prize.

Shaporin's opera *The Decembrists* occupied its composer for an even longer time that Borodin's *Prince Igor*. He began it in 1925, completely revised it after a concert performance in 1937, and as late as 1949 was reported to be still recasting some of its scenes. When the piece was finally produced, on June 27, 1953, in Moscow, an ominous occurrence which took place not on the stage but in the audience made headlines in the world press. Foreign correspondents reported that Premier Malenkov, making his first public appearance after succeeding Stalin, attended with other high officials of the Communist Party; but they also noted the conspicuous absence of Lavrenti P. Beria. Only a few days later came the startling public admission of Beria's arrest and imprisonment.

The libretto of *The Decembrists*, by the Soviet novelist, Alexey N. Tolstoy, is based on the conspiracy of December, 1825, by which a group of army aristocrats attempted to overthrow the government of Nicholas I, and in which friends of Pushkin and Glinka were involved. The leading characters are drawn from history—the country squire, Annenkov, and his wife, the French shop-girl Pauline, who devotedly followed him into exile in Siberia. Soviet critics have praised Shaporin's vivid musical characterizations in *The Decembrists*. The composer relied strongly, it is said, on Russian and gypsy folk melodies. Abraham describes the score as "a curiously satisfactory synthesis of those seeming incompatibles, Musorgsky and Tchaikovsky".

Mention should be made of Shaporin's songs, which have earned

---

[1] "The oratorio form," writes William Kozlenko, "must here be understood, of course, not as possessing its traditionally religious character, but as a special art form developed by the Soviet composer to narrate social events, with the aid of chorus, solo, and recitative."

high praise both in and out of Russia. They have been described as essentially lyrical, in the romantic vein of Tchaikovsky, Rimsky-Korsakov, and Rachmaninov. The best are said to be a cycle of five songs to words by Pushkin.

Maximilian Osseyevich Steinberg (1883–1946) was born at Vilna, and studied at the Petersburg Conservatory with Rimsky-Korsakov, Liadov, and Glazunov. He married one of Rimsky-Korsakov's daughters, and after the father-in-law's death he edited and revised his books on harmony and orchestration. Steinberg himself became an influential teacher at the Conservatory, and in 1934 was appointed its director. As a composer Steinberg began by imitating his teacher, Glazunov, then fell under the spell of Scriabin and the symbolists. In 1914 Diaghilev produced in Paris part of his ballet-triptych, *Metamorphoses*, after Ovid. Steinberg's eclectic tastes ranged over a wide field—from classic Greek subjects to Byron, Maeterlinck, and Rabindranath Tagore.

With the coming of the revolution Steinberg tried to find a place in the new order. He composed incidental music for productions of the Mamont musical group which in the nineteen-twenties made several experimental attempts to reconstruct and "sovietize" the standard operas.[1] His Third Symphony symbolized the "struggle between the principles of Individualism and Collectivism". He studied Eastern and Central Asian folk music and in 1931 published his Eighteen National Songs for Voice and Symphonic Orchestra (Op. 23). His Fourth Symphony, *Turksib*, celebrated the building of the Turkestan-Siberian railway. Steinberg also composed pieces on Uzbek and Armenian themes.

VII

Alexander Krein (1883–1951) was a native of Nijni-Novgorod. Born of a musical family, he studied 'cello and composition at the Moscow Conservatory. He composed in great abundance in a wide variety of the standard forms, but his distinction lies in his work in the field of Hebraic music. He was said to be a profound student of ancient Jewish culture, and in the early years of the century began to compose the first of a long series of works based on Hebraic and

---

[1] In Mamont productions Puccini's *Tosca* was given a sovietized title, *The Fight for the Commune*, and its action was changed to Paris and the Revolution of 1848. Meyerbeer's *Les Huguenots* was given a Russian story based on the Decembrist uprising of 1825.

Oriental themes. Krein paid his tribute to purely Communist subjects with the orchestral works, *Ode of Mourning to Lenin* (1925–26), and *U.S.S.R., the Shock Brigade of the World Proletariat* (1931–32). Krein's music is usually described as eclectic in style and romantic in spirit. He has been compared to Ernest Bloch, as a composer whose art reflects an intense, deeply-emotional nature.

Michael Gnessin, born in 1883 in Rostov-on-the-Don, is another exponent of Jewish national music. He studied at the Petersburg Conservatory under Rimsky-Korsakov and Liadov, and later spent several years in Germany. Gnessin's early works were romantic and eclectic in style. He spent much time in the Transcaucasian republics, studying the ramifications of Hebrew music in the East until he became one of the leading authorities on the subject. His opera-poem, *Youth of Abraham*, was composed in 1922 during a visit to Palestine. Gnessin's contributions to the Communist glorification literature includes his *Symphonic Monument, 1905–1917*, for orchestra and chorus, a commemoration of the two revolutions. His work in the field of song is extensive and includes a number of song cycles. Gnessin has devoted much of his life to teaching, and since 1936 has been a professor of composition at the Leningrad Conservatory. The composer's three elder sisters were founders in 1895 of a group of elementary and secondary music schools in Russia, which for many years maintained high standards of pedagogy.

One of the curiosities of Russian music is the career of Ivan Dzerzhinsky. Born in Tambov in 1909, this composer entered the Gnessin School in Moscow in 1928. He became a fluent pianist with a passion for improvising, often giving concerts at which he would "illustrate" spontaneously excerpts from classic Russian poetry. In 1930 he entered the Leningrad Conservatory. At this time Boris Assafiev, the noted musicologist-composer (known widely as a music critic under the pseudonym Igor Glebov) became Dzerzhinsky's mentor. Although exposed by Assafiev and by his teachers to the more advanced music techniques, Dzerzhinsky seemed to find that these complex systems were not suited to his own easy-going, improvisatory methods of creation. In his catalogue appear two piano concertos and a number of short piano pieces, which have been described as a naïve potpourri of imitations—of Rachmaninov, Musorgsky, Shostakovich, Prokofiev, and Medtner.

Between 1932 and 1934 the uninhibited young composer wrote his first opera, *Quiet Flows the Don*, based on the powerful story by the Soviet novelist, Michael Sholokhov. The results were astonishing.

Dzerzhinsky's piece was produced in Moscow in March, 1936, a critical juncture in the history of Soviet music. Only two months before *Pravda* had blasted Shostakovich and would soon drive his *Lady Macbeth of Mzensk* from the stage. Now the government officials, including Stalin, saw an opera of a wholly different type, by a composer whom Assafiev would describe as a "nursling of the new epoch". *Quiet Flows the Don* was rich in those official virtues which *Lady Macbeth* lacked: its theme was loftily patriotic; its melodic material was based on Cossack folk song; and its music style was as innocent of formalistic complication as a piece by Verstovsky. Stalin congratulated the composer in his box after a performance, the Soviet press rang with praise, and *Quiet Flows the Don* played for months to enthusiastic audiences.

The chief advantage of Dzerzhinsky's opera was its fund of simple, straightforward melody in the folk style. Otherwise, it was devoid of invention or originality, and so lacking in any but the most obvious technical devices that it seemed like the improvisations of a not-too-talented student.

Dzerzhinsky's second opera, *Virgin Soil Upturned*, based on another Sholokhov novel, was produced in Moscow in 1937. It did not repeat the success of its predecessor. The composer tried again with *Volochaevko Days* (1940), based on episodes of the counter-revolution in Siberia in 1923; and *The Storm*, after Ostrovsky (1941). Still later efforts include *Nadezhda Svetlova*, and *Knyas-Ozero* (Prince-Lake), the latter written for the thirtieth anniversary of the Revolution.

That Dzerzhinsky did not relish the role of a composer unable to repeat a popular success is indicated in the caustic remarks he aimed at the Soviet music critics in the course of Zhdanov's Conference of Musicians in 1948: "Nobody writes anything about me, even though, since *Quiet Flows the Don*, I have written six more operas, all of which were produced—some successfully, others less so. The question of criticism must be carefully revised; just now too many critics are, if you will excuse my saying so, nothing but flunkeys in the service of the big composers."

CHAPTER XVIII

CONCLUSION

I

DURING the last years of the dictatorship of Josef Stalin the lack of information about Soviet musicians and their work became acute. It seemed certain however that the effects of the Decree on Music published by the Central Committee of the Communist Party in February, 1948, were even more drastic than was at first feared. This was the most repressive action taken by the government against Russian composers since the revolution, and it may very well affect the growth of their art for years to come.

It transpired that reprisals were carried out against several of the most eminent Soviet composers. Shostakovich and Miaskovsky had to resign from the faculty of the Moscow Conservatory, and Shebalin was replaced as its director. Khachaturyan lost his post as Secretary General of the Union of Soviet Composers and was replaced by Tikhon Khrennikov, a composer of dubious musical gifts but a militant Communist Party member. Khachaturyan was also removed from the vice-chairmanship of the Organizational Committee, a highly influential body which works closely with the Committee on Arts of the Ministry of Education, and decides what new music shall be published by the state and virtually what shall be performed in public.

Aside from the loss of an official post, any Soviet composer who had fallen from grace with the government could be made to suffer in a variety of ways. All public performance of his music might instantly stop, whether in concert halls, opera houses, or on the radio. This would cut him off from performance fees which normally supplement the salary paid him by the government. The Union of Soviet Composers would not commission him to write a new work, for which it pays generous sums; nor would the state publishing office print any new piece by him. There would be no new recording made of his music, nor would any well-known Soviet virtuoso perform it in public. The composer would discover that whatever influence his voice once had in the affairs of the

Composers' Union is now reduced to nil; and since the Composers' Union is completely under the control of the government and is interlocked with all other cultural bodies in the U.S.S.R., the composer would find his isolation virtually complete.

With public ostracism might go other forms of reprisal, such as the loss of a comfortable apartment, or inability to secure a free vacation at one of the composers' rest homes in the country provided by the government. Certain to fall upon the composer would be a raking cross-fire of denunciation in the Soviet press, intended to pulverize any and all of his works showing the leprous spot of formalism.

Fortunately, there is a way for the Soviet composer to redeem himself from excommunication. This is the familiar form of penance which Shostakovich used with notable success after his fall in 1936 and again in 1948. The composer first makes a public admission of his errors, thanks his critics for their perspicacity and fairness in pointing out his deviations from the canons of socialist realism, and announces his firm resolve to do better in the future. To be effective the composer's words must be followed by deeds, i.e. the composition of a piece of music genuine and simon-pure in its orthodoxy.

As for the standards of socialist realism in music, the Soviet composer has at hand a fairly complete set of rules to guide him both as to subject matter and treatment. He knows for example that it would be wiser to compose vocal rather than purely instrumental music, the former being considered nearer the historical ultra-Russian concept of art music, and the latter the preoccupation of Western decadents. If he chooses an opera or oratorio his libretto should be based on some episode which glorifies Soviet war heroes or political leaders, or some phase of the government's economic programme which is supposed to bring a life of happiness to the Russian people, or some pre-Soviet subject which celebrates Russia's great historical past and her struggles against czarist tyranny. An added attraction to any libretto will be a plot development which also exposes the vice-ridden depravity of the Western countries. Carefully to be avoided would be any excess of naturalism in the treatment of Russian characters, that is, any morbid display of crime, pessimism, psychotic phenomena, or sex. No Soviet composer would even think of touching on the subject of religion. It appears that even the nationalism of the minority states of the U.S.S.R., once a subject of impeccable brightness, is now suddenly too hot for safety. In 1951 ominous blasts began to appear in *Pravda* and *Izvestia* attacking writers, poets, artists, critics, and educators from some of the non-Russian republics for their excesses of "bourgeois" nationalism; while the musicians of Tadjikistan and Azerbaijan were excoriated for concentrating on their provincially native music to the exclusion of Russian classics.

In the actual technique of composition the obedient Soviet composer will base his entire work on simply-conceived, clearly-defined melodies, preferably Russian folk melodies or something closely akin. These he will manipulate in a manner no more complex than the procedures of Tchaikovsky. In this way he can hope to please the widest possible audience among the Russian masses. Further to guide the composer, like a series of warning sign-posts along a narrow path through deadly quicksands, are innumerable directives by Soviet critics and musicologists against the evils of Western formalistic practices. These include practically all the complications, subtleties, and experiments of twentieth-century music technique—the use of dissonance, atonality, polytonality, contrapuntal complexity, and all rhythmic complications from poly-rhythms to American jazz.

The Soviet critics also maintain an *Index Expurgatorius* of Western and renegade Russian composers whose works are supposed to exemplify the utter corruption of modern Western music. The list is long and it includes Hindemith, Schönberg, Berg, Webern, Krenek, Ravel, Honegger, Milhaud, Auric, Poulenc, Messiaen, Britten, Menotti, Cowell, Copland, and various others. The name likely to lead all the rest is Stravinsky.

It was long rumoured and generally believed, both inside and outside Russia, that the standards of socialist realism in Soviet music as in all the arts, coincided exactly with the strong likes and dislikes of Josef Stalin. Even before the dictator died, however, there appears to have been some relaxation of the stifling controls of 1948. We have seen that Shostakovich, after dutifully paying off his propaganda debts, took up again the work of serious composition; Prokofiev also tried to solve the problem by working on different levels. Champions of these men were apparently able to work their way back into grace inside the Union of Soviet Composers. This body had long been a battleground between two factions—composers of international eminence like Prokofiev, Shostakovich, Miaskovsky, Khachaturyan, and Kabalevsky, who stood for high standards of composition and pedagogy; and a group of less-gifted men who were usually eager to do the work of the Communist Party.

With the death of Stalin and the emergence of Georgi M. Malenkov as Premier, there appeared a faint flush of hope that the new regime might relax some of the controls and give the artists more room to breathe. Khachaturyan was permitted to publish an article in the magazine *Soviet Music*, begging for more creative freedom for his fellow composers; he even dared to argue that "a creative problem cannot be solved by bureaucratic means". A few months later Shostakovich appeared in print in the same magazine to reinforce Khachaturyan's plea. The mere fact that the two composers were permitted to express such views at all seemed significant, forecasting a possible change of policy from above. Not many months later, however, Khachaturyan was obliged to amplify his statements to make plain that what he had been criticizing was "musical bureaucrats" and not the general Soviet policy for the arts.

As Malenkov passed into the discard and was succeeded by what appeared to be a committee of rulers, headed by Nikolai Bulganin and Nikita S. Krushchev, the world again witnessed one of the changes of costume by which the Soviet hierarchy alters its outward guise but remains always the same. At the Geneva Conference of July, 1955, the new Communist leaders substituted smiles and cordiality for the long years of Mr. Molotov's cold impassivity; there was handshaking with the Jugoslavs, the West Germans, and the Finns; the Iron Curtain was raised an inch or two to permit a few people to come in and out—but of any real concessions on the part of the Soviets which would remove the causes of world tension there was very little to be noted. At least there appeared to be a strong possibility that the new Russian rulers were shrewdly taking stock of their own affairs, and might even be preparing to jettison some of the more palpable absurdities left over from the old dictator's long reign. What this might mean for Soviet artists is at this writing a matter of speculation.

It is palpably impossible for Westerners to gauge accurately the effects of the censorship under which the composers of the Soviet Union have been working. What this code does to individual creative minds we may only guess. The Russians have lived for many generations with censorships almost as severe and the results are doubtless not as damaging to the artist's integrity and pride as they would be in the West. However, what we may judge are the collective results. A span of a third of a century should offer a reasonable time for appraisal of music under a communist state. It would appear that, whether or not the repressions of this regime have stultified Russian composers, its glories have hardly inspired them.

To be aware of the falling off in quality, vitality and originality in Russian music since the revolution we have only to compare it with the last generation to come into prominence under the old order. In a single span of twenty years, between 1872 and 1892, were born Scriabin, Rachmaninov, Stravinsky, and Prokofiev. In varying degrees and in wholly differing ways these four greatly enriched the music of the modern world ; three were among the most adventurous and influential technicians of their time. All had creative vigour coupled with high professional skill, and they advanced the progress and prestige of Russian music immeasurably.

Nothing so vital has appeared so far in the succeeding Soviet generation. These later men remind us instead of the second generation, the so-called "epigones" who marked time immediately after the Five and Tchaikovsky. Theirs is an induced rather than an original talent. It is true that with many Soviet composers craftsmanship is excellent, proving again that the pedagogy of the great music academies in Russia is not yet impaired ; a few, notably Shostakovich and Khachaturyan, have achieved moments of brilliance and some popular successes ; but none has given evidence of sustained creative power on a high level.

Significantly perhaps, Soviet music has been weakest in that very field for which the ideologists had hoped the most—the now-enormous catalogue of pieces born of political inspiration. The most conspicuous failures of the past thirty years have been the gargantuan symphonies and symphony-oratorios at which composer after composer has tried his hand. From these attempts to outdo Beethoven, Berlioz, and Mahler has come a Niagara of sound but only a trickle of substance. The value of the new literature of music based on idioms of the minor nationalities is still indeterminate. Nor can much be said at this distance of the attempt to create a new proletarian music, that is, the song, march, or dance piece, simple in style and form but rich enough in beauty to endure as part of the national heritage of folk art. Startling has been the decline of Russian opera, although this is matched by the waning of opera in the West. In general it may be said that the most interesting Soviet music has been instrumental, in the field of the purely abstract symphony, the string quartet, and the concerto.

To arrive at the conclusion that the communist yoke is at least partly responsible for this decline we need only study the plain facts of history. The century of Russian music which began with Glinka was the result of a cross-fertilization with Western culture from which Russian artists had been cut off for generations. While this intermingling was possible, all through the nineteenth and early twentieth centuries, Russia's music (like her literature and drama) became one of the most richly-productive art fields in the world. With the coming of the Communist era and the slow exclusion of Western ideas, music, like every other art, has entered a period of reaction. The largest bloc of Soviet composers now feeds upon the Russian classics—Balakirev, Borodin, Rimsky-Korsakov, Tchaikovsky, Rachmaninov. Its thought is wholly reactionary. A much smaller group began by following the lead of Scriabin, Prokofiev, and the Western moderns, but of late years and under the lash of government censorship these composers too have turned markedly conservative.

II

There is a view of history which conceives of Russia as a state part European and part Asiatic, and which explains on that premise the peculiarities of life, character, and thought which make these people so strange and so fascinating to the Western world. Russia as a kind of buffer state between Occident and Orient is a valid concept, but one not wholly revealing. There is at bottom another and more profound condition, one which continues to isolate the Russians and to immerse them in sorrow and tragedy. Russia, in a sense, is a buffer state in time. For centuries she has lain midway between the modern world of the West which represents the living and growing present, and the mediaeval, even the ancient world of the dead past. Russian history has been a series of oscillations as these people are drawn toward the politics, science, and culture of the West, and then yield to the relentless pull of their own past—of Russia's mediaeval despotism of czars and boyars, feudal landowners and uncounted numbers of slave-serfs; of the long night under the Tartar yoke; even of the mother empire, Byzantium, from which Russia's religion and so much of her ancient culture once sprang. On few other great nations of the present does the remote past hold so strong a grip. This is the true meaning of the conflict which has split Russia for generations, Slavophiles against Occidentals, and which has thrown her rulers, churchmen, and philosophers, her writers, artists, and musicians into an endlessly confusing and fruitless disputation. Igor Stravinsky speaks of "the amazement, I might even say stupefaction, into which the problem of Russia's historical fate has always plunged me, a problem that has for centuries remained a mystery".

In that conflict, the overriding fear of the extreme nationalists has always been that by embracing the culture of the West their own country must inevitably surrender all its own traditions and ancient culture, until at last the Russian identity itself may be lost. Chauvinistic pride, religion, and even a child-like fear of the unknown have all contributed to this ultra-nationalist creed. Even today we witness the spectacle of Russian Communist leaders trying to create a world dynasty and at the same time drawing over the heads of their own people the old hood of nationalism which shuts out any view of the world around them. To the modern Western mind these fears seem not only groundless but foolish. If the masters of the Russian state were but willing to consider the artists of the past century who shed lustre and glory on their country in the eyes of the whole world, they might see that Russian genius is sturdier than they think.

Pushkin was not damaged by his love for Western culture; he joined it with his own heritage to create what many of his countrymen believe is Russian art at its purest. Glinka was not overwhelmed by Italian opera; upon its basic structure he built *Ruslan and Ludmila*. Balakirev's ardour for the music of Chopin and Liszt did not dim his love for Russian folk song; Borodin could write a string quartet in the manner of Mendelssohn and still create *Prince Igor*. English poets no less than Pushkin inspired Tchaikovsky, and from an eighteenth-century Italian comedy Prokofiev created *The Love for Three Oranges*. Russian composers have read Shakespeare, Shelley, Goethe, Poe, Sheridan, Dante, Sophocles, Gide; they have gazed at the canvases of Hogarth and Böcklin—and they have not turned to stone.

The truth must be, as was set forth on the opening pages of the present book, that modern Russian music owes its profuse beauty not to one but to two phases of Russian creative genius, which permit the artist to be at once a nationalist and a cosmopolitan eclectic. The nationalist phase is the more obvious and is justly celebrated. Russian music of the nineteenth century established the validity of folk art as a basis for an intellectual art; it opened new fields of nationalist music all over Europe and America; it revived interest in the ancient modes and proved that they could blend with and interact upon the modern major-minor scale system of Western music. But beyond all technical considerations the special beauty of Russian music is its power of portrayal. No other strictly national-ist music has ever painted so spacious and so teeming a picture of an entire people and their surroundings—their history in all its darkness and violence; the stern grandeur of their ancient religion; the poignancy of their native song and the wild fantasy of their folk lore; the land itself, at once so fair and so harsh; the minds and hearts of Russian men and women—sensitive or stolid, brutal or child-like, naively humorous, eccentric, realistic, raised by mystical faiths, fatalistic in the face of endless suffering.

Hardly less remarkable is the composite nature of modern Russian music. It has borrowed from a hundred different sources beyond the borders of Russia herself—from the opera and the canzonetta of Italy, the Viennese symphony, the German music drama, the symphonic poem, and the *lied*, the ballet and the grand opera of France, the folk song of Spain, the Near East and the Orient; it has assimilated the inventions of Mozart, Beethoven, Berlioz, Chopin, Liszt, and Mahler, it has used Wagnerian chroma-ticism and French impressionism—the list is as varied as modern music itself. The test of an eclecticism of this nature is whether or not the patchwork forms itself into a unified and logical whole. Russian music has its weaknesses and its failures, the work of flaccid imitators; but at its finest it has a mosaic richness and variety which no other nationalist music has yet approached.

To consider in final summary the entire course of Russian art music, from the earliest liturgical cantilena borrowed from ancient Byzantium down to the profuse burgeoning of the past and present century, is to be aware of a kind of sermon, solemn and revelatory, disturbing and prophetic. It is the nature of art as of life itself to change. Nor can art live by feeding upon itself. We have seen that the earliest Russian art music was not at first Russian but Byzantine; but showing the powerful talent which his descendants nine centuries hence still exhibit, the mediaeval Slavic artist soon gave the chant the sound of his own voice and tongue, and then the aspiration of his own soul. The *znamenny* chant had then its golden age, only to freeze and die in a tomb of ecclesiastical restriction which would permit no inch of growth. The immutable laws of church and state had done their work and for hundreds of years Russia was to know no new music, nor any new art, poetry, or drama. After those bleak centuries there came a renaissance when once again the warming flame of a great foreign culture was able to bring vigour and growth to the native Russian arts. In scarcely more than a century and a half Russian music passed through an astonishing metamorphosis, from a few amateurish imitators of Italian opera to a great nationalist school which has produced some of the world's most potent music artists. Now, as these words are written, a third of a century after the inauguration of the Communist state, the future of Russian music again appears to be uncertain. Like the country's literature, painting, and the drama, it is being robbed of its power of original growth. As we search through the music of the Soviet era for possible hopes for its future we cannot fail to note at least one singular fact, which may explain in part its decline. This is a music which has been forcibly cut off from one of the richest of all art soils—religion. Russian music from which all trace of spirituality has been erased seems like a monstrous concept. The song of devotion and mystical celebration was never confined in this country to the church itself; it invaded and permeated a wide territory of secular music, because the Russian man could not carry on his existence without it. Nor could the Russian artist. The voice of the church which sings through great and noble works like *Boris Godunov* and *Khovanshchina*, through *The Legend of the Invisible City of Kitezh*, the *Vesper Mass*, the *Symphony of Psalms*, and through countless lesser scores, is now silent. May it be heard again!

BIBLIOGRAPHY

Abraham, Gerald E. H. *Borodin: The Composer and His Music*, William Reeves, London
—— *Eight Soviet Composers*, Oxford University Press, London, 1944
—— *A Hundred Years of Music*, Alfred A. Knopf, New York, 1938
—— *The Music of Tchaikovsky*, W. W. Norton & Co., New York, 1946
—— *On Russian Music*, William Reeves, London, 1939
—— *Studies in Russian Music*, William Reeves, London, 1936
Bain, R. Nisbet. *The First Romanovs (1613–1725)*, Archibald Constable & Co., London, 1905
Barzun, Jacques. *Berlioz and the Romantic Century*, Little, Brown & Co., Boston, 1950
Bauer, Marion. *Twentieth Century Music*, G. Putnam's Sons, New York, 1933
Belaiev, Victor. *Igor Stravinsky's "Les Noces"*, Oxford University Press, London, 1928
Berlioz, Hector. *Memoirs, 1803 to 1865*, edited by Ernest Newman, Alfred A. Knopf, New York, 1947
Bertensson, Serge. "Ludmila Ivanova Shestakova", in *The Musical Quarterly*, July, 1945
Boelza, Igor. *Handbook of Soviet Musicians*, The Pilot Press Ltd., London, 1944
Bowen, Catherine Drinker. *Free Artist*, Random House, New York, 1939
Bowen, Catherine Drinker, and Meck, Barbara von. *Beloved Friend*, Random House, New York, 1937
Brook, Donald. *Six Great Russian Composers*, Rockliff, London, 1946
Bunt, Cyril G. E. *A History of Russian Art*, The Studio, London, 1946
Calvocoressi, M. D. "Mily Balakirev on the Centenary of His Birth", in *The Musical Quarterly*, January, 1937
—— "Alexander P. Borodin", in *The International Cyclopedia of Music and Musicians*, Dodd, Mead & Co., New York, 1939
—— *Mussorgsky*, J. M. Dent & Sons Ltd., London, 1946
—— "Mussorgsky's Musical Style", in *The Musical Quarterly*, October, 1932
—— *A Survey of Russian Music*, Penguin Books, Harmondsworth, 1944

Calvocoressi, M. D., and Abraham, Gerald. *Masters of Russian Music*, Alfred A. Knopf, New York, 1944

Copland, Aaron. *Our New Music*, Whittlesey House, New York, 1941

Culshaw, John. *Sergei Rachmaninov*, Dennis Dobson Ltd., London, 1949

Debussy, Claude. *Monsieur Croche*, Lear Publishers Inc., New York, 1948

Dent, Edward J. *Opera*, Penguin Books, Harmondsworth, 1951

Downes, Olin. Interview with Serge Prokofiev, *The New York Times*, February 2, 1930

Einstein, Alfred. *Mozart: His Character, His Work*, Oxford University Press, New York, 1945

Evans, Edwin. *Tchaikovsky*, J. M. Dent & Sons Ltd., London, 1943

Ewen, David. *The Book of Modern Composers*, Alfred A. Knopf, New York, 1950

Findeisen, Nicolas. "The Earliest Russian Opera", in *The Musical Quarterly*, July, 1933

Frankenstein, Alfred. "Victor Hartmann and Modest Musorgsky", in *The Musical Quarterly*, July, 1939

Gregor, Joseph, and Fülöp-Miller, René. *The Russian Theatre*, J. P. Lippincott Co., Philadelphia, 1929

Grove, George. *Dictionary of Music and Musicians*, The Macmillan Co., New York, 1928

Habets, Alfred. *Borodin and Liszt*, Digby, Long & Co., London, 1896

Heyman, Katherine Ruth. *The Relation of Ultra-modern to Archaic Music*, Small, Maynard & Co., Boston, 1921

Hill, Ralph. *The Symphony*, Pelican Books, Harmondsworth, 1950

Ikonnikov, Alexei A. *Myaskovsky: His Life and Work*, Philosophical Library, New York, 1946

International Cyclopedia of Music and Musicians, Dodd, Mead & Co., New York, 1939

Jelagin, Juri. *Taming of the Arts*, E. P. Dutton & Co., New York, 1951

Kall, Alexis. "Stravinsky in the Chair of Poetry", in *The Musical Quarterly*, July, 1940

Katz, Adele T. *Challenge to Musical Tradition*, Alfred A. Knopf, New York, 1945

Kozlenko, William. "Soviet Music and Musicians", in *The Musical Quarterly*, July, 1937

Krehbiel, Henry Edward. *A Book of Operas*, The Macmillan Co., New York, 1920

Krenek, Ernst. *Music Here and Now*, W.W. Norton & Co., New York, 1939

Lang, Paul Henry. *Music in Western Civilization*, W. W. Norton & Co., New York, 1941

Lavrin, Janko. *Pushkin and Russian Literature*, The Macmillan Co., New York, 1948

Leyda, Jay, and Bertensson, Sergei. *The Musorgsky Reader*, W. W. Norton & Co., New York, 1947

Martynov, Ivan. *Dmitri Shostakovich: The Man and His Music*, Philosophical Library, New York, 1947

Moisenko, Rena. *Realist Music*, Meridian Books Ltd., London, 1949

Montagu-Nathan, M. *An Introduction to Russian Music*, Le Roy Phillips, Boston, 1916

Mooser, R.-Aloys. *Opéras, Intermezzos, Ballets, Cantates, Oratorios, joués en Russie durant le XVIIIᵉ siècle*, A. Kundig, Geneva, 1945

Muchnic, Helen. *An Introduction to Russian Literature*, Doubleday & Co., New York, 1947

Nabokov, Nicolas. *Old Friends and New Music*, Little, Brown & Co., Boston, 1951

Nestyev, Israel V. *Sergei Prokofiev*, Alfred A. Knopf, New York, 1946

Newmarch, Rosa. *The Russian Opera*, E. P. Dutton & Co., New York, 1914

Norman, Gertrude, and Shrifte, Miriam Lubell. *Letters of Composers*, Alfred A. Knopf, New York, 1946

Oxford History of Music, Oxford University Press, London, 1934

Pougin, Arthur. *A Short History of Russian Music*, Brentano's, New York, 1915

Ralston, W. R. S. *Russian Folk-tales*, Smith, Elder & Co., London, 1873

Reese, Gustave. *Music in the Middle Ages*, W. W. Norton & Co., New York, 1940

Riesemann, Oskar von. *Moussorgsky*, Alfred A. Knopf, New York, 1929

—— *Rachmaninov's Recollections*, The Macmillan Co., New York, 1934

Rimsky-Korsakov, N. A. *My Musical Life*, Alfred A. Knopf, New York, 1942

Rosenfeld, Paul. *Discoveries of a Music Critic*, Harcourt, Brace & Co., New York, 1936

Saminsky, Lazare. *Music of Our Day*, Thomas Y. Crowell Co., New York, 1932

Schindler, Kurt. *A Century of Russian Song*, G. Schirmer Inc., New York, 1939

Seroff, Victor I. *The Mighty Five*, Allen, Towne & Heath Inc., New York, 1948

Seroff, Victor I. *Rachmaninov*, Simon & Schuster, New York, 1950
—— *Dmitri Shostakovich*, Alfred A. Knopf, New York, 1943
Slonimsky, Nicolas. *Music Since 1900*, W. W. Norton & Co., New
     York, 1938
Stravinsky, Igor. *Stravinsky: An Autobiography*, Simon & Schuster,
     New York, 1936
—— *Poetics of Music*, Harvard University Press, Cambridge,
     Mass., 1947
Strunk, Oliver. "The Tonal System of Byzantine Music", in *The
     Musical Quarterly*, April, 1942
Swan, Alfred J. "Music of the Eastern Churches", in *The Musical
     Quarterly*, October, 1936
—— "The Nature of the Russian Folk-Song", in *The Musical
     Quarterly*, October, 1943
—— *Scriabin*, John Lane Co., New York, 1923
—— "The Znamenny Chant of the Russian Church", in *The
     Musical Quarterly*, April, July, October, 1940
Swan, Alfred J., and Swan, Katherine. "Rachmaninov: Personal
     Reminiscences", in *The Musical Quarterly*, January, April,
     1944
Tansman, Alexandre. *Igor Stravinsky: The Man and His Music*,
     G. Putnam's Sons, New York, 1949
Tchaikovsky, P. I. *The Diaries of Tchaikovsky*, edited by Wladimir
     Lakond, W. W. Norton & Co., New York, 1945
Thomson, Virgil. *Music Right and Left*, Henry Holt & Co., New
     York, 1951
Tillyard, H. J. W. *Byzantine Music and Hymnography*, The Faith
     Press, London, 1923
Toynbee, Arnold J. *A Study of History*, Oxford University Press,
     London, 1947
Veinus, Abraham. *The Concerto*, Doubleday & Co., New York, 1944
Vernadsky, George. *A History of Russia*, Yale University Press,
     New Haven, 1946
Vodarsky-Shiraeff, Alexandria. *Russian Composers and Musicians*,
     H. W. Wilson Co., New York, 1940
Weinstock, Herbert. *Tchaikovsky*, Alfred A. Knopf, New York, 1944
Werth, Alexander. *Musical Uproar in Moscow*, Turnstile Press,
     London, 1949
White, Eric Walter. *Stravinsky: A Critical Survey*, Philosophical
     Library, New York, 1948
Wilenski, R. H. *Modern French Painters*, Harcourt, Brace & Co.,
     New York, 1947

INDEX